*MATT.*

# CHRISTIANITY

## AS OLD AS THE

# CREATION:

### OR, THE

# GOSPEL

## A REPUBLICATION OF THE

## RELIGION OF NATURE

Elibron Classics
www.elibron.com

Elibron Classics series.

© 2005 Adamant Media Corporation.

ISBN 1-4021-6239-1 (paperback)
ISBN 1-4021-2556-9 (hardcover)

This Elibron Classics Replica Edition is an unabridged facsimile
of the edition published in 1731,
London.

# CHRISTIANITY
## AS OLD AS THE
# CREATION:
## OR, THE
# GOSPEL,
## A REPUBLICATION OF THE
## RELIGION of NATURE.

---

Eſt autem jus naturale adeo immutabile, ut ne quidem
a Deo mutari poteſt.
*Grot. de Jure Belli & Pacis, l. 1. c. 1. §. 10. 1. 5.*
*The* Gentiles, *which have not the Law, do by nature*
*the things contained in the Law.* Rom. ii. 14.
-- *God is no reſpecter of perſons; but in every nation,*
*he that feareth him, and worketh righteouſneſs, is ac-*
*cepted with him.* Acts x. 34, 35.
Res ipſa quæ nunc Chriſtiana Religio nuncupatur, erat
& apud Antiquos, nec defuit ab initio generis humani,
quouſque ipſe Chriſtus veniret in carne; unde vera
Religio quæ jam erat, cœpit appellari Chriſtiana.
*Aug. Oper. To. 1. p. 17. c-- Retract. l. 1. c. 13.*

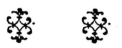

# LONDON,
## MDCC.XXXI.

Proinde perfectam illam Religionem quæ Chrifti præ-
dicatione nobis tradita eft, non novam aut pere-
grinam, fed fi verum dicere oportet, primam, folam,
veramque effe liquido apparet.

*Eufeb.* Eccl. Hift. l. 1. c. 4. *Valefius's* Tranfl.

The Religion of the Gofpel, is the true original Religion of Reafon and Nature. - - And its Precepts
declarative of that original Religion, which was as
old as the Creation.

*Serm. for prop. the Gofp. in for. parts,* by Dr. *Sherlock,*
now Bp. of *Bangor,* p. 10. & 13.

God does nothing in the government of the World
by mere Will and Arbitrarinefs. -- The Will of
God always determines itfelf to act according to
the eternal Reafon of Things. -- All rational Creatures are oblig'd to govern themfelves in A L L
their actions by the fame eternal Rule of Reafon.

Dr. *S. Clark's* Unchang. Oblig. of Nat. Relig.
Edit. 4. pag. 47, 48, 49.

# THE
# PREFACE.

THE Author of the following sheets, makes no apology for writing on a subject of the last importance, and which, as far as I can find, has no where been so fully treated. He builds nothing on a thing so uncertain as *Tradition*, which differs in most Countries, and of which, in all Countries, the bulk of Mankind are incapable of judging; but thinks he has laid down such plain & evident Rules, as may enable Men of the meanest capacity, to distinguish between *Religion*, & *Superstition*; and has represented the former in every part so beautiful, so amiable, and so strongly affecting, that they, who in the least reflect, must be highly in love with it; and easily perceive, that their Duty & Happiness are inseparable. Whether he has succeeded in this noble, and generous attempt, the Reader will be better able to judge, if he reads with the same freedom, and impartiality, as the Author has writen.

THE

# The PREFACE.

THE manner of debating a subject dialogue-wise, (as this between *A* & *B* ) was esteem'd by the Ancients the most proper, as well as most prudent way of exposing prevailing absurdities; & *Tully*'s two Discourses, *de Natura Deorum*, & *de Divinatione*, both levell'd against the Superstition of his Country-men, are living monuments of the expediency, and usefulness of this way of writing: And certainly, the Reader may be better entertain'd thus, than by that dry way of Objection & Answer, with which Controversies are usually manag'd.

*Care has been taken in this Edition to correct many typographical errors that had escaped in the former. And the pages not being the same in both Editions, I have left, in the Table of the Contents, after the Title of every Chapter, the number of the page of the quarto Edition in a parenthesis, (13) & then added the page of this new Edition; by comparing of which the Reader may easily find in this Edition any passage quoted from the 4to, which otherwise had been difficult & troublesom to find out.*

THE

# THE
# CONTENTS.

### CHAP. I.

### CHAP. II.

### CHAP. III.

### CHAP. IV.

\* 3

## CHAP. V.

## CHAP. VI.

## CHAP. VII.

## CHAP. VIII.

# The CONTENTS.

## CHAP. IX.

## CHAP. X.

## CHAP. XI.

## CHAP. XII.

## CHAP. XIII.

## CHAP. XIV.

CHRI-

# CHRISTIANITY

## AS OLD AS THE

# CREATION: &c.

## CHAP. I.

*That God, at all times, has given Mankind suffi-
cient means of knowing whatever he requires
of them; and what those Means are.*

*A.* THIS early visit, Sir, gives me hopes it will
not be a short one.

*B.* I come to talk with you on a subject, which may
perhaps keep me longer with you than you desire.

*A.* YOUR uncommon temper and candor, in debating even the most important points, will always
make your conversation agreeable, tho' ever so long;
but pray, what is to be the subject of our morning's
discourse?

*B.* I was yesterday in company with a great many
Clergy-men, it being our Bishop's primary Visitation;
where the Complaint was general, of the coldness &
indifference, with which people receiv'd the speculative points of Christianity, and all its holy rites; for
which formerly they had shewn so great a zeal. This
coldness they chiefly imputed to those *Low Church-
men*, who lay the main stress on *Natural·Religion*; and
withal so magnify the doctrine of *Sincerity*, as in effect to place all Religions on a level, where the Pro-

A                    fessors

feffors are alike fincere. The promoters of thefe notions, as wel as the notions themfelves, were expos'd with warmth; how juftly I will not determine, till we have talk'd the matter over with our ufual freedom: For which reafon, I have made you this early vifit, and wou'd be glad to know the fentiments of fo good a Judge, on thefe two important points; viz. *Sincerity*, and *Natural Religion*.

*A.* I thank you for this favour, and fhall freely tell you, I fo little agree with thofe Gentlemen in relation to fincerity, that I think a fincere examination into religious matters can't be too much prefs'd; this being the only way to difcover true Chriftianity. The Apoftles thought themfelves oblig'd, in making Profelites, to recommend an impartial fearch; they both defir'd, and requir'd Men *to judge for themfelves, to prove all things*, &c. this they thought neceffary, in order to renounce a Religion, which the force of education had imprefs'd on their minds; and embrace another directly contrary to the notions, and Prejudices, they had imbib'd. Nay, even thofe very Men who moft ridicule the doctrine of fincerity, never fail on other occafions to affert, that Infidelity is owing to the want of a fincere examination; and that whofoever impartially confiders Chriftianity, muft be convinc'd of its truth. And I might add, That cou'd we fuppofe, a fincere examination wou'd not always produce this effect, yet muft it always make Men acceptable to God; fince that is all God can require; all that it is in their power to do for the difcovery of his will. Thefe, in fhort, are my fentiments as to this point: and as to the other, I think, too great a ftrefs can't be laid on *Natural* Religion; which, as I take it, differs not from *Reveal'd*, but in the manner of its being communicated: The one being the internal, as the other the external revelation of the fame unchangeable will of a Being, who is alike at all times infinitely wife and good.

B. Su

*B.* Surely, Sir, this must be extremely heterodox. Can you believe, that *Natural* and *Revial'd* Religion differ in nothing, but the manner of their being convey'd to us?

*A.* As heterodox as I may seem at present, I doubt not, but by asking you a few questions, to let you see, I advance nothing in either of these points without reason; and in order to it, I desire to be inform'd, Whether God has not, from the beginning, given Mankind some Rule, or Law, for their conduct? And whether the observing that did not make 'em acceptable to him?

*B.* There can be no doubt, but the observing such a Law, must have answer'd the end for which it was giv'n; and made Men acceptable to God.

*A.* What more can any external Revelation do, than render Men acceptable to God? Again,

If God, then, from the beginning, gave Men a Religion; I ask, was that Religion imperfect, or perfect?

*B.* Most perfect, without doubt; since no Religion can come from a Being of infinite wisdom and perfection, but what is absolutely perfect.

*A.* Can, therefore, a Religion absolutely perfect, admit of any alteration; or be capable of addition, or diminution; & not be as immutable as the Author of it? Can Revelation, I say, add any thing to a Religion thus absolutely perfect, universal, & immutable? Besides, If God has giv'n Mankind a Law, he must have giv'n them likewise sufficient means of knowing it; he wou'd, otherwise, have defeated his own intent in giving it; since a Law, as far as it is unintelligible, ceases to be a Law. Shall we say, that God, who had the forming human understanding, as well as his own Laws, did not know how to adjust the one to the other?

If *God*, at all times, was *willing all Men should come to the knowledge of his truth;* cou'd not his infinite wisdom and power, at all times, find sufficient means, for making Mankind capable of knowing, what his infinite goodness defign'd they shou'd know?

*B.* I grant you, that God was always willing, that A L L Men shou'd come to the knowledge of true Religion; and we fay, that the Chriftian Religion being the only true, and abfolutely perfect Religion, was what God, from the beginning, defign'd for all Mankind.

*A.* I F fo, it follows, That the *Chriftian* Religion has exifted from the beginning; and that God, both *then*, and *ever fince*, has continu'd to give all Mankind fufficient means to know it; and that 'tis their duty to know, believe, profefs, and practife it: fo that *Chriftianity*, tho' the Name is of a later date, muft be as old, and as extenfive, as humane-nature; and as the Law of our creation, muft have been then implanted in us by God himfelf.

*B.* I T wou'd be too prefuming in us poor Mortals, to pretend to account for the methods Providence takes, in relation to the difcovery of its will; and, therefore, a perfon of lefs moderation might condemn your queftions as captious, prefumptuous, & founded in heterodoxy.

*A.* I F God never intended Mankind shou'd at any time be without Religion, or have falfe Religions; and there be but one true Religion, which ALL have been ever bound to believe, and profefs; I can't fee any heterodoxy in affirming, that the means to effect this end of infinite wifdom, muft be as univerfal and extenfive as the end itfelf; or that all Men, at all times, muft have had fufficient Means to difcover whatever God defign'd they shou'd know, & practife. I do not mean by this, that all shou'd have equal knowledge; but that all shou'd have what is fufficient for the cir-cumftances they are in.

*B.* S I N C E you have ask'd me queftions, let me, in my turn, demand of you, What are your fentiments

in

in this matter? Particularly, *What are those Means, which, you suppose, God has, at all times, given the whole race of Mankind, to enable them to discover what he wills them to know, believe, profess, and practise?*

*A.* I ask'd you those few questions at present, not to determine the point; but only to let you see, you had no reason to be surpris'd at my saying, *Natural and Reveal'd Religion only differ as to the manner of their being communicated.* I shall now readily answer your questions; and, as I think it my duty never to disown my religious sentiments, so I freely declare, that the use of *those faculties*, by which Men are distinguish'd from Brutes, is the only means they have to discern whether there is a God; and whether he concerns himself with human affairs, or has given them any Laws; and what those Laws are. And as Men have no other faculties to judge with, so their using these after the best manner they can, must answer the end for which God gave them, and justify their conduct: For,

I F God will judge Mankind as they are accountable, that is, as they are rational; the judgment must hold an exact proportion to the use they make of their Reason. And it wou'd be in vain to use it, if the due use of it wou'd not justify them before God; & Men wou'd be in a miserable condition indeed, if whether they us'd it, or not, they shou'd be alike criminal. And if God design'd all Mankind shou'd at all times know, what he wills them to know, believe, profess, and practise; and has giv'n them no other means for this, but the use of Reason; Reason, human Reason, must then be that Means: for as God has made us rational Creatures, & Reason tells us, that 'tis his Will, that we act up to the dignity of our natures; so 'tis Reason must tell when we do so What God requires us to know, believe, profess, and practise, must be in itself a reasonable service; but whether what is offer'd to us as such, be really so, 'tis Reason alone which

A 3         must

muſt judge; as the eye is the ſole judge of what is viſible, the ear of what is audible, ſo Reaſon of what is reaſonable. If then, Reaſon was giv'n Men to bring them to the knowledge of God's will, that muſt be ſufficient to produce its intended effect, & can never bring Men to take that for his will, which he deſign'd, they, by uſing their Reaſon, ſhou'd avoid as contrary to it.

*B.* If Men, having done all in their power, all that God requires of 'em to find out his will, ſhou'd fall into oppoſite ſentiments; muſt it not be the will of God that it ſhou'd be ſo? Can God will ſuch a previous examination, and not will what he foreknows muſt be the neceſſary conſequence?

*A.* There is, I think, no way to avoid this objection, of *God's willing contrarieties*; but by ſuppoſing he requires nothing of Men, but what is founded on the nature of things, & the immutable relations they bear to one another; & what, conſequently, they are, as far as concerns 'em, capable of knowing. But this Objection is unanſwerable by thoſe, who believe the will of God is not always thus founded; but may contain many merely poſitive things: ſince Men may, after having taken all poſſible care to be in the right, have very oppoſite ſentiments, and be oblig'd, by the Will of God, to hold, and act contrarieties.

*B.* Tho' this ſubject is attended with the utmoſt difficulties, yet I find little, or nothing ſaid to ſolve 'em. I, for my part, know not how to deny Mens being acceptable to God, whatever their opinions may be, after having us'd all the means God has endow'd 'em with for the diſcovery of his will: and yet I don't know how to admit it. For then, what Religion ſoever Men are of, if they have duly us'd ſuch means as God ordain'd for the diſcovery of his will; That, I ſay, how oppoſite ſoever to Chriſtianity, muſt be the Religion God deſign'd 'em. And on the other hand, ſhou'd I own, that the duly uſing thoſe means wou'd

have

have caus'd Men to have been all of one Religion, yet I can't see how that cou'd be the Christian Religion, except it has existed from the beginning, and all Men, at all times, have had sufficient means to discover it. For.

IF God was always willing, That *All Men should come to the knowledge of his truth*; and there never was a time, when God intended Men shou'd have no Religion; or such an imperfect Religion, which cou'd not answer the end of its being instituted by an infinitely wise Legislator; This seems to my *bewilder'd* Reason to imply, that there was from the beginning but one true Religion, which all Men might know was their duty to embrace; and if this is true, I can't well conceive, how this character can consist with *Christianity*; without allowing it, at the same time, to be *as old as the Creation*. And yet notwithstanding all these seeming difficulties, I am confident the Christian Religion is the only true Religion: but since these difficulties are of your raising, I may, in justice, expect that you shou'd solve 'em.

*A.* THIS, I must own, is a difficult point; however, I shall tell you my sentiments; which, I, far from being a *Dogmatizer*, am ready to give up, if you can frame any other *Hypothesis* not liable to the same objections; or others equally strong: tho' I may venture to say, that I take mine to be the only one, which can give any tolerable satisfaction to your present doubts. And therefore, I shall attempt to shew you, That Men, if they sincerely endeavour to discover the will of God, will perceive, that there's a *Law of Nature*, or *Reason*; which is so call'd, as being a Law, which is common, or natural, to all rational Creatures; and that this Law, like its Author, is absolutely perfect, eternal, and unchangeable; and that the design of the Gospel was not to add to, or take from this Law; but to free Men from that load of Superstition, which had been mix'd with it: So that

TRUE

TRUE CHRISTIANITY is not a Religion of yesterday, but what God, at the beginning, dictated, & still continues to dictate to Christians, as well as others. If I am so happy as to succeed in this attempt, I hope, not only fully to satisfy your doubts, but greatly to advance the honour of *external* Revelation ; by shewing the perfect agreement between *that*, and *internal* Revelation ; and by so doing, destroy one of the most successful attempts that has been made on Religion, by setting the Laws of God at variance.

BUT first, I must premise, That in supposing an external Revelation, I take it for granted, that there's sufficient evidence of a Person being sent from God to publish it ; nay, I further own, that this divine Person by living up to what he taught, has set us a noble Example ; and that as he was highly exalted for so doing, so we, if we use our best endeavours, may expect a suitable reward. This, and every thing of the same nature, I freely own, which is not inconsistent with the Law of God being the same, whether internally, or externally reveal'd.

*B.* YOUR design, I must own, is highly commendable ; but in order to succeed, you are to prove two things. *First*, That the supreme Governor of Mankind has given his Subjects an universal Law, which they, when they come to the use of Reason, are capable of knowing. *Secondly*, That the Divine precepts must be the same, whether internally, or externally reveal'd. If you prove these two points, you will entirely clear up my doubts : but I almost despair of your doing it, since you seem to me to advance a new *Hypothesis*.

*A.* HEAR the evidence, and then judge ; but before I produce it, lest the suppos'd novelty of this opinion may prejudice you, I shall put you in mind of what Archbishop *Laud* says upon a like occasion : „ * That when Errors are grown by age and con- „ tinuance to strength ; they who speak for the truth,
„ tho'

,, tho' far older, are ordinarily challeng'd for bringing
,, in new opinions; and there's no greater abfurdity
,, ftirring this day in *Chriftendom.* ,, Now,

By putting me to prove that there is a *Law of Nature*, you, I fuppofe, have a mind to hear what I can
fay on this fubject; fince none that believe there's a
God, who governs Mankind, but believe he has given
them a Law for the governing their actions; and that
this is implied in the very notion of governor, & governed; and confequently that the Law by which he
governs Men, & his government commenc'd together,
and extend alike to all his Subjects. ,, * Is it not,
,, as *Bifhop* Tillotfon *obferves*, a great miftake to think,
,, that the obligation of moral duties does folely de-
,, pend upon the revelation of God's will made known
,, to us in the holy Scriptures; it is plain, Mankind
,, was always under a Law before God made an ex-
,, ternal, or extraordinary Revelation; elfe how cou'd
,, God judge the World? Or how fhould they, to
,, whom the Word of God never came, be acquitted,
,, or condemned at the laft day; for where there is
,, no Law, there can neither be obedience, nor trans-
,, greffion.

If, then, it be abfurd to fuppofe, that Men, tho'
they liv'd ever fo impioufly and immorally, cou'd do
nothing which God has forbid them; Or if ever fo
pioufly and virtuoufly, cou'd not do any thing God
has commanded them, muft there not always have
been an univerfal Law fo fully promulgated to Mankind, that they could have no juft plea from their
ignorance not to be try'd by it; and confequently,
nothing lefs than its being founded on the nature of
things, & the relation they ftand in to God, & to one
another, vifible at all times to all Mankind, cou'd make
x thus univerfally promulgated. But further to illu-
ftrate this matter, can it be imagin'd, that if God has
been fo good to all other Animals, as to give them,

A 5                                    not

* Pref. to *Wilkins* of *Nat. Relig.*

not in one country only, but in all places whatsoever, sufficient means to act for their own preservation, that he has had less kindness for the immortal souls of those made after his own image, and has not given them at one time as well as another, and at one place as well as another, sufficient means to provide for their eternal happiness? Or,

Can it be suppos'd, an infinitely good & gracious Being, which gives Men notice by their senses, what does good or hurt to their bodies, has had less regard for their immortal parts, and has not given them at all times by the light of their understanding, sufficient means to discover what makes for the good of their Souls; but has necessitated them, or any of them, to continue from age to age in destructive ignorance, or error? To press this matter further, let me ask you, Whether there's not a clear and distinct light, that enlightens all Men; and which, the moment they attend to it, makes them perceive those eternal truths which are the foundation of all our knowledge? And is it not God himself, who immediately illuminates them? And what better reason can you assign, why infinite Wisdom shou'd act thus, except it be to give Mankind standing Rules to distinguish Truth from Falsehood; especially in matters of the highest consequence, to their eternal as well as temporal happiness?

There has, no doubt, been a great number of traditional Religions succeeding one another; and as far as we know, there is no traditional Religion, which, except in name, has continu'd the same for any long time: and tho' there are a great number of Sects, who go under the same common denomination, yet they are almost as much divided among themselves, as if they own'd different Religions, and accordingly charge one another with erring fundamentally. Yet all these agree in acknowledging a *Law of Nature*, and that they are indispensably oblig'd to obey its dictates: So that this *Light of Nature*, like that of the

Sun,

Sun, is univerfal; and wou'd, did not Men fhut the eyes of their underftanding, or fuffer others to blind them, foon difperfe all thefe mifts & fogs, which arife from falfe traditions, or falfe interpretations of the true tradition.

# CHAP. II.

*That the Religion of Nature confifts in obferving thofe things, which our Reafon, by confidering the nature of God and Man, and the relation we ftand in to him & to one another, demonftrates to be our duty; and that thofe things are plain; and likewife what they are.*

B. THAT we may the better know whether the Law or *Religion of Nature* is univerfal & the Gofpel a republication of it, & not a new Religion, I defire you will give a definition of the *Religion of Nature.*

A. By *Natural Religion,* I underftand the belief of the exiftence of a God, and the fenfe and practice of thofe duties, which refult from the knowledge, we, by our Reafon, have of him, and his perfections; and of ourfelves, and our own imperfections; and of the relation we ftand in to him, and to our fellow-creatures; fo that the *Religion of Nature* takes in every thing that is founded on the reafon & nature of things. Hence *Grotius* defines the Law *of Nature* to be * *Dictatum rectæ rationis; indicans actui alicui, ex ejus convenientia aut difconvenientia cum ipfa natura rationali, ineffe moralem turpitudinem aut neceffitatem moralem, ac confequenter ab auctore naturæ Deo talem actum aut vetari aut præcipi.*

I fuppofe you will allow, that 'tis evident by the *Light of Nature* that there is a God; or in other words,

a

* *Lib.* 1. *c.* 1. *Par.* 10.

a Being abfolutely perfect, & infinitely happy in himfelf, who is the fource of all other beings; and that
what perfections foever the creatures have, they are
wholly deriv'd from him.

B. This, no doubt, has been demonftrated over
& over; and I muft own, that I can't be more certain
of my own Exiftence, than of the Exiftence of fuch
a Being.

A. Since then, it is demonftrable there is fuch a
Being, it is equally demonftrable, that the Creatures
can neither add to, or take from the happinefs of that
Being; and that he cou'd have no motive in framing
his Creatures, or in giving Laws to fuch of them as
he made capable of knowing his will, but their own
good.

To imagine he created them at firft for his own
fake, and has fince requir'd things of them for that
reafon, is to fuppofe he was not perfectly happy in
himfelf before the Creation; and that the Creatures,
by either obferving, or not obferving the Rules prefcrib'd them, cou'd add to or take from his happinefs.

If then, a Being infinitely happy in himfelf, cou'd
not command his Creatures any thing for his own
good; nor an All-wife Being things to no end or purpofe; nor an All-good Being any thing but for their
good; it unavoidably follows, nothing can be a part
of the divine Law, but what tends to promote the
common intereft, and mutual happinefs of his rational
Creatures; & every thing that does fo muft be a part
of it.

As God can require nothing of us, but what makes
for our happinefs; fo he, who can't envy us any happinefs our nature is capable of, can forbid us thofe
things only, which tend to our hurt; and this we are
as certain of, as that there is a God infinitely happy
in himfelf, infinitely good and wife: and as God can
defign nothing by his Laws but our good, fo by being
infinitely powerful, he can bring every thing to pafs
which he defigns for that end.     From

FROM the confideration of thefe perfections, we cannot but have the higheft veneration, nay the greateft adoration and love for this fupreme Being; who, that we may not fail to be as happy as poffible for fuch Creatures to be, has made our acting for our *prefent*, to be the only means of obtaining our *future* happinefs; & that we can't fin againft him, but by acting againft our reafonable natures: Thefe reflections, which occur to every one who in the leaft confiders, muft give us a wonderful and furprizing fenfe of the divine Goodnefs, fill us with admiration, tranfport & extacy (of which we daily fee among contemplative perfons remarkable inftances) and not only force us to exprefs a never-failing gratitude in raptures of the higheft praife and thankfgiving; but make us ftrive to imitate him in our extenfive love to our Fellow-Creatures. And thus copying after the Divine original, & taking God himfelf for our precedent, muft make us like unto him, who is all perfection & all happinefs; and who muft have an inexhauftible love for all, who thus endeavour to imitate him.

THE difference between the fupreme Being, in-finitely happy in himfelf, and the Creatures who are not fo, is, that all his actions, in relation to his Crea-tures, flow from a pure difinterefted Love; whereas the fpring of all the actions of the Creatures is their own good: * *We love God, becaufe he firft lov'd us*; & confequently, our Love to him will be in propor-tion to our fenfe of his goodnefs to us. And there-fore, we can't in the leaft vary from thofe fentiments, which the confideration of the divine attributes implant in us; but we muft in proportion take off from the goodnefs of God, and thofe motives we have to love him as we ought.

OUR Reafon, which gives us a demonftration of the Divine perfections, affords us the fame concerning the nature of thofe duties God requires; not only

with

* I. John 4. 19.

with relation to himself, but to ourselves, & one another: Those we shall discern, if we look into ourselves, and consider our own natures, & those circumstances God has plac'd us in with relation to our Fellow-Creatures; & see what conduces to our mutual happiness: Of this, our senses, our reason, the experience of others as well as our own, can't fail to give us sufficient information.

WITH relation to ourselves, we can't but know how we are to act; if we consider, that God has endow'd Man with such a nature, as makes him necessarily desire his own good; and, therefore, he may be sure, that God, who has bestow'd this nature on him, cou'd not require any thing of him in prejudice of it; but on the contrary, that he shou'd do every thing which tends to promote the good of it. The health of the body, and the vigor of the mind being highly conducing to our good, we must be sensible we offend our Maker, if we indulge our senses to the prejudice of these: And because not only all irregular passions, all unfriendly affections carry their own torment with them, and endless inconveniences attend the excess of sensual delights; & all immoderate desires (human nature being able to bear but a certain proportion) disorder both mind and body; we can't but know we ought to use great moderation with relation to our passions, or in other words, govern all our actions by reason; that, and our true interest being inseparable. And in a word, whoever so regulates his natural appetites, as will conduce most to the exercise of his reason, the health of his body, & the pleasure of his senses, taken & consider'd together, (since herein his happiness consists) may be certain he can never offend his Maker; Who, as he governs all things according to their natures, can't but expect his rational Creatures shou'd act according to their natures.

As to what God expects from Man with relation to each other; every one must know his duty, who

con-

confiders that the common Parent of Mankind has the whole Species alike under his protection, and will equally punish one man for injuring others, as he would others for injuring him ; and confequently, that it is his duty to deal with them, as he expects they fhould deal with him in the like circumftances. How much this is his duty every one muft perceive, who confiders himfelf as a weak creature, not able to fubfift without the affiftance of others, who have it in their power to retaliate the ufage he gives them : And that he may expect, if he breaks thofe rules which are neceffary for Mens mutual happinefs, to be treated like a common enemy, not only by the perfons injur'd, but by all others; who, by the common ties of Nature, are oblig'd to defend, & affift each other. And not only a Man's own particular intereft, but that of his children, his family, and all that's dear to him, obliges him to promote the common happinefs, & to endeavour to convey the fame to pofterity.

ALL *Moralifts* agree, that human Nature is fo conftituted, that Men can't live without fociety & mutual affiftance ; & that God has endow'd them with reafon, fpeech, and other faculties, evidently fitted to enable them to affift each other in all matters of life ; That, therefore, 'tis the will of God who gives them this nature, & endows them with thefe faculties, that they fhould employ them for their common benefit and mutual affiftance. And the *Philofophers*, who faw that all fociety would be diffolv'd, and Men foon become deftitute of even the neceffaries of life, and be a prey to one another, if each Man was only to mind himfelf, and his own fingle intereft ; and that every thing pointed out the neceffity of mutual benevolence among Mankind ; and therefore they judg'd, that men by their nature were fram'd to be ufeful to one another; *Ad tuendos confervandosq; homines hominum naturæ effe,* fays *Cicero* *. And therefore, every Man, for the fake of

* De fin. l. 3.

of others as well as himself, is not to disable his body or mind by such irregularities, as may make him less serviceable to them.

In short, considering the variety of circumstances Men are under, & these continually changing, as well as being for the most part unforeseen; 'tis impossible to have Rules laid down by any *external* Revelation for every particular case; & therefore, there must be some standing rule, discoverable by the *Light of Nature,* to direct us in all such cases. And we can't be more certain that 'tis the will of God, that those effects which flow from natural causes shou'd so flow, than we are that 'tis the will of God, that Men shoud observe whatever the nature of things, and the relation they have to one another make fit to be observ'd, shou'd be so observ'd; Or in other words, we can't but know, if we in the least consider, that whatever circumstances Men are plac'd in, by the universal Cause of all things; that 'tis his eternal & immutable Will, by his placing them in these circumstances, that they act as these require. 'Tis absurd to imagine we are oblig'd to act thus in some cases, & not in others; when the Reason for acting thus in all is the same. This consideration alone will direct a Man how to act in all conditions of life, whether *Father, Son, Husband, Servant, Subject, Master, King,* &c. Thus we see how the reason of things, or the relation they have to each other, teaches us our duty in all cases whatever. And I may add, that the better to cause Men to observe those rules, which make for their mutual benefit, infinite Goodness has sown in their hearts seeds of pity, humanity and tenderness, which, without much difficulty, cannot be eradicated; but nothing operates more strongly than that desire Men have of being in esteem, credit, and reputation with their fellow Creatures; not to be ob-obtain'd without acting on the Principles of natural Justice, Equity, Benevolence, &c.

In

In a word, As a most beneficent disposition in the supreme Being is the source of all his actions in rerelation to his Creatures, so he has implanted in Man, whom he has made after his own image, a love for his species; the gratifying of which in doing acts of benevolence, compassion and good will, produces a pleasure that never satiates: as on the contrary, actions of ill-nature, envy, malice, &c. never fail to produce shame, confusion, and everlasting self-reproach.

And now let any one say, how 'tis possible God could more fully make known his will to all intelligent Creatures, than by making every thing within and without them a declaration of it, & an argument for observing it.

Having thus discover'd our duty, we may be sure it will always be the same; since inconstancy, as it argues a defect either of wisdom or power, can't belong to a Being infinitely wise and powerful. What unerring Wisdom has once instituted can have no defects; and as God is entirely free from all partiality, his Laws must alike extend to all times & places.

From these premises, I think, we may boldly draw this conclusion, That if Religion consists in the practice of those duties, that result from the relation we stand in to God and Man, our Religion must always be the same. If God is unchangeable, our duty to him must be so too. If human nature continues the same, and Men at all times stand in the same relation to one another, the duties which result from those relations must always be the same: And consequently, our duty to God & Man must, from the beginning of the world to the end, always be the same, always alike plain & perspicuous, & can neither be chang'd in whole or part; which demonstrates that no person, if he comes from God, can teach us any other Religion, or give us any precepts, but what are founded on those relations. *Heaven & Earth shall sooner pass away*, than *one Tittle of this Eternal Law shall either be abrogated, or alter'd.*

To

To ſum up all in few words, As Nature teaches Men to unite for their mutual defence, and Government was inſtituted ſolely for this end; ſo to make this more effectual, Religion, which reaches the thoughts, was wholly ordain'd : it being impoſſible for God, in governing the World, to propoſe to himſelf any other end than the good of the governed; and conſequently, whoever acts what is beſt for himſelf both in a publick, and private capacity, does all that either God or Man can require. Thus from the conſideration of our own imperfections, which we continually feel, and the perfections of our Creator, which we conſtantly view in all his works, we may arrive to the knowledge of our duty, both to our Creator & Fellow-Creatures. Hence I think, we may define true Religion to conſiſt in a conſtant diſpoſition of mind to do all the good we can, & thereby render ourſelves acceptable to God in anſwering the end of his creation.

## CHAP. III.

*That the Perfection and Happineſs of all rational Beings, ſupreme as well as ſubordinate, conſiſts in living up to the Dictates of their Nature.*

To make this, ( ſince all our happineſs depends on it) if poſſible, more plain; The Principle from which all human actions flow is the deſire of happineſs ; & God, who does nothing in vain, would in vain have implante  this principle, this only innate principle in Mankind, if he had not given them Reaſon to diſcern what actions make for, and what againſt their happineſs.

B. Wʜᴇʀᴇɪɴ do you take the happineſs of rational Creatures to conſiſt ? Without knowing that, this controverſy can't be determin'd; and when tis known, our diſpute muſt ſoon be ended.

A.

*A.* THE Happiness of all beings whatever confifts in the perfection of their nature; and the nature of a rational being is moſt perfect, when it is perfectly rational; that is, when it governs all its actions by the rules of right Reafon; for then it arrives to the moſt perfect, and confequently the happieſt ſtate a rational nature can afpire to: and every deviation from the rules of right reafon being an imperfection, muſt carry with it a proportionable unhappineſs: & a Man's happineſs and duty muſt confift in the ſame things, ſince no one can be oblig'd to do any thing that does not ſome way or other contribute to his happineſs; and confequently according to the ſenſe Men have of their own happineſs, and of the means which will naturally procure it, they will aſſuredly attain the knowledge of their refpective duties.

*B.* IF we know wherein the happineſs of God, who is neceſſarily happy, confifts, we might judge wherein confifts the happineſs of Man made after God's own image; and whether happineſs, or miſery are the neceſſary confequence of his Actions.

*A.* Becauſe this is a point of the higheſt confequence, I ſhall ſpeak my ſentiments (that they may the better paſs with you) in the words of the judicious Dr. *Scot*, who ſays, * ,, That which renders God ſo infinitely ,, happy in himſelf, is not ſo much the Almighty ,, power he has to defend himſelf from foreign hurts ,, & injuries, as the exact agreement of all his actions ,, with the All-comprehending Reafon of his own ,, mind. God loves nor himſelf meerly becauſe he is ,, himſelf, but becauſe he is in all refpects morally good, ,, and his Will and Power perfectly compliant with ,, the infallible dictates of his own Reafon: Hence ,, ariſes his infinite complacency in himſelf, that there's ,, nothing in him but what his own Reafon perfectly ,, approves; no inclinations in his will, or nature,

,, but

* *Chriſt. Life Part.* 2. *Vol.* I. *Ch.* I.

„ but what are exactly agreeable to the faireſt ideas
„ of his own mind.

Iϝ the perfection, & conſequently the happineſs of
God, conſiſts in the purity & rectitude of his Nature,
we, as far as we can arrive to a like purity and rectitude, muſt be ſo far neceſſarily happy; ſince by living
according to the rules of right Reaſon, we more and
more implant in us the moral perfections of God,
from which his happineſs is inſeparable. We then,
if I may ſo ſay, *live the life of God*; that is, we, in our
place and ſtation, live after the ſame manner, and by
the ſame rules as he does in his; & we do what God
himſelf wou'd do was he in our place; & there wou'd
be no other difference between his life and ours, but
what ariſes from our different ſtates and relations;
ſince the ſame rules wou'd determine our wills as determine his will: and by our repeated acts of virtue,
we ſhou'd be continually making nearer and nearer
approaches to the moſt perfect, and the moſt happy
Being. By this conduct, we, as the Scriptures aſſure us,
ſhou'd be made partakers of the *Divine nature*, *be born
of God*, and *be perfect as our heavenly Father is perfect*;
& can that be without being as happy as we are perfect? Hence we may contemplate the great dignity
of our *Rational* nature, ſince our Reaſon for kind,
tho' not for degree, is of the ſame nature with that
of God; nay, 'tis our Reaſon which makes us the
image of God himſelf, & is the common bond which
unites Heaven & Earth; the Creatures, & the Creator;
and if our happineſs is limited, 'tis becauſe our Reaſon
is ſo: 'Tis God alone, who has an unlimited Reaſon
and Happineſs.

Thᴇ excellent Author juſt now mention'd ſays,
„ * The beſt thing we can receive from God is him-
„ ſelf, and himſelf we do receive in our ſtrict com-
„ pliance with the eternal Laws of goodneſs; which
„ Laws being tranſcrib'd from the nature of God,
                    „ from

* *Chriſt. Life. Part 2. Vol. 1. Ch. 1.*

,, from his eternal righteousness & goodness, we do,
,, by obeying them, derive God's nature into our own;
,, so that while we write after the copy of his Laws,
,, we write out the perfections of his being: and his
,, Laws being the seal on which he has engraven his
,, nature, we, in obeying them, take impression from
,, them, and stamp his blessed nature on our own. ,,
Which, certainly, must make us necessarily happy,
as a contrary conduct wou'd make us unhappy. And,
I think, I may venture to say, that cou'd we suppose
God himself to act otherwise, he wou'd then be as
unhappy as he now is happy; and his omnipotency
cou'd not hinder him from being continually expos'd
to the reproach of his own infallible Reason.

FROM these premises, I think, we may conclude,
that Men, according as they do, or do not partake of
the nature of God, must unavoidably be either happy,
or miserable. And herein appears the great wisdom of
God, in making Mens misery and happiness the necessary and inseparable consequence of their actions:
and that rational actions carry with them their own
Reward, and irrational their own punishment. This,
I think, can't be deny'd, as long as there are some
actions naturally beneficial to us, & others as hurtful:
and that there's no virtue, but what has some good
inseparably annex'd to it; and no vice, but what as
necessarily carries with it some evil: and if our rational nature is to be the same in the next life, as it
is in this, our actions must produce effects of the same
kind, and that too in a much higher degree.

IN this life, 'tis true, we can't be perfectly happy
as subject to diseases and disasters. We are imperfect
ourselves, and have none to converse with but imperfect Creatures: and yet if we act according to the
dictates of right Reason, we shall receive, even here,
true inward comfort and satisfaction, and hereafter,
when we are freed from those imperfections, compleat happiness. On the contrary, the Man who aban-

dons

dons his Reason, besides the misery of all sorts an irrational conduct will bring on him, must feel in his
mind, pain, and anguish even in this life, and in the
life to come, when there are no sensual things to divert
his thoughts, insupportable grief and misery.

Tho' human Law-givers are forc'd to have recourse to punishments, which are not connected with
the things they forbid, yet a Being of infinite power
is not thus straiten'd, but may make one the necessary
consequence of the other. And, indeed, how can it
be otherwise, since good and evil have their foundation in the essential difference of things, and their nature is fix'd and immoveable: And consequently, our
happiness depends on the intrinsick nature of the one,
& our misery on the intrinsick nature of the other.

As God, whose infinite wisdom sets him above
being deceiv'd, or influenc'd by any wrong affections,
acts in constant conformity to the reason and nature
of things: and 'tis a contradiction to his nature for
him to do any thing that is not fit & reasonable : so he
wou'd have fram'd our nature in contradiction to his
own, if he had oblig'd us to act otherwise. No, God
can never give us commands repugnant to his own
nature, or require us to do what he himself abhors
to do. The end for which God has given us Reason,
is to compare things, and the relation they stand in
to each other, & from thence to judge of the fitness
and unfitness of actions: and cou'd not our Reason
judge soundly in all such matters, it cou'd not have
answer'd the end for which infinite Wisdom & Goodness
bestow'd that excellent gift, and for which we can't
enough adore the goodness of God.

Had God, from time to time, spoke to all Mankind
in their several languages, and his words had miraculoufly convey'd the same ideas to all persons, yet he
cou'd not speak more plainly than he has done by the
things themselves, & the relation which Reason shews
there is between them. Nay, since 'tis impossible in
any

any book, or books, that a particular rule cou'd be giv'n for every cafe, we must even then have had recourfe to the light of Nature to teach us our duty in most cafes: efpecially confidering the numberlefs circumftances which attend us, and which, perpetually varying, may make the fame actions, according as Men are differently affected by them, either good or bad. And I may add, that moft of the particular rules laid down in the Gofpel for our direction, are fpoken after fuch a figurative manner, that except we judge of their meaning, not merely by the letter, but by what the Law of Nature anteecedently declares to be our duty, they are apt to lead us wrong. And if precepts relating to morality, are deliver'd after an obfcure manner, when they might have been deliver'd otherwife, what reafon can you affign for its being fo, but that infinite Wifdom meant to refer us to that Law for the explaining them. Sufficient inflances of this nature I fhall give you hereafter, tho' I muft own, I can't carry this point fo far as a learned Divine, who reprefents the Scriptures more obfcure ( which one wou'd think impoffible ) than even the *Fathers.* He tells us, ,, That a ,, certain Author (viz. *Flaccus Illyricus*) * has furnifh'd ,, us with one and fifty reafons for the obfcurity of ,, the Scriptures; *adding* , ,, I think, I may truly fay ,, that the Writings of the Prophets & Apoftles abound ,, with tropes and metaphors, types and allegories, ,, parables and dark fpeeches, and are as much, nay, ,, much more unintelligible in many places, than the ,, Writings of the Ancients. ,, 'Tis well this Author, † who talks of People being ftark *Bible-mad*, ftopp'd here, and did not with a celebrated Wit ‡ cry, *The truly illuminated Books are the darkeft of all.*

B 4　　　　　　　Tн

---

* Pref. to *Reeve's* Apol. &c. p. 45, 46.
† Pref. concern. right Ufe of the Fathers. pag. 11.
‡ Tale of a Tub.

THE Writer above-mention'd suppoſes it impoſſible, that God's will ſhou'd be fully reveal'd by Books; ,, Except, *ſays he*, * it might be ſaid perhaps without ,, a Figure, that even the World itſelf could not con- ,, tain the Books which ſhould be written:,, But with ſubmiſſion to this reverend perſon, I can't help thinking, but that, (ſuch is the divine goodneſs) God's Will is ſo clearly, & fully manifeſted in the Book of Nature, that he who runs may read it.

THIS can't be deny'd, if the Book of Nature ſhews us in characters legible by the whole world, the rela- tion we ſtand in to God & our fellow-creatures, and the duties reſulting from thence: for then it muſt teach us the whole of our duty, ſince it wou'd be unjuſt and tyrannical in any Being, to require more of others than the relation they ſtand in to him makes it their duty to pay, it being that relation alone which gives him his juſt power and authority. We are en- compaſs'd with many artificial Relations, ſuch as *Go-vernor* and *governed*, *Maſter* and *Servant* *Husband* and *Wiſe*, &c. and the end of theſe relations teaches us what they require: and they being enter'd into for the ſake of each others aſſiſtance, either party is in- jur'd by the others not obſerving what theſe Relations demand, or by exacting more than the end of entring into them requires.

THO' the relation we ſtand in to God, is not ar- tificial, as moſt are amongſt Men, who want each others aſſiſtance, but is natural at leaſt on our part; yet this does not hinder, but that we may know by Reaſon the end he had in being related to us as Creator and Governor, and what he requires of his Creatures and Subjects. This the divine nature which contains in itſelf all perfection, and all happineſs, plainly points out to us. And if we are once certain of the end of God's entring into this relation with Man, we may be as certain from his wiſdom and goodneſs, and all his

Divine

Divine perfections, that he will require no more of us than the end he had in entring into this Relation requires.

IF it would be unjuſt and tyrannical in an earthly Governor, to exact things of his Subjects, that do not contribute to the end for which this relation between them was enter'd into; can we ſuppoſe a Governor of infinite Wiſdom and Goodneſs, who has always in his mind the end for which he governs Mankind, will act the Tyrant, and put them under ſevere Penalties for not obſerving ſuch things as have no relation to the end for which he created, & governs them?

THERE's no Relation among Men without a mutual obligation ariſing from it. Parents owe a duty to Children as well as Children to Parents: but are not we, in a ſtricter ſenſe, the Children of God, and Parents only inſtruments in his hands? ſince 'tis God, who from nothing brings us into being, frames us after the manner that beſt pleaſes him, imprints on us what faculties, inclinations, deſires and paſſions he thinks fit: And is not God from his innate Goodneſs & Equity, under an obligation to treat us more kindly than earthly Parents do their beſt-beloved Children, who beget them without deſigning it? Whereas God, whoſe actions are govern'd by infinite Goodneſs, could have no motive to bring us into being (which of itſelf is no bleſſing) but our good, and for the ſame reaſon preſerves us in being; nor can ſo kind & tender a Parent play the Tyrant, & impoſe commands on us, which do not flow from the Relations we ſtand in to him, and to one another.

IF we conſider what our Reaſon will inform us, of the nature of our great Creator and Governor, we can't fail of knowing our duty: for as Dr *Scott* juſtly obſerves, * „ If you will ſerve the great King of the „ World in ſuch ways as are pleaſing and acceptable „ to him, you muſt ſtudy his nature, & inform your-

selves,

* *Chriſt. Life Part 2. Vol. 1. Chap. 6. p.* 321, 322.

,, felves, which way his infinite perfections incline,
,, that you may know how to comport yourfelves
,, towards him, and to render him fuch fervices as are
,, agreeable to his nature: for there's no rule in the
,, world, but only that of his nature, by which you
,, can certainly conclude what will pleafe him. - - -
,, So that in all our enquiries what is pleafing to God,
,, our laft appeal muft be to his nature, which is the
,, great ftandard of Good & Evil, by which we are
,, to meafure what is pleafing & difpleafing to him. ,,

IF then, with this judicious Author, you allow,
that we are to meafure what is pleafing & difpleafing
to God, (which takes in the whole of Religion)
from what our Reafon teaches concerning his Nature,
you allow all I contend for.

IN fhort, if the relations between things, and the
fitnefs refulting from thence, be not the fole rule of
God's actions, muft not God be an arbitrary Being?
and then what a miferable condition will Mankind
be in! Since an arbitrary Will might change every
moment, & thofe things which entitl'd Men to God's
favour to-day, might make them incur his difpleafure
to-morrow: Nay, he might at the fame time have a
fecret Will oppofite to his reveal'd Will: or have different Wills for every different perfon: or might reveal his arbitrary commands fo obfcurely, as to caufe
the utmoft confufion. But if God only commands
what the nature of things fhews to be fit, 'tis fcarce
poffible, that Men (tho' now endlefly divided upon the
account of their different traditions) fhould miftake
their duty: fince a mind that's attentive can as eafily
diftinguifh *fit* from *unfit*, as the eye can beauty from
deformity, or the ear harmony from difcord: and if
no commands can alter the nature of things, or make
that *fit* which is in itfelf *unfit*, external Revelation muft
attend the nature and relation of things, and can only
fpeak what thofe fpeak. As for inftance, tis not in
our power, tho' ever fo often commanded, to love

the

the Deity, while we conceive him an arbitrary Being acting out of humour and caprice : nor could any commands, suppofing fuch poffible, oblige us not to love him, while we believe him a kind & beneficent Being: fo that as long as we have right notions of God, we can't but love, & adore him as we ought.

Thus, I think, I have fully prov'd from the nature of God and Man, and the Relations we ftand in to him & one another, that the Divine precepts can't vary : & that thefe Relations which are the permanent voice of God, by which he fpeaks to all Mankind, do, at all times, infallibly point out to us our duty in all the various circumftances of life.

Shou'd Revelation require lefs than thofe Relations require, wou'd it not be an imperfect rule ? And if it enjoyns more, wou'd it not argue the Author of it to be of a tyrannical nature, impofing on his Subjects, and under moft fevere penalties, unneceffary things : and likewife fhew a defign, not of being belov'd, but hated and dreaded ? And therefore, thofe who fee the confequences of things, defcribe the Chriftian Religion as requiring fuch things only, as confidering the Relations we ftand in to God and one another, are apparently for our good.

The moft accurate Dr. *Barrow* gives this character of the Chriftian Religion, * „ That its Precepts are „ no other than fuch as Phyficians prefcribe for the „ health of our bodies: as Politicians wou'd allow to „ be needful for the peace of the State: as *Epicurean* „ Philofophers recommend for the tranquility of our „ minds, and pleafures of our lives : fuch as Reafon „ dictates, and daily fhews conducive to our welfare „ in all refpects: which confequently, were there no „ Law enacting them, we fhou'd in wifdom choofe „ to obferve, and voluntarily impofe them on our- „ felves, confeffing them to be fit matters of Law, „ as moft advantagious and requifite to the good, „ general & particular, of Mankind.

That

* *Vol. of Serm. pag.* 8₄.

That great and good Man Dr. *Tillotson* says, *
,, That All the Precepts of Chriſtianity are reaſonable
,, & wiſe, requiring ſuch duties as are ſuitable to the
,, light of nature, and do approve themſelves to the
,, beſt reaſon of Mankind: ſuch as have their foun-
,, dation in the nature of God, and are an imitation
,, of the divine excellencies: ſuch as tend to the per-
,, fection of human-nature, & to raiſe the minds of
,, Men to the higheſt pitch of goodneſs & virtue. - - -
,, They command nothing that's unneceſſary, they
,, omit nothing that may tend to the glory of God,
,, or the welfare of Men, nor do they reſtrain us in
,, any thing, but what is contrary to the regular in-
,, clinations of Nature, or to our Reaſon, & true in-
,, tereſt: they forbid us nothing but what is baſe and
,, unworthy to ſerve our humours and paſſions, to
,, make ourſelves fools and beaſts. - - - In a word,
,, nothing but what tends to our private harm, or
,, prejudice, or to publick diſorder & confuſion. ,,

The late Dean of *Canterbury*, in a Sermon preach'd
in defence of Chriſtianity, ſays, † ,, What can be a
,, more powerful incentive to obedience, than for a
,, rational Creature clearly to diſcern the equity, the
,, neceſſity, the benefit, the decency and beauty of
,, every action he is call'd to do, and thence to be
,, duly ſenſible how gracious a Maſter he ſerves: One
,, that is ſo far from loading him with fruitleſs, arbi-
,, trary, & tyrannical impoſitions, that each command
,, abſtracted from his command who iſſues it, is able
,, to recommend itſelf, & nothing requir'd but what
,, every wiſe Man wou'd chooſe of his own accord,
,, and cannot, without being his own enemy, wiſh
,, to be exempted from. ,,  And this character of
Chriſtianity he makes to be eſſential to its being from
God, & therefore, muſt make it the ſame with Natural
Religion, which has this character impreſs'd on it.

There

* *Serm. Vol.* 1. *pag.* 86.
† *Boyle's* Lect. pag. 26.

„ THERE was none of the Doctrines of our
„ Saviour (*says the late Archbishop of* York *) cal-
„ culated for the gratification of Mens idle curiosities,
„ the busying and amusing them with airy & useless
„ speculations: much less were they intended for an
„ excercise of our credulity, or a trial how far we
„ cou'd bring our Reason to submit to our Faith.
„ But as on the one hand they were plain & simple,
„ and such as by their agreeableness to the rational
„ faculties of Mankind, did highly recommend them-
„ selves to our belief, so on the other hand they had
„ an immediate relation to practice, and were the
„ genuine principles and foundation, upon which all
„ human & divine virtues were naturally to be super-
„ structed. „ Does not every one see, that if the
Religion of Nature had been put instead of Christianity,
these descriptions wou'd have exactly agreed with it.

THE judicious Dr. *Scot* affirms, † „ God never im-
„ poses Laws on us *pro Imperio*, as arbitrary tests and
„ trials of our obedience. -- The great design of them,
„ *says he*, is to do us good, and direct our actions to
„ our own interest. --- This, if we firmly believe,
„ will infinitely encourage our obedience: for when
„ I am sure God commands me nothing but what my
„ own health, ease, and happiness requires, and that
„ every Law of his is both a necessary and sovereign
„ prescription against the diseases of my nature, and
„ he could not prescribe less than he has, without
„ being defective in his care of my recovery & hap-
„ piness, with what prudence & modesty can I grudge
„ to obey him?

NAY, the most considerable Men, even among the
*Papists*, do not scruple to maintain there's nothing in
Religion but what is moral. The Divines of *Port Royal*
for

* Serm. before the Queen on *Christm. Day*, 1724.
† *Christ. Life Part 2. Vol. 1. Ch. 4. p.* 173, 174.

for inſtance ſay. * „ All the Precepts, & all the My-
„ ſteries that are expreſs'd in ſo many different ways
„ in the holy volumes, do all center in this one Com-
„ mandment of *loving God with all our heart*, and in
„ *loving our Neighbours as ourſelves:* For the Scripture
„ (it is St. *Auſtin* who ſays it) forbids but one only thing,
„ which is *Concupiſcence*, or the love of the Creature;
„ as it commands but one only thing, which is *Charity*,
„ and the Love of God. Upon this double Precept is
„ founded the whole ſyſtem of the Chriſtian Religion:
„ and it is unto this, *ſay they*, according to the ex-
„ preſſion of Jeſus Chriſt, that all the ancient Law
„ and the Prophets have reference; and we may add
„ alſo, all the Myſteries, and all the Precepts of the
„ new Law: *For Love*, ſays St. *Paul, is the fulfilling
„ of the Law:* „ And theſe Divines likewiſe cite a remarkable Paſſage of St. *Auſtin* on this ſubject; *viz.*
„ † He that knows how to love God, & to regulate
„ his life by that love, knows all that the Scripture
„ propounds to be known: „ They alſo might have
quoted a known ſaying of this Father, *Omnia peccata
ſunt in univerſum contra Rationem & Naturæ Legem.*
And I might add the Authority of a greater Man, &
a *Papiſt* too, who ſays, ‡ „ Religion adds nothing to
„ natural probity, but the conſolation of doing that
„ for love and obedience to our heavenly Father,
„ which Reaſon itſelf requires us to do in favour of
virtue. And the famous *Pere Queſnel* ſays on *Acts* 2. 21.
*Le vrai culte n'eſt plus attaché à un Peuple, Le Chriſtia-
niſme eſt une Religion univerſelle.*

B. Do Divines always give this character of Chriſtianity? do they never diſtinguiſh it from the Religion
of Nature, by ſuppoſing it contains certain arbitrary
Precepts?

*A.*

* *Pref. au Nouv. Teſtamen.* † *Ibid.*
‡ Archbp. of *Cambray* Lettres ſur la Religion, p. 258.
à Paris.

*A.* WHEN they confider how repugnant'tis to the nature of God to give any arbitrary Commands, then indeed the force of truth obliges them to declare there's nothing in Religion but what tends to the good of Mankind; but if at any time they talk otherwife, 'tis for the fake of fuch things as either directly or indirectly ferve their intereft. But to remove all fcruples I fhall more fully prove,

## CHAP. IV.

*That not only the matter of all God's Laws, but the penalties annex'd to them are for the good of Mankind; even of thofe who fuffer for the breach of them.*

*B.* SHOUD I allow you, that the natural knowledge we have of God is the foundation of all Religion, and that arguing from the Divine Attributes is a moft certain way of reafoning, yet is not God's glory one of his divine Attributes? And does not the wifeft of Men fay, that * *God made all things for himfelf, and the Wicked for the Day of Evil:* and confequently God's glory, rather than the good of Man, occafion'd the Almighty to create Man, and to give him Laws?

*A.* As to this text, I fhall anfwer you from Archbifhop *Tillotfon,* that † ,, If by *God's making all things* ,, *for himfelf,* be meant, that he aim'd at & intended ,, the manifeftation of his Wifdom, Power, & Goodnefs ,, in the Creation of the World, 'tis moft true, that ,, in this fenfe *he made all things for himfelf;* but if ,, we underftand it fo, as if the goodnefs of his nature ,, did not move him thereto, but that he had fome ,, defign to ferve, ends and neceffities of his own, ,, upon his Creatures, this is far from him. But it's ,, very

* *Prov.* 16. 4.     † *Serm. Vol.* 7. *pag.* 19.

„ very probable, that neither of these are the meaning
„ of the Text, which may be render'd with much
„ better sense, & nearer to the *Hebrew* thus: *God has*
„ *ordain'd every thing to that which is fit for it, & the*
„ *Wicked hath he ordain'd for the Day of Evil*; that is,
„ the Wisdom of God hath fitted one thing to an-
„ other, Punishment to Sin, the Evil Day to the Evil
„ Doers.„ This is the sense that *Grotius*, and most of
the best Commentators put on the text. And here let
me add, that if there are innumerable places as capable of different interpretations, even with relation
to God and his Attributes, this sure, will be no argument not to adhere to what the Light of Nature
teaches us in this matter: since where texts may be
taken in different senses, things are as much left to be
determin'd by our Reason, as if there were no such
texts.   And when we meet with expressions of God's
doing any thing for is own glory, they can only mean,
that such is the transcendent excellency of his nature,
such the inexpressible marks of his Wisdom & Power
in all his works, that he cou'd not have given greater
had he design'd nothing but his own glory. And when
we impute the glory of all we do to him, we thereby
signify, that we have no power but what we derive
from him, and that we desire to acknowledge him
the Author of whatever is praise-worthy in us.

*B.* Tho' it be allow'd, that God fram'd his Laws,
& consequently the sanctions that make them Laws,
for the good of Man, yet a due regard to his own
honour, the dignity of his Laws and Government,
will oblige him to punish those, who violate his Laws,
as for an injury done to himself, distinct from the harm
that by the breach of them accrues to his Creatures.

*A.* As no Man breaks the divine Laws out of contempt to his Maker, or imagines he can do God an
injury; so God does not make Laws for one end,
& require the observing them for another; that being
inconsistent with the Dignity of the divine Legislator,

his

his Laws & Government: but as it was for the fake of Man that he gave him Laws, fo he executes them purely for the fame reafon; fince upon his own account, he can't be in the leaft affected, whether his Laws be, or be not obferv'd; and confequently in punifhing, no more than rewarding, does he act as a party, much lefs an injur'd party, who wants fatisfaction, or reparation of honour. And indeed, to fuppofe it, is highly to dishonour him, fince God, as he never can be injur'd, fo he can never want reparation; and he, who is infinitely fatisfy'd in himfelf, can gain no addition of fatisfaction by his Creatures obferving his Laws; nor can he, by their not obferving them, be reduc'd to a condition of wanting fatisfaction, or reparation of honour, or any of thofe things, which, depending on the opinion of others, are main ingredients in human happinefs: And yet even among Men none ought to be punifh'd, (fince what is paft can't be help'd) but to prevent a future breach of the Law; and all Laws being defign'd for the good of the governed, ,, The greateft Monarch is not to punifh the ,, breach of his Laws any otherwife, than the moft ,, petty State: ,, And tho all own, it would be tyranny in an earthly Governor to multiply punifhments on pretence of vindicating the honour of the Legiflator, or as the breach of Law is an injury done to him, and fuch like; yet fome are not afham'd to impute fuch tyranny to God, and thereby take off from that efteem and Love Men muft have for him, did they believe he only punifh'd when, and no further than their good requir'd.

Do not we bring God down to ourfelves, when we fuppofe he acts like us poor indigent Creatures, in feeking worfhip and honour for his own fake? nay, do we not cloath him, who has neither parts nor paffions, with the worft of our infirmities, if we reprefent him as an ambitious, fufpicious, wrathful & revengeful Being?

C Is

IF we dare confult our Reason, it will tell us that jealousy in point of honour & power, love of fame and glory can only belong to limited Creatures; but are as necessarily excluded from an unlimited, absolutely perfect Being, as anger, revenge, and such like passions, which would make the Deity resemble the weak, womanish, and impotent part of our nature, rather than the manly, noble, and generous.

Cou'd God strictly speaking, be made angry, provok'd, or griev'd by the conduct of us wretched Mortals, he wou'd not enjoy a moment's quiet, but must be much more miserable than the most unhappy of his Creatures. Or,

HAD God any comfort, or satisfaction to gain from the thoughts and actions of his Creatures, he wou'd never have been without an infinity of them jointly contributing to this end.

IF Religion in general, & every part of it was not useful to Mankind, there wou'd be no reason why they shou'd know it more than other Animals, who, tho they have wonderful talents (in many of which they exceed Men) given them by God for preserving themselves and their species, yet are utter strangers to Religion, as a thing wholly useless to them.

THE sum of what I have been saying is fully express'd by *Job* in these words, * *If thou sinnest, what dost thou against him? Or if thy transgressions be multiply'd, what dost thou unto him? If thou be righteous, what givest thou him? Or what receiveth he at thy hands? Thy wickedness may hurt a Man as thou art, and thy righteousness profit the Son of Man.* Or, as *Esdras* says, † *What is Man that thou shouldst take displeasure at him? Or what is a corruptible Generation, that thou shouldst be so bitter towards it?*

OUR greatest felicity consists in having such an impartial & disinterested Judge as well as Legislator, that whether he punishes, or rewards, he acts alike for our

good;

* Chap. 35. 6, &c.    † II, Esdr. 8. 34

good; That being the end of all his Laws, and consequently of the penalties as well as rewards which make them Laws; whereas your common systems of Divinity represent him full of wrath and fury, ready to glut himself with revenge for the injuries he has suffer'd by the breach of his Laws.

*B.* Is not God's Justice as well as his Mercy a divine Attribute, and will not that as much oblige him to punish the Breakers of his Laws, as if he had been, as he is sometimes represented, full of anger, wrath, and revenge?

*A.* Tho' Justice & Mercy can't at the same time be exercis'd in one & the same instance on the same Subject, yet your System Writers, left they shou'd limit these two Attributes in God, extend them alike to all persons, which is making him neither just, nor merciful; because these Attributes drawing contrary ways must hinder each other's effect.

*B.* I must confess, I do not see how the same act can be an act both of Justice and Mercy in relation to the same person; or how it can be said that God does Justice on a Sinner, when he shews Mercy to him; and yet we must suppose the Justice as well as Mercy of God to be infinite,

*A.* The Justice by which God is righteous in all his actions, and the Mercy by which he is good or beneficent are infinite, and eternally inherent in the divine nature; but these oblige not God either to punish, or pardon any further than his infinite Wisdom sees fit; and such punishing & pardoning are transient acts, the effects of his Will, not properties belonging to his nature. Justice and Mercy among Men relate to different subjects: When the Magistrate punishes a Criminal, 'tis an act of Justice to the publick; and when he pardons him 'tis an act of mercy to the criminal, tho' an act of injustice to the publick; except in such circumstances, where he has ground to believe that pardoning him may be no disadvantage to the

publick,

publick, whose interest it is not to lose a useful member.

THE greatest difference in this case between God and Man is, that the most powerful Monarch on earth is of the same nature with his Subjécts, and his good involv'd in the good of the whole, & by the breach of his Laws may be injur'd; and as a party injur'd may exact reparation & satisfaction: But this without blasphemy can't·be said of God, whose nature is infinitely superior to that of Man; and who as he was infinitely happy in himself before there was any Creature to adore him, or be obedient to his will; so he must still be such, tho' none of them did obey his Laws, or acknowledge his being: and therefore, in doing acts of Justice he can't, like the Monarchs of this world, propose any security to himself, but acts purely for the good of his Creatures; and the effects of his Justice (they never extending to annihilation) must not only be for the good of others, but even of the persons punish'd; because God, whose Love infinitely exceeds that of mortal Parents, chastises his Children, (and all Mankind are alike his offspring) because he loves them, & designs their amendment; & the reason why God in Scripture is said to be *Love*, must be because all his acts, by what name soever you call them, are acts of pure, impartial, & disinterested Love.

ALL Punishment for punishment's sake is meer cruelty and malice, which can never be in God; nor can he hate any thing he has made, or be subject to such weakness or impotence as to act arbitrarily, or out of spite, wrath revenge, or any self-interest; and consequently, whatever punishment he inflicts, must be a mark of his Love, in not suffering his Creatures to remain in that miserable state, which is inseparable from sin & wickedness.

As God's infinite goodness appears in the sanctions as well as matter of his Laws, so his infinite Wisdom
know

knows how to adjuſt the puniſhment to the offence; that it may be exactly fitted to produce the deſir'd amendment.

B. Does not your ſuppoſing that God has no other motive in executing his Laws, than he had in making them; *viz.* the Good of his Creatures; and that all puniſhment muſt bear an exact proportion to the offence it is deſign'd to amend, ſtrike at the abſolute eternity of Hell-torments? ſince there's no proportion between temporary injuries done to all Men, & eternal miſery of but one Man; nor can everlaſting torment work amendment.

*A.* I ſhall at preſent refer you to Dr. *Burnet, de Statu mortuorum;* and only ſay with Archbiſhop *Tillotſon*
,, The right that God hath in his Creatures is founded
,, in the benefits he hath conferr'd on them, and the
,, obligation they have to him on that account. Now
,, there's none, who becauſe he has done a benefit,
,, can have, by virtue of that, a right to do a greater
,, evil than the good he has done amounts to; & I
,, think it next to madneſs to doubt, whether extreme
,, & eternal miſery be not a greater evil than ſimple
,, being is a good. ,, But at a proper time I ſhall conſider what may be ſaid from Scripture as well as Reaſon, for the doctrine of the abſolute eternity of torments; and what will be the condition of thoſe who dye before they are capable of undergoing a tryal, or knowing any thing of Religion. A ſubject, which, I think, has ſcarce been conſider'd by any one.

* *Serm. Vol.* 6. *pag.* 211. *& pag.* 621.

CHAP.

# CHAP. V.

*That God requires nothing for his own sake; no not the Worship we are to render him, nor the Faith we are to have in him.*

B. YOUR arguing from the Nature of God, that every thing, consequently Faith in him, and even the worship and service we render to him, is wholly for our own sake, will hardly go down with the bulk of Mankind, who imagine, they by those acts do him some real service.

*A.* IF they think so, 'tis a sign they have not been well instructed : the most eminent of our Divines wou'd teach them, that Prayer itself, God knowing beforehand what we will ask, chiefly becomes a duty, as it raises in us a due contemplation of the divine Attributes, & an acknowledgement of his great & constant goodness, and serves to keep up a constant sense of our dependance on him ; and as it disposes us to imitate those perfections we adore in him, in being kind & beneficent to one another. There are few so gross as to imagine, we can direct infinite Wisdom in the dispensation of Providence, or perfuade him to alter those Laws he contriv'd before the Foundation of the World for putting things in a regular course.

„ TIS, says Archbishop *Tillotson,* * a great con-
„ descention and goodness in him, to accept our im-
„ perfect praises, and ignorant admiration of him ;
„ & were he not as wonderfully good, as he is great
„ and glorious, he wou'd not suffer us to sully his
„ great & glorious name by taking it in our mouths ;
„ and were it not for our advantage & happiness to
„ own & acknowledge his benefits, for any real hap-
„ piness and glory that comes to him by it, he cou'd
　　　　　　　　　　　　　　　　　　　　　　„ well

* *Vol.* 7. *pag.* 28. *To.* 2. 681.

,, well enough be without it, and difpenfe with us
,, for ever entertaining one thought of him; & were
,, it not for his goodnefs might defpife the praifes of
,, his Creatures, with infinitely more reafon than wife
,, Men do the applaufe of Fools. ,,

,, To imagine, as Dr. *Scot* obferves, * that God
,, needs our fervices, and requires them to ferve his
,, own intereft, is to blafpheme his All-fufficiency,
,, and fuppofe him a poor indigent being, who for
,, want of perfect fatisfaction within himfelf, is forc'd
,, to roam abroad, and raife taxes on his Creatures,
,, to enrich and fupply himfelf: So that whatfoever
,, fome high-flown Enthufiafts may pretend, that 'tis
,, fordid and mercenary to ferve God for our good,
,, I am fure, to ferve him for his good is profane &
,, blafphemous. ,,

As able a Divine as this, or perhaps any other Age
has produc'd, obferves, that † ,, Nothing can be more
,, falfe, or contrary to the nature of the Gofpel, than
,, to fancy God in part defign'd to fhew he was Mafter,
,, by enjoining fome Commands, which have no re-
,, lation to the good of Mankind; Religion was re-
,, veal'd for us, and not for God, who, abfolutely
,, fpeaking, neither wants what we think of him, nor
,, the worfhip we pay him, but has manifefted him-
,, felf to us, only to make us happy. ,,    And, therefore, if from excefs of Devotion, a Man neglects the
duties of civil life, he is fo far from doing a thing
acceptable to God, that he miftakes the end of Religion, which is to render him as perfect as may be in
all moral duties whatever.

If any Command was ever given for the fake of
God, it muft certainly be that relating to the inftitution of the *Sabbath*; and yet we find it faid, *The Sabbath is made for Man, and not Man for the Sabbath.*

* *Scot's* Chrift. Life. Part 2. Vol. 1. Ch. 6.
† *Le Clerk's* Cauf. of Incred. Eng. Tranfl. p. 2

So true is it in Divinity as well as Politicks, that *the good of the People is the supreme Law.*

IN short, the worship God requires, is either for his own sake, which supposes his happiness some way or other depends on it; or else (except he requires things to no purpose) for the sake of Men, to raise & keep in their minds the contemplation of an infinitely good Being, and of his Laws, all founded on a disinterested Love to the whole race of Mankind. To imagine the worship of God is ordain'd on any other account, not only destroys one of the greatest motives of Mens doing good to one another, but supposes God not sufficient for, or infinitely happy in himself, but subject to the passions of ambitious & vain-glorious Mortals.

THE Generality of Christians not only believe, that in worshipping God they do him real service, but think he is extreamly uneasy, if publick worship is not perform'd in such a manner, & with such rites and ceremonies; & being endlesly divided about these trifles, think they make their court to Heaven, and and highly oblige an omnipotent Being, in destroying those formidable Enemies of God, who presume, without their leave, to worship him after that manner they judge agreeable to his will. And,

THERE are no measures, tho' ever so destructive, but what they, who do not consider the end of God's Laws, may be brought into; as all History sufficiently proves. The *Jews* not only thought that doing the greatest good on their Sabbath, was profaning the day; but were so superstitious as to think, * that all self-defence was then unlawful; and therefore durst not lift up their hands against their Enemies, who butcher'd them as they pleas'd: And many of the primitive Fathers thought the Gospel forbid all self-defence; and herein they are follow'd by a modern Sect, who are their strict imitators in most things.

TIS

* *Maccab.* 2.

'TIS no wonder, if some Ecclesiasticks have not been very forward to teach People, that what worship God requires of them, is for their own sakes; since then they cou'd not on pretence of that worship, have claim'd such powers and privileges, as are inconsistent with the common good: & People might then think it their duty so to regulate matters, as that their Priests, upon the whole, considering the charge of maintaining them, and other incidents, shou'd do more good than hurt; which can never happen, till Men are taught 'tis their duty to do good to all, notwithstanding their widest differences as to worship, or any other matter of meer Religion: & 'tis to the honour of our Clergy at present, that so many of them now endeavour to infuse such human and penevolent Principles into a People, who not long since; thought they shew'd a sufficient zeal for Religion, in hating those their Priests hated, without knowing wherefore; and fir'd by their pulpit invectives, thought it their duty to pull down houses of religious worship, & were ready at the direction of their impious leaders, to have perpetrated worse crimes.

*B.* THERE's one difficulty, which to me seems insuperable; how to make the Faith requir'd by the Religion of Nature & that of the Gospel, to have the same views, and tend to the same end.

*A.* IF Faith in God himself, no more than any other act of Religion, is requir'd for God's sake, but our own; can Faith in one sent by God be requir'd for any other end? Especially considering, that no Person is ever the more known to posterity, because his Name is transmitted to them: when we say, *Cæsar* conquer'd *Pompey*, we having no idea of either can only mean, Some-body conquer'd Some-body; and have we more distinct ideas of *Jesus* & *Pilate?* And tho' we had a personal idea of the former, he cou'd receive no advantage or disadvantage by what we thought of him. And if Faith in him was requir'd

C 5                                    for

for a caufe antecedent to his being fo fent, founded
in his & our nature, & the relation we always ſtood
in to him, wou'd not the eternal Reafon of things
have made it manifeſt? That which concern'd all,
muſt be knowable by all, for which reafon the Apoſtle
fays, *That which may be known of God* (and none can
know that which may not be known) *was manifeſt
in the Gentiles.* And,

THE end of Chriſt's coming feems not to teach
Men new duties, but (repentance being the firſt thing
preach'd by him and his Apoſtles both to *Jews* and
*Gentiles*) to repent of the breach of known duties.
And Jefus does not fay, He was *fent to all Ifrael,* *
*but to the loſt Sheep of the Houfe of Ifrael*; and that the
† *Son of Man is come to fave that which was loſt*: And
his Parable about the *loſt Sheep,* ‡ fuppos'd all were
not loſt. And when it was objected to him, that he
kept company with Sinners, he owns the charge, &
fays, § *The whole need no Phyſician, but they that are
fick*; which wou'd have been an improper anfwer, if
he thought that all ſtood in need of him, and his ſpiritual phyſick. And to confirm this, he adds, ¶ *I am
not come to call the righteous, but Sinners to repentance*
and that *There's more joy in Heaven for one Sinner that
repents, than ninety nine juſt perfons that need no repentance.* Which is dividing Mankind into two parts,
the *whole* or *righteous,* and the *fick* or *Sinners*; & that
his bufineſs was intirely with the latter. The not obferving this diſtinction has been the occafion of many
uncharitable & grofs miſtakes & 'tis fomewhat ſtrange;
that Jefus, who beſt knew how far his Commiſſion
extended, fhou'd not be credited in this matter; eſpecially confidering that in Religion there are no *noſtrums,*
or fecrets, but all may know what God requires of all;
and there is but one univerfal remedy for all fick perfons, *Repentance* and *Amendment.* And if *God, who is*

nc

* *Mat.* 15. 24.    † 18. 11.    ‡ *Luke* 15. 7.
§ *Mat.* 9. 12.    ¶ *Ibid. Verf.* 13.

*no respecter of persons, will judge the world in righteou-*
*ness*, and *they that in every nation fear him*, *and work
righteousness shall be accepted of him*, they, certainly,
are whole, and need no Physician, who do of themselves what will make them acceptable to him, living
as those whom Christ came to reform were taught to
live. Is it not absurd to suppose, that till then none
had sufficient means given them to answer the end for
which all were created ?

,, The Catholick Epistle of St. *Barnabas* will inform
you of the sentiments of the Ancients on this head.
This great Apostle (as translated by Dr. *Wake*) says, *
,, That Jesus, when he chose his Apostles, which were
,, afterwards to publish his Gospel, took Men who
,, had been very great sinners, that thereby he might
,, plainly shew, that † *He came not to call the righteous,*
,, *but Sinners to Repentance.* The words are fuller in
the Original, ὄντας ὑπὲρ πᾶσαν ἁμαρτιαν ἀνομωτέρους.

B. There's may be a forg'd passage.

A. *Origin* owns it to be genuine, for when *Celsus*
(I will give you his words in the *Latin* Translation)
says, ‡ *Jesum ascitis decem undecimve famosis hominibus, publicanis nauiisquo nequissimis, cum his ultro ostroque fugitasse, corrogantem cibos sordid ac turpiter* Origen
says, § *Extat sane in Barnabæ Catholica Epistola scriptum, Jesum ad Apostolicam functionem elegisse homines omni iniquitate iniquiores.* And it may be said in support of
St. *Barnabas*, that the Apostles first became Jesus's
Disciples upon temporal motives; and the belief of
Christ's temporal Kingdom was so firmly rooted in
them, that Jesus neither during his life, nor even after
his resurrection was able to remove it. At the last
Supper there was a strife amongst them, ¶ *Who should
be accounted the greatest ?* ,, The meanest (as Bishop *Parker*
,, expresses it) hoped at least to have been made Lord
,, Mayor

* *Wake's* Transl. §. 5. p. 272.    † *Mat.* 9. 13.
‡ *Origen* cont. *Celsum.* l. 1. p. 47.    § *Ib. p.* 49.
¶ *Luke* 22. 24.

,, Mayor of *Capernaum.* ,, And even at his Ascension the only Question his Disciples ask'd was, * *Lord, wilt thou at this time restore again the Kingdom to* Israel?

BUT to take away all subterfuges, what can be more requir'd than such qualifications as will make *Jesus* in the last day declare, *Come ye blessed of my Father, inherit the Kingdom prepared for you from the beginning of the World?* And what are those qualifications, but living up to the Law of Reason, in exercising acts of benevolence, goodness, &c? That this was the *Unum necessarium* is plain from his answer, *Depart from me ye that work iniquity,* made to those who had omitted these things, tho' they pleaded, † *They had prophecy'd in his name, and in his name cast out Devils, and done many wonderful works.* St. *Paul* in the first Chapter to the *Romans* is very large, in shewing that the *Gentiles* cou'd not plead ignorance of their duty, either to God or Man, and as sinning against knowledge were inexcusable; & persuing the same subject in the second, he says, that *God who is no Respecter of Persons* will deal with every one both *Jew* & *Gentile* according to their deeds; and those by which they are to be judg'd are either moral or immoral; and had there been any thing else requir'd by the written Law, it cou'd not be said that *the Gentiles, who were not ignorant of their duty either to God or Man, did by Nature the things contained in the Law.*

AND does not St. *Paul,* in another place, put our future state on the same foot, in supposing we shall be dealt with at the last day ‡ *according to what we have done in the body, whether good or bad.* In short, if the tree is to be known by its fruit, and it brings forth good fruit, the means by which this good fruit is produc'd are not material; but if it does not, no means whatever can hinder it from being *hewn down, & cast into the fire.* § ,, The grand deciding question

(says

---

* *Acts* 1. 6.          † *Mat.* 7. 22, 23.

‡ *2 Cor.* 5. 10.        § *Mat.* 7 19.

(*says Dr.* South) ¶ ,, at the laſt day will be, not what
,, you have ſaid, or what you have believ'd; but what
,, you have done more than others. * God is pleas'd
,, to vouchſafe the beſt he can give, only to the beſt
,, we can do. ,, But to go the bottom of this matter,

Faith conſider'd in itſelf can neither be a Virtue,
nor a Vice, becauſe Men can no otherwiſe believe
than as things appear to them: Nay, can there be an
higher affront to God than to ſuppoſe, he requires Men
to judge otherwiſe than the faculties he has given
them enable them to do? Or what can be more abſurd
than to imagine, that God will ſhew his favour to one
for believing what he could not but believe; and his
diſpleaſure to another for not believing what he could
not believe? & therefore Faith is only to be eſteem'd
by the works it produces; for the ſtrongeſt Faith may
be worſe than no Faith at all. *The Devils themſelves,*
(who are held the moſt wicked beings in the Univerſe)
*believe, & tremble* Happy had it been for *Chriſtendom,*
if zeal for what the prevailing parties call'd, *The Orthodox Faith,* had made none but themſelves to
tremble.

Dr. *Whitby* expreſſes himſelf very accurately on this
point. † ,, Belief, or disbelief can neither be a Virtue,
,, or a Crime in any one, who uſes the beſt means in
,, his power of being inform'd. If a propoſition is
,, evident, we cannot avoid believing it, and where
,, is the merit or piety of a neceſſary aſſent? If it is
,, not evident, we cannot help rejecting it, or doubting
,, of it: And where is the crime of not performing
,, impoſſibilities, or not believing what does not ap-
,, pear to us to be true? ,, What worſe opinion can
we have of the divine Goodneſs, than to imagine a
mean denial of our Reaſon, or a wretched affectation
of believing any point too hard for our underſtanding,
can entitle us to the favour of God.

I F

I f Charity, which comprehends doing all possible good to our Fellow - Creature, is to be destroy'd for the sake of Faith; or if incapacities, fines, imprisonments, rods, gibbets, racks, and fire, are marks of Charity, the Christian world has outdone all Mankind in acts of charity: but the description St. *Paul* gives of Charity, is so far from requiring us to make others suffer, that itself ✠ *suffers long, seeks not her own, bears all things, endures all things*; and strictly enjoins us so to do.

H e r e is the practice of the Christian World on the side of Faith, sacrificing Charity, and all that's valuable to it; & on the other side, Christ & his Apostles preferring Charity before it. St. *Paul*, speaking of himself, says, * *Tho I have the gift of prophecy, & understand all mysteries, & all knowledge; And tho' I have all faith, and could remove mountains, & have no charity, I am nothing: Or tho' I give my body to be burnt* ( which shews the highest act of Faith) *and have not charity, it profiteth nothing.* And in another place he says, † *Above all things put on Charity, which is the bond of perfectness.* And again, ‡ *The End of the commandment is Charity;* § *and Love is the fulfilling of the Law.* And, ¶ *If any provide not for his own, especially those of his own house* (which is but one species of Charity) *he has denied the Faith, and is worse than an Infidel.* And St. *Peter* likewise speaks as highly of it in saying, ✠ *Above all things have fervent Charity among yourselves, for Charity shall cover a multitude of Sins;* which can't be said of *Faith*, because that *without Charity profiteth nothing*, in not answering the end for which it was given. And St. *James* * calls Love *the Royal Law.* And St. *John* says, † *If any Man says I love God, & hateth his Brother, he is a liar.* And is not he likewise a liar, who shews all the marks of hatred to his
Brother,

✠ 1 *Cor.* 13.          * *Ibid.*          † *Col.* 3. 14.
‡ 1 *Tim.* 1. 5.          § *Rom.* 13. 10.          ¶ 1 *Tim.* 5. 8.
✠ 1 *Pet.* 4. 8.          * *James* 2. 8.          † 1 *John* 4. 20,

Brother, & yet pretends to love him, & makes those very marks an argument of his love. *In Jesus Christ,* says the Apostle *Paul,* * *neither circumcision, nor uncircumcision availeth any thing, but faith which worketh by Love.* - - † *For all the Law is fulfilled in one word, even in this, Thou shalt love thy Neighbour as thy self.* And Christ, in saying, ‡ *By this shall all Men know ye are my Disciples, if ye love one another,* supposes Mens loving one another so essential to Christianity, as by that token alone all Men may know who are his Disciples; and if they who thus love one another are of course his Disciples, whose Disciples then are they, who, as all Men know, make people hate, & harrass one another, and pretend Christ's commission for so doing?

*Origen* speaking of the Faith of Christians, cou'd not (was there any thing peculiar in their Faith) have said, „ § 'Tis the conformity of our Faith with the com-„ mon innate notions of all Mankind, that has given „ it entrance into the minds of candid & ingenuous „ hearers. And.

Our Divines (since the liberty they enjoy has enabl'd them to think, and speak their thoughts more freely than formerly) when they write in defence of Christianity, endeavour to shew that the Faith the Scripture requires, is conformable to what *Origen* calls, *The common, and innate notions of Mankind.* I do not find, that the Dean of *Sarum* is censur'd for affirming in defence of Christianity, that ¶ „ The Scripture „ notion of Faith is very plain and obvious, *viz.* not „ a speculative and philosophical, but a religious and „ practical Faith; and 'tis built on this principle, „ That God *is,* and that *he is a rewarder of them that* „ *diligently seek him;* That religious Faith is a full „ conviction of mind, that an eternal, immense Being; „ in-

* *Gal.* 5. 6.     † *Ver.* 14.     ‡ *John* 13. 35.
§ *Origen* contra *Celsum.* l. 3. p. 135.
¶ *Origin of Moral Evil:* pag. 90.

,, infinitely wife, juft, & good, not only actually exifts.
,, but is the Governor of the World; prefcribes Laws
,, to the confciences, & to the actions of Men; takes
,, notice of their compliance with, or tranfgreffion
,, of them; & will certainly reward, or punifh them,
,, according as their works have been. To live under
,, this fenfe and expectation, is to live a life of Faith,
,, and is co-incident with a life of Virtue.   All the
,, fpecies, or particular inftances of Faith may be re-
,, duc'd to this, as fo many branches fpringing from it:
,, And to explain them in any other fenfe, as if Faith
,, & Reafon were oppos'd to each other, & Religion
,, and Virtue two different things, is to blind Mens
,, underftandings, and to confound the plaineft, and
,, moft numerous texts of Scripture.

A N O T H E R learned Divine, in defence of the Chriftian Religion, fays, * ,, If it fhould happen, that we
,, cannot fo fatisfactorily evince the certainty of the
,, Scripture-Hiftory againft fcrupulous, nice, & fcepti-
,, cal Wits, yet we find ourfelves oblig'd to the belief
,, & practice of what is really the Chriftian Religion;
,, becaufe tis nothing elfe, as to the Faith & Morals
,, of it, but Natural Religion.

T H E great *Grotius*, in a Difcourfe own'd to be the
beft that was ever writ in defence of Chriftianity, lays
it down as a Maxim, that † ,, 'Tis abfolutely repugnant
,, to the goodnefs of God, that thofe, who without
,, refpect to worldly advantage, feek after the way
,, which leads to eternal happinefs, imploring withal
,, the divine affiftance, and fubmitting themfelves in-
,, tirely to his Providence, fhould not be able to find it.
,, And if this is too evident to be deny'd, can there
,, be any thing eafier in relation to Faith or manners
,, in the way that leads to eternal happinefs, but may
,, be found at all times & places of every one, who
,, diligently fearches after it.

AND

* *Nye* of Nat. & Reveal. Relig. pag. 127.
† *Grotius* de Verit. Chr. Relig. lib. 6. Sect. 2.

AND an eminent Divine, who is not look'd on to have altogether so extensive a charity as *Grotius,* yet says, * ,, I think we may pronounce safely in this ,, matter, that the goodness & mercy of God is such, ,, that he never deserts a sincere person, nor suffers ,, any one that shall live (even according to these ,, measures of sincerity) up to what he knows, to ,, perish for want of any knowledge necessary; and ,, what is more, sufficient to save him ,, Which supposes no Faith, or knowledge necessary to salvation, but what all are capable of acquiring by virtue of that † *Light, which lighteth every Man that cometh into the World.* And our Saviour himself says, ‡ *Seek, and ye shall find.* By this you may see what Faith is requir'd, and for what end.

IF Man, as our Divines maintain against *Hobbs,* is a social creature, who naturally loves his own species, and is full of pity, tenderness, & benevolence; and if Reason, which is the proper nature of Man, can never lead Men to any thing but universal love & kindness, and there be no part of Natural Religion, or any Faith it requires, but highly tends to improve this kind and benign temper; how comes it to pass, that what is taught for Religion in so many places of *Christendom,* has transform'd this mild & gentle Creature into fierce and cruel; and made him act with rage & fury against those who never did or intended him the least harm? Is not this chiefly owing to such a *Faith* as *works* not *by love;* and such a Zeal as, not being according to knowledge, has destroy'd all good works, & is utterly inconsistent with the end of all Religion. But no wonder if Men, who most uncharitably damn one another for such matters of Faith as they dare not trust Reason to judge of, shou'd hate & persecute each other on the same account.

D

THE

---

* *South's* Serm. Vol. 1. pag. 298.
† *John* 1. 9. ‡ *Mat.* 7. 7.

THE *Epicureans*, tho' they had exalted notions of their Gods, yet becaufe they afferted it beneath their dignity to concern themfelves with human affairs, were at all times cenfur'd as Atheifts; which fhews that 'twas accounted much the fame to believe no Gods, as to believe them ufelefs to Mankind. But certainly, believing the Deity to be indolent, can't be fo bad as believing him fo cruel, as to oblige Chriftians to perfecute, ruin, & deftroy even their Brethren, for things too, no ways contributing to the good of Mankind; fince this is downright *Demonifm*: And yet in what Age of the Church, wou'd not thofe confcientious people that chanc'd to be undermoft, have thought themfelves happy, if the Men in power had not had a worfe notion of the Deity than that of indolence.

## CHAP. VI.

*That the Religion of Nature is an abfolutely perfeEt Religion ; and that external Revelation can neither add to, nor take from its perfeEtion : and that true Religion, whether internally or externally reveal'd, muft be the fame.*

HAVING prov'd, That God requires nothing for his own fake; I fhall now, the way being thus prepar'd, fhew you, *That the Religion of Nature is abfolutely perfeEt ; & that external Revelation can neither add to, nor take from its perfeEtion :* And in order to it let me ask you, Why you believe the Gofpel a Law of abfolute perfeEtion, incapable of any addition, diminution, or alteration?

*B.* BECAUSE 'tis the laft Law of God's giving.

*A.* WAS it not fuch in itfelf, that cou'd not make it fo: fince the Law given to the *Jews* was for many ages the only external Law : And yet, I fuppofe, you grant

grant that this abrogated Law was far from deserving such a character. But were there any thing in this argument, it makes wholly for the Law of Nature: since that is not only the first, but the last Law of God's giving: if that can be said to be last, which is eternal: a Law, by which God governs his own actions, and by which he expects all the rational world shou'd govern theirs. And therefore, notwithstanding the promulgation of the Gospel, he continues daily to implant it in the minds of all Men, Christians as well as others: and consequently, 'tis as necessary for them as for others; as necessary since, as before the coming of Christ: And I may add too, not only necessary to be observ'd in this World, and ten thousand more, were there so many, but in Heaven itself, & that too for ever.

*B.* Shou'd I grant that my argument, from the Gospel's being the last Law of God's giving, does not fully prove its absolute perfection; yet it will undeniably follow from the great agreement there is between that & the Law of Nature; it neither forbiding what that requires, nor requiring what that forbids; and in a Word, containing nothing in it unworthy, but every thing worthy of an absolutely perfect Law giver.

*A.* In saying this, you own the Law of Nature to be the standard of perfection: and that by it we must judge antecedently to any traditional Religion what is, or is not a Law absolutely perfect, & worthy of such a Being for its Legislator.

*B.* Indeed, it must be own'd, that Divines as well as others, make the same concessions in relation to Natural Religion, which Dr. *Prideaux* does in his celebrated Letter to the *Deists* at the end of *Mahomet*'s Life: ,, * Let what is written in all the Books of the New ,, Testament be try'd by that which is the Touch- ,, stone of all Religions, I mean that Religion of ,, Nature and Reason, which God has written in the

* *Pag.* 127. *Edit.* 7. *octavo.*

,, hearts of every one of us from the first creation;
,, and if it varies from it in any one particular, if it
,, prescribes any one thing, which may in the minutest
,, circumstances thereof be contrary to its righteous-
,, ness, I will then acknowledge this to be an argu-
,, ment against us, strong enough to overthrow the
,, whole cause, and make all things else that can be
,, said for it totally ineffectual for its support.

*A.* I desire no more than to be allow'd, that there's
a Religion of Nature & Reason written in the hearts
of every one of us from the first Creation, by which
all Mankind must judge of the truth of any instituted
Religion whatever: and if it varies from the Religion
of Nature and Reason in any one particular, nay, in
the minutest circumstance, that alone is an argument,
which makes all things else that can be said for its
support totally ineffectual. If so, must not Natural
Religion and external Revelation, like two Tallies,
exactly answer one another, without any other difference between them, but as to the manner of their
being deliver'd? And how can it be otherwise? Can
Laws be imperfect, where a Legislator is absolutely
perfect? Can time discover any thing to him, which
he did not foresee from eternity? And as his Wisdom
is always the same, so is his Goodness: & consequently
from the consideration of both these his Laws must
always be the same. - - Is it not from the infinite
Wisdom and Goodness of God, that you suppose the
Gospel a most perfect Law, incapable of being repeal'd,
or alter'd, or of having additions? And must not you
own the Law of Nature as perfect a Law, except you
will say, that God did not arrive to the perfection of
Wisdom and Goodness till about seventeen hundred
years since?

To plead, that the Gospel is incapable of any additions, because the Will of God is immutable, and
his Law too perfect to feel them, is an argument,
was Christianity a new Religion, which destroys itself:
since

since from the time it commenc'd, you must own God is mutable; and that such additions have been made to the all-perfect Laws of infinite Wisdom, as constitute a New Religion. The Reason why the Law of Nature is immutable, is, because it is founded on the unalterable reason of things: but if God is an arbitrary Being, and can command things meerly from Will and Pleasure, some things to-day, and others tomorrow, there is nothing either in the nature of God, or in the things themselves, to hinder him from perpetually changing his mind. If he once commanded things without reason, there can be no reason why he may not endlessly change such commands.

I think, no Man has more fully done justice to the Law of Nature, than a Divine of that Church which requires so many things contrary to that Law; I mean the celebrated *Charron*, in his Treatise *of Wisdom*, whose authority is certainly not the less for being translated by the late Dean of *Canterbury:* He says, *
,, The Law of Nature, by which I mean Universal
,, Reason and Equity, is the candle of our Maker,
,, lighted up in every breast, to guide, and shine per-
,, petually. This is the dictate of God himself, he is
,, the King, & this the fundamental Law of the Uni-
,, verse; a ray and beam of the divine Nature, which
,, flows from, & has a necessary connexion & depen-
,, dance upon that eternal & immutable Law, which
,, the Almighty prescribes to his own actions. A Man,
,, who proceeds on this principle is his own rule;
,, for he acts in agreement with the noblest, & most
,, valuable part of his nature: This Man's honesty is
,, essential to, & inseparable from him, not precarious
,, and uncertain, and owing meerly to chance & oc-
,, casion; for this Light & Law is born with, & bred
,, in us; a piece of our frame & constitution; & from
,, thence obtains the name of Nature, and the Law
,, of Nature: Such a Man, by consequence, will be a

D 3　　　　　　good

* *Lib. 2. cap. 3. pag. 69.*

„ good Man conſtantly, and at all times, his virtue
„ will be uniform, & every place, every emergency
„ will find him the ſame; for this Law of Nature is
„ perpetual, the obligation of it is laſting & inviolable,
„ the equity and reaſon of it are eternal, written in
„ large & indelible characters; no accident can deface
„ them, no length of time waſte, or wear them out.
„ — — Theſe firſt principles, which are the ground of
„ all moral inſtitutions, admit of no change, no in-
„ creaſe, no abatement, no fits, no ſtarts, no ebbings
„ & flowings. — — Why then, vain Man, doſt thou
„ trouble thyſelf to ſeek abroad for ſome Law or Rule
„ to Mankind? What can Books, or Maſters tell thee,
„ which thou might'ſt not tell thyſelf? What can ſtudy,
„ or travel ſhew, which without being at the expence
„ of ſo much pains, thou might'ſt not ſee at home,
„ by deſcending into thy own conſcience, and hear-
„ kening attentively to its own admonitions?

„ To what purpoſe is all this labour and coſt?
„ The toilſom tumbling over of Codes & Inſtitutes?
„ — — The two Tables of *Moſes,* the twelve Tables
„ of the *Greeks,* the Law written in the heart of them
„ who had no Law, & in ſhort all the rules of equity
„ & good Laws, that have any where been enacted,
„ and obtained in the world, are nothing but copies
„ & tranſcripts produc'd in open Court, and publiſh'd
„ from that *original,* which thou keepeſt cloſe within
„ thee; and yet all the while pretendeſt to know
„ nothing of the matter, ſtifling & ſuppreſſing as much
„ as in thee lieth the brightneſs of that Light, which
„ ſhines within thee. As this inviſible fountain within
„ is more exuberant & plenteous, ſo it is more lively,
„ pure, and ſtrong, than any of the ſtreams deriv'd
„ from it; of which we need but this ſingle teſti-
„ mony, that when any diſputes ariſe about the right
„ meaning of any poſitive Law, the conſtant, & beſt
„ method of underſtanding the equity & true intent
„ of it, is by running back to its head, & obſerving
          „ what

„ what is moſt agreeable to the Law of Nature: This
„ is the teſt & touch, this is the level, & the truth,
„ by which the reſt are to be judged.

And in truth all Laws, whether the Law of Nations, or thoſe of particular Countries, are only the
Law of Nature adjuſted, & accommodated to circumſtances; nor can Religion, even in relation to the
Worſhip of God, as it is a reaſonable ſervice, be any
thing, but what neceſſarily flows from the conſideration of God, and the Creatures. 'Twas this made the
great Mr. *Selden* ſay, in an expreſſion ſomewhat homely,
„ * That Men look after Religion, as the Butcher
„ did after his knife, when he had it in his mouth.

The Religion of Nature is ſo entirely calculated
for the good of human ſociety, that tho' a Man,
hurry'd with the violence of his paſſions, breaks it himſelf, yet he wou'd have all others moſt ſtrictly obſerve
it: and accordingly all Legiſlators puniſh the breach
of it. Whereas no Man rejects any poſitive Inſtitution
himſelf, but is willing that all others ſhou'd do ſo too:
which plainly ſhews, Men do not apprehend it to be
for the general good of Mankind. And the contending
Parties in Religion, with equal confidence, cry,
„ That if our Religion be not true, God muſt be
„ wanting to Mankind, in what concerns their eternal
„ happineſs; he muſt be wanting to himſelf, and to
„ his own attributes of Goodneſs, Juſtice, & Truth:
„ It's repugnant to the very Notion of a God, to let
„ Men be ignorant in a matter of ſuch importance
„ without any help or remedy. „ This reaſoning,
if true, neceſſarily infers ſome univerſal Law knowable
at all times; and can't be apply'd to any partial Religion unknown to the world for many Ages, and, as
not being diſcoverable by Reaſon, ſtill unknown to
the greateſt part of it.

In a word, if the higheſt internal excellence, the
greateſt plainneſs & ſimplicity, unanimity, univerſality,

D 4     anti-

* *Table-Talk, pag.* 162.

antiquity, nay, eternity, can recommend a Law; ah these, 'tis own'd do, in an eminent degree, belong to the Law of Nature: A Law, which does not depend on the uncertain meaning of words & phrases in dead languages, much less on types, metaphors, allegories, parables, or on the skill or honesty of weak or designing transcribers (not to mention Translators) for many Ages together, but on the immutable relation of things always visible to the whole world. And therefore Dr. *Scot* justly says, * ,, Moral Obligations ,, are not founded like positive ones upon mutable cir- ,, cumstances (which suppose they can only oblige in ,, certain circumstances) but upon firm & everlasting ,, reasons; upon reasons that to all eternity will carry ,, with them the same force & necessity: as long as ,, we are Creatures of an infinitely perfect Creator, ,, it will be as much our duty as 'tis now, to submit ,, our will and affections to our Reason: & as long ,, as we are related to other reasonable Creatures, it ,, will be as much our duty as now to be kind, just, ,, and peaceable in all our intercourses with them: ,, So that these are such duties as no will can dispense ,, with, no reason abrogate, no circumstances disannul; ,, but as long as God is what he is, & we are what ,, we are, they must, and will oblige us.

I could, from many other considerations, shew you the absolute perfection of Natural Religion. For instance, must we not, except we speak without any meaning, or have no true meaning of the Word *God*, intend by it a Being of all perfections, free from all those defects, which belong even to the most perfect Creatures? And must we not have an idea of these Perfections, before we can know whether there is any Being who has enjoy'd them from eternity; & must we not know there s such a Being from our Reason, before we can come to this question, *Whether he has made any external Revolation?* Nay, examining into
this

* *Scot*'s Chrst. Life. Part 2. Vol. 1. Ch. 1. p. 66.

this queſtion wou'd be to very little purpoſe, except we cou'd know whether this Being is bound by his external word, & had not either at the time of giving it a ſecret will inconſiſtent with his reveal'd will; or has not ſince chang'd his will. This can't be known from any external Revelation, tho it expreſs'd itſelf ever ſo plainly; becauſe the queſtion being, *Whether God is oblig'd to do, as he in it ſays he will do*, this muſt be reſolv'd antecedently by the light of Nature, which muſt diſcover to us the veracity of God, and the immutability of his will: & the ſame reaſons which will prove he cou'd not change his will ſince he made an external Revelation, will prove his will was always unchangeable, and at all times the ſame; whether internally, or externally reveal'd. Nor cou'd we take a ſtep towards proving the veracity of God, or the immutability of his will, or indeed, any of his perfections beſides Power, without knowing that the will of God is always determin'd by the nature & reaſon of things: Otherwiſe falſehood and mutability might be the will of God, and there cou'd be no ſuch thing in Nature as Good and Evil, but an arbitrary will wou'd govern all things.

Were we not capable by our Reaſon of diſtinguiſhing Good from Evil, or knowing from the conſideration of the invariable perfections of God, what the divine Goodneſs cou'd command, or forbid his Creatures antecedently to any external Revelation, we cou'd not diſtinguiſh the true inſtituted Religion from the many falſe ones: or if by accident we ſtumbl'd on it, avoid running into many abſurdities in the interpretation of it, thro' the difficulties that muſt attend a Book writ in a dead language, & ſo many ages ſince; & where thro' the vaſt variety of readings we might miſtake the true reading: and tho' we were certain of the Letter, even *the Letter killeth.* *

D 5

IF

* 2 *Cor.* 3. 6.

I f Man had not natural abilities to diftinguifh between Good & Evil, or to know what is pleafing, or difpleafing to God, how cou'd we fay he was a moral Agent, or even an accountable Creature?

D i d we not allow that Men, by the Light of Nature, are capable of forming a found judgment in matters of Religion, they might be fo impos'd on by controverted, or mifinterpreted, not to fay forg'd Texts, as to admit feveral objects of divine worfhip in their practice, while in their words they own but one: or, in order to advance a fupernatural Charity, deftroy all natural Humanity, and believe our Love to God may be beft fhewn by our hatred to our Fellow-Creatures: and introduce fuch abominable notions, as may make Religion, inftead of a benefit, become a mifchief to Mankind.

W h e r e a s, if we allow the Light of Nature fufficient to enable us to judge rightly in thefe matters, and confequently to diftinguifh truth from falfehood, we muft own, fince there can be no difagreement in truth, that there's an exact conformity between internal & external Revelation, with no other difference but as to the manner of their being reveal'd: Or in other words, that the Gofpel, fince 'tis impoffible for Men at the fame time to be under different obligations, can't command thofe things which the Law of Nature forbids, or forbid what that commands; nor can any thing be a part of Religion by one Law, which by the other is Superftition: nor can external Revelation make that the Will of God, which the Light of Nature continually reprefents as unworthy of having God for its Author.

T h e judicious Writer of the *Rational Catechifm* lately reprinted fays, * „That one of the moft uni-
„ verfal caufes of the great differences among Men in
„ matters of Religion, is, that they have not examin'd
„ things to the bottom; they have fail'd in their
„ foun-

,, foundation-work; they have too much flighted that
,, Philofophy which is the Natural Religion of all Men;
,, and which being natural, mult needs be univerfal &
,, eternal: - - They have forfaken the Rule of right
,, Reafon, which is only capable to produce true fym-
,, metry in their intellectual buildings; and they have
,, apply'd themfelves without any Rule to the inter-
,, pretation of words and phrafes, which being eafily
,, fufceptible of various fenfes, have produc'd as many
,, deform'd irregularities.

Tho' all parties alike pretend to aim at truth, yet
none of them, I think, inform us what Truth is, or
wherein it confifts. Now if Truth in general, implies
an agreement of our ideas with the things themfelves,
Religious Truth, or true Religion mult confift in the
agreement of our ideas with thofe things which are
the fubjects of our religious inquiry, *viz.* the nature
of God. and Man; and falfe Religion mult confilt in
having ideas that are not agreeable to, or do not truly
reprefent thofe fubjects: and this agreement which we
call Truth in refpect to *Theory*, is what we term, in
relation to *Action*, fit, jult, good, or reafonable. Thus
God is frequently ftyl'd in Scripture the *God of Truth*,
becaufe his ideas of things and the things themfelves
exactly correfpond; & all his actions are agreeable to the
relation things have to one another: And when our
actions are fuch, we do all that's fit, juft, & reafonable,
all that God or Man can require; & from hence too
it follows, that Iniquity is the fame in action, as Fal-
fity is in theory.

CHAP.

## CHAP. VII.

*That Natural and Reveal'd Religion having the same End, their Precepts must be the same.*

B.  ALLOWING that the natural knowledge we have of God, ourselves, & our fellow Creatures, is the foundation of all Religion, may not external Revelation, building on this foundation, erect a larger & nobler edifice, by extending it to such things as the light of Nature cou'd not reach, without contradicting any thing it teaches?

*A.* I thought I had obviated this objection, by proving that the Religion of Nature was so perfect, that nothing cou'd be added to it; & that the truth of all Revelation was to be judg'd of by its agreement with it. However, since this objection is the most plausible of any you have yet made, I reply, That if our natural notions of the divine perfections demonstrate, that God will require nothing of his Creatures but what tends to their good; whatsoever is of this kind, is a superstructure that belongs to the Law of Nature; or, in other words, what the reason, or nature of the things themselves plainly point out to us: and for all other matters, which have no such tendency, you must seek another foundation, another Nature very different from the divine, to build *your hay & stubble upon.* And

I F it be evident from the Light of Nature, what are those relations we stand in to God & our Fellow-Creatures, and that neither God nor Man, without acting tyrannically, can require more than those require; can external Revelation any more than internal exceed these bounds?

I F original Revelation comprehends every thing obligatory on the account of its excellency; that is, every thing which tends to the honour of God, or the good of Man, (and these are the only ends of *Traditional*

*tional* Religion) no arbitrary, or merely positive precepts, as not tending to the honour of God, or the good of Man, can belong either to Natural, or Reveal'd Religion.

By the Law of Nature as well as the Gospel, the honour of God, and the good of Man, being the two grand, or general Commandments, all particular Precepts must be comprehended under these two, & belong alike to the Law of Nature as well as the Gospel; and what does not, can belong to neither. Thus any particular Precept, if by change of circumstances it ceases to contribute to the honour of God, or the good of Man, much more if it become prejudicial to either, must lose its obliging force.

There must be some Rule, or Rules, which bind without exception, *because every exception to a Rule is built on some Rule or other*; & as there can't be Rules, so there can't be Exceptions *ad infinitum*; and I suppose, you will not deny, but that these two grand Rules, or Commandments, *the Honour of God*, & *the Good of Man*, are obligatory without exception. And yet these would be to little purpose, cou'd not Reason tell Men how to apply them in all conditions, & circumstances of life.

*B.* Supposing no particular Precepts can oblige, if they chance to clash with either of those Commandments, yet what is to be done if these two interfere with one another; must the Good of Man, or the Honour of God take place?

*A.* These two grand Laws are in effect the same, since what promotes the Honour of God necessarily promotes the Good of Man: The more we love and honour God, the more we shall imitate him in our extensive love to our Fellow-Creatures, who are equally the children of God. The greater our veneration is for our Maker, the more it will excite us to copy those perfections of Goodness & Benevolence we adore in him: so that the duty of a truly-religious person, and

of

of a good subject and citizen are the same with relation to God and Man; for the more he honours God, the more zealous will he be to act the Patriot; & the more he does that, the more he honours God; because the happier Men are, the more reason they have to honour that God, who made 'em so. The way to * *glorify your Father which is in Heaven*, is to *let your light so shine before Men, that they may see your good works*. And † *herein is my Father glorify'd, that ye bear much fruit*. And indeed, nothing can be plainer from Scripture, than that these two great Duties of the *Love of God, & our Neighbour*, include each other. *If*, says the Apostle, ‡ *a Man say I love God, and hateth his Brother, he is a Liar*. And, § *If we love one another, God dwelleth in us, & the Love of God is perfected in us*. Again, ¶ *Let us love one another; every one that loveth is born of God, and knoweth God. He that loves not, knoweth not God.* ✠ *But whoso hateth this world's goods, and seeth his Brother have need, & shutteth up his bowels of compassion from him, how dwelleth the Love of God in him?* And it was this consideration, that made that great Emperor and Philosopher *Marcus Antoninus* say, *

„ Thou wilt never do any thing purely humane in a
„ right manner, unless thou knowest the relation it
„ bears to things divine; nor any thing divine, unless
„ thou knowest all the ties it has to things humane.

In a word, As Man is by Nature qualify'd to answer all the purposes of a social life, and to act a part agreeable to Reason, so in doing this he gives glory to his Maker, by fulfilling the end of his creation: but if he goes contrary to the Light of Nature in acting an unsociable and hurtful part, he reflects dishonour on his Creator by defeating as far as in him lies, the design of God in making him a social Creature. But

B E-

---

* *Mat.* 5. 16.    † *John* 15. 8.    ‡ 1 *John* 4. 20.
§ *Ib. Ver.* 12.    ¶ *Ib. Ver.* 7. 8.    ✠ 1 *John* 3. 17.
⁑ *Lib.* 3. c. 12. in Mr. & Madam *Dacier's* Version.

BECAUSE Bigots represent these two grand Obligations as frequently clashing; & oppose things which are for the good of Man, on pretence that the Honour of God will either directly, or indirectly suffer by it; & on this pretence have frequently done such mischiefs to their fellow-Creatures, as to give occasion for that proverbial saying, *In nomine Domini incipit omne malum*; Give me leave to say, that we can no otherwise honour God, since that consists in having the most exalted ideas of him, than by supposing him benevolent in the most universal & impartial manner: and consequently, to imagine he can command any thing inconsistent with this universal benevolence, is highly to dishonour him; 'tis to destroy his impartial Goodness, and make his Power & Wisdom degenerate into cruelty & craft.

THO we have receiv'd our all from God, we can give him nothing, nor do him the least kindness, much less return kindness for kindness; & therefore, the only way we have to shew our real gratitude to our great Creator & Benefactor, is to be as useful as we can to his Creatures, whom we ought to love as ourselves: and if there can now be a Sin against the Holy Ghost, I shou'd not scruple to say, it is making Religion the means of destroying the end of all Religion, & rendring the Creature miserable on pretence of doing Honour to the Creator; who, as he has imprefs'd on *bodies*, in order to preserve the natural World, a tendency to each other, so he has implanted in *minds*, the better to support the moral world, a tendency to be kind & beneficent to one another. And so deep is the impression of benevolence, that we can't but applaud a person who does brave & generous actions, even tho' we suffer by them; & as much condemn him who acts basely & treacherously, tho' we are ever so great gainers.

,, Is there then (*says a noble Author*) * a natural
,, Beauty of Figures, and is there not as natural a one
,, of

„ of Actions ? No sooner the eye opens upon *Figures*,
„ the ear to *Sounds*, than straight the *Beautiful* results,
„ and *Grace* & *Harmony* are known, & acknowledg'd;
„ no sooner are Actions view'd, no sooner the *human*
„ *Affections* and *Passions* discern'd (and they are most
„ of them as soon discern'd as felt) than straight *an*
„ *inward eye* distinguishes, and sees the *fair* & *shapely*,
„ the *amiable* and *admirable* apart from the *deform'd*,
„ the *foul*, the *odious*, or the *despicable*. How is it possible therefore not to own, „ that as the *distinctions*
„ have their foundation in *Nature*, the discernment
„ itself is *natural*, and from *Nature* alone.

B. Th is, I own, is a beautiful description of human nature, and a strong evidence of the goodness of
its Author: But do Men act as if they had such an innate love for Virtue, or such a benevolent disposition ?

*A.* An execrable Superstition has in many Christian
countries, in a manner, extinguish'd these kind sentiments, and even all humanity and pity; insomuch
that the tender Sex can rejoice to hear the shrieks,
and see the agonies of Men expiring under the most
cruel tortures; and there's scarce any place, so much
does this cursed bigotry prevail, where we do not almost daily see too much reason to cry,

*Tantum Religio potuit suadere malorum.*

Th e Noble Author now quoted justly observes,
„ * If there be a Religion that teaches the adoration
„ & love of a God, whose character it is to be cap-
„ tious, and of high resentment, subject to wrath &
„ anger, furious, revengeful, and revenging himself,
„ when offended, on others than those who gave the
„ offence; and if there be added to the character of
„ this God, a fraudulent disposition, encouraging deceit
„ and treachery among Men; favourable to a few,
„ tho' for slight causes, & cruel to the rest; 'tis evident
„ that such a Religion as this being strongly enforc'd,
„ must

* *Characteris. Vol. 2. pag. 48.*

„ muft of neceffity raife even an approbation & repect
„ towards the vices of this kind, & breed a fuitable
„ difpofition, a capricious, partial, revengeful, & deceit-
„ ful temper. For even *irregularities & enormities* of
„ a heinous kind muft in many cafes appear illuftrious
„ to one, who confiders them in a Being admir'd &
„ contemplated with the higheft honour & veneration.
„ - - * Whenfoever, therefore, a Religion teaches
„ the love and admiration of a Deity, that has any
„ apparent character of *ill*; it teaches at the fame time
„ a love and admiration of *that ill*, & caufes that to
„ be taken for good & amiable, which is in itfelf hor-
„ rid & deteftable.

Archbishop *Tillotfon*, than whom none better
underftood human nature, fays, that † „ According as
„ Mens notions of God are, fuch will their Religion
„ be; if they have grofs & falfe conceptions of God,
„ their Religion will be abfurd and fuperftitious: If
„ Men fancy God to be an ill-natur'd being, arm'd
„ with infinite power, who takes delight in the mifery
„ and ruin of his Creatures, and is ready to take all
„ advantages againft them, they may fear him, but
„ they will hate him; & they will be apt to be fuch
„ towards one another, as they fancy God to be
„ towards them: for all Religion doth naturally in-
„ cline Men to imitate him whom they worfhip.

Dr. *Scot*, to root out all fuch injurious notions as
derogate from the goodnefs of God, very juftly obferves, that ‡ „ God being infinitely good in his own
„ nature, it is impoffible we fhou'd conceive him to
„ be better than he is; & therefore every falfe notion
„ we entertain of his goodnefs muft detract from it;
„ and fo much as we detract from his goodnefs, fo
„ much we detract from the principal reafon & mo-
„ tive of our loving him.

E

AND

* *Characterif. Vol.* 2. *pag.* 47.
† *Serm. Vol.* 1. *pag.* 181. *& To.* 1. *pag.* 60.
‡ *Chrift. Life.* P. 2. *Vol.* 1. *pag.* 320.

AND indeed, power & knowledge of themselves can't engage our love : if they cou'd, we shou'd love the Devil in proportion to his power and knowledge. 'Tis goodness alone which can beget confidence, love, and veneration; and there's none of those questions, whether relating to God or Man, but what may be easily determined, by considering which side of the question carries with it the greatest goodness : since the same light of Nature, which shews us there is such a good Being, shews us also what such goodness expects. And did Men consider how repugnant 'tis to his goodness, to require any thing of them which they had no reason to obey, but because they had no power to disobey, they must abhor the notion of all arbitrary commands.

AND therefore, I shall not scruple to affirm, That he who stedfastly adheres to what the Light of Nature teaches him concerning the divine goodness, as he will avoid the comfortless prospect of the Atheist, * the perpetual anxiety of the Superstitious, the wild perturbation of the Enthusiast, and the pernicious fury of the Bigot; so he can't fail of the true Religion, happily seated in the middle between these extreams. And, as such a person can't but love God as he ought, so in imitation of the divine goodness, which influences all his actions, he will contribute his utmost to the good of others : and his love & kindness will be as extensive as Human-nature; and going on rational & evident principles, which must give him entire satisfaction, he will act a steady uniform part. And what can be wanting to a Man, who has this heavenly, this god-like disposition, which renders him happy in himself, & as far as it in his power, makes the whole World so too ?

AND since 'tis not easy to part with a subject, which one can scarce think of without rapture, I must
say,

* See *Plutarch* de Superstitione, Op. To. 2. p. 171. E. Edit. Francofurt.

say, that Men can never have true sentiments of the goodness of the divine Legislator, or esteem his Laws as they ought, till they are convinc'd he requires nothing of them but what is for their good; & that they can't but be miserable as long as they swerve from rules so essential to their happiness; & that the longer they do so, the more difficult will it be to acquire a contrary habit. These notions early inculcated, will cause Men with joy to obey the divine Laws, & make them in reality love God as well as be belov'd by him; who has the chief regard to the heart, and above all things requires the purity of the mind; and that Men shou'd act, not out of a principle of slavish fear, but from *perfect love void of all fear.*

*Plutarch* speaking of Religion, as it stood in the Heathen Church, & in his own time, represents it as full of satisfaction, hope, joy, and delight; and *says,* *
,, It is plain, and evident from most demonstrable
,, testimonies, that neither the societies, nor publick
,, meetings in the Temples, nor any other diverting
,, parties, sights, or entertainments are more delight-
,, ful, or rejoicing, than what we ourselves behold,
,, and practice in the Church worship. - - Our dis-
,, position & temper is not on this occasion, as if we
,, were in the presence of worldly Potentates, dread
,, Sovereigns and despotick Princes; nor are we here
,, found meanly humbling ourselves, crouching in
,, fear & awe, and full of anxiety and confusion, as
,, wou'd be natural to us in such a case; but where
,, the Divinity is esteem'd the *nearest,* and most im-
,, immediately present, there horrors & amazement
,, are the furthest banish'd; there the heart, we find,
,, gives the freest way to pleasure, to entertainment
,, -- and this even to excess. ,, And,

CHRISTIANS in addressing to the divine Majesty, must be fill'd with inexpressible joy & delight, did they

E 2     con-

* Treatise ag. *Epicurean* Atheism. To. 2. pag. 1101.
D, E.

conſider the true notion of God; ,, Who, *as Arch-*
,, *biſhop* Tillotſon *ſays,* * wou'd appear to be ſo lo-
,, vely a Being, ſo full of goodneſs and all deſirable
,, perfections, that even thoſe who are of ſo irregular
,, underſtanding, as not to believe there is a God,
,, yet could not refrain from wiſhing with all their
,, hearts there was one -- Who takes particular care
,, of every one of us, & loves us, & delights to do
,, us good. -- Who underſtands all our wants, & is
,, able & willing to relieve us in our greateſt ſtreights.
,, -- Is it not every Man's intereſt, that there ſhould
,, be ſuch a Governor of the world as really deſigns
,, our happineſs, and has omitted nothing neceſſary
,, to it? as governs us for our advantage, and will
,, require nothing of us but what is for our good;
,, & yet will infinitely reward us for doing of that
,, which is beſt for ourſelves; that will puniſh any
,, Man that ſhall go about to injure us, or to deal
,, otherwiſe with us than himſelf in like caſes would
,, be dealt withal. -- We have reaſon to believe God
,, to be ſuch a Being, if he be at all.

*B.* Are not the laſt words too bold in ſuppoſing
there cou'd be no God, were he not ſuch as he deſcribes him?

*A.* With Submiſſion, I think not; ſince there can
be nothing in God but what is God-like, he either
muſt be perfectly good, or not be at all.  It wou'd
be well, if all who in words give this character of the
Deity, were conſiſtent with themſelves, and did not
impute ſuch actions to him, as make him reſemble the
worſt of beings, & ſo run into downright *Demoniſm,*
And let me add, Men of good ſenſe, and who mean
well, will naturally fall into the ſame ſentiments;
a *Shaftsbury* will ſay the ſame as a *Tillotſon.*

,, If there be, *ſays that* Noble Author, † *a general*
,, *Mind,* it can have no *particular* intereſt: But the
,, general good, and the good of the whole, and its
,, ,, own

---

* *To.* I. *p.* 24.    † *Letter concer. Enthuſiaſm. p.* 40, 41.

,, own private good, must of necessity be one and
,, the same. It can intend nothing besides, nor aim
,, at any thing beyond, nor be provok'd to any thing
,, contrary. So that we have only to consider, whether
,, there be really such a thing as a *Mind that has re-*
,, *lation to the whole,* or not. For, if unhappily there
,, be *no Mind,* we may comfort ourselves, however,
,, that Nature has *no malice:* If there be really a MIND
,, we may rest satisfy'd, that it is *the best natur'd one*
,, *in the world.* The last case, one wou'd imagine,
,, shou'd be the most comfortable; & the notion of a
,, *common Parent* less frightful than that of *forlorn Na-*
,, *ture,* and a *fatherless World.* Tho' as Religion stands
,, amongst us, there are many good people who wou'd
,, have less fear in being thus expos'd, and wou'd be
,, easier, perhaps, in their minds, if they were assur'd
,, they had only mere *Chance* to trust to. For no body
,, trembles to think there shou'd be *no God,* but rather,
,, that there *shou'd be one.* This however wou'd be
,, otherwise, if *Deity* were thought as kindly of as
,, *Humanity*; and we cou'd be persuaded to believe,
,, that if there really was a GOD, *the highest Goodness*
,, must of necessity belong to him, without any of
,, those defects of passion, those meannesses & imper-
,, fections, which we acknowledge such in ourselves;
,, which, as good Men, we endeavour all we can to
,, be superior to, and which, we find, we every day
,, conquer as we grow better.

IN recapitulating what I have said of the agreement
of Natural & Reveal'd Religion, I can't do it more
fully than in the words of Dr. *Sherlock* ( now Bishop
of *Bangor*) who, in a Sermon for propagating the Gospel
( where we may expect every thing which recommends it ) says, * that ,, The Religion of the Gospel
,, is the *true original Religion* of *Reason* and *Nature.* --
,, That the doctrine of repentance, with which the
,, Gospel set out in the world, had reference to the

* *Serm. before the Society for Propag. the Gospel. p.* 16. &c.

,, *Law of Reason* and *Nature*, againſt which Men had
,, every where offended; and ſince repentance infers
,, the neceſſity of a future reformation, and a *return*
,, to that duty and obedience, *from which*, by tranſ-
,, greſſion we are fallen: the conſequence is mani-
,, feſtly this, that the *Goſpel* was a *Republication of the*
,, *Law of Nature*, and its *precepts declarative* of that
,, *original Religion*, which was as *old* as the *Creation*.

,, THIS, *continues he*, will appear, by conſidering
,, the nature of the thing itſelf. The *notions* of good
,. and evil are eternally and unalterably the *ſame*;
,, which notions are the rules & meaſures of all moral
,, actions, and are conſequently neceſſary, and con-
,, ſtituent parts of Religion: And therefore, if the *Re-*
,, *ligion of Nature* in her primitive ſtate was *pure* and
,, *uncorrupt*, which will not, I preſume, be deny'd,
,, tho there was ſufficient reaſon for a *Republication*
,, of it, becauſe of the great ignorance & Superſtition
,, which had grown upon the world, yet there cou'd
,, be no reaſon for any *alteration* of it: For tho' the
,, world was the worſe for abuſing the *Religion of Na-*
,, *ture*, & might want to be reform'd by a divine in-
,, ſtructor, yet the *Religion of Nature* was not the worſe
,, for being abus'd, but *ſtill* retain'd its firſt *purity* &
,, *ſimplicity*. The duties of Religion, conſider'd as the
,, rules of action, flow from the relation we bear to
,, God, and to one another; and Religion muſt ever
,, be the ſame, as long as theſe relations continue un-
,, alterd. If our firſt Parent was the Creature of God,
,, ſo are we; and whatever ſervice & duty he ow'd
,, in virtue of this dependance, the *ſame* is due from
,, us: nor can this *relation* be ever made the ground
,, of *different* duties in his caſe, & ours. If therefore,
,, *Nature* rightly inſtructed him at firſt how to *ſerve*
,, his Maker, our obligations being the ſame with his,
,, our rule muſt be the *ſame* alſo. The caſe is the ſame
,, with reſpect to the duties owing from Man to Man;
,, and it would be as reaſonable to ſuppoſe, that the
,, three

,, three angles of a triangle fhould be equal to two
,, right ones in one age, & unequal in another, as to
,, fuppofe, that the duties of Religion fhould differ in
,, one age from what they were in another, the ha-
,, bitudes and relations from which they flow con-
,, tinuing always the fame.

,, THAT the cafe is in fact what I have repre-
,, fented it to be, might be fhewn from the *particular*
,, Laws of the Gofpel, and their dependance *on* the
,, maxims & principles of *Natural Religion*. -- I will
,, content myfelf with one general proof, which reaches
,, to *every* part of the *Chriftian* doctrine. -- If the Law
,, and the Prophets hang on thefe two grand com-
,, mandments, *viz.* The *Love* of God, and the *Love*
,, of our Neighbour, then the Doctrine of our Saviour,
,, which is the perfection of the Law & the Prophets,
,, muft hang on *them* likewife: Now, if you will allow,
,, that the Love of God, & the Love of our Neighbour
,, are *fundamentals* in the Law of Reafon & Nature
,, ( as *undoubtedly* they are ) you muft alfo allow,
,, that whatever may be deduc'd from them by ratio-
,, nal confequence, muft be a *Precept* of the Law of
,, *Nature*. Whatever, therefore, hangs on thefe two
,, Commandments, muft neceffarily be a part of *Na-*
,, *tural* Religion ; & that *all* the Law & the Prophets
,, do fo hang, and confequently, the Doctrine of the
,, Gofpel, which is the perfection of them, you have
,, had our Saviour's *exprefs* teftimony. Since then it
,, appears ( as I think ) that the *Religion* of the *Gofpel*
,, is the *true original* Religion of *Reafon & Nature* ; --
,, That it has, as fuch, a claim to be receiv'd *inde-*
,, *pendent* of thofe *Miracles*, which were wrought for
,, its confirmation, will be admitted by all, who allow
,, the force & obligation of *Natural Religion* ; & can
,, be deny'd by none who know, or underftand them-
,, felves. The principles of Religion are interwoven
,, with the very frame & make of our minds, & we
,, may as well run from ourfelves, as from the fenfe
,, of the obligations we are under.

E 4                                R.

*B.* Bᴜᴛ does not this Right Reverend Prelate in this Sermon affirm, that there are Doctrines in Christianity, which, tho' not different, yet are distinct from the Principles of Reason and Nature?

*A.* Tʜᴇʀᴇ's nothing more common with learned Authors, than distinctions without any difference; yet the Bishop very cautiously words what he says, ,, That the Doctrines of Christianity, tho' not different, ,, are distinct from the principles of Reason & Nature; but he does not say they are distinct from those doctrines, which flow from the principles of Reason and Nature: And what he immediately adds, that ,, Our Saviour came into the World to supply the ,, defects, not of Religion, which continu'd in its ,, purity & perfection, but of Nature; ,, plainly shews, that he thinks nothing cou'd be added by our Saviour, to a Law that had no defects; and that the defects of Nature cou'd only be supply'd, by obliging people to live up to this natural Law of unchangeable purity & perfection.

Tʜɪꜱ is doing justice to Reveal'd as well as Natural Religion, and shews the Author of both to be at all times equally wise, good, & beneficent; & the Bishop ought to be valu'd for speaking thus plainly. *O si sic omnia dixisset.*

Aɴᴅ to this Right Reverend Father, I may add the Authority of the late Most Reverend Archbishop *Sharp,* who says, * ,, That Religion (taking that word ,, as it signifies that universal duty we owe to God, ,, and by which we are to recommend ourselves to ,, his favour) is not so variable, uncertain, & arbitrary ,, a matter, as some Men do perhaps suppose it; but ,, is a constant, fixed, permanent, immutable thing. ,, The same now that it was in the days of the old ,, Law; and the same then that it was in the days ,, before the Law was given; & the same both then ,, and now that it shall be a thousand years hence,
                                                      ,, if

* *Serm. Vol. 4. pag.* 208 – 211.

„ if the World fhould laft fo long.   True Religion,
„ and that which is from God, was, & is, and ever
„ will be the fame, in fubftance in all Countries, and
„ in all Nations, & among all forts & conditions of
„ Men whatfoever; and the fum of it is, *To love the*
„ *Lord our God with all our hearts, and with all our*
„ *minds, and with all our ftrength; and* next to that,
„ *To love our Neighbour as ourfelves.*   This was the
„ Religion that the Patriarchs, and all the pious Men
„ of old lived in, and by which they obtained God's
„ favour and acceptance, when as yet there was no
„ reveal'd inftituted Religion in the world. -- That
„ this is the fum of the Chriftian Religion, no Man
„ can in the leaft doubt that has ever read the New-
„ Teftament. -- In our Saviour's inftitution there is
„ hardly any one thing recommended to us, that doth
„ not directly relate to this matter; that is not either
„ an inftance wherein we are to exprefs our love to
„ God, & our Neighbour, or a means whereby we
„ may be furthered in the practifing of thofe duties,
„ or an argument, & motive, & encouragement to
„ excite us to the practifing of them. It is the defign
„ of all his Doctrines to give us right notions of God,
„ and our Neighbour; to teach us how excellent,
„ how good God is in himfelf, and how kind, how
„ gracious to us, and therefore, what infinite reafon
„ we have to love, and ferve him, and to love and
„ ferve all Mankind (who are our Neighbours) for
„ his fake. --
„ We have an eafy, & a true notion of that Reli-
„ gion which is from God, and we can never be at
„ a lofs to find out in what it doth confift: it is not
„ a thing to be alter'd at pleafure; both the Law of
„ Nature, and the Law of God; both the natural
„ difpenfation under which all Men are born, & the
„ reveal'd difpenfation as we have either in the Old
„ or New Teftament, do fuffiiently inftruct us in the
„ main heads of it.   Nay, I dare be bold to fay,

E 5                    „ fo

„ so long as Mankind do retain their nature, & are
„ not transform'd into another sort of creatures than
„ what God made them at first, it is impossible that
„ there should be any true Religion, but what may
„ be summed up in these two things; to love God,
„ and our Neighbour.

## CHAP. VIII.

*That the not adhering to those notions Reason dic-*
*tates concerning the Nature of God, has been*
*the occasion of all Superstition, & of all those*
*innumerable mischiefs, that Mankind, on the*
*account of Religion, have done either to them-*
*selves, or to one another.*

HAVING in general shewn the absurdity of not
being govern'd by the reason of things in all
matters of Religion, I shall now in particular, shew
the fatal consequences of not adhering to those notions
Reason dictates concerning the nature of God.

*Charron*, tho' a Priest of that Church which abounds
with superstition, the most pernicious as well as absurd,
seems to have a right notion of Superstition as well
as justly to abhor it, in saying, that * „ Superstition,
„ and most other errors and defects in Religion, are,
„ generally speaking, owing chiefly to want of be-
„ coming, & right apprehensions of God : We debase,
„ and bring him down to us, we compare, & judge
„ him by ourselves, we cloath him with our infir-
„ mities, and then proportion, and fit our fancy ac-
„ cordingly. -- What horrid prophanation and blas-
„ phemy is this !

T is to this absurdity of debasing God, & cloathing
him with our infirmities, and judging of him by ourselves,

* *Charron* of Wisdom, Eng. Transl. pag. 131.

felves, that the mediatory Gods amongft the Heathen owe their rife. Had they believ'd a fupreme Being was every where, & at all times knew their thoughts, they cou'd never have taken fuch a round-about way of addreffing him, who not only knew what they defir'd, but their real wants, & what would relieve them better than any mediatory Beings whatever.

*B.* THEY addrefs'd to mediatory Beings, to fhew their greater refpect to the fupreme Being, and their own unworthinefs to approach him.

*A.* THIS fhews what unworthy notions they had of the fupreme Being, fince it wou'd be an affront even to a temporal Prince, if he was prefent, & heard every thing you faid, not to addrefs to him, but to another, to let the Prince know what you wanted from him.

THE Heathens muft think, if they thought at all, that thofe mediatory Gods cou'd either fuggeft to the fupreme God fome reafons he before was ignorant of, or that by their importunities they cou'd prevail on his weaknefs, to do what otherwife he was not willing to do.

THIS Heathen notion, as it fuppos'd the fupreme God either ignorant or weak, fo it made the mediatory Gods to have a greater kindnefs for, & readinefs to do good to Mankind, and that their follicitations made him better-natur'd than otherwife he wou'd be: This of courfe took off their love from the Supreme, and plac'd it on thofe mediatory Gods, upon whofe powerful interceffions they fo much depended. However, thefe Heathens, allowing one, & but one Moft High God, did not fo far derogate from the honour of the one true God, as to pretend that the moft diftinguifhed among their feveral Mediators was equal to him, *equality* and *mediation* being as inconfiftent as *equality* & *fupremacy*: And they wou'd have made their Religion an errant jumble, if they had worfhipp'd thefe Gods fometimes as Mediators only,

fome-

sometimes as sovereign disposers of things, & sometimes as both together.

Had the Heathens believ'd God to have been a purely-spiritual, invisible Being, they cou'd never have suppos'd him visible to mortals, or have thought that an unlimited Being cou'd appear under the limited form of a Man, or other animal: or that an omnipresent Being cou'd any more be present in one place, or creature, than another; or that such a Being cou'd be confin'd to a small spot of earth, while another equally omnipresent was in Heaven, and a third descending from thence, &c. Or that one God cou'd be sent on the errand of another God, after the manner that God *Mercury* was by God *Jupiter*: tho' there was nothing too absurd for the Heathens to believe, after they had destroy'd the unity of God, except it was, that *Jupiter* & *Mercury*, the *Sender* and the *Sent* were the same God.

The primitive Fathers bitterly inveigh'd against these heathenish Notions: *Justin Martyr* for instance says, *
,, None, who have the least sense, will dare to affirm,
,, that the Maker & Father of the Universe did appear
,, in a small spot of earth; the God of the Universe
,, can neither ascend, nor descend, or come into any
,, place. *Tertullian* says, † He wou'd not believe the
,, sovereign God descended into the womb of a
,, Woman, tho' even the Scripture itself should say it.
'Tis impossible, says *Eusebius*, ‡ ,, that the eyes of
,, Mortals should ever see the supreme God; *viz.*
,, Him, who is above all things, & whose essence is
,, unbegotten & immutable. *Again*, § 'Tis absurd,
,, and contrary to all Reason, that the unbegotten &
,, immutable nature of the Almighty God should take
,, the form of a Man; or that the Scripture should
                                                    ,, forge

---

* *Justin* Oper. p. 207. Ed. 1593. Al. p. 283. B. p. 356 E.
† *Adv. Prax. c.* 16.     ‡ *Demon. Evan. l.* 5. *c.* 20. *p.* 248.
§ *Eccl. Hist. l.* 1. *c.* 2. *pag.* 6. C.

,, forge such like falsities. *Minutius Felix* in his Apology says, * ,, That the Deity can't dye, nor can any
,, thing which is born be a God: That only is divine,
,, which has neither beginning nor end: If the Gods
,, get Children, they would get them immortal: We
,, must conclude those Gods to be Men, of whose
,, birth & burial we are fully satisfy'd. ,,   Thus the
Fathers expos'd the Pagan *Polytheism.*

A great deal more, as you may well imagine, might
be said on this head; but now I shall briefly consider
what pernicious effects the having wrong & unnatural
conceptions of the Deity, has occasion'd among Men
with relation to themselves, & one another.

If we take a general view of those mischiefs
Mankind have at all times practis'd on a religious account, either upon themselves or others, we shall find
them owing to their entertaining such notions of God,
as are intirely inconsistent with his nature, and contrary to what their Reason, if attended to, wou'd inform them of the Design & End of the Laws of God.

Had not numbers in all ages thought, that God
delighted in the pain and misery of his Creatures,
they cou'd never have imagin'd, that the best way to
render them acceptable to him, was by tormenting
themselves with immoderate watchings, fastings, pe-
nances, and mortifications of all sorts; & the greater
the more pleasing.   And even at present there are
among *Christians*, *Mahometans*, and *Pagans*, numbers
of Men who devote themselves to exercises full of pain
& corporal sufferings, and either wound, or mangle
their own persons, or find other ways of tormenting
themselves: & indeed, the Superstitious every where
think, the less mercy they shew to their bodies, the
more mercy God will shew to their souls.

Many of the primitive Christians, instead of flying,
as the Gospel directs, not only ran voluntarily to execution, but provok'd their Judges to do them that favour.

And

* *Reeve*'s Transl. p. 121, Ed. Dav. c. 23.

And under *Traian*, all the Chriſtians in a City in *Aſia* came in a body to the Proconſul, & offer'd themſelves to the ſlaughter; which made him cry, * *O! ye unhappy People, if ye have a mind to dye, have ye not halters and precipices enough to end your lives, but ye muſt come here for Executioners.* This was a general practice under the *Antonini*; † & *Marcus Antoninus* ſeverely reflects on the obſtinacy of the Chriſtians, in thus running headlong to death. And St. *Cyprian* labours to comfort thoſe who might be ſo unhappy, by the ceaſing of the then Perſecution, to miſs the Crown of Martyrdom : tho' one wou'd think there were but few who wanted this conſolation; ſince he ſays, *Many of the Clergy, & the far greater part of the Laity apoſtatiz'd.* But when by the Empire's becoming Chriſtian, the Crown of Martyrdom .was no longer to be obtain'd by the prevailing party of Chriſtians, then exerciſing cruelties on themſelves was eſteem'd the next beſt thing ; & many Devotees put monſtrous hardſhips on themſelves, while others choſe poverty, rags, & naſtineſs ; or elſe retir'd to caves, deſarts, and other ſolitary places to ſigh away their miſerable lives. And Eccleſiaſtick Hiſtory is full of Miracles done by ſuch Madmen as *Simeon Stylites*, who had no other dwelling than a pillar, on which he ſpent the beſt part of his life ; and 'twas owing to theſe ſuperſtitious notions, that ſuch numbers of *Monaſteries* & *Nunneries* were ſoon founded to the great oppreſſion & depopulation of the Chriſtian World : not but that the impudent Forgeries of *Athanaſius*, ‡ & other ſuch like Saints about Miracles done

by

* *Tertul.* ad *Scap.* cap. 5. pag. 11.

† See *Marc. Antonin.* de rebus ſuis, *lib.* 11. *cap.* 3. And *Lucian* de morte *Peregrin.* To. 2. p. 567, 568. And *Arrian.* Epict. *l.* 4. *c.* 7. *p.* 500. Edit. Cantab. *Le Clerk*'s Life of *Cypr.* Bib. Un. To. 12. p. 248, 249. Ep. 14. p. 31. Edit. Oxon.

‡ See *Athanaſius*'s Life of *Anthony* the Monk, To. 2. p. 455. A & d. *Jerom* of the Miracl. of *Paul* & *Hilarion* two Monks, To. 1. p. 237. & d. & p. 241, & d.

by *Monks*, help'd to increase this superstition; whilst the Prelates, tho' they encourag'd those severities on others, were far from practising any on themselves.

HAD such notions been adher'd to concerning the divine Goodness, as the Light of Nature dictates, the *Egyptians*, and some other Pagan Nations cou'd never have thought that *cutting off the foreskin* (not to be perform'd without great pain & hazard) cou'd have been esteem'd a religious duty acceptable to a good & gracious God; who makes nothing in vain, much less what requires the cutting off, even with extream danger as well as anguish. Had Nature requir'd such an operation, Nature, being always the same, wou'd still have requir'd it.

THIS Institution, as is prov'd by *Marsham*, * and others, seems to be owing to the *Egyptians*, who thought all to be profane who us'd it not: & it was after *Abraham* had been in *Egypt*, that *Circumcision* was instituted; in order, 'tis likely, to recommend his Posterity to the *Egyptians*, on whom they were for some ages to depend: and what makes this the more probable, is, that 'twas not till after the Lord had order'd *Moses* into *Egypt*, that † *the Lord met him by the way in the Inn, and sought to kill him* for not circumcising his Son. And upon *Joshua*'s circumcising the *Israelites* (circumcision not being observ'd during their stay in the wilderness, when they had no communication with *Egypt*) the Lord himself says, ‡ *This day have I rolled away the reproach of* Egypt *from off you.*

THE Heathen World must have very gross conceptions, not only of their inferior Gods, but of the Father of Gods and Men; when they imagined him of so cruel a nature, as to be delighted with the butchering of innocent animals; and that the stench of burnt flesh shou'd be such a *sweetsmelling savour in his nostrils*, as to atone for the wickedness of Men: and
wicked

* *Can. Chron. t.* 73. *& d. Edit. Francof.*
† *Exod.* 4. 14.     ‡ *Josh.* 5. 2 - 9.

wicked, no doubt, they were, when they had such an atonement at hand. So that the *harmless* were burnt to save the *hurtful*; and Men, the less *innocent* they grew, the more they destroy'd the innocent beasts.

*Non Bove mactato Cœlestia Numina gaudent;*
*Sed, qua præstant'a est, & sine teste, Fide.*
Ovid Epist. p. 89. Ep. 20. v. 181.

If the *Pagans* believ'd beasts were not given them for food, why did they eat them? Or, if they thought they were, why did they ungratefully throw back the gifts of God on the donor? Or, why did they not drown, or bury them, rather than make such a stench in burning them, as many times by the number of Sacrifices, might infect the very air?

'Tis probable, that the Heathen Priests who shar'd with their Gods, and reserv'd the best bits for themselves, had the chief hand in this as well as in all other gainful superstitions; while the deluded People, who many times suffer'd by the scarcity of provisions, caus'd by the great number of Sacrifices, were at vast expence in maintaining these holy butchers, whose very trade inspir'd them with cruelty.

And 'tis probable, this absurd notion prevail'd like all other absurdities by degrees, and at first Sacrifices were only religious Feasts, either in commemoration of some national benefit, where after God, their great benefactor, was celebrated, they commemorated their particular benefactors; or else Feasts were made on a private account by the Master of a Family, upon shearing his Sheep, gathering in the fruits of the Earth, &c. where those that assisted him were entertained, & joyfully join'd in giving thanks to the Author of those blessings, without destroying, or burning any part of the creature given for their use; and, the Master of the Family was, no doubt, Master of the Ceremonies at his own Feast: But this simple method not pleasing certain Persons, who were resolv'd to have the best

share

share in all those religious Feasts, they persuaded the People that it was necessary some part of the flesh of Animals should be burnt to feed the hungry nostrils of the Deity, delighted with the sweet savour of burnt flesh; and the better part to be reserv'd unburnt for themselves, to whom the slaying of the animals, & the offering them up was appropriated. 'Tis then no wonder the number of the Gods multiply'd, since the more Gods, the more Sacrifices, and the Priests had better fare: and that they might not want plentiful feastings, the People were made to believe, that they cou'd learn their fortunes from the intrails of the beasts they sacrific'd; and this method continues to this day in those places, where they have not found out an easier and better way of cheating the People.

*B.* You seem to be of the sentiments of the Poet, who says,

*Natural Religion was easy first, and plain;*
*Tales made it mystery, offerings made it gain;*
*Sacrifices and shews were at length prepar'd,*
*The Priests eat roast meat, and the people star'd.*

*A.* The *Pagans* sacrificing of beasts was not so bad in itself, as what it soon occasion'd, *human Sacrifices*; which, Men being of greater value than beasts, were believ'd to be more acceptable; and Parents, stifling all natural affections, offer'd up their own Children, as the most precious gifts they cou'd bestow on the Gods, except offering up their own lives, and sacrificing themselves. And as this Sacrifice was thought most meritorious, so the more excellent the Persons, the more agreeable the Sacrifice. And there are even at this day, a number of superstitious People in *India*, who out of great devotion throw themselves under the wheels of those heavy chariots, which carry the Images of their Gods, & are crush'd to death; & others, out of the same mistaken zeal, cut off their flesh, & mangle their limbs till they fall down dead; which

F makes

makes the People rejoice at their sufferings, and reverence them as most holy Martyrs; concluding that
nothing but the truth of their Religion cou'd enable
them to shew such terrible marks of zeal on themselves, and become voluntary Martyrs.

*B.* I pity those deluded People, & wonder how Men
can persuade themselves, that the mercy of Heaven
can be purchas'd by such barbarities, as human-nature
left to itself wou'd start at.

*A.* THAT the Priests were every where for human
Sacrifices is no wonder; since they had the appointing
the Men, whom the Gods did the great honour to
accept for Burnt-offerings: And indeed, after People
once gave themselves up to believe in their Priests,
there was nothing too absurd to be receiv'd as divine.
When the *Ethiopians,* for instance, were once persuaded that their Priests were intimately acquainted
with the will of the Gods, it was too late to dispute
any orders they pretended to bring from them; and
therefore, their Kings as well as private persons, well-
knowing that the commands of the Immortal Gods
were not to be disputed by Mortals, * most religiously
executed themselves as soon as the pleasure of the
Gods was signify'd to them by those sacred Messengers
of their will.   And this blind-devotion might have
continu'd till now, had not an Infidel Prince, bred up
in the profane Philosophy of the *Creeks,* put a stop to
it by surprising, & destroying at once all those holy
Impostors.

WE learn from *Bernier* & others, that it has been
an immemorial custom in *Indostan,* for the Women
(so great a power has Superstition even over that fear-
ful Sex) to burn themselves with their dead Husbands,
adorn'd with all the incombustible riches they cou'd
procure on their own account; or that the folly of
others wou'd send by them to their dead friends:
These their Priests secure to themselves, by telling
the

* *Diod. Sic. l. 3. p.* 102. *B, & d.*

the credulous people that the afhes of the dead, and all burnt with them, are too facred to be touch'd by any but themfelves.

*B.* Tho' human Sacrifices obtain'd among the Heathen, yet fure the *Levitical* Law did not approve, or countenance any fuch practices.

*A.* A u t h o r s are divided, & they who maintain the affirmative fay, that the *Levitical* Law diftinguifhes between ordirary Vows, and thofe Vows where any thing is *devoted* to the Lord; and this they pretend is plain from *Levit.* 27. where after many furprifing things about common Vows, by which the things themfelves, or money in lieu of them, were to be given to the Prieft; at *Ver.* 28 it comes to things devoted, and fays, *Notwithflanding, no devoted thing that a Man fhall devote unto the Lord, of all that he hath, both of Men and Beafts, and of the field of his pof-feffion, fhall be fold or redeem'd; every thing devoted is moft holy unto the Lord.* And what is meant by being *moft holy unto the Lord,* is explain'd in the next verfe, *None devoted, which fhall be devoted of Man fhall be redeem'd; but fhall furely be put to death.* And they fay it was before declar'd, that whatever was the Lord's, as the Firft-born of Man and Beaft, was to be flain; if God did not order its redemption. * *The Firft-born of Man was to be redeem'd;* and that of *an Afs, if not redeem'd by a Lamb, was to have its neck broke;* & the *Captives taken in War, which fell to the Lord's fhare,* there being no order for redeeming, *were,* as is own'd by all, *to be flain.*

T h e Prophet *Micah* reckons the putting every devoted thing to death among the *Jewifh* inftitutions, in faying, † *Wherewith fhall I come before the Lord, & bow myfelf before the High God? Shall I come before him with burnt-offerings, with calves of a year old? Will the Lord be pleafed with thoufands of rams, or with ten*

F 2 *thou-*

---

* Exod. 30. 12, 13. & 34. 19, 20.    † Mic. 6. 6. & 8.

*thousand of rivers of oil? Shall I give my First-born for my transgression; the fruit of my body for the sin of my soul? He hath shewed thee, O Man, what is good; and what doth the Lord require of thee; but to do justly, & to love mercy, & to walk humbly with thy God?*

HERE the sacrificing of a Man's own Children is mention'd equally with the sacrificing of beasts, which is allow'd to be a *Jewish* institution: how absurdly must the Prophet be suppos'd to have argu'd, after he hath preferr'd Justice & Mercy to a thing commanded by God, if he shou'd go on to prefer it before a thing abhorr'd by God!

IF there cou'd be any doubt in this matter, *Jeptha's* Vow wou'd clear it up; for this *Jewish* Hero made the Vow when the Spirit of the Lord came upon him, & after making it he wrought a great deliverance for *Israel*. The words of the Vow are, *Whatsoever* ( or rather *Whosoever* ) *cometh forth of the doors of my house to meet me, when I return in peace from the Children of* Ammon, *shall surely be the Lord's; and I will offer it up to him for a burnt-offering.* A Vow made by such an extraordinary person, and upon such an extraordinary occasion, looks as tho' something extraordinarily pleasing to God, was design'd by that Vow; which, tho' domestick animals might have been sacrific'd, must relate to persons capable of acting with design; *viz.* of coming out of his house to meet him after the victory; which to his great grief his only Child did. Had there been any way of dispensing with this solemn Vow, he, since he had two month's time to consider, wou'd, no doubt, have found it out: but he says, *I have opened my mouth unto the Lord, & I cannot go back;* and he did with her according to his Vow. And his Daughter, worthy of a better fate, was willing her Father shou'd execute his cruel Vow, only regretting that she dy'd without being a Mother in *Israel* for that reason she was yearly mourn'd by by the Daughters of *Israel.*

ST.

St. *Jerome*, as well as the Author of the *Questions to the Orthodox*, * thinks that *Jeptha*'s piety in sacrificing his Daughter, was the reason of St. *Paul*'s numbring him among the just persons. And,

Bishop *Smalridge*, in his Sermon about *Jeptha*'s Vow, says, „ That all the Fathers, as well as our own „ *Homilies*, own that he sacrific'd his Daughter.

The *Jews* cou'd not think it absolutely unlawful for a Father to sacrifice an innocent Child; since *Abraham* was highly extoll'd for being ready to sacrifice his only Son, and that too without the least expostulation: tho' he was importunate with God to save an inhospitable, idolatrous, and incestuous City.

No wonder that a single person in the power of another might be devoted to God, since free, & independent Nations were so devoted; & it was by virtue of such a Vow, which *Israel* vowed unto the Lord, that the *Canaanites*, who had never done *Israel* the least injury, † Men, Women, and Children were to be utterly destroy'd.

Had the Author of the Epistle to the *Hebrews*, ‡ who reckons *Jeptha* among the *Jewish* Heroes, thought the *Jews* abhorr'd all human Sacrifices, he wou'd not, at least, without some apology for the lawfulness of human Sacrifices, have declar'd one such Sacrifice, where the same person was both Sacrificer & Sacrifice, to have been of infinite value, in saying, that *Christ offer'd up himself*; § and that *He put away Sin by the Sacrifice of himself*; ¶ and endeavours to shew the *Hebrews*, that the blood of the beasts that were sacrific'd was of no value in comparison of ✠ *the blood of Christ, who, thro' the eternal Spirit, offer'd up himself without spot to God.* *

F 3                B. An-

---

*B.* ADMITTING the *Jewish* Law allow'd human Sacrifices, yet the Christian Religion, sure, forbids (since *Christ*, according to the Apostle, *sacrific'd himself*) all human sacrifices.

*A.* IF putting innocent, and conscientious Men to death on account of Religion, may be call'd *sacrificing* them, there have been more human Sacrifices than ever were before in the world, & those too not offer'd up to God, but to the Devil, by burning their bodies, and sentencing their souls to Hell. And even at this day the *Papists* to persuade the Spectators, that those they condemn to the flames immediately go to Hell, dress them up in a *San-benito*, or a coat painted all over with flames and Devils; and then take their leave of each sufferer with this charitable expression, *Jam animam tuam tradimus Diabolo.*

*B.* I must own, this bigotry, which has had such terrible effects among Christians, was little felt, or known in the *Pagan* world.

*A.* Is not this cursed bigotry owing to the most unworthy notions bigots have entertain'd of the divine perfections, imagining they do service to the Creator, by hurting, and destroying his Creatures? The fiery zeal of such wretches is capable of any mischief: Most other Men, tho' ever so wicked, have some remains of pity and humanity, some checks of conscience, and tho' ever so much provok'd, time will asswage their anger: but the Bigot feels not the least remorse, nor can time abate his fury, & he is so far from having any pity, that he glories in the cruellest actions, & thinks the more hellish facts he commits, the more he merits Heaven: and very often gets the reputation of a Saint for acting the part of a Devil. So that his notions of God and Religion, serve only to make him infinitely a worse Man, than if he had been without any belief: for then he could have no motives from the next world for doing mischief; nor wou'd his disbelief strip him of his humanity, or hinder
him,

him, if he judg'd rightly of his own interest, from acting so by his Fellow-Creatures, as, taking in the whole of his life, was best for him to do.

B. You represent bigotry more odious than it is, in making it worse than Atheism itself.

A. As Bigotry is the worst sort of Superstition, so you know the Philosophers in general suppose Superstition to be worse than Atheism itself. *Plutarch*, in particular, makes it his business in his Tract of *Disidemony*, or *Superstition*, * to prove that Atheism, tho' an opinion false, & even stupid, yet is far less hurtful to Men than Superstition; & reflects less dishonour on the Deity itself: For he interprets *Disidemony*, to be the † *continual dread of a Deity no less mischievous than powerful*; which is the most odious character that can belong to any intellectual Being, & *has given birth to those shocking notions, & dismal rites in divine Worship, that have either run Men into Atheism, and expos'd Religion itself to ridicule & contempt; or made Mankind the dupe of designing knaves, and taught fierce bigots to exercise, and then sanctify the most inhuman barbarities.* --

„ The Atheist, *says he*, ‡ knows no God at all;
„ the Superstitious none but what is monstrous and
„ terrible; mistaking for dreadful, what is most kind
„ & beneficent; for tyrannical, what is truly paternal;
„ for mischievously inclin'd, what is full of providen-
„ tial care; nay, for a Being brutally savage & fierce,
„ what is meer Goodness itself. Shall then, *adds he*, §
„ the Atheist be counted impious, & not this super-
„ stitious Person much more so? I, for my part, had
„ rather Men should say there is no such Person as
„ *Plutarch*, than that he is a Man inconstant, fickle,
„ prone to anger, ¶ ready to revenge himself upon
„ the slightest occasion, & full of indignation for meer
„ trifles, &c. And yet this is no more than what the

F 4                         *super-*

---

„ superstitious think of the Deity ; whom of conse-
„ quence they must as well hate as fear : They worship,
„ indeed, & adore him ; and so do Men even those
„ very Tyrants they wou'd be glad of an oppor-
„ tunity to destroy.   * The Atheist contributes not
„ in the least to Superstition : but Superstition having
„ given out so hideous an idea of the Deity, some
„ have been frighted into the utter disbelief of any
„ such Being ; because they think it much better,
„ nay, more reasonable, that there shou'd be no Deity,
„ than one whom they see more reason to hate, &
„ abominate, than to love, honour, and reverence,
„ † Thus inconsiderate Men, shock'd at the defor-
„ mity of Superstition, run directly into its opposite
„ extream *Atheism*, heedlessly skipping over true Piety,
„ that is the golden mean between both. „ So much
for this Philosopher of the *Gentiles*,  I shall now quote
a noble Christian Philosopher, who says, ‡ „ Atheism
„ leaves a Man to sense, to Philosophy, to natural
„ pity, to laws, to reputation ; all which may be guides
„ to an outward moral virtue, tho' Religion were not :
„ But Superstition dismounts all these, & erecteth an
„ absolute Monarchy in the minds of Men.   There-
„ fore Atheism did never perturb States ; for it makes
„ Men wary of themselves, as looking no further ;
„ And we see the times inclining to Atheism (as the
„ Time of *Augustus Cæsar*) were civil times.   But
„ Superstition hath been the confusion of many States,
„ & bringeth in a new *Primum Mobile*, that ravisheth
„ all the Spheres of Government.

I grant that next to a real Bigot, an Atheist in
masquerade may do most mischief ; but then it is by
hiding the Atheist, & personating the Bigot, & under
colour of promoting Religion, advancing Priest-craft.
And there are no small number of these Atheists, if
what the famous *Scaliger* says is true, § *Quicumque Je-*
*suitæ*

---

*  *Pag.* 171. *A,* &c.        † *Ibid. E.*
‡ *Bacon's* Essays, p. 96.        § *Scaligerana*, p. 126.

*suite vel Ecclesiastici Romæ in honoribus vivunt. Athei sunt.*
And Men must have a great deal of charity to think
better of any Protestant, whose pretended zeal carries
him, contrary to the principles of his Religion, into
persecuting measures.

Had the Heathen distinguish'd themselves by *Creeds*
made out of spite to one another, & mutually persecuted each other about the worship of their Gods,
they wou'd soon have made the number of their
Votaries as few as the Gods they worshipp'd; but we
don't find (except in *Egypt* that motherland of Superstition) they ever quarrell'd about their Gods; tho
their Gods sometimes quarrell'd, and fought about
their Votaries: No, it was a Maxim with them,
*Deorum injuriæ, Diis curæ.*

By the universal liberty that was allow'd amongst
the Ancients, * ,, Matters (*as a noble Author observes*)
,, were so ballanc'd, that Reason had fair play; Lear-
,, ning, and Science flourish'd; wonderfull was the
,, harmony & temper, which arose from these con-
,, trarieties. Thus Superstition, & Enthusiasm were
,, mildly treated; and being let alone, they never
,, rag'd to that degree as to occasion bloodshed, wars,
,, persecutions, and devastations: but a new sort of
,, policy, -- has made us leap the bounds of natural
,, Humanity, and out of a super natural Charity, has
,, taught us the way of plaguing one another most
,, devoutly. It has rais'd an antipathy, that no tem-
,, poral interest could ever do, and entail'd on us a
,, mutual hatred to all eternity. † And savage zeal,
,, with meek and pious semblance, works dreadful
,, massacre; & for Heaven's-sake (horrid pretence)
,, makes desolate the Earth.

And as this noble Author observes, ‡ ,, The Ζεὺς
,, ξένιΘ, (or the *Jupiter* of Strangers) was, among
,, the Ancients, one of the solemn characters of Di-

F 5                                                   vinity,

* *Letter of Enthusiasm. p. 18. al. 28, 29.*   † *Ib. 388.*
‡ *Characterist. Vol. 3. pag. 153, 154.*

,, vinity, the peculiar attribute of the supreme Deity;
,, benign to Mankind, and recommending universal
,, love, mutual kindness and benignity between the
,, remotest, & most unlike of human race. Such was
,, the ancient Heathen Charity, & pious duty towards
,, the whole of Mankind, both those of different
,, nations & different worship.

But, good God! how different a character do
Bigots give us of the Deity, making him an unjust,
cruel, and inconsistent Being; requiring all Men to
judge for themselves, and act according to their consciences, and yet authorising some among them to
judge for others, and to punish them for not acting
according to the consciences of those Judges, tho' ever
so much against their own.

These Bigots thought they were authoris'd to
punish all those that differ with them in their religious
worship, as God's Enemies; but had they consider'd,
that God alone cou'd discern Mens hearts, and alone
discover whether any, by conscientiously offering him
a wrong worship, cou'd become his Enemies; & that
infinite Wisdom best knew how to proportion the
punishment to the fault, as well as infinite power how
to inflict it; they wou'd, surely, have left it to God
to judge for himself, in a cause which immediately
related to himself; and where they were not so much
as parties concern'd, and as likely to be mistaken as
those they wou'd punish. Can one, without horror,
think of Mens breaking through all the rules of doing
as they wou'd be done unto, in order to set themselves
up for standards of truth for God as well as Man?
Do not these impious wretches suppose, that God is
not able to judge for himself; at least, not able to
execute his own judgment? And that therefore, he
has recourse, forsooth, to their superior knowledge or
power; & they are to revenge his injuries, root out
his Enemies, & restore his lost Honour, tho' with the
destruction of the better part of Mankind? But,

To

To do the Propagators of thefe blafphemous notions juftice, they do not throw this load of fcandal on the *Law of Nature*, or of much as pretend from thence to authorife their execrable principles; but endeavour to fupport them by Traditional Religion, efpecially by mifinterpreted texts from the Old Teftament; & thereby make, not only Natural & Reveal'd Religion, but the Old & New Teftament (the latter of which requires doing good both to *Jews* & *Gentiles*) contradict each other. But to return.

IF what the Light of Nature teaches us concerning the divine perfections, when duly attended to, is not only fufficient to hinder us from falling into Superftition of any kind whatever, but, as I have already fhown, demonftrates what God, from his infinite Wifdom and Goodnefs, can, or cannot command; how is it poffible that the Law of Nature and Grace can differ? How can it be conceiv'd, that God's Laws, whether internally, or externally reveal'd, are not at all times the fame, when the Author of them is, and has been immutably the fame for ever.

# CHAP. IX.

*Human Happinefs being the ultimate defign & end of all Traditional, as well as Original Revelation, they muft both prefcribe the fame means; fince thofe means, which at one time promote human happinefs, equally promote it at all times.*

B. SHOU'D I grant you, that *Natural & Reveal'd Religion*, as they have the fame Author, *muft have the fame ends*; & that *the ultimate end of all God's Laws, and confequently, of all Religion, is human happinefs*: yet there are feveral things to be confider'd as fubordinate ends; And here, may not Original and

Tra-

Traditional Religion differ? since 'tis allow'd by all, that how immutable soever these subordinate ends are, yet the means to promote these ends are various and mutable.

*A.* You r allowing these means to be various & mutable, supposes no such means so prescrib'd in the Gospel; but that, agreeably to the Law of Nature, they are to be vary'd as best suits that end for which they were ordain'd: To imagine the contrary, is to make things, dependent on circumstances, independent; things that are proper only under some circumstances, necessary under all circumstances; nay, to make ends mutable, and means immutable; and that these are to continue the same, tho' by change of circumstances they become prejudicial, nay, destructive to the end for which alone they were ordain'd. The more necessary any *End* is, there's the more reason for people to be left at liberty to consider in the vast variety of circumstances, and those too perpetually changing, what means may be most proper for obtaining that End; since these having no worth in themselves, can only be valu'd according as they more or less conduce to the purpose they were intended for: & where God does not interpose, it is incumbent on human discretion, chiefly ordain'd for this end, to make such alterations as the reason of things requires.

Did not God always employ the most fit & most suitable means, he wou'd act contrary to the rules prescrib'd him by his own unerring Reason; & so he wou'd, did he not leave men at liberty to use such means, as their Reason, given for that purpose, told them was fittest to be used, in all those circumstances in which he had plac'd them; because that wou'd be requiring of them a conduct contrary to his own, & consequently, a conduct highly irrational: And therefore to alter one's conduct, as circumstances alter, is not only an act of the greatest prudence & judgment, but is consistent with the greatest steadiness.

As

As far as Divine Wisdom excels human, so far the divine Laws must excel human Laws in clearness & perspicuity, as well as other perfections. Whatever is confus'd and perplex'd, can never come from the clear fountain of all knowledge, nor that which is obscure from the Father of inexhaustible Light: & as far as you suppose God's Laws are not plain to any part of Mankind, so far you derogate from the perfection of those Laws, & the wisdom, & the goodness of the divine Legislator; who, since he has the framing of the understanding of those to whom he dictates his Laws, can't but adapt one to the other. But how can we say that infinite Wisdom speaks plainly to Mankind thro' all generations, except we allow that his commands extend not beyond moral things; and that in all matters of a mutable nature, which can only be consider'd as means, he obliges them to act according as they judge most proper for bringing about those ends.

Upon any other *Hypothesis*, human Laws have vastly the advantage of the divine; as being publish'd in the language the Subjects understand, in a plain simple style, without any allegorical, metaphorical, hyperbolical, or other forc'd way of expression: & if time discovers any inconvenience, or any unforeseen difficulties want to be clear'd up, the Legislature is ready at hand; or if in the mean time, any doubts about interpreting the Laws arise, there are standing Judges (accountable to the Legislature) in whose determinations people are to acquiesce. But Mankind are not to expect, that the divine Legislator will, from time to time, make any change in his Laws, & communicate them to all Nations in the languages they understand: nor can there be any Judges with a power to oblige people by their determinations; because such a power being without any appeal, is the same as a power to make divine Laws: & consequently, the only Tribunal God has erected here on Earth
(distinct

(diftinct from that he has mediately appointed by Men for their mutual defence) is every Man's own Confcience; which, as it can't but tell him, that God is the Author of all things, fo it muft inform him, that whatever he finds himfelf oblig'd to do by the circumftances he is in, he is oblig'd by God himfelf, who has difpofed things in that order, and plac'd him in thofe circumftances. 'Tis for want of obferving this rule, that the divine writings are render'd fo obfcure; and the infinity of Sermons, Notes, Comments & Paraphrafes, which pretend to fpeak plainer than God himfelf, have encreas'd this obfcurity. If whatever tends to the honour of God, & good of Man, is evident from the Light of Nature, whence comes all this uncertainty, perplexity, doubts & difficulties? Is it not chiefly owing to the denying people that liberty, which God, out of his infinite goodnefs, has allow'd them by the Law of Nature: & hindring them from judging for themfelves of the means, which beft tend to promote this end; and impofing on them, by the terrors of temporal & eternal punifhment, fuch needlefs fpeculations and ufelefs obfervances, as can't be confider'd either as means or ends?

B. You know that Divines, tho' they can't deny what you fay to be true in general, yet they think there's an exception as to Church-matters; and that here Men are not permitted to ufe fuch means as they themfelves think beft, but fuch only as thofe, who fet up to be their *Spiritual Governors,* fhall appoint.

A. Nothing can be more abfurd, than to fuppofe God has taken this power from the people, who have an intereft to preferve Religion in its purity (every deviation from it being to their prejudice) & plac'd it uncontroulably in the hands of Men, who, having an intereft in corrupting it, do, generally fpeaking, fo manage matters, as if Religion was the means, and their power the end for which it was inftituted. We do not find, that the *Mahometan* Clergy

caufe

cause any confusion or disorder among the *Muſſelmen*, & the *Pagan* Prieſts are ſcarce taken notice of in Story, ſo little miſchief did they do ; while all *Church-Hiſtory* is full of the vileſt, and moſt pernicious things perpetrated by *Chriſtian* Prieſts. The Chriſtian Morals, you muſt own, are too pure and plain to cauſe this difference ; what then can it be imputed to, but that independent power, which thoſe Prieſts uſurp'd ? which, tho' they claim'd it as deriv'd from Heaven for promoting godly Diſcipline, has occaſion'd general diſorder & confuſion. Endleſs have been the quarrels ambitious Prieſts have had with Princes upon the account of this Power, to the ſtopping of juſtice, and ſubverſion of almoſt all civil polity. Nor have the Eccleſiaſticks been leſs embroil'd among themſelves, each Set ſtriving to engroſs a Power which can belong to no Mortal. And the Biſhops, when they had no others to conteſt with, have ever contended among themſelves about *Superiority*, the *rights of their Sees*, and the *limits of their Juriſdiction :* and when their choice depended on the People, they frequently, eſpecially in their contentions about the greater Sees, run things on to blood & ſlaughter. And I appeal to their own Hiſtorians , whether the Eccleſiaſticks ever ſcrupl'd any method to obtain this Power : & whenever they got it, whether an inſupportable tyranny over body and mind, with the utter ruin of Religion, was not the conſequence? And whether it had not, where exercis'd to the height, more fatal effects than all the Superſtition of the *Gentiles?* Look the world round, you ſhall every where find Men more or leſs miſerable, as they have been more or leſs debarr'd the right of acting according to the beſt of their underſtanding in matters relating to Religion.

While every Church, or Congregation of Chriſtians, as in the Apoſtolical days, choſe, & maintain'd their own Miniſters, and order'd among themſelves whatever requir'd a ſpecial determination, no inconveniences happen'd; but as soon as this simple and natural method was broke, & the Clergy were form'd into a closely-united body, with that subordination & dependance they had on one another, the Christian world was enslav'd, and Religion forc'd to give way to destructive Superstition.

Which cou'd never have happen'd, if the Christians had observ'd these general rules, obligatory by the Light of Nature, as well as the Gospel; & which are alike given to every Christian, & oblige one as well as another; such as, ,, Doing all things for the ,, honour of God, for edification, for order, for de- ,, cency; for fleeing false Teachers, seducers, decei- ,, vers for avoiding scandal, & offending weak bre- ,, thren, &c. ,, And here since *every one* must judge for himself, & can't make over this right to any other, must not all Church-matters be manag'd by common consent?

In a word, If we consider the infinite variety of circumstances, the different manners & customs that prevail in different places, the prejudices of the weak, ignorant, and superstitious, and the designs of ambitious Men, there's nothing of a mutable nature, if once esteem'd immutably fix'd by God, but must sometimes become prejudicial to the end 'twas intended to promote; especially in a Religion design'd to be extended over the whole World, as well as to last to the end of it. There are but two ways of avoiding this inconvenience; either to suppose that the Founder of this Religion will, from time to time, himself ordain such alterations in things of a mutable nature, as those circumstances, which are different in different places, do require: or else, that he has left the parties concern'd, to act in all places according to discretion in such mutable matters.

*B.* You labour this point, but there are few of your sentiment.

*A.* If

*A.* If you mean Ecclefiafticks, perhaps you are in the right; tho' I'm fure, I have the Church of *England* on my fide, if judicious *Hooker* may be allow'd to underftand its Conftitution, as well as the nature of *Ecclefiaftical Polity.* He, in the tenth Section of his third Book, maintains this Propofition, that „ Neither „ God being the Author of Laws, nor his commit- „ ting them to Scripture, nor the continuance of the „ end for which they were inftituted, is reafon fuffi- „ cient to prove they are unchangeable: „ Where he admirably well diftinguifhes between things in their own nature immutable, & matters of outward order & polity, which he fuppofes daily changeable; & favs, „ The nature of every Law muft be judg'd by the „ end for which it was made, and by the aptnefs of „ the thing therein prefcrib'd to the fame end. - - „ When a thing does ceafe to be available to the end „ which gave it being, the continuance of it muft „ appear fuperfluous. - - That which the neceffity „ of fome fpecial time doth caufe to be enjoin'd, „ binds no longer than that time, but does afterwards „ become free. Laws, tho' both ordain'd of God „ himfelf, & the ends for which they were ordain'd „ continuing, may notwithftanding ceafe, if by al- „ teration of time, or perfons, they are found infuf- „ ficient to attain to that end. In which refpect why „ may we not prefume, that God doth even call for „ fuch a change or alteration, as the very nature of „ the things themfelves doth make neceffary? - - „ God never ordain'd any thing which could be bet- „ ter'd, yet many things he hath, that have been „ chang'd, and that for the better; that which fuc- „ ceedeth as better now, when change is requir'd, „ had been worfe, when that which is now chang d „ was inftituted. - - In this cafe, Men do not pre- „ fume to change God's ordinance, but yield there- „ unto, requiring itfelf to be chang'd. „ And he ap- plies this reafoning honeftly in faying, „ The beft way

G                                                        for

„ for *us* were to hold, even as they do, that in the
„ Scripture there muſt needs be found ſome particular
„ Form of Church-Polity, which God has inſtituted,
„ and which, for that very cauſe belongeth to all
„ Churches, to all times; but with any ſuch partial
„ eye to reſpect ourſelves, and by cunning to make
„ thoſe things ſeem the trueſt, which are the fitteſt
„ to ſerve our purpoſe, is a thing we neither like,
„ nor mean to follow.„ And let me add, that moſt,
if not all our Divines from the *Reformation* till the
time of the *Laudean* Faction, were in the ſame ſentiments; & from the mutability of ſuch things as are
means to an end, prov'd there cou'd be no particular
Form of Church-Polity eſtabliſh'd by divine authority: And they argu'd from the example of good King
*Hezekiah*, who, without regard to the ſalutiferous virtue
the *Brazen Serpent* once had, broke it to pieces when
perverted to a ſuperſtitious uſe.    And,

A l l, who believe *means* in their own nature are
mutable, muſt, if conſiſtent with themſelves, agree
with Mr. *Hooker*. This is ſo very apparent, that nothing
but intereſt can make any one talk otherwiſe; therefore, I ſhall only quote the late Dean of *Canterbury*,
who, in a Sermon preach'd before the Univerſity of
*Cambridge*, & publiſh'd at their requeſt, ſays, * „ That
„ the very temper, & compoſition of the Scripture
„ is ſuch, as neceſſarily refers us to ſome other Rule;
„ for this is a ſyſtem of mix'd, & very different duties,
„ ſome of eternal & univerſal obligation, others oc-
„ caſional & particular, limited to times & circum-
„ ſtances; and when theſe occaſions & circumſtances
„ ceas'd, the matter or the command was loſt, and
„ the whole reaſon and force of it ſunk of courſe:
„ Now thoſe things being oftentimes deliver'd pro-
„ miſcuouſly, & in general terms, Men muſt of ne-
„ ceſſity have recourſe to ſome other Rule to diſtin-
„ guiſh, & guide them in making the juſt difference
„ between the one, & the other ſort.

A n d

* *Serm. at the Commen. at* Cambr. *p.* 12.

And what other Rule is there, by which we can diftinguifh rightly in this important matter, but what arifes from the things themfelves? Thofe which have an innate worth and goodnefs are of an eternal and univerfal obligation; others, which have no fuch worth, can be confider'd only as means occafionally accommodated to particular times, places, perfons, and circumftances; which, of courfe, muft ceafe to oblige, when they ceafe to conduce to the end for which they were appointed, or others become more conducive. And this will more fully appear, if we confider, as the above-mention'd Author obferves, that * ,, The cir-,, cumftances of human life are infinite, and depend ,, on a multitude of accidents not to be forefeen, & ,, confequently not to be provided againft. Hence ,, Laws muft run in general terms, & fometimes the ,, intent of the Law is beft fulfill'd by running con-,, trary to the letter; & therefore, Reafon & Honefty ,, muft guide us to the fitnefs of the thing, & a great ,, fcope muft be left to Equity and Difcretion. ,, And furely, we muft not fuppofe, that Reafon, Honefty, Equity, and Difcretion will teach us one thing, and the Traditional Law another; efpecially confidering that in all God's-Laws, 'tis the Reafon of the Law that makes it Law.

B. By the reafoning of fuch Divines, I can't perceive the ufe of any occafional Commands, fince they fuppofe thefe can't oblige people longer than they judge it fit to obferve them: otherwife there cou'd be no difference between occafional and eternal Precepts; and what they judge fit & proper to be done, they are oblig'd to do without any occafional Commands; fo that according to them, whether there are, or are not any occafional Commands, human Difcretion is left at liberty to judge what is fit, or not fit to be obferv'd; which, I think, is fuppofing all fuch Commands needlefs. Yet the Authors you quote fup-

G 2                                         pofe,

pofe, contrary to your *Hypothefis*, there have been fuch Commands, particularly in relation to the *Jewish* State.

*A.* THE *Jews*, taking the ftory to be literally true, being upon their coming out of *Egypt* a free People, had a right by the Law of Nature to choofe what Government and Governor they pleas'd; and God wou'd not act fo inconfiftent a part, as to deprive them of any of thefe rights he had given them by the Law of Nature; & therefore did not take upon him the civil adminiftration of their affairs, till he had obtain'd their exprefs confent: fo that here he acted not as Governor of the Univerfe, but by a power deriv'd from the People by virtue of the *Horeb* Covenant; and the prefumption is, that where there is no fuch Contract, God will not exercife fuch a power; efpecially confidering that tho' the *Jews* rejected God himfelf from reigning over them, & were for choofing a new King, yet he bids *Samuel* * thrice in the fame Chapter to *hearken to the voice of the People.* But of this, and all other arguments of this nature, more fully hereafter.

*B.* THE Reafons you have given do not fully fatisfy me, but that fome things may be requir'd by God as Governor of the Univerfe, which are meerly pofitive; nay, that *Rites, & Ceremonies, Signs,* or *Symbols* might be arbitrarily enjoin'd, and fo intermix'd with matters of Morality, as to bind the Confciences of all Men at all times; and therefore, if you pleafe, we will review this point.

*A.* WITH all my heart, for this alone is the point that muft decide this Queftion, *Whether Natural and Reveal'd Religion do really differ?* As for *Natural Religion,* that, as you well know, takes in all thofe duties which flow from the Reafon and Nature of things, and the Relations we ftand in to God & our Fellow-Creatures; and confequently was there an inftituted Reli-

* I *Sam.* 8. 4. *&c.*

Religion which differs from that of Nature, its Precepts muſt be arbitrary, as not founded on the Nature and Reaſon of things, but depending on meer will and pleaſure; otherwiſe it wou'd be the ſame with Natural Religion. And tho' 'tis difficult to prove a negative, yet, I think, I can fully ſhew you, by adding other reaſons to thoſe already mention'd, that God, the great Governor of the Univerſe, can't give Mankind any ſuch Precepts : and conſequently, that *Natural & Reveal'd Religion* only differ in the manner of their being deliver'd.

## C H A P. X.

*God does not act arbitrarily, or interpoſe unneceſſarily; but leaves thoſe things, that can only be conſider'd as Means (& as ſuch are in their own nature mutable) to human Diſcretion, to determine as it thinks moſt conducing to thoſe things, which are in their own nature obligatory.*

IN order to ſettle this point, 'tis neceſſary to ſee how far this Natural Law extends. It not only commands that *Evil-doers ſhould be puniſh'd*, but that Men, according to the different circumſtances they are under, ſhou'd take the moſt proper methods for doing it, & vary as exigences require; ſo it not only requires that Juſtice ſhou'd be done Men as to their ſeveral claims, but that the readieſt, & moſt effectual way of doing it ſhou'd be taken; and the ſame may be ſaid of all other inſtances of this nature. If God interpoſes further, and preſcribes a particular way of doing theſe things, from which Men at no time, or upon no account ought to vary, he not only interpoſes unneceſſarily, but to the prejudice of the end for which he thus interposes. And as to matters relating to the Worship of God, it is the voice of Nature that God shou'd be publickly worshipped; & that Men shou'd do this in the most convenient way, by appointing amongst themselves time, place, persons, and all other things which require special determination. And, certainly, there's as much reason that things of this nature shou'd be left to human Discretion, as any other whatever; considering the different conditions & circumstances which Christians may be under, and the handle designing Men might otherwise take, to impose upon weak persons what they please, on pretence of divine right.

This being premis'd, the sole question is, Whether God, who, for many Ages, did not command, or forbid any thing, but what was moral or immoral; nor yet does so to the greatest part of Mankind, has, in some places & in some cases, broke into the rule of his own conduct, & issu'd out certain Commands which have no foundation in reason, by obliging Men to observe such things as wou'd not oblige were they not impos'd; or if the imposition was taken off, wou'd immediately return to their primitive indifference?

To suppose then such Commands, is it not to suppose God acts arbitrarily, and commands for commanding-sake; & that too under the severest penalties? Can such Commands be the effects of infinite Wisdom & Goodness? Or, if there be no reason why a thing shou'd be done at all, or if to be done, why it shou'd be done rather this way than that way; or why Men shou'd not vary means, as they judge most conducive to the end, for whose sake alone they were design'd; can there be any cause, why a Being, which never acts unnecessarily, and whose Commands are all the effects of infinite Wisdom, shou'd interpose? 'Tis so far from being necessary for God to interpose in such cases as these, that it only serves for a handle to human im-

imposition: for there's nothing so indifferent, but may, if believ'd to have Divinity stamp'd upon it, be perverted by designing Men to the vilest purposes; and in truth, there's nothing of this nature introduc'd into Religion, but what, I am afraid, has been some time or other so perverted.

ONE wou'd think it a thing wholly indifferent, who sprinkl'd an Infant, or from whose hands we receiv'd the Sacramental Bread & Wine, as long as the rules of decency & order were observ'd; yet has there not been a Set of Men, who, on pretence of a divine right to do those things, have made the Christian World believe, they have a discretionary power to bestow, or with-hold the means of Salvation; and, by virtue of this claim, have over-aw'd them into a slavish obedience, & a blind Submission?

THERE's no good or hurt in drawing two lines across one another, & yet what have not Priests made the poor people believe they cou'd do by virtue of it, as *curing diseases, driving away Devils*, and doing an infinity of other miracles? And in short, they have made it one of the chief engines of their craft, for the better carrying on of which, they persuaded the People to adore the *Cross*, miraculously found after it had been bury'd about three hundred years; & the wood of it has since so wonderfully encreas'd, as to be able to make innumerable Crosses, whereof each bit contain'd the virtue of the whole.

CONFESSION *of sins* to honest & judicious persons, might be of service, by the prudent advice they gave how to avoid the like sins for the future; but the *Popish Priests* claiming a power by divine right to *absolve people upon Confession*, have been let into the secrets of all persons, & by virtue of it have govern'd all things, and have made the *sins of the people*, not to be pardon'd but on their terms, the *harvest* of the *Priests*.

AMONG the *Jews*, the *Anointing with oil* was look'd on as very medicinal, and generally us'd in sickness; they pray'd & anointed the sick in hopes of a recovery: But tho' the Anointing in these colder climates is thought of no use in sickness, yet the *Papists* have built a most superstitious practice on it, which, for the greater reverence, they call the Sacrament of *Extreme Unction;* and which their Priests are not to administer as long as there's hopes of recovery.

WHAT can be more indifferent, or harmless, consider'd in themselves, than the Ceremonies of *oiling the heads of Kings*, & *laying hands on the heads of Elders* or *Presbyters?* & yet what absurd pretences have not Priests, who have the art of turning the most indifferent things to a superstitious use, drawn from thence to the prejudice of both Church and State?

IT was an ancient custom among the *Hebrews*, when they pray'd for a blessing on any person, to lay hands on him: Thus *Jacob* laid his hands on the Sons of *Joseph*, & *Moses* on *Joshua*. And among the primitive Christians, when any Congregation chose their Minister, they pray'd that he might duly execute that office, to which they had ordain'd him, & in praying, he that was the Mouth of the Congregation (the whole Assembly not being able conveniently to do it) laid his hands on him.

THIS gave a rise to the Clergy to pretend, that their *Laying on of hands upon a Man*, was necessary to qualify him for the Ministry; they by that act having given him the Holy Ghost, & an indelible character with certain spiritual powers; so that the People must either be without Ministers, or take one they had thus ordain'd, however unqualify'd they might think him.

IT's a thing indifferent in itself, whether *Men meet to pray in this*, *or that place;* but the Christians out of a superstitious reverence to the Reliques of the Martyrs, usually praying at their Tombs, came by degrees, as their reverence for them increas'd, to offer their

their prayers to them; which was a great change from their praying for them among the other dead, as was in the first Ages a general practice; & which, some of our High-church Priests are zealous for restoring, & pretend we have better proof for its being a Catholick doctrine, than for the authority of several Books of Scripture.

THE primitive Christians frequently consulting their Clergy in relation to Marriages, gave them a handle to set up for Judges by divine right in all matrimonial causes; and many prohibited Degrees as well as spiritual Relations, such as *God fathers* & *God-mothers*, &c. were introduc'd, to give the Clergy frequent opportunities to grant, at their own price, dispensations; by which means the succession & inheritance not only of private estates, but of Principalities & Kingdoms, in a great measure depended on them. And as an appendix to this spiritual usurpation, they hook'd in the cognizance of all *carnal causes*, *incontinence* in single as well as married persons. Thus you see, how easily Mankind may be abus'd, where 'tis believ'd, that Religion can require any thing inconsistent with the rights and liberties God has allow'd them by the Law of Nature; and how dangerous 'tis to trust any thing with Men, who pretend a divine right to whatever they can lay hands on. To give an instance how severely this divine right was exerted by the Pope, as Head of the Church: * „ *Robert*, King of *France*, „ having marry'd a Lady of the House of *Burgundy*, „ a match very advantageous to the State, & tho' he „ had the consent of his Bishops, yet he, & the whole „ Kingdom were excommunicated by the Pope, be- „ cause this Lady was in the fourth degree of con- „ sanguinity, and the King had been God-father to „ her Child by a former Husband; which so distress'd „ the poor King, that all his Servants, except three „ or four, deserted him, and no one wou'd touch

G 5 the

* *Puffend.* Intr. to History, pag. 170.

,, the victuals which came from his table, which were,
,, therefore, thrown to the dogs.

I shall give one instance more, Men are oblig'd to
avoid as much as conveniently they can the infectious
conversation of immoral persons; & it was, no doubt,
at first a duty in a special manner, for Christians, com-
pass'd round with *Pagans*, to observe this rule in relation to their own body, & agree to shun any such
person as one who had his *Father's Wife*: & tho' this
is no more than what is daily done in private societies,
& was easily practis'd amongst Christians when they
were but few, yet because the Minister might collect
the votes, and declare the opinion of the Assembly,
the Clergy by degrees not only excluded the Congregation from this their natural right, but claim'd,
as giv'n them by Heaven, a power to excommunicate
whom they pleased, even their own Sovereign, and
that too for things relating to their own interest:
And they order'd not only their own Congregations,
but all Christians, on peril of their Salvation, to *avoid
all commerce with the Excommunicated*, and ordain'd,
that *if he did not in forty days give the Church satisfaction, the Magistrate was bound to imprison him, and
confiscate his Estate.* And the Princes, instead of re-
senting these incroachments on their power, had so
little sense as to pass this into a Law; not imagining
this treatment wou'd reach them: but they soon felt,
that the Church claim'd the same power over them as
over other Christians, looking on all to be alike subject to their spiritual power. And accordingly Kings
were often excommunicated, their Subjects absolv'd
of their oaths of allegiance, & their dominions given
to more orthodox Princes to be held of the Church,
which, no doubt, was in a flourishing Condition,
when she, as often as her interest requir'd it, absolv'd
Princes of their oaths to their Subjects, & Subjects of
theirs to their Sovereigns, and by Virtue of her spiritual power, dispos'd, as she thought fit, of Mens Estates,
Honours,

Honours, and even Lives. *What has been may be!* And in all probability wou'd be, were the Clergy as united among themselves as formerly.

In a word, there's nothing in itself so indifferent, either as to matter or manner, but if it be engrafted into Religion, and monopoliz'd by the Priests, may endanger the substance of it. This has been plainly shewn by those Divines, who, at the *Reformation*, & since, have argu'd against all impositions : they have prov'd that most of the corruptions of *Popery* began at some rites, which seem'd at first very innocent, but were afterwards abus'd to Superstition and Idolatry, and swell'd up to that bulk, as to oppress, & stifle true Religion with their number & weight. And, indeed, there's no Sect, but complains how superstitiously Rites and Ceremonies are us'd by all, except themselves. And since I am defending the Liberties given by God to Mankind, & which, without ingratitude to the donor, as well as injury to ourselves, we can't give up, I do not doubt you will hear me with patience, because if I prove my point, I shall, it may be hoped, in some measure put an end to those otherwise endless disputes, which divide, & distract the Christian World.

Whatsoever is in itself indifferent, whether as to matter or manner, must be so to an All-wise Being, who judges of things as they are; & for the same reason that he commands things which are good, and forbids those which are evil, he leaves Men at liberty in all things indifferent; & 'tis in these only, that our liberty of acting as we please consists.

Things, which are of no value in themselves, can be no motives to an All-wise Being to punish us, or to clog our happiness with any such needless observances: And consequently, Men, as far as they assert our future happiness, or any part of it, to depend on such things, do so far derogate from the Wisdom & Goodness of God, and from those motives we have to love, & honour him. The arbitrary Commands

of

of a Tyrant may be obey'd out of fear, but juſt and rational Laws alone can move the affection of rational creatures.

Is it reaſonable to believe, an All-wiſe & Gracious Being is ſo fond of indifferent things, that he ſubjects his Children to ſuffer even in this life on their account? And yet you muſt own, if he has made theſe the ſubject of his Commands, they ought to ſuffer every thing rather than not obſerve them: but if God will not have Men puniſh'd in this world, and much leſs in the next, upon the account of things indifferent, they can never be the ſubject of his Commands.

Tho' a judicious Author ſuppoſes a Form of divine Worſhip in itſelf indifferent, may be requir'd by God for the ſake of peace & unity, yet at the ſame time he contends, that * „ God does not expect we „ ſhou'd comply with that Form, if it brings miſery „ on ourſelves, or confuſion to the publick; becauſe „ that wou'd be preferring a thing in itſelf indifferent „ to the happineſs of our lives, and the peace of the „ Publick; and that to ſuppoſe the contrary, wou'd „ be breaking in upon the ſpotleſs character of our „ heavenly Father, by repreſenting him not as a wiſe „ and good, but a peeviſh and ill-natur'd Being; „ who takes an unreaſonable reſentment at the pru- „ dent conduct of his Children. „   But will not this as ſtrongly infer, that God cou'd not command the obſerving ſuch things, which, if obſerv'd, wou'd deſtroy his moral Character; and which, inſtead of preſerving peace & unity, wou'd bring miſery on private perſons, and confuſion the Publick? whereas theſe bleſſings of peace and unity can never be obtain'd by a forc'd conformity, nor by any other method than allowing People their natural liberty in all ſuch matters.    And,

If Religion conſiſts in imitating the Perfections of God, what Perfection of God do the ſuperſtitious imi-

tate,

* *Chub*'s Suppl. to his Prev. Queſt. 27, 28.

tate, when they contend, as *pro Aris & Focis*, for Forms, Rites, and Ceremonies?

IF in Heaven there's no room for arbitrary Precepts, to incumber that moral goodnefs which is the fole bufinefs of the blefs'd above, what cou'd hinder us, did we but make that too our only concern here, from enjoying a fort of Heaven on Earth, free from all tyrannical impofitions, and endlefs quarrels about indifferent things?

IN a word, If there's nothing in a Religion which comes from God, but what is moft excellent, what room can there be for indifferent things? Can fuch things as have no worth or excellency, contribute to the worth, or excellency of Religion? If they cou'd, the more they abounded, the more excellent wou'd Religion be; which yet is fo far from being true, even in the opinion of thofe who contend for fuch things, that even they, when they are to fhew the excellency of the Chriftian Religion, recommend it for having but few of thofe things; which is fuppofing it lofes of its excellency in proportion to what it has of this nature; and that they have a higher & more honourable conception of it, who believe it has no fuch mixture to fpoil its beauty, and deftroy its fimplicity; but that, like its Author, 'tis wholly fpiritual, & as fuch, worthy its divine original.

ONE wou'd think thefe men muft appear ridiculous to themfelves, who, tho' they recommend the Chriftian Religion, as purely fpiritual, in oppofition to the carnal Religion of the *Jews*, yet at the fame time contend, it has fome ordinances as little fpiritual as any the *Jews* had; and put a greater ftrefs upon 'em, than ever the *Jews* did on any of theirs.

IF God's works fhew infinite Wifdom, there's no reafon to imagine but his Laws do the fame; but then they muft be moral Laws, for thefe alone can fpeak his Wifdom as plainly to all Mankind as his works do: They both alike have the character of infinite

finite Wifdom imprefs'd on them, & both alike difcover their divine original.

If all God's Laws are of a piece, muft they not
all be built on the eternal Reafon of things? Nay,
if that be fufficient to determine him in one cafe, it
muft be fo in all. But on the contrary, if God acts
arbitrarily in any one inftance, he muft, or at leaft may,
do fo in all; fince no foreign caufe, nothing but his
nature, cou'd make him act fo. But God forbid we
fhou'd imagine, that any of his Laws have not imprefs'd
on them the fame character of the higheft Wifdom
and Goodnefs, that is imprefs'd on the whole frame
of Nature, and on every part of it.

'Tis impoffible Men fhou'd have any juft idea of
the Perfections of God, who think that the dictates
of infinite Wifdom do not carry their own evidence
with them; or are not by their own innate worth
difcoverable to all Mankind. Were it not fo, how
cou'd they be diftinguifh'd from the uncertain opinions
of weak and fallible Men; not to fay the whimfies &
reveries of crack-brain'd Enthufiafts? How fhocking
is it to hear Divines cry, that * ,, Certain things,
,, were they not to be ador'd as Myfteries, ought to
,, be exploded as Abfurdities.

If we fuppofe any arbitrary Commands in the
Gofpel, we place Chriftians in a worfe condition than
thofe under no Law but that of Nature, which requires nothing but what is moral; and confequently
the greateft part of Mankind, who are to be judg'd
by the Law they know, & not by the Law they do
not know, are, on this fuppofition, in a better condition as to the next world than Chriftians; becaufe
they do not hazard the favour of God by any miftakes,
or omiffions in fuch matters.

To fuppofe fome Men, who, tho' they exactly obey
the Law of Nature, may yet be punifh'd, even eternally, for not obeying another Law befides, wou'd be
to

* _South_'s Serm. Vol. 3. pag. 316.

to make God deal infinitely lefs mercifully with them,
than with thofe that have no other Law: And yet in
this miferable cafe are all Chriftians involv'd, if the
Gofpel requires fuch things as the Law of Nature
does not; and that too under the fevereft penalties.
And I may add, that even as to temporal happinefs,
they who think original and traditional Revelation
don't differ, are in the better ftate; fince they muft
delight in their duty, as having nothing requir'd of
them, but what they moft evidently fee tends to their
good, & confequently are free (no fmall happinefs)
from all panick fears; while they, who believe there
are things meerly pofitive in Religion, of which Reafon
affords no light how they are to be perform'd, or even
what they are, muft lye under endlefs doubts & fears,
and according to the meafure of their fuperftition, be
wrought upon by defigning Men to hate, damn, and
perfecute one another about fuch obfervances; as we
fee is actually done every where by the different Sect,
who are fo abfurd as to believe a God of infinite
Wifdom & Goodnefs can give his Creatures arbitrary
Commands.

When Men are at a lofs to know from the nature
and reafon of things, what to believe, and what to
practice, and fee every where endlefs divifions, they
muft be in continual dread of fuch an arbitrary Being,
as their unmanly & irrational fears reprefent God to be.
*Plutarch* makes this difference between the Atheift &
Superftitious; * ,, One believes no Deity, the other
,, wifhes there was none; if he believes, 'tis againft his
,, will; miftruft he dares not, or call his thoughts in
,, queftion, but could he, with fecurity, at once throw
,, off that oppreffive fear, which, like the rock of
,, *Tantalus*, impends, & preffes over him, he would
,, with equal joy fpurn his enflaving thoughts, and
,, embrace the Atheift's ftate & opinion, as the hap-
,, pieft deliverance. Atheifts are free of fuperftition,
                                            ,, but

* *Treatife of Superftition.* To. 2. *pag.* 170. E, F.

,, but the Superstitious are in will and inclination ,, Atheists, tho' impotent in thought, and unable to ,, believe of the divine Being as they willingly would. And I am afraid, this now is the case with most of these superstitious persons, who represent God as a most cruel Being, damning Men to eternity, even for mistaken opinions, or about such things too as have no foundation in Reason. And perhaps, the endeavouring to drown all thoughts of such a tyrannical Deity, is no small occasion of that gross immorality, which does every where prevail, & must ever do so where superstition abounds.

'Tis Mens not being govern'd by the reason of things, which makes them divided about trifles, and lay the utmost stress on such things as wise Men wou'd be asham'd of. Tis on the account of these, that the different Sects set the highest value on themselves, & think they are the peculiar favourites of Heaven, while they condemn all others for opinions & practices not more senseless, than those themselves look on as essentials. And were it not in so serious a matter, it wou'd be diverting to see how they damn one another, for placing Religion in whimsical notions, and fantastical Rites & Ceremonies, without making the least reflection on what they themselves are doing.

What reason has a *Papist*, for instance, to laugh at an *Indian*, who thinks it contributes to his future happiness to dye with a Cow's tail in his hands, while he lays as great a stress on rubbing a dying Man with oil? Has not the *Indian* as much right to moralize this action of his, and shew its significancy, as the *Papist* any of his mystick rites, or *Hocus Pocus* tricks? which have as little foundation in the nature or reason of things.

Suppose one came from the furthermost parts of the Earth, vouching it as a divine Revelation, that the nails of our Children are, at a certain time, to be par'd by certain Persons with certain ceremonies, in order

order to make them capable of Salvation; and that such as dy'd before their nails were thus par'd, remain'd for ever in a very wretched ſtate; wou'd not every one here, without examining into this Man's miſſion, or without regard to thoſe ſpiritual things ſignify'd under paring of nails, reject this belief as unworthy of having God for its Author? And yet as abſurd as this may appear to us, the ſuperſtitious *Mahometans* * think they are oblig'd to have their nails par'd during their ſickneſs, if they apprehend it to be mortal.

THEY muſt be very little acquainted with the nature of a ſpiritual Religion, who think it can any ways conſiſt in not going to reſt when Men are ſleepy; not eating, when they are hungry; or abſtaining from, or uſing certain meats & drinks at ſtated times; and in waſhings, ſprinklings, and luſtrations by blood or water; and yet theſe things were in ſo high a repute with moſt of the *Pagans*, that they thought they wou'd atone for the greateſt immoralities.

*Ah nimium faciles, qui triſtia crimina cædis*
*Fluminea tolli poſſe putetis aquâ.* Ovid. Faſt. l. 2. 45.

THE *Taurobolia*, or the bedawbing a Man in a pit, all over with the blood of a Bull, which fell on him thorow holes made in the plank on which the beaſt was ſlain, was believ'd to waſh away all his ſins, & he, happy Man, regenerated to eternity, provided that once in twenty years he renewed this myſtical regeneration: & not only great Perſons, but whole Cities might perform this religious Ceremony by deputation, and receive the benefit. A ſhort account of this you meet with in *Fontenelle*'s Hiſtory of Oracles, taken from *Prudentius.* †

THO' the Heathen Prieſts made the People believe they cou'd be clean from their ſins by ſacrifices, and
H                    other

* *Hide*'s Pref. to *Bobovius* of the *Turkiſh* Liturgy, &c.
† *Peri Stephanon, de Romano,* p. 135, 136. *See Salmaſ. ad Heliotab. cap.* 7.

other external things, yet it was as themselves had the application of them, they were the Persons to whom the Gods had committed the *religious rubbing brushes*; tho' the Men of sense among the *Pagans* were not thus to be impos'd on, which made *Tully* say,

*Animi labes nec diuturnitate evanescere, nec amnibus ullis elui potest.* De Leg. l. 2. c. 10.

*Lactantius* seems to be of another opinion, in saying, ,, * Give us one that is unjust, foolish, & a sinner, ,, and in one instant he shall be just, prudent, & in- ,, nocent; with one laver all his wickedness shall be ,, wash'd away.

In a word, while Priests of what denomination soever pretend authority to absolve sinners, and the people are so void of sense as to rely on their absolu- tion, Natural Religion, which puts the whole stress on internal penitence & true virtue in the soul, will be despis'd, allowing no *succedaneum*, no commuting, or compounding with Heaven. And, indeed, all such commuting, or compounding powers, wherever they are suppos'd to be lodg'd, serve as a Bank of credit for the transgressors, and are a mighty incitement to all manner of villany. And in former days, the great Men, after having oppress'd and plunder'd people, thought to compound with Heaven, by letting the Clergy share in the spoil; and 'tis on this notion so many Abbies & Monasteries have been founded; & the superstitious, as long as they are persuaded there is any virtue in externals, will, as we see by constant expe- rience, chiefly depend on such things. And I may add,

This Doctrine, that one Man may not only merit for himself by doing more than God requires of him, but that the merit of such actions may be transfer'd to another, who has done less than God requires of him, has been a great incitement to wickedness; and those who have acted a most immoral part during their

* *Institut. l. 3. c. 26. n 9.*

their whole lives, have believ'd they might comfortably rely on it; nothing being thought too hard for merit & mediation.

There are none, I think, now so abſurd, as in words to maintain, that there's the leaſt variableneſs in God, much leſs that he is an arbitrary Being, commanding things for commanding-ſake: yet are not they, who aſſert there are meerly poſitive things in the Chriſtian Religion, guilty of this abſurdity; in ſuppoſing that God, who had the goodneſs for a long time, not to confine Mankind to any indifferent things, yet at length chang'd his mind, & repented of this great goodneſs; & arbitrarily depriv'd, they will not ſay, all Mankind, but no ſmall number of this liberty; and requir'd of them the belief of certain uſeleſs ſpeculations, & the practice of certain indifferent things on the ſevereſt penalties? And when they lament that the Chriſtian World, even from the earlieſt days, has been in perpetual broils about ſuch things, do they not ſuppoſe that God can give arbitrary Commands, & that thoſe Commands are involv'd in great obſcurity? Whereas, if merely poſitive things were requir'd, thoſe, not being like matters of morality, diſcoverable by their own light, wou'd be made as plain as infinite Wiſdom could render them; & to prevent their being perverted to ſerve ill purpoſes, we ſhou'd have been punctually told when, how, and by whom, thoſe arbitrary things ſhou'd be apply'd, as well as that they were to be obligatory for ever.

*B.* If God has reveal'd any thing in a way liable to be miſtaken, he can't be diſpleas'd with ſincere people for miſtaking it.

*A.* That's very true, but certainly the end of God's giving any Precepts, was not to deliver them ſo obſcurely that people might be faultleſs if they miſtook, but to make 'em ſo plain that they could not well miſtake: And this is agreeable to infinite Wiſdom directed by infinite Goodneſs, which, certainly, will

H 2 give

give us equal degrees of evidence for religious truths which so much concern us, as it has done for truths of less importance.

For my part, I can't help being of the sentiments of a learned Divine, who, after having prov'd at large, that Morality is capable of Demonstration, concludes with saying, * „ I shall only here repeat, that Man „ being a reasonable agent, Reason is the Law & Rule „ of his actions ; there's no truth in *Mathematicks* „ more clear, & incontestable than this. Now 'tis as „ easy for him, when he examines his actions by this „ Rule, to see whether they agree together, as to „ know when two lines are compar'd, whether they „ are of the same, or a different length. -- Why „ should demonstration then be confin'd only to „ numbers & figures? -- Nay, if we argue from the „ importance of Morality, it will be found much more „ agreeable to the goodness of God, who gave us „ our intellectual faculties, that the truths which are „ of the greatest concern to us, should, if we make „ a due use of those faculties, admit of the greatest „ evidence. „ I think, I need only add, that was there any thing but Morality necessary to constitute true Religion, we might be certain that the Goodness of God wou'd give us a demonstration for it, equal to that he has given us for Morality. But,

If there are now things which are not moral in Religion, does not that suppose a change of mind in God, and then where will you stop? For if change-ableness was not a perfection, it wou'd not be in him; and if all his Perfections are infinite, must not this be so too? And is it not as reasonable to suppose, he may command some indifferent things to-day, and others to-morrow; or some in this part of the world, and some in another; as at first to command moral, and then super-add indifferent things? If indifferent things can contribute to the perfection of Revelation, there may

* *Fiddes's* Body of Divinity Par. 2. B. 1. c. 11.

may be endless Revelations; & the laſt always more
perfect, as having new indifferent things. It was not
about things of a moral nature, that there were ſuch
diviſions in the primitive times, and that *Montaniſm*
ſpread itſelf over a great part of the Chriſtian world;
the followers of *Montanus*, as *Euſebius* writes, * boaſting
that he was the Paraclet, & that *Priſcilla* & *Maximilla*
his companions were his Propheteſſes. And *Tertullian*,
as is own'd by the Tranſlator of his Apology, ſays, †
,, That the Law, & the Prophets were to be look'd
,, on as the infancy, and the Goſpel, as it were, the
,, youth; but that there was no compleat perfection
,, to be found, but in the inſtruction of the Holy Ghoſt,
,, who ſpake by *Montanus*:,, But to make ſome apology for his laps'd Father, he ſays, ,, The Arch-
,, Heretick *Montanus* ſupported the character of a
,, moſt holy, mortify'd, & extraordinary perſon for a
,, conſiderable time; the world rung with the viſions
,, and prophecies of him, & his two damſels; & the
,, face of ſeverity and ſaintſhip conſecrated their re-
,, veries, & made real poſſeſſion paſs for inſpiration.--
,, The Churches of *Phrygia*, and afterwards other
,, Churches, divided upon the account of theſe new
,, Revelations; & even the very Biſhop of *Rome* him-
,, ſelf for ſome time eſpous'd the vanity, and made
,, much of the Impoſtor.,, And had he continu'd to
do ſo, it might, perhaps, have obtain'd; ſince we find
the Chriſtians in the primitive times came intirely into
a more groſs impoſture, and had faith for the moſt
palpable forgery of the *Sybilline* Oracles being writ by
real Propheteſſes under divine inſpirations. And the
whole Chriſtian world for more than the two firſt
centuries believ'd the *Millenarian* Hereſy, as it is now
call'd; for which, indeed, they pretended other proofs
than the divine authority of the *Sybils*. And there has
ſcarce been an age ſince, but where ſome ſuch attempt

H 3                                               has

* *Eccl. Hiſt. l. 5. c. 14.*
† *Reeve*'s Prelim. Diſc. to *Tertul.* Apol. p. 149.

has been made; & that of *Popery*, which is the grossest attempt on the credulity of Mankind succeeded; tho' the *Monks* in the twelfth Century were not satisfy'd even with that, & therefore, endeavour'd to introduce a new Gospel, call'd *Evangelium eternum*, or the *Gospel of the Holy Ghost*; * and affirm'd, that this Gospel of the Spirit excell'd that of Christ's, as much as the light of the Sun does that of the Moon.

In short, to this belief, that there may be things in Religion not founded on Nature & Reason, & that these may be reserv'd for this, or that period of time, are owing all the visions & reveries among the *Papists*, & other Enthusiastick Christians; & upon this absurd notion is founded the most spreading Religion of *Mahomet*, who pretended to be the Paraclet promis'd by Jesus to compleat, & perfect all things: And,

In a word, to this belief are owing all the false Revelations that ever were in the world; and except we allow there are certain tests flowing from the nature of things, whereby the meanest capacities may distinguish truth from falsehood, we shall for ever be liable to be impos'd on by Mad-men as well as Impostors.

If God can command some things arbitrarily, we can't be certain, but that he may command all things so; for tho' some Commands should relate to things in their own nature good, yet how can we know that an arbitrary Being commands them for this reason; & consequently, since an arbitrary will may change each moment, we can never be certain of the will of such a Being. And,

To suppose that God by the Law of Nature leaves Men at liberty in all indifferent things, and yet by a positive Law restrains this liberty in certain parts and ages of the world, is to suppose God determines one way by immediate, & another way by mediate Revelation; both Laws too subsisting at the same time.

B.

* *Usser.* de Chris. Eccles. successione & statu. l. 9. Sect. 2.

B. WE fay that the Law of Nature, however immutable as to Good & Evil, has enjoin'd nothing in relation to indifferent things; fo that there's a large field, in which all Legiflators, human as well as divine, may exert their power.

A. IT's true, the Law of Nature leaves Men at liberty to act as they pleafe in all indifferent matters; and if any traditionary Law abridges this liberty, fo far 'tis contrary to that of Nature, & invades thofe rights which Nature & its Author has given Mankind.

HUMAN Legiflators are fo far from having a right to deprive their Subjects of this liberty, that their main end in fubmitting to government is, to be protected in acting as they think fit in all fuch cafes where no one is injur'd; & herein the whole of human liberty confifts, the contrary being a ftate of meer vaffalage: & Men are more or lefs miferable, according as they are more or lefs depriv'd of this liberty; efpecially in matters of meer Religion, wherein they ought to be moft free.

To fuppofe God has *in thefe laft days*, as they are call'd in Scripture, depriv'd any part of Mankind of that Liberty which before was granted to all, wou'd be to make him act unreafonably; fince all thofe reafons which oblig'd him to command good, or forbid evil things, muft wholly ceafe in relation to a fubject, which by being indifferent partakes of neither: and was there any reafon to deprive Men of their liberty in indifferent things, they wou'd then ceafe to be indifferent; on the contrary the fame reafons which oblige him to interpofe in things, whofe nature is either good or evil, forbids it in indifferent things, fince Mens happinefs depends on their liberty in all fuch things. Whatever is unreafonable for God to do, is contrary to the eternal Law of his nature; and confequently, to deprive Men in any of thefe cafes, is to make the dictates of his Nature, & his revealed Will to clafh.

IN

IN short, the Law of Nature either is, or is not, a perfect Law: if the firſt, 'tis not capable of additions; if the laſt, does it not argue want of wiſdom in the Legiſlator, in firſt enacting ſuch an imperfect Law, and then in letting it continue thus imperfect from age to age; and at laſt thinking to make it abſolutely perfect, by adding ſome merely poſitive and arbitrary Precepts? To what end does God continually impreſs on Chriſtians as well as others this Law of Nature? ſince that was needleſs, had they another more perfect, & more plainly reveal'd.

IF Men have been at all times oblig'd to avoid Superſtition, and embrace true Religion, there muſt have been at all times, ſufficient marks of diſtinction; which cou'd not ariſe from their having different objects, ſince God is the object of both, but from the having different notions of him & his conduct. Nay, allowing that the Light of Nature was ſufficient to teach Men, that true Religion conſiſts in entertaining ſuch notions of God as are worthy of him, & Superſtition in ſuch as are unworthy of him; yet that alone wou'd not enable Men, when they came to particulars, to diſtinguiſh one from the other: And, therefore, the ſame Light of Nature muſt teach them what notions are worthy, and what unworthy of having God for their Author. But how can there be ſuch marks flowing from the nature of Religion & Superſtition, if what is Superſtition by the Light of Nature, can, notwithſtanding theſe marks, be made a part of Religion by Revelation?

IF he, who reſembles God moſt is like to underſtand him beſt, is it not * „ becauſe, as Biſhop *Tillot-* „ *ſon* obſerves, he finds theſe perfections in ſome „ meaſure in himſelf, which he contemplates in the „ divine Nature; and nothing gives a Man ſo ſure „ a notion of things as practice and experience; „ every good Man is in ſome degree partaker of the
divine

* *Serm. Vol.* 3. *pag.* 42.

,, divine Nature, and feels that in himself, which he
,, conceives to be in God, so that this Man does ex-
,, perience what others do but talk of; he sees the
,, image of God in himself, & is able to discourse of
,, him from an inward sense & feeling of his excel-
,, lency.,, But this would not be just arguing, if God
was an arbitrary Being, & cou'd command his Creatures things which carried no perfection or goodness
with them.

In a word, if the essence of Religion consists in
believing and practising such things, as have a real
worth & excellency in them, tending to the honour
of God, and the good of Man, the essence of Superstition, which is its opposite, must consist in imagining
to propitiate an allwise and gracious Being by such
things as have no worth or excellency in them, such
as may as well not be done, as done, or as well done
this as that way. Superstition is defin'd by Dr. *H. More*
(& all our Divines speak to the same purpose) * *to be
that impiety, by which a Man considers God to be so light
or passionate, as with trivial things, either to be appeas'd,
or else mov'd to wrath.* Can any thing be more trivial, than useless speculations, & unnecessary obser-
vations?

How numerous soever Christians may be, tho' they
are but few in comparison of the rest of Mankind,
yet the Church of Christ, by the confession of all parties, is a very small body of Men; each Sect, tho'
they complain of one another's uncharitableness, yet
they, excluding all other Sects, either as *Schismaticks*
or *Hereticks*, confine Salvation to their own Church.
Dr. *Scot* says, † ,, While Men behold the state of Re-
,, ligion thus miserably broken and divided, and the
,, professors of it crumbl'd into so many Sects & par-
,, ties, and each party spitting fire and damnation at

H 5                             ,, its

* *The Abridgm. of his Morals or Account of Virtue l. 2.
p. 122.*    † *Christ. Life, P. 11. Vol. 1. c. 3. p. 112.*

,, its adversary, so that, if all say true, or, indeed,
,, any two of them in five hundred Sects, which there
,, are in the world, (& for ought, I know, there may
,, be five thousand) it is five hundred to one, but that
,, every one is damn'd, because every one damns all
,, but itself, and itself is damn'd by four hundred &
,, ninety nine.,, How, I say, can these differences
be avoided, as long as Men take into their notion of
Religion, nay, make unnecessary things necessary parts
of it; and if many of our Divines have got rid of
these absurd notions, is it not because they are, what
in contempt they are call'd, *Rationalists?*

THE pious Bishop *Taylar* says, * ,, He could not
,, expect, but that God wou'd some way or other
,, punish Christians, by reason of their pertinacious
,, disputing of things unnecessary, undeterminable &
,, unprofitable; and for their hating and persecuting
,, their brethren (which shou'd be as dear to them as
,, their own lives) for not consenting to one anothers
,, follies & senseless vanities.

BUT, is there any certain way of judging what are
unnecessary or unprofitable things, but by the rules
here laid down, of judging of things from their nature & tendency? Without observing this rule, there's
nothing so trifling, or senseless, but People may be
persuaded to place Religion in, and be in continual
broils about it.   If a dispute between two Preachers,
whether the first words in the Lord's Prayer shou'd
be translated *Father our*, or *Our Father*, cou'd cause
such disturbances, as it lately did at *Hamburgh*, what
is there so indifferent, if once believ'd to belong to
Religion, but may have pernicious effects? And there
are a number of instances in all ages, where things
as trifling have occasion'd strange disorders.

And the primitive times were not free from them:
the memorable Mr. *Hales* gives this account of the
then quarrel about the time of keeping *Easter*;
,, It

* *Epistle Dedic. to Liberty of Prophesying.*

,, It being, *says he,* * upon error taken for necessary,
,, that an *Easter* must be kept, and upon worse than
,, error, if I may so speak, (for it was no less than a
,, point of *Judaism* forc'd upon the Church) thought
,, further necessary, that the ground for the time of
,, our keeping that Feast, must be the rule left by
,, *Moses* to the *Jews*; there arose a stout question,
,, Whether we were to celebrate it with the *Jews*
,, on the fourteenth Moon, or the Sunday following.
,, This matter, tho' most unnecessary, most vain, yet
,, caus'd as great a combustion as ever was in the
,, Church; the *West* separating from the *East* for many
,, years together. In this fantastical hurry, I can't
,, see but all the world were *Schismaticks*; neither can
,, any thing excuse them from that imputation, ex-
,, cepting only this, that we charitably suppose that
,, all parties, out of conscience did what they did.
,, A thing which befel them, thro' the ignorance of
,, their Guides; and because thro' sloth and blind
,, obedience Men examin'd not the things they were
,, taught, but like beasts of burden patiently couch'd
,, down, & indifferently underwent whatever their
,, superiors laid upon them.

,, And can we, says Dr. *Burnet*, † think without
,, astonishment, that such matters, as giving the Sa-
,, crament in leavened or unleavened bread; or an
,, explication of the Procession of the Holy Ghost,
,, whether it was from the Father and the Son, or
,, from the Father by the Son, cou'd have rent the
,, *Greek* and *Latin* Churches so violently one from
,, another, that the *Latines,* rather than assist the other,
,, look'd on till they were destroy'd by the *Ottoman*
,, Family?

AND other instances he gives of fatal disturbances
from disputes about trifles; as the removing the pictures of certain Bishops out of a Church occasion'd
Image-worship; for those who oppos'd their removal,

went

* *Tract of Schism.*   † *Burnet's* Serm, Ann. 1681.

went so far as to maintain, that Pictures ought not only to be set up, but worshipp'd; which caus'd not only great disorders in the *East*, but made *Italy* to revolt at the Pope's instigation. This contest too begat another, Whether the Sacrament was only the image, or the very substance of Christ?

I might add, that the dispute between the *Lutherans* & *Calvinists* about the Sacrament, tho' it has created such fierce animosities, is meerly verbal, since both sides are against any change in the elements, & both sides maintain a real presence of the body of Christ.

I need not have gone to distant times and places for instances, our own late divisions and persecutions about such trifling things, as Rites and Ceremonies, nay, habits & postures, wou'd in all likelyhood have ended in the utter ruin both of Church and State, had not the blessed Revolution interpos'd.

*B.* I wou'd not have you treat what you call postures so irreverently: ought not People to kneel at their devotions?

*A.* The whole Christian World for many ages thought not; & the *Anti-Nicene* Fathers, * as well as the Council of *Nice*, forbad kneeling, on all sundays, & all other days between *Easter* & *Whit-sunday*.

In a word, if those sentiments must be true, which tend most to make Men love & honour God, by giving the brightest and noblest ideas of his Wisdom and Goodness, and which free him from the imputation of change and inconstancy, and from imposing from time to time arbitrary Commands, & from partiality and respect of persons, what I have laid down must be true, & the contrary, not only false, but impious; But however, since this is a point of the utmost consequence, I shall proceed to other arguments, & shew how inconsistent it is with the good of Mankind, to suppose any merely positive things to be part of the ingredients which constitute true Religion.

* *Daillee* of the Fathers, l. 2. c. 6. p. 336, 337.

CHAP.

## CHAP. XI.

*The suppofing Things meerly pofitive to be made the Ingredients of Religion, is inconfiftent with the Good of Mankind as well as the Honour of God.*

THE Happinefs of human fociety, and of every particular member confifling in the due obfervation & practice ot Morality, whatever diverts, or difcourages that, mult be highly injurious. Now 'tis certain, that the mind may be over loaded as well as the body, & the more it is taken up with the obfervation of things, which are not of a moral nature, the lefs it will be able to attend to thofe that are; which requiring the application of the whole Man, can never be rightly perform'd, while the mind, by laying ftrefs on other things, is diverted from attending on them; efpecially, if it be confider'd, that Superftition, if once fuffer'd to mix with Religion, will always be gaining ground. If Reafon is to be heard, no unneceffary things will be admitted; but if it be not, where fhall we ftop? If people are once brought to believe fuch things are good for any thing, they will be apt to believe they are good for all things; at leaft, pretences will never be wanting for a thoufand things of this nature; and there's nothing of this kind that men will not come into, if they are made to beheve they carry any merit with them. Thefe they will be punctual in obferving, in hopes to atone for indulging themfelves in their darling vices; which they, not knowing how to leave, and yet willing to fecure their future happinefs, hope by the help of fuch expedients, to compound with Heaven; & then vainly imagine, they cannot have too many things of this nature, or fhew too great a zeal for the practice
of

of them, when affur'd by their Priefts, (who, as they fondly imagine, know the whole counfel of God) that they are acceptable to the Deity, & tend to make him propitious to religious obfervers of them.

THE *Banditti*, & Bravoes moft religioufly obferve the orders of their Church, about *not eating flefh*, &c. and inftances of this nature might be produc'd from the moft immoral in all Churches, who, not fatisfy'd with practifing fuch things themfelves, think it highly meritorious to compel others to do the fame. And, indeed, the fubftance of Religion has been deftroy'd in moft places, to make room for Superftition, immo-morality, & perfecution; which laft, when Men want reafon to fupport their opinions, always fupplies its place. And are there not even now, numbers in the beft reform'd Churches, of the fame fentiments with thofe Dr *Scot* complains of? ,, Who, *he fays*, * per-,, fuade themfelves, that God is wonderfully concern'd ,, about fmall things, about trifling opinions and in-,, different actions, and the rites and modes, and ap-,, pendages of Religion; & under this perfuafion they ,, hope to atone for all the immoralities of their lives, ,, by the forms & outfides of Religion; by uncom-,, manded feverities, & affected fingularities; by con-,, tending for opinions, and flickling for parties; and ,, being *pragmatically* zealous about the borders and ,, fringes of Religion. And,

I'M afraid 'tis but too true, as is obferv'd in the *Letters concerning Infpiration*; that †,, Men have thought ,, it an honour to be ftil'd that which they call zealous ,, orthodox, to be firmly link'd to a certain party, ,, to load others with calumnies, and to damn by an ,, abfolute authority the reft of Mankind; but have ,, taken no care to demonftrate the fincerity & fer-,, vour of their piety, by an exact obfervation of the ,, Gofpel Morals; which has come to pafs by reafon
,, that

---

* *Chrift. Life Vol.* 1. P. 2. c. 6. p. 376.
† *Eng. Tranfl. pag.* 108.

„ that orthodoxy agrees very well with our paſſions;
„ whereas the ſevere Morals of the Goſpel are in-
„ compatible with our way of living. „ And one
wou'd be apt to think, that zeal for ſpeculative opinions, and zeal for morality were ſcarce conſiſtent,
ſhou'd he form his Judgment from what he ſees moſt
practiſ'd. „ Moral goodneſs ſays Dr. *Scot,* * is the
„ great ſtamp & impreſs that renders Men current in
„ the eſteem of God, whereas on the contrary, the
„ common brand by which Hypocrites & falſe pre-
„ tenders to Religion are ſtigmatiz'd, is their being
„ zealous for the poſitives, and cold & indifferent as
„ to the Morals of Religion.

„ AND, † in general, we find mere moral prin-
„ ciples of ſuch weight, that in our dealings with Men,
„ we are ſeldom ſatisfy'd by the fulleſt aſſurance giv'n
„ us of their zeal in Religion, till we hear ſomething
„ further of their character. If we are told a Man
„ is religious, we ſtill ask *What are his Morals?* But if
„ we hear at firſt that he has honeſt moral Principles,
„ and is a Man of natural juſtice, and good temper,
„ we ſeldom think of the other queſtion, *Whether he*
„ *be religious and devout?*

IT is a general obſervation in Hiſtory, that where
any thing has had the appearance only of piety, and
might be obſerv'd without any Virtue in the Soul, it
eaſily found entertainment among ſuperſtitiousNations.
Hence *Tacitus* ſays, ‡ „ Men extremely liable to Su-
„ perſtition are at the ſame time as violently averſe to
„ Religion. „ *Le Clerc* not only makes the ſame remark, but ſays, § „ Thoſe who had a confus'd notion
„ of chriſtian piety, believ'd it could not maintain it-
„ ſelf without the help of outward objects, & I know
„ not what heatheniſh pomp, which at laſt extin-
guiſh'd

* *Chriſt. Life P.* 2. *Vol.* 1. *c.* 1. *p.* 53.
† *Inq. concern. Virtue & Merit. Treat.* 4. *l.* 1. *p.* 6.
‡ *Hiſt.* 5. 13. -- § Life of *Prudentius* pag. 317.
Eng. Tranſl. & Bibl. Univ. To. 12. p. 173, 174. --

„ guiſh'd the ſpirit of the Goſpel, and ſubſtitufed
„ *Paganiſm* in its room.

WHATEVER appearance it might have of piety,
what virtue did it require in the practice, to make
war with the *Saracens* for the *Holy-Land*; (tho' conſidering the impieties committed there, it might be
call'd *Unholy*;) yet ſo highly meritorious was this
project for ſeveral Ages thought to be, that vaſt ſhoals
of *Bigots* for its ſake have frequently gone from the
*Weſt* to fight Men in the *Eaſt*, who never did them
any harm; and thoſe *Bigots*, preſuming on the merits
of this ſacred Expedition, were moſt enormouſly flagitious.

*B.* IF this was Superſtition, it was built on a notion which had long before prevail'd, of believing it
a piece of piety to viſit *Jeruſalem*, & the holy places
there.   The great St. *Jerome* ſays, *Certe adoraſſe ubi
ſteterunt pedes Domini, pars Fidei eſt*, &c. *  „ That it
„ was undoubtedly a part of faith, to go, & worſhip
„ in thoſe places, where the feet of our Saviour had
„ once ſtood, & to have a ſight of the tracks, which.
„ at this day continue freſh, both of his Nativity,
„ Croſs, & Paſſion.

*A.* I believe St. *Jerome*, when he ſays, *We ought
to worſhip where the feet of our Lord ſtood*, chiefly intended his laſt footſteps when he mounted up to Heaven;
*the print of which*, ſays Sulpicius Severus, † *remain to
this day. Quæcunque applicabantur, inſolens humana ſuſ-
cipere terra reſpueret, excuſſis in ora apponentium ſæpe
narmoribus. -- Et cum quotidie confluentium Fides cer-
tatim Domino calcata diripiat, damnum tamen arena
non ſentiat: & eadem adhuc ſui ſpeciem, velut impreſſis
ſignata veſtigiis, terra cuſtodit*.   And *Paulinus* ſays the.
ſame.

A ſtrict obſervance of ſuch things as require no
virtue in the practice, and may with great eaſe he
punc-

---

* Ep. 144. ad *Deſider*. To. 3. p. 198. D.
† *Sulp. Sever. Sacred Hiſt. l. 2. p.*100, 101. *Edit. Elzev.*1642

punctually obferv'd, makes the fuperftitious liable to be evety where cheated by your *Tartuffs*, or *Mackworths*, while Men who put the whole ftrefs on Morality, are reprefented not only as enemies to Religion, but even as encouragers of immorality, and meer Libertines, becaufe they are for liberty in thinking; tho this can't fail to make Men fee the folly of licentioufnefs in acting.

AND, indeed, we fhall generally find thofe Ecclefiafticks, who inveigh moft againft *Free-thinking*, are the real encouragers of immorality; by fcreening, not only the moft immoral of their own Order on pretence of preferving the Honour of the Church, tho' to the dishonour of Religion; but alfo by laying the moft moral, if they differ from them in fpeculative points, under conftant fufferings, to enforce them to play the hypocrites with God and Man: and who is it that the corrupt part of the Clergy fhew more inveteracy againft, than the very beft Men of their own Order, for not approving thefe methods?

IT's worth while to remark, how differently Men are treated for civil & ecclefiaftical offences: * „ In „ *civil cafes*, as a Right Reverend & excellent Author „ obferves, the Offender, if his crime be not capital, „ fuffers a *temporary* punifhment, proportion'd to the „ fault he has committed; and when he has under- „ gone that, nothing further is requir'd of him, „ except in fome cafes to find fecurity for his good „ behaviour for the future: But in cafes of *Herefy*, „ there is no regard to the degree of the offence, „ in the punifhment inflicted, nor is there any end. „ of it. 'Tis not enough to have fuffer'd the fevereft „ punifhment, tho' for the fmalleft offence; 'tis not „ enough to give fecurity of not offending for the „ future: The innocent offender muft declare (what „ 'tis oftentimes impoffible he fhould declare) that he

I                          has

* *Diffic. & Difcouragments of fludying the Scriptures,* pag. 23, 24.

„ has chang'd his sentiments, & is become *Orthodox*;
„ and this, tho' perhaps no methods of conviction
„ have been used, except that of punishment be one.
„ This is the miserable condition of a Convict Here-
„ tick: The punishment which fell on him for ex-
„ pressing thoughts heretical, he must continue to
„ endure for barely thinking; which is a thing not
„ in his own power, but depends on the evidence
„ that appears to him: He must for ever (cruel *Justice*!)
„ for ever suffer for his private thoughts (tho' they
„ go not beyond his own heart) the punishment
„ which some overt-act has once drawn upon him.
„ To punish *toties quoties*, as often as those overt-acts
„ are repeated, will not satisfy the *Holy Office*. — —
„ \* If an offender can't be convicted of *Heresy*, he
„ may however be convicted of writing, or speaking
„ *against* the establish'd Doctrine of the Church, and
„ that will draw on him all the same consequences,
„ that *Heresy* would do. — † Well does this Author
„ advise, whatever you do be *Orthodox*: *Orthodoxy*
„ will cover a multitude of sins, but a cloud of virtues
„ cannot cover the want of the minutest particle of
„ *Orthodoxy*. — ‡ It may, I doubt not, be demon-
„ strated with the greatest evidence, that all Christian
„ Churches have suffer'd more by their zeal for Or-
„ thodoxy, & by the violent methods taken to pro-
„ mote it, than from the utmost efforts of their greatest
„ enemies. But for all that, the world will still think
„ the same methods necessary.

A Man, who has, or pretends to have a blind zeal
for those things which discriminate his Sect, tho' he
be ever so immoral, too often finds countenance and
credit from them; & tho' thought a Devil by others,
passes for a Saint with his own party: So that the
superstitious lye under strong temptations to be vicious,
& the vicious to act superstitiously. Nay,

T H E

---

Footnotes\* *Ibid. pag.* 26.    † *Ibid. pag.* 22.    ‡ *Ibid. pag* 29.

,, The way that Men are apt to take to pacify
,, God, is, as Archbishop *Tillotson* observes, * by some
,, external piece of Religion. -- Such as were sacri-
,, fices among the *Jews* & *Heathens*. -- The *Jews*
,, pitch'd upon those which were most pompous and
,, solemn, the richest, & most costly; so they might
,, but keep their sins, they were well enough content
,, to offer up any thing else to God; they thought
,, nothing too good for him, provided he would not
,, oblige them to become better.

,, And thus it is among ourselves, when we appre-
,, hend God is displeas'd with us. -- We are content
,, to do any thing, but to *learn righteousness*.

,, As to the Church of *Rome*, -- He *says*, They
,, (as they pretend) are the most skilful people in the
,, world to pacify God. -- I do not wrong them by
,, representing them enquiring after this manner:
,, Shall I go before a *Crucifix*, and bow myself to it,
,, as to the *High God?* -- To which of the Saints or
,, Angels, shall I go to mediate for me, & interceed
,, on my behalf? Will the Lord be pleas'd with
,, thousands of *Paternosters*, or with ten thousands of
,, *Ave-Maries?* Shall the Host travel in Procession,
,, or myself undertake a tedious *Pilgrimage?* Or shall
,, I list myself a Soldier for the *Holy War?* Shall I
,, give my Estate to a *Convent?* Or chastise, & punish
,, my body for the sin of my soul?

The Heathen Priests, knowing what would render
them most acceptable to the People, made the chief
part of their Religion to consist in gaudy shews,
pompous ceremonies, and such other tricks as serv'd
to amuse, and divert them, who, provided they entertain'd such notions as created a reverence for their
Priests, & believ'd they could discover to them the
will of their Gods, might be as leud, and wicked as
their Gods themselves: ,, Are the Gods angry? Must
,, we repent of our crimes, and re-enter into the

I 2    paths

* *Tillotson's* Serm. Vol. 4. p. 5, 6. & to. 2. p. 334.

,, paths of Natural Juſtice to divert their thunder?
,, Not at all; only take a Calf of ſuch a colour,
,, calv'd at ſuch a time, & let his throat be cut by a
,, religious Butcher, in ſuch a dreſs, with a conſecrated
,, knife, & the Gods, as you will find by the entrals,
,, will be ſtrait appeas'd.

THE *Mahometans* make the going a Pilgrimage to
*Mecca*, the higheſt act of Religion; and there, out of
deep devotion, play many Monkey-tricks, & then,
they return cleanſed from all impurity. As to the
*Jewiſh* Prieſts, & the Doctors, who depended on them,
we learn from our Saviour, how they made the moral
Law void by their vain Traditions; & that the Temple
then, as the Church in after-times, was made the
grand pretence. And what vile things has not the
abus'd name of the Church patronis'd? Nay, even in
the beſt conſtituted Church, have we not lately had
numbers of Men fond of the name of *High-Church*,
whoſe Religion chiefly conſiſted in drinking for the
Church, curſing, ſwearing, and lying for the Church,
railing riots, tumults, & ſedition, in favour of a *Popiſh
Pretender*, and all for the ſecurity of the *Proteſtant*
Church of *England*; & in having a profound veneration for black Gowns, no matter what the wearers are;
and a great contempt for Men in black cloaks, how
deſerving ſoever; and in firmly believing, that thoſe
who go to places with ſteeples can never be in the
wrong, & that thoſe who go to places without them
can never be in the right; without knowing what
either hold, or ſo much as what is the true meaning
of even the word *Church?*

WHAT advantage have not the Popiſh Prieſts gain'd
by their arts of reconciling the practice of vice, with
the proſpect of Heaven. The *Jeſuits*, tho' the youngeſt
Order, yet flouriſh moſt, being the moſt expert in this
artifice; as may be ſeen in Monſieur *Paſcal's Provin-
cial Letters*. But all the Popiſh Prieſts agree, in defending their Superſtition by fire & faggot; while their

Churches

Churches are open Sanctuaries for the moſt flagitious; which ſhews how ſenſible they are, that Superſtition & Immorality ſupport each other. And perhaps, tis but reaſonable, that the places, where they learn vile things, ſhou'd protect them, when they have committed the vileſt. Tis by theſe means that Holy Church gets a terrible party, who can't refuſe to maim or murder, as their ſpiritual Protectors direct, for fear of being deliver'd up to civil Juſtice: & not only your mean Rogues, but even the greateſt have been frequently ſcreen'd this way.

The ſuppoſing indifferent things equally commanded with matters of morality, tends to make Men believe they are alike neceſſary: Nay, the former will, by degrees, get the better with the ſuperſtitious, and acquire ſuch a veneration by age, as to make Men have recourſe to them upon all occaſions, tho' ever ſo unſeaſonable. If People can be ſo far impos'd on, as to admit ſuch things into their Religion, they will as eaſily be perſuaded to put a greater ſtreſs on things, tho' of ſmall uſe in Religion, than their nature will bear; to the confounding things of the greateſt moment with thoſe of the ſmalleſt; & if this is reckon'd Superſtition, much more ought the other to be thought ſo.

The not diſtinguiſhing means from ends, has been the occaſion of endleſs Superſtition; and there have been numbers, in all ages, eſpecially of the female Sex, who have thought themſelves very religious, if they, tho' to the neglect of their family-concerns, went from Church to Chappel, from Chappel to Church, & were punctual in obſerving all Church-ceremonies, without regarding the end, for which alone they cou'd be inſtituted; ſo that inſtead of being humble, affable, & good, they have prov'd big with the worſt ſort of pride, ſpiritual pride, cenſuring and deſpiſing their neighbours, tho' ever ſo good, if they were not as punctual as themſelves in obſerving thoſe things;

and

and the conceit they had of their own godliness, has made them as troublesome at home as abroad, as bad Wives, as Neighbours.

UPON the whole, nothing can be of worse consequence, than thus to depreciate Morality, by mixing things of an indifferent nature with it; because, as experience shews, Men are more or less vertuous according to the value they put on Virtue: & can a Man, who acts contrary to Reason not be an enemy to a Religion founded on Reason? The precepts of natural Religion, & the Rules of right Reason, can't but make strong impressions on rational Creatures: what is fix'd on the minds of Men, & wrought in as it were with their very constitution, can't easily be broke thorow; human-nature is apt to start, and recoil at any such attempt: And yet some have found a most effectual way to break through it, by teaching Men, that the most moral actions, without a right notion forsooth in certain things of another nature, are to be look'd on as *splendida peccata*, & partaking of the nature of sin.

IT is the chief business of preachers, to shew the reasonableness of the Doctrines they teach, as the most effectual way of operating on rational Creatures; and all the Laws of natural Religion being built on their own reasonableness, they, who attend to the dictates of their Reason, can scarce fail to pay a ready and chearful obedience to all its Laws: but when Men take things meerly on authority, & would have taken the contrary on the same authority, Reason is discarded and rational motives cease to operate; nor can Men any longer perform moral duties with a free & chearful mind, but slavishly obey, out of fear, the suppos'd arbitrary commands of a Being, too mighty to be contended with, and that only with a view to atone for Immoralities.

As long as Men believe the good of the Society is the supreme Law, they will think it their duty to be govern'd by that Law; & believing God requires nothing

nothing of them but what is for the good of Mankind, will place the whole of their Religion in benevolent actions, & to the utmost of their abilities copy after the divine original; but if they are made to believe there are things, which have no relation to this good, neceffary to falvation, they muft fuppofe it their duty, to ufe fuch means as will moft effectually ferve this purpofe, & that God, in requiring the end, requires all thofe means as will beft fecure and propagate it. And,

'Tis to this principle we owe the moft cruel Perfecutions, Inquifitions, Crufades & Maffacres; & that *Princes* have endeavour'd, not only to deftroy their Subjects, but to difinherit their own Iffue, to make room for fuppofititious Children. And,

'Tis to this Principle we alfo owe innumerable tumults, feditions, & rebellions, even againft the beft of Princes, as well as endlefs feuds & animofities in private familes, and among the neareft relations. They who are govern'd by this Principle can't be good Men, good Subjects, good Citizens, or good Neighbours; no ties of friendfhip or gratitude, no vows or oaths can bind them, when the intereft of fuch things, as they think they are oblig'd to promote on pain of God's difpleafure, requires the contrary conduct.

The *Jews,* as they were moft fuperftitious, fo were they moft cruel; and as the *Papifts* have, beyond all other Chriftians, introduc'd into Religion, things which are far from contributing to the good of Mankind; fo they have exercis'd a matchlefs cruelty for the fupport of them : And no wonder, fince their Priefts gain by the fuperftition of the People, & confequently, infpire them with a proportionate hatred againft all, who will not comply with it. And,

Among *Proteftants* of what denomination foever, they who lay the greateft ftrefs on ufelefs fpeculations, rites, modes & ceremonies, are for the moft part four, ill-natur'd persons, ready to come into any persecuting measures for their sake: But nothing has done so much mischief as that most monstrous opinion of *Imperium in Imperio*. Those, who pretended to a spiritual Empire, claim'd, as well they might, a divine right to judge of the extent of that Empire, & to do all they judg'd necessary for its support; and consequently, that they had a right, since temporal things must give place to spiritual, to depose the Governors of the State, whenever they judg'd it necessary for the safety of the Church. Tis from hence there have been so many tumults, seditions, insurrections, rebellions, civil-wars, murders & massacres upon the pretence of Religion, and which at last ended in the inflaving of the Christian World to the *Pope*, as head of the Church, whose power of deposing heretical Princes, was for many ages universally allow'd; * *no Nation no University declaring against it*; *nor so much as one Divine, Civilian, or Casuist.* Nor were things mended when, by reason of the great Schisms about the *Popedom*, Councils pretended to govern the Church: † They then carry'd their power to such a height, as dispos'd Princes to enter into agreements with the *Popes*, to whom they yielded a great deal, to be protected in what they had reserv'd to themselves. They, therefore, who maintain, that People may forfeit their properties by *Schism, Heresy, Infidelity*, &c. play the hypocrites, when they pretend the power of Princes is more sacred than the properties of the People, for whose sake they have all their power: And, therefore, we may justly conclude, that they, who are for soliciting Kings, and Magistrates to assist the Church in punishing Misbelievers, are equally enemies to the power of Kings, as well as to the rights of the People; and they have never fail'd to shew it, whenever they have found it their interest.

AND

* *Burnet's* Exp. of the Art. 19. p. 187. — *Ibid.* Art. 21. p. 200. † *Ibid.* Art. 37. p. 385.

And tho' at firſt thoſe Princes were idoliz'd, who where the inſtruments of their cruelty; yet when by their means, the People were intirely at the devotion of the Clergy, they too were ſoon forc'd to ſubmit; and had juſt cauſe to curſe their own, & Predeceſſors bigotry, which enabl'd the *Eccleſiaſticks* to inſult them as they pleas'd. And what diſturbances have not your *Beckets*, *Lauds*, &c. created here, when they got into power, & became then as inſolent, as before they were ſubmiſſive. Father *Paul*, no Stranger to our Conſtitution, in one of his Letters writ in the Reign of King *James* I. ſays thus; * ,, As for the *Engliſh*, I am in ,, fear; the great Power the Biſhops have, tho' under ,, a King, makes me very jealous; for ſhould they ,, have an eaſy Prince, or an Archbiſhop of an high ,, ſpirit, the Kingly power muſt ſink by the Biſhops ,, aſpiring to an abſolute dominion.

I believe you will allow, that in the late times, Men were as much in earneſt about Religion as ever, & yet by their mixing ſeveral things, not of a moral nature with it, & thinking all means proper to promote them lawful, Impoſture & Zeal, Bigotry and Hypocriſy, were ſtrangely blended together. And as we are aſſur'd by an eminent Hiſtorian, it was the opinion of *Cromwell*. that † ,, the Moral Laws were ,, only binding in ordinary caſes; but that upon ex- ,, traordinary ones theſe might be ſuperſeded; he, & ,, that Set of Men, juſtifying their ill actions from ,, the practice of *Ehud* & *Jael*, *Sampſon* & *David*.

Here, indeed, they were no Hypocrites, but frankly confeſs'd what at the bottom influences all thoſe, who, tho' they have not the grace to own it, make things, not of a moral nature, neceſſary ingredients of Religion; & thereby give too juſt occaſion

I 5 for

---

* *Eng. Tranſl. Pref. pag.* 51.    † *Bp. Burnet's* Sum. of Affairs before the Reſtora. pag. 46. - 79. -

for this remark of Archbishop *Tillotson* , * ,, That it
,, will be hard to determine, how many degrees of
,, innocence & good nature, or of coldness and in-
,, difference in Religion, are necessary to overbalance
,, the fury of a blind zeal; since several zealots had
,, been excellent Men, if their Religion had not hin-
,, der'd them, if the doctrines & principles of their
,, Church had not spoil'd their natural disposition. ,,
What can be a greater satyr on any Religion, than
that it is able to spoil the best disposition, and that,
if it does not make Men arrant Devils, 'tis only because Nature is too hard for Principles?

B. These sure are uncommon Principles.

A. Not so uncommon , as you may imagine ,
since all Religion inclines Men to imitate what they
worship; and they who believe that God will damn
Men for things *not Moral*, must believe, that in order
to prevent damnable opinions from spreading , & to
shew themselves holy, as their heavenly Father is holy,
they can't shew too much enmity to those, against
whom God declares an eternal enmity , or plague
them enough in this life, upon whom in the life to
come God will pour down the plagues of eternal vengeance. Hence it is, that animosity, enmity, & hatred,
has over-run the Christian-world , and Men, for the
sake of these notions, have exercis'd the utmost cruelties on one another, the most *cursing* and *damning*
Churches having always prov'd the most *persecuting* :
The *Papists*, tho' they declare it to be their duty to
love their own Enemies, yet looking on all *Protestants*
as God's Enemies, think it meritorious to murder
them; and *Protestants* had no sooner renounc'd those
persecuting Principles of *Popery*, but they too shame-
fully practis'd the same themselves, for the support
of such trifling notions, as the publick had not the
least interest in.   And before the happy Revolution,
the Spirit of Persecution was so outragious, that *Pro-*
                                                  *testants*

* *Serm. Vol.* 3. *p.* 26, 27. & *Ta.* I. *p.* 208, 209. -

*teftants* ruin'd *Proteftants* upon the account of rites, ceremonies, habits, *&c.* to the great joy of the common Enemy. And,

THO' there may be, even now, fome, who will not forgive their being debarr'd the exercife of their former Tyranny, and wou'd be glad, at any rate, to deftroy that hated liberty we are now blefs'd with; yet, I may venture to fay, that all, who have fo juft an opinion of Religion, as to think it requires nothing but what is for the good of Mankind, are to a Man zealous for the prefent Government eftablifh'd on the principles of civil and reiigious Liberty.

To preferve which, the Legiflature has not only excluded all *Papifts*, as Men of perfecuting principles from the Crown, but, by affording protection to *Diffenters*, has fet the differing Churches in *South* and *North-Britain* on a level; well knowing, that neither Civil nor Ecclefiaftical Liberty can be preferv'd on any other foot. Had they gone a ftep further, and excluded on the ftricteft tefts, Men of perfecuting Principles from inferior Pofts, as well as the perfecuting *Papifts* from the higheft, they had acted up to thofe Principles of *Proteftantifm* upon which the Revolution is founded. And all, who are in earneft about Religion, wou'd have been highly pleas'd to have feen it an eftablifh'd Maxim, that *no Man ought te fuffer in his perfon, his property, or reputation, for his opinion in matters of meer Religion.*

THEY, who think force lawful for the fupport of fuch opinions as can't be fupported by Reafon, (as what Church, when it has power, does not?) can't but think fraud fo too; efpecially when 'tis us'd not only for Mens eternal but temporal good, & to prevent fuch feverites, as otherwife wou'd be thought *wholfome* & neceffary. How can Men of thefe Principles think any untruth not lawful, when 'tis neceffary to guard fundamental Truths? Nay, muft they not think it much more their duty to deceive Men,

for

for the fake of their eternal good, than to deceive Children or fick People for an infinitely lefs good; efpecially when the temporal intereft of the deceivers is join'd with the fpiritual intereft of the deceiv'd; who, happy Men, have the good luck to be cheated into Paradife, and by the ftratagem of a pious fraud to obtain an heavenly Crown? If it be lawful to deceive melancholy perfons, who defign to poifon themfelves, and put a remedy in the place of the poifon; can any think fuch an artifice unlawful, when he believes 'tis to hinder millions from imbibing fuch notions, as are rank poifon to their immortal fouls?

'Tis with an ill grace that thofe *Proteftants*, who are for reftraining the Liberty of the Prefs, or fuffering nothing to be printed, but what has undergon their fponges, rail at the *Papifts* for their *Index expurgatorius:* Thefe Men may, indeed, plead authority; fince as *Daillé* obferves, * ,, This opinion has always been
,, in the world; that to fettle a certain & affur'd eftimation upon that which is good and true, (that is
,, to fay, upon what we account to be fuch;) it is
,, neceffary to remove out of the way whatfoever
,, may be an hindrance to it: Neither ought we to
,, wonder, that even thofe of the honeft, innocent,
,, primitive times made ufe of thefe deceits, feeing
,, for a good end they made no fcruple to forge whole
,, Books.

They, indeed, (& fuch there are, to the honour of the prefent time, not a few) who think fincerity will carry Men to Heaven, lie under no temptation no ufe pious frauds; but for Men of other Principles, tho' they go under the Name of Fathers and Saints, there's no depending on them; fince a defire to deceive people into their opinions, will hold in proportion to the zeal they have for propagating thofe opinions.

I v

* *De ufu Patrum l. 1. c.* 3.

IF thofe Men, in whofe hands the facred Books from time to time have been chiefly depofited, did allow that every Man was to judge for himfelf of their meaning, in order to make him acceptable to God, there could be no danger of their being defignedly corrupted: But if they believ'd, that a certain fet of opinions was neceffary to falvation, then they muft have thought themfelves in charity oblig'd, to take the moft proper methods to bring Men to embrace them, and confequently, muft have believ'd it their duty to fubftitute fome words of their own, which would beft exprefs thofe opinions, on which Mens falvation depended, in the room of others, which were apt to lead them into fatal errors; fince by thus changing of founds, they might fave millions of Souls, who, they were confident, wou'd otherwife everlaftingly perifh. Muft not the fame Principle, that oblig'd them to impofe their own words, inftead of the words of God, in their *Creeds* and *Articles* on pain of damnation, equally oblige them to act the fame part in relation to the Scripture? And if Men have ftuck fo clofe to this Principle, that they have, (wherever they had a convenient opportunity) left out, added to, or altered all other books of Religion whatever, which have fallen into their hands; there can be no reafon to think, they would not do the fame with the Bible, where the motives were fo much ftronger. ,, 'Tis no wonder, * fays that primitive ,, Father, *Dionyfius*, Bifhop of *Corinth*, that fome at- ,, tempt to adulterate the holy Writings of our Lord, ,, fince they have bafely falfify'd fuch as are of an ,, inferior authority: ,, And it muft be either to put a ftop to, or prevent this practice, that the *Revelation* concludes with a curfe on all who fhould make any alteration in that Book. And 'tis morally impoffible, that they, who thought it their duty to commit the moft barbarous acts of cruelty for propagating of

opi-

* *Eufeb.* Eccl. Hift. l. 4. c. 23. in fine.

opinions, fhou'd not think it lawful to ufe deceit for the fame end; which they can never imagine to be an evil, while they fuppofe it fo ufeful for the faving of Mens Souls, without giving up all the other indirect methods, they took to hinder Men from feeing what may be faid for, or againft any opinions.

No r is there any one thing in which all parties agree, but in taking it for·granted, that their Adverfaries will fcruple no means to gain credit to their own opinions, or to difcredit thofe of their Adverfaries; and in order to it, mifreprefent their perfons as well as opinions, and make Men Saints or Devils, as it ferves their caufes: which, as you will find in Church-Hiftory, hath afforded a number of miracles for the *Orthodox*, and as many judgments on the *Heterodox*: And if there be miracles on both fides, ours to be fure are divine, and yours diabolical.

I f ever the words of *David*, that *All Men are Liars*, were literally true, it has been in this cafe; and all Hiftory fhews the juftnefs of my Lord *Bacon*'s remark: * *Maxime habenda funt pro fafpectis, quæ pendant quomodecunque a Religione; at Prodigia Livii.*

T h e *Arabian* Writers are full of miracles done by *Mahomet*, which they impote on people, by telling them, that † ,, *Mahomet*'s Enemies would not invent ,, them; & his Friends are forbid telling lies of him ,, on pain of damnation.

B. Y o u may make as bold as you will with *Mahometans*, but can you charge Proteftant Writers, much lefs the holy Fathers, with any fuch practices?

A. I hope, 'tis no crime to take notice, that one of the ten *reafons* the celebrated *Chillingworth* gives for his turning *Papift*, is, ‡ ,, Becaufe the Proteftant ,, caufe is now, and hath been from the beginning, ,, maintain'd with grofs falfifications and calumnies, where-

* *Nov. Org. l. 2. Aph. 29.*
† *Mahom.* Life in Eng. before *Reland's Mahom.* p. 32.
‡ *Pref.*

,, whereof the prime Controverſy-Writers are noto-
,, riouſly, & in a high degree, guilty.,, And upon
his return to the Church, he ſays, *Iliacos intra muros
peccatur & extra*; which is in plain Engliſh, *Prieſts of
all denominations will lie alike.* And I may add, that
it is ſo fully prov'd in the *Hiſtorical Eſſay of the Thirty
nine Articles*, that, that clauſe in the twentieth Article,
that *the Church has power to decree Rites & Ceremonies,
and authority in Controverſies of Faith*, had neither the
ſanction of Parliament or Convocation, that no one
has offer'd the leaſt Reply, tho' for the honour of
thoſe good Church-men who firſt forg'd it, and thoſe
who ſince defended it, we might expect all that could
be ſaid, tho' the Clauſe had not given them a power
which can only belong to Parliaments, of *decreeing
Rites and Ceremonies*, and another power, which can
belong to no mortal, *Authority in Controverſies of Faith.*
What credit ought to be given to the repreſentations
of modern Divines, we may, in ſome meaſure, learn
from a Pamphlet entitul'd, * *The Repreſentation of the
preſent ſtate of Religion; with regard to the late exceſſive
growth of Infidelity, Hereſy & Profaneneſs, as it paſs'd
the lower Houſe of Convocation*; where there are almoſt
as many notorious falſehoods, as there are paragraphs;
not to ſay any thing of a *certain Paſtoral Letter.* And
if we look into Church-Story, we ſhall find it to have
been the conſtant practice of a certain ſet of Men,
not only to impute to their Adverſaries opinions which
they diſown'd, but to repreſent thoſe opinions as ready
to prevail, was it not for their interpoſition: By which
means they hop'd not only to be highly reverenc'd
for their great zeal, but to have new powers granted
them to oppreſs Mankind. Thus the conſequence of
belying the Followers of *Wickliff*, was the Statute *de
Haretico comburendo*, granted at the petition of the
Clergy;

* See a Pamphlet in two Parts, entittul'd, *The Nation
vindicated from the Aſperſions caſt on it in that Repreſentation.*

Clergy; and the belying the *Albigenses, Waldenses*, &c. rais'd a Crusado against those poor people.

A s for the holy Fathers, They, as *Daillé* * has a whole Chapter to prove, did not think themselves in their controversial writings (and most of theirs were such) oblig'd to speak the truth; but that every thing was lawful which serv'd to gain the victory. They thought they might, by way of oeconomy or dispensation, say one thing & mean the contrary: ,, *Origen,* ,, *Methodius, Eusebius, Apollinaris,* (says St. *Jerome*) † ,, have writ largely against *Celsus* & *Porphyry*; Do but ,, observe, *says he*, the manner of their arguing, and ,, what slippery problems they us'd. They alled'gd ,, against the *Gentiles*, not what they believ'd, but ,, what they thought necessary; *Non quod sentiunt,* ,, *sed quod necesse est*, dicunt. And adds, I forbear ,, mentioning the Latin-Writers, as *Tertullian, Cyprian,* ,, *Minutius, Victorinus, Lactantius,* and *Hilary*; lest I ,, should seem rather to accuse others, than defend ,, myself: ,, And yet he goes on charging, not only St. *Paul*, but even *Jesus Christ* himself with the same practice. And there was nothing so sacred that cou'd escape being chang'd, either in whole or in part; even the Canons of the famous Council of *Nice*, as well as the Canons of other Councils, have been falsify'd; and those forg'd Canons of *Nice* the *Popes* for many ages impos'd on the *Christian World* as genuine; & the antient *Liturgies*, tho' things of daily use, underwent divers alterations: Nay, even the *Creeds* themselves, tho' thought to be the sacred *depositum* of the Faith, have had the same fate. ,, 'Tis well known, *says* an eminent Divine, ‡ ,, that the *Apostles Creed* ,, has receiv'd various additions to the original Form; ,, That the *Nicene Creed* was enlarg'd by the *Constan-* ,, *tinopolitan* Fathers, & has also, with respect to the ,, *Filioque*, been interpolated by the *Latin* Church; that

* *L. 1. c 6. See p.* 159. &c.    † *To.* 2. *p.* 105, 106.
‡ *Bennet's* Directions for studying the 39 Articles, p. 66.

,, that 'tis probable, the *Latin* Church has interpolated
,, the *Athanasian Creed* too, with respect to the *Filio-*
,, *que*; nay, the *Athanasian Creed* itself, as Bishop
*Burnet* * has shown, was a forgery of the eighth
Century: Nor did they confine their forgeries to
Church matters, but practis'd on the imperial Laws,
and inserted in the *Theodosian Code*, † a Rescript of
*Constantine*, relating to the power of Bishops, long
before repeal'd.

THE further back we go, the greater was their
recourse to pious frauds. *Scaliger* speaking of the primitive Christians, says, ‡ *Omnia, quæ putabant Chri-*
*stianismo conducere, bibliis interseruerunt.*   And as he
supposes nothing certain of the Church till the times
of *Pliny*, so he says, speaking of the second Century,
§ *Adeo verbum Dei inefficax esse censuerunt, ut regnum*
*Christi sine mendacio -- promoveri posse diffiderunt, ut qui*
*utinam illi primi mentiri cœpissent.*  And *Casaubon* says,
⌡ *Illud me vehementer movit, quod videam primis Ec-*
*clesiæ temporibus quam plurimos extitisse, qui facinus pal-*
*marium judicabant, cœlestem veritatem figmentis suis ire*
*adjutum; quo facilius nova illa doctrina Gentium sapien-*
*tibus admitteretur.*   And the learned *Blondel* says, ✠
,, That the second Century of Christianity, whether
,, you consider the immoderate impudence of Im-
,, postors, or the deplorable credulity of Believers,
,, was the most miserable time, & exceeded all others
,, in holy cheats; and that, to the disgrace of Chri-
,, stianity, there was a greater aversion to lying, more
,, fidelity, & a greater simplicity not to depart from
,, the truth, to be found in profane Authors, than in
,, the Christian Writers.

K                    OUR

* *Art.* 8. *p* 106.    † *Selden*'s Dissert. on Fleta. c. 5. N. 6.
‡ *Scaligerana,* Art. Siloe.    § *Epist. ad Casaubon, p.* 303.
⌡ *Exercit.* 1. *ad Appendix pag.* 54. *a.* --
✠ Epist. ad C. Arnoldum, apud *Ouvrages des Savans,*
Anno 1701.

Our moſt learned Biſhop *Stillingfleet*, ſays, * „That „ Antiquity is moſt defective where it is moſt uſeful; „ namely, in the times immediately after the Apoſtles: „ And that the Fathers were often deceiv'd with pious „ frauds; † but then it was when they made for the „ Chriſtians.„  And the pious Biſhop *Fell* does not ſpeak quite ſo tenderly in ſaying, ‡ *Tanta fuit primis ſeculis fingendi licentia, tam prona in credendo facilitas, ut rerum geſtarum fides exinde graviter laboraverit; nec orbis tantum terrarum, ſed & Dei Eccleſia de temporibus ſuis myſticis merito queratur.*

How unhappy were we of the Laity, had we not the Reaſon and Nature of things (which no Prieſts can alter) to depend on; and were intirely oblig'd to take our religious ſentiments from Men, who as far as we have any account of things, have, even from the earlieſt times, not ſcrupl'd to forge, not only whole paſſages, but whole books, and left nothing entire on which they cou'd lay their foul hands? Which, as that great and honeſt Critick *Daillé* obſerves, § „ has render'd the writings & venerable monuments „ of antiquity ſo imbroil'd, & perplex'd, that it will „ be the hardeſt matter in the world for any Man to „ make out any clear or perfect diſcovery of thoſe „ things, which ſo many ſeveral Artiſts have endea- „ vour'd to conceal from us.„  As to this impoſing temper of the Eccleſiaſticks, I ſhall only ſay, that it is plain from Hiſtory, that the ambitious, domineering part of the Clergy, the impoſers of *Creeds*, *Canons* & *Conſtitutions*, have prov'd the common plagues of Mankind, and the true authors & fomenters of the moſt general & moſt fatal calamities, which have be- fallen the Chriſtian World.  What the conſequence was of impoſing *Creeds*, may be learnt from an eminent Father, who flouriſh'd when this trade of *Creedmaking* was

* *Iren. pag.* 296.    † *Orig. Sacr. pag.* 29.
‡ In præmiſſâ monit. Conſeſſ. Suppos. *Cypriani, p.* 53.
§ *De uſu Patrum c.* 4. *in fine c.* 120. --

was at its height. ,, It is, *says* St. *Hilary*, * a thing
,, equally deplorable & dangerous, that there are at
,, present as many *Creeds*, as there are opinions among
,, Men. -- We make *Creeds* arbitrarily, and explain
,, them as arbitrarily. -- We can't be ignorant, that
,, since the Council of *Nice*.,, ( there it seems the
fatal mischief began ) ,, we have done nothing but
,, made *Creeds*. -- We make *Creeds* every year, nay,
,, every moon; we repent of what we have done;
,, we defend those that repent; we anathematize those
,, we have defended; we condemn the doctrine of
,, others in ourselves, or our own in that of others;
,, and reciprocally tearing one another in pieces, we
,, have been the cause of one another's ruin.

THUS you see, how fraud & force are unavoidable,
when 'tis believ'd things, having no foundation in Nature or Reason, are necessary parts of Religion; and
Ecclesiastical History contains a continued scene of
villany, for the support of such notions: And the more
good sense, piety, and virtue any Man was endow'd
with, the more, if he did not come into those notions,
was he hated and persecuted as a most dangerous
Enemy. But,

BEFORE I leave this melancholy subject, I must
observe, these Men have done their best to justify a
remark of *Uriel Acosta*, who, in his *Exemplar vitæ humanæ*, says, † ,, That when Men depart ever so little
,, from Natural Religion, it is the occasion of great
,, strifes and divisions; but if they recede much from
,, it, who can declare the calamities which ensue? ,,
And can Men more depart from it, than by imposing
on their Brethren, either by fraud, or force, things
no ways tending to the good of Mankind?

THO' we cry up the great advantage we have
above all other Animals, in being capable of Religion,
yet those Animals we despise for want of it, herd

K 2 most

* *Hil. ad Constant. p.* 217. *Basil Edit. al. p.*211, 212 -
† *P.* 351. *sub finem Amic. Collat. Limborch.*

moſt ſocially together : except ſuch carnivorous Creatures which neceſſity ſeparates.   The *Ants*, notwithſtanding they have ſtings, are crouded in vaſt numbers in the ſame hillock ; &, having all things in common, ſeem to have no other contention among them, but who ſhall be moſt active in carrying on the common intereſt of their ſmall Republick. And much the ſame may be ſaid of *Bees*, and other Animals ; yet Men, tho' they can't ſubſiſt but in ſociety, and have hands, ſpeech, & reaſon to qualify them for the bleſſing of it above all other Animals, nay, what is more, have Religion, deſign'd to unite them in the firm bonds of Love & Friendſhip, and to engage them to vie with one another in all good offices ( and the good natur'd Laity too have, at a vaſt expence, hir'd perſons to inculcate theſe generous notions ) yet alas ! in ſpite of all theſe helps & motives, Religion has been made by theſe very perſons, a pretence to render Men unſociable, fierce, and cruel , and to act every thing deſtructive to their common welfare : And the greater the number of theſe religious, & the more expence people have been at in maintaining them, the more of theſe miſchiefs have they moſt ungratefully occaſion'd to their generous benefactors.

*B.* Granting that a deluge of every thing that's ill has overflow'd *Chriſtendom*, & does ſo ſtill in moſt places ; and that Religion has been made a handle for ſuch barbarities, as human-nature, left to itſelf, wou'd ſtartle at , yet how is this to be remedy'd?

*A.* Education is juſtly eſteem'd a ſecond nature, & its force ſo ſtrong, that few can wholly ſhake off its prejudices, even in things unreaſonable & unnatural , and muſt it not have the greateſt efficacy in things agreeable to Reaſon, and ſutable to humane-nature? Let thoſe, therefore, who have the education of Youth, recommend Morality as the end of all Religion , and let every thing not tending to promote the Honour of God and the Good of Man, be accounted

counted Superstition; let the Youth be taught to join
the ideas of Virtue with the ideas of beauty, pleasure,
& happiness, and the ideas of Vice with those of deformity, grief, and misery; there wou'd then be little
room for so odious a thing as Vice to take possession
of peoples minds, & justle out Virtue so firmly rooted:
For these ideas thus early associated, wou'd by degrees
become inseparable, especially if Men, as they grew
up, were frequently shewn the necessary connexion
between these ideas, and how essential Virtue is to
the felicity of nations, families, and private persons,
and on the contrary, how miserable Vice must render
Men in every station of life.

'Twas after this manner, that the Heroes of old,
those benefactors to Mankind, were educated, & the
discourses of the Philosophers, who had the instructing
them, were full of the intrinsick loveliness of Vertue,
& deformity of Vice, and taught them to direct all
their actions to the common good, as to a common
centre, and that their future as well as present happiness depended on it: But afterwards the education
of the Youth being committed to Men of another
stamp, devoted to the interest of their own Order,
they, instead of infusing these noble sentiments into
them, persuaded them that their separate interest,
with the things on which it depended, which they
call'd *the good of the Church*, was to be their chief aim:
and so little regard have some Men had to the common good, that they have industriously dress'd up Vice
in such lovely, and Virtue in such odious colours, as
to maintain, that bating the consequences of a future
state, they wou'd act like Fools, who did not indulge
themselves in a vicious course. And I believe, Men
of such Principles can't boast of much more Virtue,
than a late Prelate of uncommon parts and learning,
who from the Pulpit endeavour'd to prove, that * *In
this life the virtuous Man is most miserable;* and who,

* *Atterbury's* Fun. Sermon on Mr. *Bennes.*

by all his actions, especially, by his late monstrous practices, shew'd how firmly he believ'd his own doctrine, & how resolv'd he was, that Virtue shou'd not make his present life miserable.

*B.* I grant you, 'tis of the utmost consequence to the Common-wealth, that Youth shou'd be rightly instructed in all such principles as promote the common good, but can you imagine Pagan Philosophers cou'd infuse more generous sentiments into them, than Christian Clergy-men?

*A.* I do not think so, when they are such Clergy-men as those who at present have the instructing our Youth, otherwise I can't help giving into the sentiments of a noble Author, who, speaking of the education of Youth, when instructed by Philosophers, says, * ,, It tended to make them as useful to the
,, Society they liv'd in as possible. There they were
,, train'd up to exercise & labour, to accustom them-
,, selves to an active life, no Vice was more infamous
,, than sloth, nor any Man more contemptible, than
,, he who was too lazy to do all the good he could.
,, The lectures of their Philosophers serv'd to quicken
,, them up to this, they recommended above all
,, things the duty to their Country, the preservation
,, of the Laws and publick Liberty, subservient to
,, which they preach'd up moral Virtues, such as for-
,, titude, temperance, justice, a contempt of death, *&c.*
,, They taught their Youth how, and when to speak
,, pertinently; how to act like Men, to subdue their
,, passions, to be publick-spirited; to despise death,
,, torments and reproach, riches, and the smiles of
,, Princes as well as their frowns, if they stood be-
,, tween them & their duty. This manner of educa-
,, tion produc'd Men of another stamp than appears
,, now upon the theatre of the World, such as we
,, are scarce worthy to mention, & must never think
,, to imitate, till the like manner of institution grows
                                                  again

* Preface to the Account of *Denmark.*

„ again into reputation; which in enſlav'd Countries
„ 'tis never like to do, as long as the Eccleſiaſticks,
„ who have an oppoſite intereſt, keep not only the
„ education of Youth, but the conſciences of old Men
„ in their hands.

B. This, I confeſs, is the right way to prevent immorality; but if every thing, as you contend, ought to be look'd on as ſuperſtitious which is not of a moral nature, Superſtition has ſpread itſelf over the face of the earth, & prevail'd more or leſs in all times & places.

A. This is no more than what has been own'd long ago by a very good Judge, who ſays, * *Superſtitio fuſa per gentes, oppreſſit omnium ferè animos, atque hominum occupavit imbecillitatem.* And the univerſality of Superſtition is in effect own'd by every Sect, in affirming that Superſtition is crept into all other Sects, & that 'tis the chief buſineſs of their reſpective Teachers to promote it: And is it poſſible to be otherwiſe, as long as Men are taught to build their Religion on a narrower foundation, than that on which the univerſal Being has univerſally laid it?

'Tis the obſervation of *Naturaliſts*, that there is no ſpecies of creatures, but what have ſome innate weakneſs, which makes them an eaſy prey to other Animals, that know how to make their advantage of it: Now the peculiar foible of Mankind is Superſtition, which at all times has made them liable to be practis'd on, not by creatures of different ſpecies, but by thoſe of their own; who, by a confident pretence of knowing more than their neighbours, have firſt circumvented the many, the credulous & unwary, and afterwards forc'd the free-thinking few into an outward compliance: And as far as we have an account of things, we ſhall find that moſt of the prevailing Superſtitions have been erected on this foundation and to it owe their whole ſupport. And whoever knows any thing

K 4 of

* *Cicero* l. 2. de Divinat. c. 72.

of *France* & *Italy*, not to mention other Countries, can't but know that the better fort are fenfible of the prevailing abfurdities, but, over-aw'd by the Priefts & mob, are forc'd to fubmit. And,

THE more Superftition the people have, the eafier they may be impos'd on by defigning Ecclefiafticks; and the lefs Religion the Clergy have, the more un-animous they will be in carrying on their common intereft: and when the Clergy are without Religion, and the People abound in Superftition, the Church, you may be fure, is in a flourifhing condition; but in great danger, when Men place their Religion in Mo-rality: For then all indifferent things are look'd on as they are in their own nature, indifferent; then the People have no fuperftitious veneration for the perfons of Men, & the Clergy are efteem'd only in proportion to the good they do; and every evil they commit is reckon'd a breach of truft, they being maintain'd by the People chiefly to fet them good examples. But this method of gaining all that reverence & authority they pretend to, has, it feems, been thought too la-borious & fervile. They have (I mean where *Popery* prevails) as mafters of the religious ceremonies, moft effectually gain'd their end, by introducing fuch things into Religion, as have promoted a fuperftitious vene-ration to themfelves; and made people believe, that the chief means to obtain their *eternal* happinefs, were of a different nature from thofe which caus'd their *temporal* happinefs, and only to be difpens'd by them, in order to get the fole management of *fpiri-tuals* to themfelves; and confequently, (fince there can't be at the fame time two fupreme Powers) of temporals *alfo:* And fo well have they fucceeded, that, in moft places, the temporal intereft of the Clergy paffes for the fpiritual of the Laity.

THERE are two ways which never fail to make Superftition prevail; myfteries to amufe the enthu-fiafts, efpecially the pretenders to deep learning, and

all

all that admire what they do not underſtand; & gaudy
ſhews & pompous ceremonies, to bewitch the vulgar:
And the *Popiſh* Church, whoſe conduct ſhews how
well they underſtand their intereſt, may vie with the
old *Egyptian* Church for myſteries; and *Pagan Rome*
muſt yield to *Chriſtian Rome* in ſuch ſhews, rites, and
ceremonies as dazzle the eyes of the people, & in-
ſenſibly gain their hearts: and the more there are of
theſe in any Church, the more the Clergy, the holy
diſpenſers of them, are reverenc'd, not to ſay, ador'd
by the unthinking multitude, as they are in the Church
of *Rome*. * „ That Church has, *as Archbiſhop* Tillotſon
„ *obſerves*, weaken'd the force of Chriſtianity upon
„ the hearts & lives of Men, by amuſing them with
„ *external rites*, which they have multiply'd to that
„ exceſſive degree, as to make the *Yoke* of Chriſt
„ really *heavier* than that of *Moſes*; and the Chriſtian
„ Religion a more *external* and *carnal commandmens*
„ than that of the Law; & have diverted the minds
„ of Men from the main deſign of Chriſtianity. - -
„ They have had no leiſure to think of being good
„ Men, & to mind the *great* & *ſubſtantial* duties of
„ the Chriſtian Life -- The *Simplicity* of the *Chriſtian*
„ *worſhip* they have incamber'd with ſo many tri-
„ volous *rites* and *obſervances*, as not only render it
„ more burthenſom, but leſs apt to make Men *in-*
„ *wardly*, & *ſubſtantially* good, than *Judaiſm* itſelf.
Th<small>IS</small> great Man obſerves, that † „ Thoſe things
„ which are agreeable to our nature, our reaſon, and
„ our intereſt, are the great things which our Reli-
„ gion requires of us. -- And that Mankind might
„ have no pretence left to excuſe them from theſe,
„ the Chriſtian Religion has ſet us free from thoſe
„ many outward poſitive obſervances, that the *Jewiſh*
„ Religion was incumber'd withal; that we might
„ be wholly intent on theſe great duties, and mind

K 5                                           nothing

,, nothing in comparison of the real, and substantial ,, virtues of a good life. ,, If so, can we suppose the Christian Religion has superadded any outward positive things of its own, to hinder us from being wholly intent on these duties?

THE Popish Priests are so far from giving the People any just idea of God, that they represent him as an arbitrary & tyrannical Being, imposing, on the highest pain, the practice of ridiculous, ceremonies, & the belief of absurd doctrines; as a fantastical Being, angry without cause, & pleas'd without reason; as a vain-glorious Being, fond of having his Ministers & Favourites, that is, themselves, live in pomp, splendor, & luxury, to the miserable oppression of the People. But 'tis no wonder, that they are made to believe, that God requires the observing indifferent things on the severest penalties; since their Priests claim the same power, in making such things necessary to the communicating in their holy Church, out of which, they affirm, salvation is not to be had. I wish I cou'd say, the Popish Priests only were guilty of this horrid impiety, & that some others had not been as zealous for imposing such things, by making them necessary terms of communion, & damning those that durst not comply with them; & who seem to be of the same Spirit with the famous Bishop *Gunning*, * who, when the *Presbyterians* urg'd that *Lights*, *Holy Water*, & such like, might as well be impos'd as the *Cross* and *Surplice*; reply'd, *The more the better.* But if *external rites*, as Archbishop *Tillotson* observes, *have eat out the heart of Religion in the Church of* Rome, by parity of reason, Religion should seem to have made the deepest impression on the *Quakers*, who are the most averse to things of this nature, and are therefore hated by the *Formalists* of all Churches.

B. Sensible things make a deeper impression on the minds of the common People than words; & therefore

* **Life of** *Baxter* c. 8. p. 175. *Calamy's* Abridgment.

fore, the using symbolical representations being for the advantage of Religion, why may they not be ordain'd of God?

*A* IF you must have recourse to words, to explain the signification of such symbols, are they not arbitrary marks, whose meaning cannot be known, but from words; and, not being capable of expressing things more fully than words, wholly needless as to that purpose? Nay, words themselves being but arbitrary signs, to multiply such signs needlesly would be very absurd.

As to sensible things making a deeper impression on the common people, that, I presume, is a just reason against their use in Religion; because the vulgar, who generally look no further than externals, do not use them barely, as they do words, to express their meaning, but conceive in them, I know not what internal holiness, and think such symbolical representations as necessary as the things represented by them; nay, by degrees, forgetting the reason of their institution, come to idolize them, as the *Israelites* did the brazen Serpent: And this the People have always done in all Religions whatever, where these symbolical representations have been used.

THE chief cause of the *Egyptians* falling into grosser Idolatries than other less knowing Nations, was, no doubt, owing to the use of *Hyeroglyphicks* in their religious worship: An *Ox*, that laborious and useful animal, was at first only a symbolical representation; the meaning of which, the People in time forgetting, fell to down-right adoring the beast; and, perhaps, it was for the same reason that *Leeks* & *Onions*, and other garden-stuff came likewise to be worshipped. But without looking into the *Pagan* world, & shewing by what degrees they came to worship those sensible representations, statues and images, whoever reflects on the use the *Papists* have made of such things, must see how fatal it is to bring them into Religion: The

Images

Images & Pictures of Saints, and Crosses were first introduced, on pretence, that being sensible representations, they might serve to excite peoples devotion; but that end was soon forgotten, & the superstitious Vulgar worshipp'd the very Images, Pictures, & Crosses. I need not tell you what *Transubstantiation*, *Consubstantiation*, *Real Presence*, & other absurdities of that nature are owing to; and what mischiefs they have occasion'd: But supposing such symbolical representations might be occasionnally used, is it not, for the reasons already given, incumbent on the parties concern'd, to appoint, alter, and vary them as occasion requires?

*B.* I f God has delegated to the Clergy a power to confecrate Persons & things, can any, whether Prince or People, dispense with this power, and substitute things unconfecrated?

*A.* A s God alone is absolutely holy, so Men may be said to be more or less holy, according as they imitate him; and as this holiness consists in a good & pious disposition of mind, so Mens actions are no otherwise holy, but as they flow from, and are signs of this holy disposition. Inanimate things can only be said to have a relative holiness, as made use of in actions, by which Men express that holy disposition of mind; and can last no longer than they are thus employ'd. What holiness, either real or relative, wou'd the Ark now have? tho' it once had such a legal holiness, that more than fifty thousand Reapers were destroy'd for peeping into it. * Nay, Persons who want all real holiness, may yet have a relative holiness, as Ministers employ'd by the Congregation about holy things; but this can be no more than a derivative holiness, & can last no longer than the holy action they are about; and belongs equally to those from whom 'tis deriv'd. Thus all the relative holiness which concerns publick worship, whether as to persons,

places,

* I *Sam.* 6. 19.

places, or things, must be deriv'd from the Congregation; and nothing sure, can be more absurd, than to imagine the Clergy, by any form of words, can bestow any permanent holiness, whether real or relative, on timber, stone, *&c.* And therefore, the method us'd by Archbishop *Laud*, in confecrating of a Church, was generally cry'd out on as profane, and tending to justify those Consecrations us'd in the *Greek* & *Latin* Churches, whereby they cheat the People of immense fums. But 'tis no wonder, if they, who claim this power in relation to inanimate things, shou'd pretend to convey to Men, tho' ever so wicked, a real inherent, nay, *indelible* holy character; tho' wherein that confifts, they themselves can't tell. But,

WHAT the Priefts aim at by this cant, is to make People believe their prayers are of greater efficacy than those of the unfanctify'd Laity; very well knowing, that if the People were so weak as to believe it, they wou'd be thought necessary on all occasions, especially to persons on their death-beds. What advantages they have made by being then thought thus necessary, none can be ignorant of. I do not wonder, that so loose an haranguer as St. *Chrysostom* shou'd say, *The prayers of the People, which are weak in themselves, laying hold on the more prevailing prayers of the Priefts, may, by them, be convey'd to Heaven.* But I admire, that the judicious Bishop *Potter,* * the King's Professor of Divinity at *Oxford*, should maintain the same position, & think to support it by this Father's authority. But this is modeft in comparison of what *Hicks*, *Brett,* & others of that ftamp, affign to Priefts, in suppofing they have such transcendent privileges by virtue of their *indelible* character, that they can blefs, or curfe *authoritatively*; nay, that their very prayers to God himfelf are *authoritative Prayers.*

*B.* THO some have had too little regard for Natural Religion, as being too ftubborn to yield to any

felfish

* Of *Church Governm,* pag. 250.

felfifh views, yet that will not justify you for levelling your arguments against the divine Omnipotency. Are we not God's Creatures, & may not our Creator give us what arbitrary Commands he pleases?

*A.* N o t to repeat what I have said already, I shall only ask you, Why may not God deceive us? Tell us one thing, & act the contrary? Is not his Power absolute? And *his Will, who can refift?* Would you not reply, that God as he is infinitely good & happy, can have no motive to deceive us? And that he could do whatever he thought fit for the good of his Creatures, without having recourse to fuch mean shifts? And will not this reason equally hinder him from burthening us with arbitrary Commands? Is not one as much as the other, inconfistent with his Wifdom & Goodnefs, by which his Power is always directed? And of the two, it fhou'd feem lefs abfurd, that God might deceive People for their good, than impofe arbitrary things on them for their hurt, by annexing fevere penalties on non-obfervance.

*B.* M a y not God give us arbitrary Commands to try our obedience?

*A.* A M a n, who knows not the hearts of others, nor forefees how they will act, may think it prudent to try people in things of little or no moment, before he trufts them in greater; but God, who foreknows what Men will do on all occafions, can need no fuch trial. If earthly Kings, who may be deceiv'd, & for the moft part are fo, wou'd be juftly efteem'd Tyrants, if they required things of their Subjects meerly to try their obedience, how can we think this of the Omnifcient, infinitely Glorious King of Kings? Tho' was a trial neceffary, moral & immoral things wou'd be the moft proper fubjects for it; becaufe we can't practife one, or refrain from the other, without fubduing our lufts & paffions: But what speculative articles will not an ill Man profefs? Or what indifferent things will he not practife, to be indulg'd in any one darling vice? A n d

AND now don't you think we may juſtly conclude, that whatſoever God requires of us to believe, or practiſe, is purely for our good; and conſequently, that no belief, or practice, which does not contribute to that good, can come from God; and therefore, as long as we adhere to what Reaſon reveals to us concerning the Goodneſs of God, by admitting every thing into Religion which makes for the Good of Man, & nothing that does not, we can't miſtake our duty either to God, or Man.

AND therefore, I ſhall conclude this head with a quotation from a noble Author, * ,, To believe, ,, that every thing is govern'd, order'd, or regulated ,, *for the beſt*, by a deſigning Principle, or Mind, ne- ,, ceſſarily good and permanent, is to be a perfect ,, THEIST.

,, To believe no one ſupreme deſigning Principle, ,, or Mind, but rather two, three, or more, (tho' in ,, their nature good) is to be a POLYTHEIST.

,, To believe the governing Mind, or Minds, not ,, abſolutely & neceſſarily good, nor confin'd to what ,, is beſt, but capable of acting according to meer will ,, or fancy, is to be a DÆMONIST.

* *Characteriſt. Vol. r. pag. 11.*

## CHAP. XII.

*That they, who, to magnify Revelation, weaker the force of the Religion of Reaſon & Nature, ſtrike at all Religion: and that there can't be two independent Rules for the government of human actions.*

B. IN my opinion, you lay too great ſtreſs on fal- lible Reaſon, & too little on infallible Revela- tion: And, therefore, I muſt needs ſay, your arguing wholly from Reaſon wou'd make ſome of leſs candor than myſelf, take you for an arrant *Free-Thinker*.

A.

*A.* WHATEVER is true by Reafon, can never be falfe by Revelation; & if God can't be deceiv'd himfelf, or be willing to deceive Men, the light he hath given to diftinguifh between religious truth & falfehood, cannot, if duly attended to, deceive them in things of fo great moment.

THEY, who do not allow Reafon to judge in matters of opinion, or fpeculation, are guilty of as great abfurdity as the *Papifts*, who will not allow the fenfes to be judges in the cafe of *Tranfubftantiation*, tho' a matter directly under their cognizance: nay, the abfurdity, I think, is greater in the firft cafe; becaufe Reafon is to judge, whether our fenfes are deceiv'd; and if no texts ought to be admitted as a proof in a matter contrary to fenfe, they ought, certainly, as little to be admitted in any point contrary to Reafon.

IN a word, to fuppofe any thing in Revelation inconfiftent with Reafon, &, at the fame time, pretend it to be the will of God, is not only to deftroy that proof, on which we conclude it to be the will of God, but even the proof of the being of a God; fince if our reafoning faculties duly attended to can deceive us, we can't be fure of the truth of any one propofition, but every thing wou'd be alike uncertain, and we fhou'd for ever fluctuate in a ftate of univerfal fcepticifm. Which fhews how abfurdly they act, who, on pretence of magnifying Tradition, endeavour to weaken the force of Reafon, (tho' to be fure they always except their own,) and thereby foolifhly fap the foundation, to fupport the fuperftructure. But as long as Reafon is againft Men, they will be againft Reafon. We muft not, therefore, be furpris'd, to fee fome endeavour to reafon Men out of their Reafon: tho' the very attempt to deftroy Reafon by Reafon, is a demonftration Men have nothing but Reafon to truft to. And,

AND

AND to suppose any thing can be true by Revelation, which is false by Reason, is not to support that thing, but to undermine Revelation; because nothing unreasonable, nay, that is not highly reasonable, can come from a God, of unlimited, universal, and eternal Reason. As evident as this Truth is, yet that shall not hinder me from examining in a proper place, whatever you can urge from Revelation. And give me leave to add, that I shall not be surpris'd, if for so laudable an attempt, as reconciling Reason & Revelation, which have been so long set at variance, I shou'd be censur'd as a *Free-Thinker*; a title, that, however invidious it may seem, I am far from being asham'd of; since one may as well suppose, a Man can reason without thinking at all, as reason well without thinking freely. But,

THE irreconcilable enemies of Reason, seeing it too gross, in this reasoning Age, to attack Reason openly, do it covertly under the name of *Free-Thinking*; not despairing, but that the time may come again, when the Laity shall stifle every thought rising in their minds, tho with ever so much appearance of truth, as a suggestion of Satan, if it clashes with the real, or pretended opinions of their Priests.

B. THO you talk so much about Reason, yet you have not defin'd what you mean by that word.

A. WHEN we attribute any operation to it, as distinguishing between truth & falsehood, *&c.* we mean by it the rational faculties; but when we ascribe no such operation to it, as when we give a reason for a thing, *&c.* we then understand by it, any medium, by which our rational faculties judge of the agreement, or disagreement of the terms of any proposition; and if an Author writes intelligibly, we may easily discern in which of these two senses he takes the word. But to go to the bottom of this matter,

IT will be requisite to give a more distinct account of *Reason* in both these senses. By the rational facul-

ties

ties then, we mean the natural ability a Man has to *apprehend, judge,* and *infer:* The *immediate objects* of which faculties are, not the things themselves, but the *ideas* the mind conceives of them: While our *ideas* remain single, they fall under the *apprehension,* & are express'd by *simple terms;* when join'd, under the *judgment,* & are express'd by *propositions;* when so join'd as to need the *intervention* of some other *idea* to compare 'em with, in order to form a *judgment,* they become by that *intervention,* the subject of *inference,* or *argumentation;* and this is term'd, *syllogism* or *argument.* It must be observ'd too, that all the *ideas* we have, or can have, are either by *sensation* or *reflection:* by the first, we have our *ideas* of what passes, or exists without : by the second, of what passes, or exists within the mind: And in the view, or contemplation of these consists all our knowledge; that being nothing but *the perception of the agreement, or disagreement of our ideas;* & any two of these, when join'd together, so as to be affirm'd or deny'd of each other, make what we call a *proposition;* when consider'd apart, what we call the *terms* of that *proposition;* the *agreement,* or *disagreement* of which *terms* being express'd by the rightly affirming, or denying 'em of each other, is what we call *Truth;* the perception of their agreement or disagreement, is what we term *knowledge.* This knowledge accrues either immediately on the bare intuition of these two *ideas,* or *terms* so join'd, & is therefore styl'd *intuitive knowledge,* or, self-evident *truth;* or by the intervention of some other idea, or ideas, as a common measure for the other two, & is therefore call'd the *medium,* by which Reason judges of their agreement, or disagreement; & this is called *demonstrative knowledge,* which is never to be had without the help of the other. For,

IF there were not some propositions which need not to be prov'd, it would be in vain for Men to argue with one another, because they then could bring no
proofs

proofs but what needed to be prov'd. -- Those propositions which need no proof, we call self-evident; because by comparing the ideas signify'd by the terms of such propositions, we immediately discern their agreement, or disagreement: This is, as I said before, what we call intuitive knowledge, & is the knowledge of God himself, who sees all things by intuition; and may, I think, be call'd *divine inspiration*, as being immediately from God, and not acquir'd by any human deduction, or drawing of consequences. This, certainly, is that divine, that uniform Light, which shines in the minds of all men, and enables them to discern whatever they do discern; since without it there could be no Demonstration, no Knowledge, but invincible obscurity, & universal uncertainty.

Where a proposition can't be made evident, by comparing the two ideas, or terms of it with each other, it is render'd so by intermediate ideas or terms, whereby the agreement, or disagreement of the ideas under examination, or the truth of that proposition is perceiv'd; and when there is an intuitive perception of the agreement, or disagreement of the intermediate ideas in each step of the progression, then, and not till then, it becomes demonstrative Knowledge; otherwise it can rise no higher than probability, which consists not in a certain, but a likely connexion between the terms of a proposition, & the intermediate proofs of it: So that every proposition that's only probable, must have a proportionable degree of uncertainty, otherwise it would amount to demonstration; & consequently, Probability, as well as Certainty, is founded on the relation it has to self-evident truths; because where no relation to them of any sort can be discover'd, there is no room for Certainty, or Probability.

Hence we see that all wrong reasoning is the effect of rashness, and consists either in taking propositions to have a certain connexion with self-evident

truths,

truths, when they have but a probable one, or imagining there's a probable connexion, when there's no
connexion at all, or else mistaking the degrees of
probability.

*B.* The *Quakers* are very positive, that there is in
all Mankind, a principle of action distinct from Reason,
(& which is not inspiration) by which all are to be
govern'd in matters of Religion, as they are by Reason
in other matters, and which they commonly call *the
Light within.*

*A.* Was there any such principle, Men destitute
of all Reason were as capable of knowing all matters
of Religion, as if they had been ever so rational.
'Tis strange, that all Mankind shou'd have a principle
of acting, of which they never were sensible; nor can
these modern discoverers tell them what it is, or how
it operates; nor do they themselves ever use it in any
of their debates about Religion, but argue like other
Men from principles that are common to all Mankind,
& prove propositions that are not self-evident by those
that are so; and confute false & bad reasons (of which
they can only judge by Reason) by true and good
reasons; which supposes that Reason, however fallible
it may be, is all rational Creatures have to trust to;
and that 'tis the highest commendation of Religion,
that it is a *reasonable service.* And since this is an Age,
where words without meaning, or distinctions without
difference, will not pass current, why shou'd they,
who otherwise appear to have good sense, thus impose on themselves, and be expos'd by others, for
such senseless notions, as can only serve to prejudice
people against their other rational principles? But 'tis
the fate of most Sects to be fondest of their ugliest
brats. But not to deviate,

Were it not for those self-evident notions, which
are the foundation of all our reasonings, there could
be no intellectual communication between God and
Man; nor, as we are fram'd, can God ascertain us
of

of any truth, but by fhewing its agreement with thofe
felf-evident notions, which are the tetts by which we
are to judge of every thing, even the Being of a God
and Natural Religion; which, tho' not knowable by
intuition, are to be demonftrated by fuch proofs,
which have, mediately or immediately, a neceffary
connexion with our felf-evident notions. And therefore, to weaken the force of demonftration, is to
ftrike at all Religion, & even at the Being of God;
and not to give probability its due weight, is to ftrike
at the authority of that Revelation you contend for;
becaufe, that God reveal'd his Will by *vifions, dreams,
trances*, or any other way befides the light of Nature,
can only come under the head of Probability. And,

If it be but probable, that God made any external
Revelation at all, it can be but probable, tho' perhaps,
not in the fame degree of probability, that he made
this or that Revelation: And this evidence all pretend to, fince, perhaps, there never was a time or
place, where fome external Revelation was not believ'd,
& its Votaries equally confident, that theirs was a
true Revelation: And, indeed, the prodigious numbers
of Revelations, which from time to time have been
in the world, fhew how cafily Mankind may in this
point be impos'd on. And as there can be no demonftration of the Revelation itfelf, fo neither can
there be any of its conveyance to pofterity; much
lefs that this or that, has been convey'd entire to diftant
times & places, efpecially, if a Revelation be of any
bulk, and which may have gone thorow the hands
of Men, who not only in the dark ages of the Church,
but even in the beginning, if we judge by the number
of corrupted paffages, and even forg'd books, were
capable of any pious fraud. Nay, the very nature of
Probability is fuch, that were it only left to time itfelf, even that wou'd wear it quite out; at leaft if it be
true what *Mathematicians* pretend to demonftrate, *viz.*
That the probability of facts depending on human

tefti.

teftimony, muft gradually leffen in proportion to the diftance of the time when they were done. And we have a Reverend Divine, * who has publifh'd, as he thinks, a demonftration of this, with relation to facts recorded in Scripture, and has gone fo far, as to fix the precife time, when all probability of the truth of the hiftory of Chrift, will be entirely fpent, and exhaufted.

ARCHBISHOP *Laud* fays, † that ,, the affent we ,, yield to this main point of Divinity, that the ,, Scripture is the word of God, is grounded on no ,, compelling or demonftrative ratiocination, but relies ,, on the ftrength of Faith more than any one prin- ,, ciple whatever. ,,   And by the confeffion of the beft *Proteftan.* Writers, the internal excellency of the Chriftian doctrines is the main proof of their coming from God; and therefore, Mr. *Chillingworth* fays, ‡ ,, For my part, I profefs, if the Doctrine of the ,, Scripture was not as good, & as fit to come from ,, God, the fountain of Goodnefs, as the miracles, ,, by which it was confirm'd, were great, I fhould ,, want one main pillar of my faith, and for want ,, of it, I fear, fhould be much ftagger'd in it.

THIS, I think, may be fufficient to fhew, what a folly they are guilty of, who, in order to advance the credit of Revelation, endeavour to weaken the force of Reafon.

*B.* I don't think, we ought to have the fame regard for Reafon, as Men had formerly, when that was the fole Rule God had given them for the government of their actions; fince now we Chriftians have two fupreme, independant Rules, *Reafon* and *Revelation,* and both require an abfolute obedience.

*A.*

* *Craig's* Principia Mathematica Theologiæ Chriftia- næ, *pag.* 23. - & d. Edit. *Londini* 1699.

† *Laud* againft *Fifher*, pag. 110.

‡ *Relig. Proteft. Part. I. cap. 2. pag.* 53.

*A.* I can't fee how that is poffible; for if you are to be govern'd by the latter, that fuppofes you muft take every thing on truft, or meerly becaufe it's faid by thofe, for whofe dictates you are to have an implicit faith; for to examine into the truth of what they fay, is renouncing their authority: As on the contrary, if Men are to be govern'd by their Reafon, they are not to admit any thing further than as they fee it reafonable. To fuppofe both confiftent, is to fuppofe it confiftent to take, and not to take, things on truft.

To receive Religion on the account of authority fuppofes, that if the fame authority promulgated a different Religion, we fhou'd be oblig'd to receive it: And indeed, it's an odd jumble, to prove the truth of a book by the truth of the doctrines it contains, & at the fame time conclude thofe doctrines to be true, becaufe contain'd in that book; & yet this is a jumble every one makes. who contends for Mens being abfolutely govern'd both by Reafon & Authority.

What can be a fuller evidence of the fovereignty of Reafon, than that all Men, when there is any thing in their traditional Religion, which in its literal fenfe can't be defended by Reafon, have recourfe to any method of interpretation, tho ever fo forc'd, in order to make it appear reafonable. And do not all parties, when prefs'd, as they are all in their turns, fay with *Tertullian*, ,, we ought to interpret Scripture, not by ,, the found of words, but by the nature of things. ,, *Malo te ad fenfum rei, quam ad fonum vocabuli exerceas.* * But fometimes the letter of the Scripture is fuch an authority, as can't be parted with without facrilege, and fometimes 'tis a *letter which killeth.*

In a word, when Men, in defending their own, or attacking other traditionary Religions, have recourfe to the Nature or Reafon of Things, does not that fhew, they believe the truth of all traditionary

L 4

Reli-

* *Adv. Prax. c. 3.*

Religions is to be try'd by it; as being that, which must tell them what is true or false in Religion? And were there not some truths relating to Religion of themselves so evident, as that all must agree in them, nothing relating to Religion cou'd be prov'd, every thing wou'd want a further proof; and if there are such evident truths, must not all others be try'd by their agreement with them? And are not these the tests, by which we are to distinguish the only true Religion from the many false ones? And do not all alike own, there are such tests drawn from the nature of things, each crying their Religion contains · every thing worthy, and nothing unworthy of having God for its Author; thereby confessing, that Reason enables them to tell what is worthy of having God for its Author: And if Reason tells them this, does it not tell them every thing that God can be suppos'd to require?

In short, nothing can be more certain, than that there are some things in their own nature good, some evil, and others neither good nor evil; and for the same reason God commands the good, & forbids the evil, he leaves Men at liberty in things indifferent; it being inconsistent with his wisdom to reward the observance of such things, and with his goodness to punish for not observing them. And as he cou'd have no end in creating Mankind, but their common good, so they answer the end of their creation, who do all the good they can; and to enable Men to do this, God has given them Reason to distinguish Good from Evil, useful from useless things: Or in other words, has made them moral agents, capable of discerning the relations they stand in to God and one another, & the duties resulting from these relations, so necessary to their common good: And consequently, Religion, thus founded on these immutable relations, must at all times, & in all places, be alike immutable, since external Revelation, not being able to make any change

change in thefe relations, & the duties that neceffarily refult from them, can only recommend, & inculcate thefe duties; except we fuppofe, that God at laft acted the Tyrant, and impos'd fuch Commands, as the relations we ftand in to him, & one another, no ways require.

To imagine any external Revelation not to depend on the Reafon or Things, is to make Things give place to Words, and implies, that from the time this Rule commenc'd, we were forbid to act as moral agents, in judging what is good, or evil, fit, or unfit; and that we are to make no other ufe of our Reafon, than to fee what is the literal meaning of texts, & to admit that only to be the will of God, tho' ever fo inconfiftent with the Light of Nature, & the eternal Reafon of Things. Is not this to infer, there's nothing good or evil in itfelf, but that all depends on the Will of an arbitrary Being, which, tho' it may change every moment, is to be unalterably found in fuch a Book?

ALL Divines, I think, now agree in owning, that there's a Law of Reafon, antecedent to any external Revelation, that God can't difpenfe, either with his Creatures or himfelf, for not obferving, and that no external Revelation can be true, that in the leaft circumftance, or minuteft point, is inconfiftent with it. If fo, how can we affirm any one thing in Revelation to be true, till we perceive, by that underftanding, which God has given us to difcern the truth of things, whether it agrees with this immutable Law, or not?

IF we can't believe otherwife than as things appear to our underftandings, to fuppofe God requires us to give up our underftandings (a matter we can't know but by ufing our underftanding) to any authority whatever, is to fuppofe he requires impoffibilities. And our felf-evident notions being the foundation of all certainty, we can only judge of things, as they are found to be more or lefs agreeable to them.

To

To deny this on any pretence whatever, can serve only to introduce an universal Scepticism. And therefore Bishop *Taylor* very justly observes, * „ 'Tis Reason „ that is the Judge, and Fathers, Councils, Tradition, „ & Scripture the Evidence. „ And if Reason be the Judge, can it form a right judgment, without examining into every thing which offers itself for evidence? And wou'd it not examine in vain, if it had not certain tests, by which it cou'd try all evidences relating to religious matters.

*B.* Tho' Reason may be the Judge, yet the Scripture, we say, is the Rule, by which Reason must judge of the truth of things.

*A.* If it be such a Rule, must it not have all the qualifications necessary to make it so? But if Reason must tell us what those qualifications are, & whether they are to be found in Scripture, & if one of those qualifications is, that the Scripture must be agreeable to the nature of things, does not that suppose the nature of things to be the standing Rule, by which we must judge of the truth of all those Doctrines contain'd in the Scriptures? So that the Scripture can only be a secondary rule, as far as it is found agreeable to the nature of things, or to those self-evident notions, which are the foundation of all knowledge, & certainty.

In short, no Man can any more discern the objects of his own understanding, & their relations, by the faculties of another, than he can see with another Man's eyes; or than one Ship can be guided by the Helm of another: And therefore, he, who demands a Man's assent to any thing, without conveying into his mind such reasons as may produce a sense of the truth of it, erects a tyranny over his understanding, & demands an impossible tribute. No opinion, tho' ever so certain to one Man, can be infus'd into another as certain, by any method, but by opening his understanding,

* *Pelem. Disco. pag.* 507.

standing, so that he may find the reasonableness of it in his own mind; & consequently, the only *Criterion*, by which he tries his own reasonings, must be the internal evidence he has already of certain truths, & the agreeableness of his inferences to them. And,

To suppose a Creature to have Reason to direct him, and that he is not to be directed by it, is a contradiction: and if we are religious as we are rational, can Religion oblige us not to be govern'd by Reason, tho' but for a moment? Nay, what is the Religion of all rational Beings, but what the Scripture terms it, *a reasonable service?* Or, their Reason employ'd on such subjects, as conduce to the dignity of the rational nature? So that Religion & Reason were not only given for the same end, the good of Mankind, but they are, as far as such subjects extend, the same, & commence together. And if God can no otherwise apply to Men, but by applying to their Reason, (which he is continually doing by the Light of Nature) does he not by that bid them use their Reason? And can God at the same time forbid it, by requiring an implicit faith in any person whatever?

If you allow, that Men by their reasoning faculties are made like unto God, & fram'd after his image, and that Reason is the most excellent gift God can bestow, do they not destroy this likeness, deface this image, and give up the dignity of human Nature, when they give up their Reason to any person whatever.

Can we lay too great a stress on Reason, when we consider, 'tis only by virtue of it God can hold communication with Man? Nor can otherwise, if I may so speak, witness for himself, or assert the Wisdom & Goodness of his conduct, than by submitting his ways to Mens cool deliberation, & strict examination? since 'tis from the marks we discern in the Laws of the Universe, and its Government, that we can demonstrate it to be govern'd by a God of infinite

Wisdom

Wisdom & Goodness. He, whose Reason does not enable him to do this, can neither discern the Wisdom, Goodness, or even the Being of a God.

They only answer the end for which their Reason was given them, who judge of the Will of God, by the reasonableness & goodness of doctrines; & think his Laws, like his works, carry in them the marks of Divinity; and they likewise do the greatest honour to the Scripture, who suppose it deals with Men as with rational Creatures; and therefore admit not of any of its doctrines without a strict examination; and those, who take a contrary method, wou'd, if they liv'd in *Turky*, embrace *Mahometism*, and believe in the *Alcoran*.

And indeed, a blind submission is so far from doing credit to true Religion, that it puts all Religions on the same foot; for without judging of a Religion by its internal marks, there's nothing but miracles to plead; and miracles true or false, if they are believ'd (& where are they not?) will have the same effect. Nay, if miracles can be perform'd by evil, as well as by good Beings, the worst Religion may have the most miracles, as needing them most. And it was a proverbial saying among the Philosophers of *Greece*, Θαύμαζα μώροις: *Miracles for Fools, and Reasons for wise Men*. The *Beotians* were remarkable for their stupidity, and the number of their Oracles; and if you look no further than the Christian World, you will find, that ignorance, and the belief of daily miracles go hand in hand; and that there's nothing too absurd for the Peoples belief. And if the most learned *Huetius* * gives us a true account of things, there are no miracles recorded in the Bible, but many of the like nature are to be found in Pagan Histories.

Wou'd not Christians themselves, think it a sufficient proof of a Religion's not coming from God, if it
                                        wanted

* *See his* Alnetanæ Quæstiones de Concordia fidei & rationis.

wanted any of thofe internal marks, by which the truth of all Religion is to be try'd, without inquiring into its miracles, or any other external proofs? and confequently, wherever thele internal marks are found, are not external marks needlefs? But,

How can we maintain, that the Scripture carries with it all thofe internal marks of truth, which are infeparable from God's Laws, and at the fame time affirm, it requires an implicit faith, & blind obedience to all its dictates? If it does fo, how could we have examin'd whether it had hofe internal marks? Or how can we fay, we can't know without the Scripture, what are the internal marks of truth; and at the fame time fuppofe, we muft by our Reafon know what are thofe marks, before we can tell whether they are to be found in the Scripture?

If our Nature is a rational Nature, and our Religion a *reafonable fervice*, there muft be fuch a necef-fary, and clofe connexion between them, as to leave no room for any thing that is arbitrary to intervene: And confequently, the Religion of all rational beings muft confift, in ufing fuch a conduct to God, & their fellow-Creatures, as Reafon, whatever circumftances they are in, does direct.

We find St. *Paul* himfelf faying, that *Tho' we,* (the Apoftles) *or an Angel from Heaven, preach any other Gofpel, let him be accurfed:* * And is not this laying the whole ftrefs on its internal marks? Since there's nothing in the nature of fuch things as have not thofe marks, to hinder them from being chang'd every moment.

And as to thofe who deprefs Reafon, in order to exalt Revelation, I wou'd ask them; what greater proof the Scripture can give us of the rectitude of human underftanding in religious matters, than cal-ling it the *Infpiration of the Almighty;* † or than God's fo frequently appealing to it, for the juftification of his own conduct?

I i5

* *Gal* 1. 8.        † *Job* 32. 8.

I n the Prophet *Isaiah*, God repréfenting his own conduct towards his People, under the parable of a vineyard, exprefly fays, * *O ye Inhabitants of* Jerufalem, *and Men of* Judah, *judge, I pray you, between me and my Vineyard.*  And in *Ezekiel*, God, after a long vindication of his carriage towards his People, appeals to them, faying, † *Hear now, O Houfe of* Ifrael, *is not my way equal? Are not your ways unequal?*  And in the Prophet *Micah* he fays, ‡ *He will plead with them; asks what he has done; & bids them teftify againft him.*  And in the Prophet *Ifaiah*, after the Lord had faid, § *Wafh ye, make ye clean, put away the evil of your doings from before mine eyes; Ceafe to do evil, learn to do well; feek judgment, relieve the oppreffed; judge the Fatherlefs, plead for the Widow:* he adds, *Come near, let us reafon together, tho' your fins be as fcarlet, they fhall be as white as fnow.*  Does not God here appeal to their Reafon for the fufficiency of moral things, to wafh away their fins, tho' of the deepeft die? And cou'd God & Man reafon together, except there were fome notions in common to both; fome foundation for fuch reafoning? Otherwife how cou'd *Job* fay, *I defire to reafon with God?* ¶  And certainly, the next thing to reafoning with God, is reafoning with one another about God & Religion; that being the chief end, for which our Reafon was giv'n us. *Thus Paul* * *reafon'd in the Synagogue every Sabbath.*  And again, † *He reafon'd with them out of the Scriptures.  And as he reafon'd of Righteoufnefs, Temperance, and Jugdment to come,* Felix *trembl'd:* ‡ Which, certainly, he had never done, had *Paul* talk'd about Types, Allegories, Rites, and Ceremonies, &c.

B.  Y o u argue, as if we had no certain way of knowing the will of God, except from the light of Nature, and that eternal rule of Reafon, by which,

you

---

* *Ifa.* 5. 3.    † *Ezek.* 18. 25.    ‡ *Mic.* 6. 2, 3.
§ *Ifa.* 1. 16. 18.       ¶ *Job* 13. 3.
* *Acts* 18. 4.    † *Chap.* 17. 2.    ‡ *Chap.* 24, 25.

you fuppofe, God governs all his own actions, and expects Men fhou'd govern all theirs; but may not God take what method he pleafes, to communicate his mind?

*A.* THIS all traditional Religions with equal confidence affert; and they wou'd have equal right to plead it, if Reafon did not afford Men certain *criteria* to know God's will by, which way foever reveal'd.

IF God created Mankind to make them happy here, or hereafter, the Rules he gave them, muft be fufficient to anfwer that benevolent purpofe of infinite Wifdom; and confequently, had Mankind obferv'd them, there cou'd have been no occafion for an external Revelation; and its great ufe now is, to make Men obferve thofe neglected Rules, which God, of his infinite wifdom and goodnefs, defign'd for their prefent, and future happinefs.

*B.* Do not our Divines fay, Mankind were for many Ages in a deplorable ftate, for want of an external Revelation?

*A.* IF God does every thing that's fit for him to do, cou'd Men be in fuch a ftate, becaufe God did not do a thing, which was not fit for him to do? *viz.* make a Revelation, before it was fit for him to make it? Or can the greateft part of Mankind be now in that deplorable condition, for want of a Revelation, which God, out of his infinite Wifdom, has not as yet thought fit to communicate to them; at leaft with that evidence, as is neceffary to make them believe it?

MUST not thefe Gentlemen fuppofe, that either God, in creating Mankind, did not defign their future happinefs, tho' he gave them immortal fouls capable of it; or elfe, that tho' he defign'd it, he prefcrib'd them fuch means, or gave them fuch rules, as either were not fufficient at firft, or in procefs of time became infufficient for that end? but that after Men had been, for many Ages, in this miferable condition, God thought fit to mend the eternal, univerfal Law

of

of Nature, by adding certain obfervances to it, not founded on the Reafon of things; and that thofe, out of his partial goodnefs, he communicated only to fome, leaving the greateft part in their former dark & deplorable ftate? But,

Is it not incumbent on thofe, who make any external Revelation fo neceffary to the happinefs of all Mankind, to fhew, how it is confiftent with the notion of God's being univerfally benevolent, not to have reveal'd it to all his Children, when all had equal need of it? Was it not as eafy for him to have communicated it to all Nations, as to any one Nation, or Perfon? Or in all languages, as in any one? Nay, was it not as eafy for him to have made all Men, for the fake of this noble end, fpeak in one, and the fame language; as it was at firft, to multiply languages, to prevent their building a Tower up to Heaven? Nay, I fee not how God can have any need at all of language, to let Mankind know his will; fince he has at all times communicated his mind to them without it.

*B.* THESE, I confefs, are confiderable difficulties; but as to the laft difficulty, did not God give Laws to the *Jews*, of which other Nations knew nothing?

*A.* NOR were they concern'd to know, or when known, oblig'd to obferve them; nor did they bind the *Jews* themfelves, but for a time; and even then, they were for the moft part impracticable, out of the Land of *Canaan*; where God, as I fhall fully fhew hereafter, acted, not as Governour of the *Univerfe*, but as King of the *Jews*, by virtue of the *Horeb Covenant*, which he obtain'd at his own requeft. But when God acts as Governour of the *Univerfe*, his Laws are alike defign'd for all under his government; that is, all Mankind; and confequently, what equally concerns all, muft be equally knowable by all. And if the univerfality of a Law, be the only certain mark of its coming from the Governour of Mankind, how

can

can we be certain, that that which wants this mark, comes from him? And if Religion belongs to us, as we are Men, must we not, as Men, be capable of knowing it? And if all Mankind are Creatures of the same Creator, & Fellow-creatures with one another, must not all their religious duties, as they are Creatures of the same God, and Fellow-Creatures with one another, be the same? And let me add, that

IF Men are religious, as they are rational, must they not be capable, when they come to the use of their Reason, of knowing a Religion founded on Reason? Or must they be oblig'd to leave their country, and endlesly rove up & down, in search of such opinions, as have no foundation in Reason? Or, if they are forc'd to stay at home, be ever examining into all the arbitrary precepts, which are to be met with in any of the traditional Religions they can come at? And shou'd they do so, must they not, since Reason cou'd not direct them in things not depending on Reason, perpetually remain in a state of uncertainty?

I might go further, and ask you, Whether it is consistent with that impartiality which is essential to the Deity, not to make those, he designs should know his Will by Revelation, capable of knowing that Revelation, and consequently, his Will contain'd it, at one time as well as another? Which cou'd not be, if that which was plain at first, became obscure by reason of the change of languages, customs, the distance of time & place, the errors of Transcribers & Translators, & an hundred other things too long to mention. Can these difficulties be avoided, without supposing, that Religion, which way soever reveal'd, carries such internal marks of truth, as, at all times & places, plainly shews itself, even to the meanest capacity, to be the Will of a Being of universal & impartial benevolence.

B. THE greater stress you lay on Reason, the more you extol Revelation; which being design'd to exalt

M                              and

and perfect our rational nature, muſt be itſelf highly reaſonable.

*A.* I grant you this is the deſign of Religion; but have not the Eccleſiaſticks in moſt places entirely defeated this deſign; and ſo far debas'd human-nature, as to render it unſociable, fierce & cruel? Have they not made external Revelation the pretence of filling the Chriſtian World with animoſity, hatred, perſecution, ruin & deſtruction; in order to get an abſolute dominion over the conſciences, properties & perſons of the Laity? But paſſing this over, If the perfection of any Nature, whether human, angelical, or divine, conſiſts in being govern'd by the Law of its Nature; & ours, in acting that part, for which we were created; by obſerving all thoſe duties, which are founded on the relation we ſtand in to God & one another; can Revelation any otherwiſe help to perfect human-nature, but as it induces Men to live up to this Law of their Nature? And if this Law is the teſt of the perfection of any written Law, muſt not that be the moſt perfect Law, by which the perfection of all others is to be try'd? And,

If nothing but reaſoning can improve Reaſon, & no Book can improve my Reaſon in any point, but as it gives me convincing proofs of its reaſonableneſs; a Revelation, that will not ſuffer us to judge of its dictates by our Reaſon, is ſo far from improving Reaſon, that it forbids the uſe of it; and reaſoning faculties unexercis'd, will have as little force, as unexercis'd limbs: He that is always carry'd, will at length become unable to go: And if the *Holy Ghoſt*, as Biſhop *Taylor* ſays, * *works by heightening, & improving our natural faculties*, it can only be by uſing ſuch means as will improve them, in propoſing reaſons & arguments to convince our underſtanding; which can only be improv'd, by ſtudying the nature and

reaſon

* *Liberty of Prophecy, cap.* 18, *pag.* 19.

reaſon of things: *I apply'd my heart* (ſays the wiſeſt of Men) *to know, and to ſearch, & to ſeek out wiſdom & the Reaſon of Things.* *

So that the Holy Ghoſt can't deal with Men as rational Creatures, but by propoſing arguments to convince their underſtandings, & influence their wills, in the ſame manner as if propos'd by other agents; for to go beyond this, would be making impreſſions on Men, as a ſeal does on wax; to the confounding of their Reaſon, & their liberty in chooſing, and the Man would then be merely paſſive, and the action would be the action of another being acting upon him, for which he could be no way accountable: But if the Holy Ghoſt does not act thus, & Revelation itſelf be not arbitrary, muſt it not be founded on the Reaſon of Things? And conſequently, be *a Republication, or Reſtoration of the Religion of Nature?* And ſince that takes in every thing thus founded, all the help any authority whatever can afford a reaſonable Being, is the offering him arguments, of which his own Reaſon muſt judge; and when he perceives their agreement with his ſelf-evident notions, 'tis *then*, & only *then*, he can be ſure of their truth. And tho' Men cou'd not miſtake, as we ſee they daily do, a natural for a ſupernatural ſuggeſtion, yet whether that ſuggeſtion comes from a good or evil Being, (continually tempting people) can only be judg'd by the nature of the things ſuggeſted. For 'tis in vain to have recourſe to miracles, if evil as well as good Beings have the power of doing them? And ſome are ſo heterodox, as to imagine, one reaſon why evil Beings are permitted to do miracles, is, leaſt from the report of miracles, (which is alike ſpread every where, & for every Religion) Men might be tempted not to rely on the Reaſon & Nature of Things, and ſo run into endleſs ſuperſtitions.   And,

M 2

GOD.

* *Eccleſ. 7. 25.*

God, in the Old Testament, * is said to suffer miracles to be done by false Prophets, in order to prove his People; and in the New, such miracles, as wou'd, *if it were possible, deceive the very Elect.* †

In short, Revelation either bids, or forbids Men to use their Reason, in judging of all religious matters; if the former, then it only declares that to be our duty, which was so independent of and, antecedent to Revelation; if the latter, then it does not deal with Men as with rational Creatures, but deprives them of that inestimable blessing.

*B.* Who, I pray, maintains, that Revelation forbids us the use of our Reason, in judging of the truth of any religious matters?

*A.* Is not every one of this opinion, that says, we are not to read the Scripture with freedom of assenting, or dissenting, just as we judge it agrees, or disagrees with the Light of Nature, & the Reason of Things? And this, one wou'd think, none cou'd deny was absolutely necessary, in reading a book, where 'tis own'd that the *Letter killeth.* Nay, do not all in effect own as much, who will not allow the Scripture any meaning, how plain soever, but what is agreeable to their Reason? which shews, that in their opinion, Reason was rather given to supply the defects of Revelation, than Revelation the defects of Reason. Is there a Divine, who, tho' he pretends ever so high a veneration for the Scripture, but will own there are many places, where 'tis necessary to recede from the letter, and find out a sense agreeable to his Reason; which supposes it is that, & not the authority of the Book (for that's the same in both cases) which makes him approve the literal sense in one case, & condemn it in another. And were Men not govern'd by their Reason, but by some external Revelation, they had nothing more to do, but to take the words of that Revelation, in its literal, obvious, & plain meaning,

how

* *Deut.* 13. 1. 3.     † *Mat.* 24. 24.

how abfurd foever it might appear to their carnal Reafon.

B. We may take the words of fallible Men in the plain, literal fenfe; but if any thing is faid by infallible Men, which in the obvious meaning of the words is inconfiftent with Reafon, we muft have recourfe to an allegorical fenfe; or if that will not do, we muft put no meaning at all on the words; thus we fupport the dignity of both Revelation & Reafon.

A. Is not this owning you take not your Religion from thofe infallible Men, but you endeavour to impofe that Religion your Reafon tells you is true, upon their words, by allowing them no other meaning, how plain foever, but what you antecedently know by the Light of Nature to be the Will of God.

There's no Book, but you may own its infallibility, and yet be entirely govern'd by your Reafon, if you, as often as you find any thing not agreeable to your Reafon, torture it, to make it fpeak what is fo. Would you think a *Mahometan* was govern'd by his *Alchoran*, who, upon all occafions fhould thus depart from the literal fenfe; nay, would you not tell him, that his infpir'd Book fell infinitely fhort of *Cicero's* uninfpir'd writings, where there is no fuch occafion to recede from the letter?

The *Moammarites*, a famous Sect among the *Mahometans*, and the *Myfticks*, very numerous in *Turky*, fenfible of the difficulties & uncertainties that attend all traditional Facts, maintain, * ,, That God can ,, never difcover himfelf with certainty any other way, ,, than by fpeaking to the Reafon and Underftanding ,, of Men: For if we depend, fay they, on oral Tradition, ,, dition, we lay ourfelves open to the greateft falfi- ,, ties & impofitions; there being nothing fo liable to ,, infinite changes & alterations, numberlefs miftakes, ,, additions & fubftractions, according as Mens opi-

M 3 nions

* *Mahom.* Life in Eng. before *Reland's Mahom.* pag. 39, 40.

„ nions vary by the change of times & circumstances.
„ Nor are Books more exempt from such doubt-
„ fulness & uncertainty; since we find so much dis-
„ agreement among Books wrote by different Men,
„ in different parts & different ages ; & even among
„ the different Books of the same Men. But suppose,
„ continue they, we should resolve all our Faith into
„ the sole text of the *Alchoran*, the difficulty & un-
„ certainty will still remain ; if we consider, how
„ many *Metaphors*, *Allegories*, and other *Figures* of
„ speech ; how many obscure, ambiguous, intricate
„ and mysterious *passages* are to be met with in this
„ infallible Book ; & how different are the opinions,
„ expositions and interpretations of the most subtle
„ Doctors, and learned Commentators on every one
„ of them.   The only sure way, then, add they, to
„ come to the certain knowledge of the truth, is to
„ consult God himself, wait his inspirations, live just
„ & honest lives, be kind and beneficent to all our
„ Fellow-creatures, & pity such as differ from us in
„ their opinions about the authority, integrity, and
„ meaning of the *Alchoran*.

T H E *Mahometans*, tho they own the Law of Christ,
yet they make it of no use, because they suppose,
the Law of *Mahomet* is more perfect, and tis that
they must stick to : And do not some Men, by arguing
much after the same manner in relation to the Gospel,
render the Law of Nature useless ? But if we are still
moral agents, and as such are capable of judging between Religion & Superstition, can we think otherwise of the Gospel, than that it is design'd, not to
free us from the eternal Law of Nature, but from
those absurdities, which the folly or knavery of Men
have introduc'd in opposition to it ? Hence it is, that
the Scripture speaks in general terms, without de-
fining those things which it commands, or forbids;
because it supposes Men moral agents, capable by their
Reason to discern Good from Evil, Virtue from Vice,
Religion from Superstition.                                    I v

IF Mr. *Lock* reasons justly, * ,, No Mission can be
,, look'd on to be divine, that delivers any thing de-
,, rogating from the honour of the once, only, true,
,, invisible God, or inconsistent with Natural Reli-
,, gion & the Rules of Morality: Because God having
,, discover'd to Men the unity and majesty of his
,, eternal Godhead, & the truths of Natural Religion
,, & Morality by the light of Reason, he cannot be
,, suppos'd to back the contrary by Revelation; for
,, that would be to destroy the evidence and use of
,, Reason, without which, Men cannot be able to
,, distinguish divine Revelation from diabolical Im-
,, posture.

DOES not this suppose, *First*, that no Mission can
be divine, or its Revelation true, that admits of more
than one, only, true, invisible God? *Secondly*, That
Men, by their Reason, must know, wherein the honour
of this one, only, true, invisible God consists; otherwise, they might (for ought they know) be oblig'd
by Revelation to admit what is derogatory to his
honour? *Thirdly*, They must know by the light of
Reason, what are the truths of Natural Religion &
rules of Morality; because otherwise they might be
oblig'd to admit things inconsistent with them: And
that to suppose the contrary, wou'd be to destroy the
use & evidence of Reason, without which, Men would
not be able to distinguish divine Revelation from diabolical Imposture; which implies, that in things tending
to the honour of God, and the good of Mankind,
the *dernier* resort is to Reason; whose dictates, as they
need no miracles for their support, so all doctrines
inconsistent with them, tho' they plead endless miracles, must be look'd upon as diabolical Impostures.
And

WHEN the Apostle says, † *Whatsoever things are
true, whatsoever things are honest, whatsoever things are
just, whatsoever things are pure, whatsoever things are
lovely,*

M 4

* *Posthumous Works, pag. 226.*    † *Phil. 4. 8.*

*lovely, whatsoever things are of good report, if there be any virtue, if there be any praise, think on these things;* is not this referring us to the Light of Nature, to know what these things are, which shew themselves to be the will of God by their natural excellency?

*B.* OUR Divines, tho' they own Reason may do tolerably well in things between Man & Man, yet in matters relating to God, Reason, *they say,* must submit to Faith; and that the chief end of Revelation is to give Men, especially the common People, just conceptions, & right notions of the nature & perfections of God; which they cou'd never have from the dim Light of Nature, without the help of Revelation.

*A.* THO' they argue thus, yet at the same time they find themselves oblig'd to own, that the Scripture, when taken literally, gives the vulgar false and unworthy notions of the divine Nature, by imputing almost every where to God, not only human parts, but human weakness & imperfections, and even the worst of human passions. To this, indeed, they have two answers, which seem inconsistent: First, That 'tis necessary to accommodate things in some measure to the gross conceptions of the Vulgar. The other is, that Reason has given all Men such just conceptions of the divine Nature, that there's no danger that even the common People shou'd take these expressions literally.

*B.* THO' Reason, on which you lay such stress, may demonstrate, that there are not more Gods than one, yet Reason can never tell us, that there's more than one that is God: tho' Reason tells us, that there are not three Gods, yet Reason cou'd never tell us, that, tho' in the idea of a divine person the idea of God be included, each Person being by himself God, yet that the multiplying of divine Persons, was not the multiplying of Gods: And tho' Reason declares, there's a difference between three & one, yet Reason will never discover, that there's no more in three

Persons,

Perfons, than in one, all three together being the fame numerical God, as each is by himfelf. Reafon will never be able to find out a middle between a numerical, and a fpecifick unity, between one in number, and one in kind; and yet without it, how can we fuppofe the fame God to be felf-exiftent, & not felf exiftent, &c. Reafon can as little difcover a *medium* between a nominal, and a real difference; and yet without it how can we avoid *Sabellianifm* on the one hand, or *Polytheifm* on the other? There's nothing Reafon can tell us more plainly, than that God & a Man are two diftinct, intelligent perfons; but can Reafon tell us they may become one intelligent perfon, even while their perfonal natures and properties remain infinitely diftinct and different? Thus you fee, how Reafon muft fubmit to Faith.

*A.* I, for my part, not underftanding thefe orthodox paradoxes, can only at prefent fay, I do not disbelieve them, but muft add, that as I am a rational Creature, & God requires of me a *reafonable fervice*, I ought not, nay, I cannot have any faith, which will not bear the teft of Reafon; and therefore, notwithftanding your maxim of Reafon's fubmitting to Faith, I will venture to affirm, if a Book affert (fuppofing the words of it are taken in their plain, literal fenfe) immoral, or impious doctrines, and there are not in that Book certain marks to tell us, where they are to be taken literally, & where figuratively, or, what is the figurative fenfe, that Men in thefe points are as much to be determin'd by their Reafon, as if there was no fuch book.

*B.* This, fure, can't be the cafe with relation to the Scriptures.

*A.* I fhall only tell you what the moft celebrated Fathers fay on this head. *Athanafius* fays, * „ Should „ we underftand a great part of the facred Writ li„ terally, we fhould fall into moft enormous blafphe-

M 5                                                          mies.

* *Quæftiones ad Antiochum. To.* 2. *pag.* 357. D.

mies. St. *Cyril* fays \* much the fame. St. *Gregory*
the firft fays, † ,, The Scripture is not on!y dead,
,, but deadly ; for it is written, *The letter kills, but the*
,, *fpirit quickneth*; and this is what the whole divine
,, letter does. ,, And in another place ‡ he compares
them to beafts who regard the letter. And St. *Jerom*
fays, § ,, If we adhere to the flefh of the letter, it
,, will be the occafion of many evils. ,, And *Gregory*
*Nyffen* ¶ makes the like reflection.

*B.* I durft not have made fo bold with the Scriptures , as thefe Fathers ; but content myfelf with
faying with the excellent Bifhop of *Litchfield*, ✠ that
,, God, was he to fpeak with Men, muft not only
,, fpeak their very language , but according to the
,, conceptions of thofe, he fpeaks to : To rectify their
,, fentiments in *natural* , *hiftorical* , or *chronological*
,, matters, to mend their *Logick* , or *Rhetorick* when
,, 'tis defective, but has no ill influence on piety, is
,, not the bufinefs of Revelation. -- Needlefly to
,, contradict innocent vulgar notions, is the furc way
,, to lofe the peoples affections, and to forego a
,, prudential way of gaining them.

*A.* With fubmiffion to this learned Author, is
there no difference between God's not rectifying Mens
fentiments in thofe matters, and ufing himfelf fuch
fentiments as need to be rectify'd ? or between God's
not mending Mens *Logick*, or *Rhetorick*, where 'tis defective, & ufing fuch himfelf ? or between God's not
contradicting vulgar notions, and confirming them,
by fpeaking according to them ? Or can the God of
Truth, ftand in need of Error to fupport his Truth,
his eternal Truth ? Or can infinite Wifdom defpair of
gaining, or keeping Peoples affections, without having
re-

---

\* *Lib.* 9. *contr. Julian, p.* 303, 304. *to.* 6. *Oper.*
† *Comm. on* 2 *Kings c.* 7.    ‡ *Prolog. in Cant. Cantie.*
*fol.* 256. *col.* 1. *B.*    § *In Gal. c.* 5. *p.* 84. *B.*
¶ *De vita Moyfis, To.* 1. *p.* 235. *D. & d.*
✠ *Defence of Chriftian. p.* 363.

recourse to such mean arts? No wonder, if Men use pious frauds, when they think God himself has recourse to them. In this case, must not Men by their Reason judge, when God makes use of defective *Logick*, or *Rhetorick*, and speaks in *Natural*, *Historical*, & *Chronological* matters, not according to the truth of things, but according to the conceptions of those of the vulgar, to whom he directs his speech? Nor can I think of any falsehood, suppos'd to be authoris'd by the God of truth, but may be made use of to some ill purpose: in *Divinity* as well as *Mathematicks* it's a certain Maxim, *Uno absurdo dato mille sequentur*.

St. *Austin* argues after another manner, in saying, *
,, Should Unbelievers know us to be mistaken in such
,, things as concern the natural world, & alledge our
,, Books for such vain opinions, how shall they be-
,, lieve the same Books, when they speak of the re-
,, surrection of the dead, & the world to come?

D r. *Prideaux*, speaking of the marks of imposture,
says, † ,, If there be but one known truth in the whole
,, scheme of Nature with which it interferes, this must
,, make the discovery; & there's no Man, that forgeth
,, an *imposture*, but makes himself liable to be this
,, way convicted of it. ,, The Doctor, sure, wou'd
not have asserted this so roundly, had he not compar'd
the philosophical, & scriptural scheme of Nature, and
perceiv'd their exact agreement. But,

N o t only Dr. *Burnet* in defence of his *Archæologia*,
but all, who maintain, that the Sun is immovable,
& that 'tis the Earth which moves, sufficiently shew,
that the scriptural & philosophical account of natural
things seldom agree: However, to give one instance,
there's scarce a Country-man so ignorant, as not to
know, that if the seed thrown into the earth is kill'd
by drought, or dies by any other accident, it never
rises;

* *Gen. ad Lit. l. 1. c. 19.*
† *Letter to the Deists. p. 139. Edit. 7. 8vo.*

rifes; but St. *Paul* (without regard to that judgment, which our Saviour denounces againſt a Man who calls his Brother *Fool*; ) ſays, * *Thou Fool, that which thou ſoweſt is not quickned, except it die:* And our Saviour himſelf ſays, † *Verily, verily, I ſay unto you, except a corn of wheat fall into the ground, & die, it abideth alone; but if it die, it bringeth forth much fruit.* And the *Greek* Church, at this day, make uſe of boil'd corn at their commemoration of the dead, to ſignify the *Reſurrection of the body.* ‡

To convince you how entirely we are to depend on Reaſon in matters of Religion, I will only ask you, Why you ſuppoſe it ſo abſurd in the *Papiſts* to ſay, that Men bred up in their Church, are oblig'd intirely to depend on its infallibility; & that they, who have not had the happineſs to be thus educated, ought, indeed, to uſe their Reaſon to bring them into their Church; but that then they are no longer to be govern'd by it, but with the reſt of the members, equally to rely on the Church's infallible deciſions.

*B.* Because this ſuppoſ'd Infallibility puts it in the power of that Church, to make their Votaries believe Vertue to be Vice, and Vice, Virtue, or any other abſurdity whatever; ſince they have no way to know, whether it does not require ſuch things, but by examining, by their Reaſon, all her doctrines; & if Reaſon be ſufficient to diſcover the Being and Will of God, and that their Church holds no doctrines diſagreeable to his Will, (for this they muſt own Reaſon capable of diſcovering, before it could bring Men into their Church) they, in ſpight of their pretences to infallibility, put the whole ſtreſs on Reaſon. And if afterwards, they teach Men to renounce that Reaſon, by which before they would have them wholly govern'd, it can be for no other cauſe, but to prevent their diſcovering in that Church ſuch errors, as they

cou'd

* 1 *Cor.* 15. 36.          † *John* 12. 24.
‡ The Works of *Gregory* of *Chriſt Church*, p. 141.

cou'd not well know before; and which, if known, wou'd have hinder'd them from coming into it.

*A.* THE *Papiſts*, you know, reply, that if this reaſoning is good, it ſtrikes at all implicit faith in St. *Peter*, as well as his ſucceſſors, & equally concludes againſt Mens giving up their Reaſon to any perſons in former ages, as well as the preſent; ſince 'tis by that alone they are able to judge, whether their doctrines are conſiſtent with the light of Nature, & free from ſuperſtition, and contain nothing in them unworthy of a divine original: Before examining what Men teach, there's no reaſon to have an implicit faith in one ſet of Men more than another; and examination deſtroys all implicit faith, & all authority whatever; ſince if they then embrace the opinions of others, whether Apoſtles or not, 'tis becauſe they appear agreeable to their Reaſon.  If you ſay, the Apoſtles wou'd by Reaſon bring Men into their Religion, & after that, have them wholly govern'd by their authority, may not the *Papiſts* retort on you your own anſwer? and cry, ,, That if Reaſon is ſufficient to dif-
,, cover the Being & Will of God, & that the Apoſtles
,, taught no doctrines, but what are agreeable to his
,, Will; (for this, *ſay they*, you muſt allow Reaſon
,, capable of diſcovering, otherwiſe it cou'd never
,, lead Men to believe what the Apoſtles taught;)
,, You alike put the wole ſtreſs on Reaſon: And you
,, muſt own, either that Men are intirely to be go-
,, vern'd by Reaſon, & then you deſtroy all authority
,, whatever; or elſe not to be govern'd by it, & then
,, you can't, by Reaſon, ſhew the abſurdity of that
,, implicit faith, the Catholick Church requires.

*B.* YOU know, that in anſwer to all objections of this nature, we ſay as Biſhop *Burnet* does, in his expoſition of the *Articles* of our Church, * ,, That if
,, we obſerve the ſtyle & method of the Scriptures,
,, we ſhall find in them all over a conſtant appeal to
Mens

* *Expoſ. of the* 19*th Article, pag.* 183.

„ Mens Reafon, and to their intellectual faculties.
„ If the meer dictates of the Church, or of *infallible*
„ *Men*, had been the refolution & foundation of Faith,
„ there had been no need of fuch a long thread of
„ reafoning and difcourfe, as both our Saviour us'd
„ when on Earth, & the Apoftles us'd in their Wri-
„ tings. We fee the way of authority is not taken,
„ but explanations are offer'd, proofs, & illuftrations
„ are brought, to convince the mind; which fhews
„ that God, in the cleareft manifeftation of his will,
„ wou'd deal with us as with rational Creatures,
„ who are not to believe, but on perfuafion; and to
„ ufe our Reafon, in order to the attaining that per-
„ fuafion.

*A.* THIS is all I contend for; & had not what the
Bifhop fays, (tho' it amounts to giving up all implicit faith) been agreeable to the whole tenor of the
Scriptures, and the doctrines of our Church, fome of
thofe, who have fo nicely examin'd into all parts of
his *Expofition* of the Articles, wou'd never have let
this paffage efcape without remarks. And, therefore,
fince 'tis in defence of the *Proteftant Religion*, & the
whole current of Scripture, I fhall add, to what this
excellent Father of the Church has faid; that when
any perfon has recourfe to arguments and reafonings,
he does, in thofe inftances, difclaim all authority, and
appeals to the Reafon of thofe he means to perfuade,
&, in order to it, wou'd have them judge of the force
of his arguments, by thofe common, & felf-evident
notions, upon which the validity of all proofs depend;
and Men, in examining what he fays by that Reafon
to which he appeals, wholly anfwer the end for which
he argues with them, tho', upon examination, they
are not convinc'd by his reafons. To require more,
wou'd be to require impoffibilities; fince 'tis not in
Mens power, after they'have confider'd things as well
as they are able, to believe otherwife than they do.
And had the Apoftles faid to thofe they defign'd to
con-

convert; „ It will be an affront to our infallibility,
„ not to have an implicit faith in us, not to take on
„ content whatever we fay; You are, therefore, no
„ longer to act as moral agents, or to have recourfe
„ to the effential difference of Good & Evil; to the
„ Light & Law of Nature, or to the eternal Reafon
„ of things, to judge of the truth of what we declare.
„ No, this is the Faith, and thus you muft believe,
„ or perifh everlaftingly. „ Had the Apoftles, I fay,
talk'd after this manner, do you think they could
have gain'd one reafonable Convert? No, they knew
full well, that this was not the way to deal with rational Creatures; they, on the contrary, as I fhall
fully fhew hereafter, every where fpeak to this effect,
„ * We defire you would, with the utmoft freedom,
„ examine our doctrines; fince if they are, as we
„ affirm, true, they will not only bear the teft of Reafon,
„ but the more they are try'd, the brighter they will
„ appear: † This will be *enobling* yourfelves, & doing
„ juftice to your own underftanding, as well as to
„ our doctrines. „ If Men have any authority, 'tis
then only, when they renounce all peremptory authority; & inftead of claiming *dominion over Mens Faith,*
defire they would prove every thing by thofe tefts
God had given them, in order to difcern Good from
Evil, Truth from Falfehood, Religion from Superftition; thus the Apoftle feeks to maintain his credit &
Authority with the *Theffalonians; Prove all things,*
fays he, *hold faft that which is good.*

*B.* Do not you, by laying fuch a ftrefs on Reafon,
in effect, fet afide Revelation?

*A.* No, if Revelation be a reafonable Revelation,
the greater ftrefs we lay upon Reafon, the more we
eftablifh Revelation.

*B.* But not on the foot of its own authority,
but only as you judge it agreeable to Reafon; and
therefore I queftion, whether any of our eminent Divines

* 1 Thef. 5. 21.     † Acts 17. 11.

vines talk thus in commendation of Reason, to the
disparagement of Authority.

*A.* IF Reason is all we rational Creatures have to
trust to, being that alone which distinguishes us from
Brutes, incapable of Religion, Divines, even those of
the most narrow principles, however they may shufflie
a while, must make Reason their *dernier* resort; but
however, since Reason alone will not satisfy you,
but you must have authority even against authority,
I shall mention what some of our most eminent Divines say, when they are defending Revelation against
the attacks of *Infidels*; or writing against the *Papists*,
or Men *popishly* affected.

DR. *J. Clarke*, Dean of *Sarum*, in defending Christianity against the attacks of *Infidels*, who charge it
with requiring an implicit faith, thinks this such a
scandal to Christianity, that a good part of his *Boylean*
Lectures are to clear it from that charge; ,, We find,
*says he,* * ,, no Command in Scripture to lay aside
,, our Reason or Understanding, but directly the con-
,, trary is there affirmed of the Christian Religion, *viz.*
,, that it is our *reasonable* service: † And therefore
,, the method in which Christ and his Apostles taught
,, *this service,* was agreeable to Reason, *viz.* by ex-
,, horting Men to *attend seriously,* to *weigh diligently,* ‡
,, their doctrines and precepts, *&c. and then asks.*
,, § Are these, & such like expressions calculated to
,, enslave Mens understandings, & to induce a blind
,, and implicit obedience? Such methods may serve
,, the purpose of Superstition, but true Religion can
,, gain nothing by them.

DR. *Whitchcot* does this justice to external Revelation, as to say, ¶ ,, The Scripture's way of dealing
,, with Men in matters of Religion, is always by evi-
,, dence of Reason & argument; *&very judiciously adds,*
,, I reckon, that which has not Reason in it, or for it,
is

* *Orig. of Moral Evil, p. 88.* † *Rom. 12. 1.* ‡ *Mat. 11. 15.*
§ *Orig. of Moral Evil, p: 89.* ¶ *Vol. of Serm. p. 117.*

,, is Man's Superstition, and not Religion of God's ,, making :,, What an infinity of disputes would this rule have cut off. What I pray, was the grand occasion of so many monstrous *Heresies*, even in the primitive times, but their believing the Scripture's way of dealing with Men was not by evidence of Reason. And if any now think otherwise, are they not in danger of making no better distinction between Religion & Superstition, than a modern Philosopher, who thus concisely distinguishes them; * *Tales publickly allow'd, Religion; not allow'd, Superstition.*

Bp. *Hoadly*, the strenuous assertor of our religious, as well as civil Rights, *says*, † ,, Authority is the ,, greatest & most irreconcilable enemy to *Truth* & ,, *Argument*, that this world ever furnish'd out.   All ,, the *sophistry*, all the *colour* of *plausibility*, all the ,, *artifice* & *cunning* of the subtilest *disputers* in the world, ,, may be laid open, and turn'd to the advantage of ,, that very truth, which they design'd to hide, or to ,, depress; But against *Authority* there is no defence. And after having shewn, that it was *Authority* that crush'd the noble sentiments of *Socrates* and others; & that it was by *Authority*, that the *Jews* & *Heathens* combated the truth of the Gospel; he says, ,, When ,, *Christians* were increas'd to a *majority*, & came to ,, think the same method to be the only proper one, ,, for the advantage of *their* cause, which had been ,, the enemy and destroyer of it; *then*, it was the ,, *Authority* of *Christians*, which, by degrees, not only ,, laid waste the honour of *Christianity*, but well nigh ,, extinguish'd it among Men. -- It was *Authority*, ,, which wou'd have prevented all *Reformation*, where ,, it is; & which has put a *barrier* against it, wherever ,, it is not. -- How indeed, can it be expected, that ,, the *same thing*, which has in all ages, and in all ,, countries, been hurtful to *truth*, and *true Religion*,

N

amongst

* Hobbes.    † Answ. to the *Represen. of the Comitt. of the lower-House of Convoc.* p. 312, 313, 314, 315.

,, amongſt Men, ſhou'd in *any* age, or *any* country,
,, become a friend & guardian of them. ,,  And to
obviate an objection eaſily foreſeen, he ſays, ,, It was
,, *Authority*, which hinder'd the voice of the *Son* of
,, *God* himſelf from being heard; and which alone
,, ſtood in oppoſition to *his* powerful *arguments*, and
,, his divine *doctrine*. ,,  Which ſuppoſes there's no
Chriſtian doctrine, but what has powerful arguments
to ſupport it; or in other words, has divinity ſtamp'd
on it, ſhewing itſelf by its innate excellency to be the
will of God : ſince to put its credit on meer Authority, is to put its credit on that, which has been, and
always will be, an enemy to truth.  Nay, he ſuppoſes,
that were it poſſible, that Authority & Truth cou d
conſiſt together, & the latter be receiv'd for the ſake
of the former, it cou'd not avail.  His words are,
,, Where *Truth* ſhappens to be receiv'd for the ſake
,, of Authority, there is juſt ſo much diminiſh'd from
,, the love of Truth, & the glory of Reaſon, & the
,, acceptableneſs of Men to God, as there is attri-
,, buted to *Authority*. ,,   And,

  Archbishop *Tillotſon* ſays, * ,, All our reaſonings
,, about divine Revelation are neceſſarily gather'd by
,, our natural notions about Religion; & therefore,
,, he, who ſincerely deſires to do the Will of God,
,, is not apt to be impos'd on by vain, and confident
,, pretences of divine Revelation, but if any Doctrine
,, be propos'd to him, which is pretended to come
,, from God, he meaſures it by thoſe ſure, & ſteady
,, notions, which he has of the divine Nature and
,, Perfections, and by theſe he will eaſily diſcern,
,, whether it be worthy of God or not, & likely to
,, proceed from him : He will conſider the nature &
,, tendency of it, or whether it be a Doctrine ac-
,, cording to godlineſs, ſuch as is agreeable to the
,, divine Nature & Perfections, and tends to make us
,, like unto God: if it be not, tho' an Angel ſhould
                                                    bring

* *Serm. Vol.* 3. *pag.* 40.

,, bring it, he would not receive it. ,, And if no miracles, no, not the preaching of an Angel, ought to make us receive any Doctrine that does not carry those internal marks; no miracles, certainly, ought to make us reject any Doctrine that has these internal marks. And much to the same purpose, our judicious Doctor *Claget* says, * ,, When Men pretend to work
,, Miracles, and talk of immediate Revelations, of
,, knowing the truth by inspiration, & of more than
,, ordinary illumination, we ought not to be frighted
,, with those big words, from looking what is und r
,, them, nor to be afraid of calling these things in'o
,, question, which are set off with *high-flown* pretences.
,, From hence it has come to pass, that Superstition
,, and Idolatry, Enthusiasms and Impostures have so
,, much prevail'd in the world. It is somewhat strange,
,, that we should believe Men the more, for that very
,, reason upon which we should believe them the
,, less. ,

I shall give you the Sentiments of one judicious Divine more, since they contain a summary of what I have been saying; his words are, † ,, It could not
,, be avoidable, but that this natural reverence for
,, divine Revelations, & proneness of believing them,
,, would produce some ill effects, prejudicial to the
,, Reason and interest of Mankind, a fatal credulity
,, would creep into the world, & possess the minds
,, of the more ignorant persons, and induce them
,, blindly to believe every bold pretender to Revela-
,, tion. After a laborious & fruitless search of future
,, happiness, Men were apt to embrace any System
,, of Religion presented to them; if it flatter'd their
,, hopes of future felicity, they were loth to discover
,, the error and illusion of any pleasing revelation;
,, they wish'd it might be true, & what at first, they

N 2  wish'd,

* *Claget's* Persuasive to an ingen. Trial of Opin. p. 19.
† Enthusiasm of the Ch. of *Rome.* p. 234. suppos'd to be *Stillingfleet's.*

„ wish'd, they at last believ'd to be true. -- Many
„ fear'd they should be injurious to the divine Majesty,
„ & incur the guilt of *Atheism*, if they should scru-
„ pulously examine what pretended to carry the stamp
„ of his authority, & to have been reveal'd by him.
„ To entertain scruples in this case, was thought no
„ less than sacrilege, & every doubt was esteem'd an
„ affront to God: to which may be added, that they
„ should contract no small merit, & ever lay an obli-
„ gation on God, if they immediately resign'd up
„ their judgment to his suppos'd Revelation, & blindly
„ receiv'd it without any doubt or hesitation.

„ T h i s in all Ages, open'd a wide gap, & prepar'd
„ a way for error & Superstition; while the whimsies
„ of every foolish *Enthusiast*, & the follies of every
„ bold *Impostor* were propos'd under the venerable
„ name of *divine Oracles.* -- Hence all the absurdities
„ of the *Pagan* Religion found belief, and entertain-
„ ment in the world, and the most extravagant *im-*
„ *postors* never wanted *Proselytes.* Hence the most
„ pernicious errors of *Heretcks,* found admission into
„ the Church, and the pretence of new Revelations,
„ seduc'd some part of the *Christian* world.

„ T o this fatal credulity, and danger of illusion
„ arising from it, God & Nature have prescrib'd an
„ excellent remedy; the use of our Reason, which
„ may examine the grounds and testimonies of all
„ pretended Revelations, enquire into their truth,
„ and after a scrupulous trial, pass sentence on them.
„ This, the interest of Truth, & the honour of our
„ Nature requires us to perform, that we may neither
„ prostitute the former, nor depreciate the latter. --
„ Without this precedent enquiry, our belief would
„ become unlawful; for to obviate the rules of con-
„ duct, prescrib'd to our understanding, were to over-
„ throw all the Laws of Nature, to debase the dignity
„ of Mankind, and to efface the image of God im-
„ planted in us. Those Rules assure us, that God

can't

„ can't command any thing foolifh or ridiculous. --
„ No greater injury can be offer'd to the Deity,
„ than to believe him the author of any Religion,
„ which prefcribes, or encourages foolifh, or fuper-
„ ftitious practice. -- Juftly does *Plutarch* wonder,
„ why *Atheifm* fhould rather be accus'd of impiety,
„ than Superftition, fince few are mov'd by any de-
„ fect in the order of government, to call in queftion
„ the Exiftence of God, but the tricks & cheats of
„ fuperftitious perfons, their *Enthufiaftick* motions,
„ ridiculous actions, exorcifms, & luftrations, & fuch
„ like, give them occafion to believe it better there
„ fhould be no God, than fuch a God, as the Author
„ of fuch a fuperftitious Religion muft neceffarily be.

I f this Author reafons juftly, as all *Proteftants* will
allow, at leaft when they write againft the *enthufiafm*
of the Church of *Rome*, does it not follow, that 'tis
our duty, before we embrace any inftituted Religion,
to examine by that Light which God has given us,
into every part of it, & after a fcrupulous trial, pafs
fentence on it? If the intereft of Truth, & the honour
of Man's Nature require them to perform this grand
duty, muft not their Reafon, antecedently to all external Revelation, afford certain tefts to diftinguifh
between truth and falfehood in all religious matters?
'Twould be ridiculous to tell Men, that 'tis a crime
worfe than *Atheifm*, to admit a Religion, which prefcribes, or encourages foolifh or fuperftitious practices,
unlefs upon a fuppofition, that their Reafon can tell
them what are fuch practices, & thereby hinder them
from embracing a Religion, which requires things of
this nature. And if Men are apt to embrace any
Religion (the *Mahometan* for inftance) which flatters
their hopes of future felicity, & makes them loth to
difcover the pleafing illufion, does it not follow, that
the more any Religion does fo, the more caufe Men
have critically to examine into its reafonablenefs?
Becaufe without fuch a precedent enquiry, their belief

would

would be irrational & unlawful, debasing the dignity of Mankind, & effacing the Image of God implanted in them.  And,

IF the abfurdities, not only of the *Pagan* Religion, but even the moft pernicious errors among *Chriftians*, have been occafion'd thro' want of previous examination, nothing can be requifite to difcover true Chriftianity, and to preferve it in its native purity, free from all Superftition, but, after a ftrict fcrutiny, to admit nothing to belong to it, except what our Reafon tells us is worthy of having God for its Author. And if it be evident, that we can't difcern whether any inftituted Religion contains every thing worthy, and nothing unworthy of a divine original, except we can antecedently by our Reafon difcern what is, or is not worthy of having God for its Author, it necef-farily follows, that natural & reveal'd Religion can't differ; Becaufe whatever Reafon fhews to be worthy of having God for its Author, muft belong to Natural Religion; and whatever Reafon tells us is unworthy of having God for its Author, can never belong to the true Reveal'd Religion.  Tis upon this very plan, that I have endeavour'd to fhew you wherein true & genuine Chriftianity confifts.

*B.* BY the reafoning of thefe Divines, Religion is the plaineft thing in the world: We, it feems, have nothing to do, but to examine what notions are worthy of God, in order to know his will: but do they tell us, how we may certainly know what thofe notions are?

*A.* ALL Divines of what denomination foever agree, at leaft in words, that God can't act arbitrarily in the government of the world, or command things for commanding-fake; but that all his Laws, being calculated for the good of Mankind, carry with them the marks of confummate Wifdom and Goodnefs. However, I fhall mention two.

THE

The incomparable Archbishop *Tillotson* says, *
,, It wou'd be little lefs than an horrid and dreadful
,, blafphemy, to fay, that God, out of his fovereign
,, will & pleafure, can do any thing which contra-
,, dicts the nature of God, or the effential perfections
,, of the Deity; or to imagine that the pleafure and
,, will of the holy, juft, & good God, is not always
,, regulated, and determin'd by the effential and in-
,, difpenfable Laws of Goodnefs, Holinefs and Righ-
,, teoufnefs.

The judicious Dr. *Scot* affirms, † ,, That to fup-
,, pofe the will and power of God is not perfectly
,, fubject to his moral perfections, is to fuppofe him
,, a very defective & imperfect Being; a lawlefs will
,, & power being the greateft defect in Nature; where-
,, fore to fecure our minds againft all injurious appre-
,, henfions of God, this is a moft neceffary rule, that
,, we conceive him to be fuch a Being as can never
,, will, nor act any thing, but what his own effential
,, Wifdom, Goodnefs and Juftice do approve. - -
,, To affirm, he is not oblig'd to regulate himfelf by
,, Wifdom, Juftice & Goodnefs, or that he can do
,, otherwife, is to attribute to him a power to will,
,, or act foolifhly, &c.

B. I fhou'd readily approve what the Authors you
quote have faid, to fhew the reafonablenefs of the
divine Law in every inftance, were there not in
Religion, propofitions to be believ'd, which are above
Reafon.

A. If I do not underftand the terms of a propofition, or if they are inconfiftent with one another,
or fo uncertain, that I know not what meaning to
fix on them, here is nothing told me, & confequently
no room for belief: But in all cafes, where I am capable of underftanding a propofition, 'tis Reafon muft
inform me, whether 'tis certain, probable, or uncertain; & even in propofitions relating to fuch facts

N 4 as

* *Vol.* 6. *p.* 216.  † *Chrift. Life, Part.* I. *Vol.* I. *p.* 362.

as we learn from report, 'tis by our Reason alone, in comparing circumstances, &c. that we must judge of their probability.  But,

ALTHO' designing Men very well know, that it's impossible to believe, when we know not what it is we are to believe; or to believe an absurd, or contradictory proposition; yet they, because without examination, people may be brought to fancy they believe such things, and it being their interest to confound Mens understandings, and prevent all inquiry, craftily invented the notion of believing things above Reason: Here the ravings of an *Enthusiast* are on a level with the dictates of infinite Wisdom, & nonsence is render'd most sacred; here a contradiction is of great use to maintain a doctrine, that, when fairly stated, is not defensible; because by talking backward & forward, by using obscure terms, & taking words in different senses, they may easily amuse, & puzzle the People.  On this foundation *Transubstantiation* is built, & most of those mysterious propofitions, about which in former days Christians so frequently murder'd each other.  But,

IF the Scripture was defign'd to be understood, it must be within the reach of human understanding; and consequently, it can't contain propositions that are either above, or below human understanding; and if there are no propositions in the Bible, but what have certain ideas, by common usage annex'd to the words, how can we suppose some are defign'd to be understood, & some not? or know which are, and which are not? And indeed, if the end of God's giving a Revelation was to direct Mens thoughts and actions, it must (as necessary to that end) be deliver'd in such a way, as is plain & easy to be understood, even by mean capacities; and consequently, to suppose it dark and mysterious in any part, is to represent it as unworthy of having God for its Author. And,

ONE,

ONE wou'd think, that Men, when they knew they had truth on their side, wou'd speak after the plaineſt manner, and not ſtudy to diſguiſe it by unnatural ways of expreſſing themſelves; eſpecially, when they reflect on others for ſo doing.

THE *Chriſtians* ſaid, the *Heathens* were conſcious their Religion was abſurd, by their having recourſe to allegorical, ænigmatical, and myſterious explications; and conſequently, that it cou'd not be deſign'd for the common people, incapable of ſuch explications; and that their Prieſts, inſtead of defending it, render'd it uncertain; ſince where the literal ſenſe is quitted, there may be many allegorical, or ſpiritual ſenſes, oppoſite to one another; and indeed, the wiſe Men among them, as *Tully,* &c. own'd as much.

NOR did the *Heathens* fail to retort the like objection upon the *Chriſtians*; &, in truth, they equall'd, if not out-did them in allegoriſing away, not only the plaineſt texts, but even matter of fact; which prov'd the occaſion of innumerable Hereſies.

*Du Pin,* ſpeaking of the extravagant opinions, which obtain'd among ſilly people in the primitive times; ſays, * ,, That they ſprang from the principles of the ,, *Pagan* Philoſophers, and from the myſteries, which ,, crack-brain'd Men put on the Hiſtory of the Old ,, and New Teſtament, according to their imagina- ,, tions; the more extraordinary theſe opinions were, ,, the more did they reliſh, and the better did they ,, like them; and thoſe who invented them, publiſh'd ,, them gravely as great Myſteries to the ſimple, who ,, were all diſpos'd to receive them. ,, But cou'd any crack-brain'd Writers have found out more Myſteries in the Old and New Teſtament, than the primitive Fathers; (who interpreted them according to their imaginations, and jumbl'd them together with that

Pagan

---

* *Short Hiſt. of the Church Vol.* 2. *c.* 4.

Pagan Philofophy they were educated in?) Or have publifh'd their myfterious reveries with greater gravity, to fimple people, always difpos'd to receive what they do not underftand?

T H E fame Author, fpeaking of St. *Barnabas*'s Catholick Epiftle in anfwer to this objection, ,, That it ,, was incredible fo great an Apoftle, full of the Holy ,, Ghoft, & Colleague of St. *Paul*, fhou'd be the Author ,, of fuch forc'd Allegories, and extravagant Explica- ,, tions of Scripture ; of thofe various fables con- ,, cerning animals, with divers other conceits of the ,, like nature ; *fays*, * ,, They have but little know- ,, ledge of the *Jewifh* Nation, and of the primitive ,, Chriftians educated in the Synagogues, who obfti- ,, nately believe, that fuch fort of notions cou'd not ,, proceed from them ; that on the contrary, it was ,, their very character to turn the whole Scripture ,, into Allegory.　And,

I think, none of our celebrated Writers reject this Epiftle as fpurious, becaufe of the allegories it abounds with : Our excellent Archbifhop fays, † ,, Even St. *Paul* ,, himfelf in his *Epiftles*, receiv'd by us as *Canonical*, ,, affords us not a few inftances of this, which is fo ,, much found fault with in St. *Barnabas*: As I might ,, eafily make appear from a multitude of paffages ‡ ,, out of them, were it needful for me to enlarge ,, myfelf on a point, which every one, who has read ,, the *Scriptures* with any care, cannot choofe but ,, have obferv'd. ,,　And thofe Chriftians St. *Paul* mentions, for *believing the refurrection was paft*, were, no doubt, great Allegorifts.

T H E primitive Fathers exactly follow'd the prece- dent fet them by the Apoftle *Barnabas*, & other Apoftolical

---

* *Du Pin*'s Life of *Barnabas* p. 6. col. 2 - & 7 col. 1.-
† *Wake*'s Life of *Barnabas*, pag. 73.
‡ See 1 *Cor.* 10. 1. 4.　*Gal.* 4. 21.　*Eph.* 5. 31.
　*Heb.* 9. 8. 23, 24. & 10. 1. &c.

ftolical Men: *Clemens* of *Alexandria* fays, * ,, The
,, œconomy of the Law, is typical and prophetical;
,, & that *Mofes* & the Prophets, wrote all in *Parables.*
So *Tertullian*, ,, The Law is fpiritual & prophetical,
,, and almoft in all points figurative.,, And *Le Clerc*
obferves, that † ,, The Fathers did not content them-
,, felves with interpreting the Old Teftament allego-
,, rically, but they did the fame as to the New.,, --
But becaufe,

Origen was famous for this allegorical method, and
by virtue of it efteem'd the greateft Champion of
Chriftianity, next to the Apoftles, & fince what he
fays, was not only his own, but the fenfe of the then
Church, it will not be improper to cite him. ,, If we
,, adhere, *fays he*, ‡ to the letter, or underfland what
,, is written in the Law of God, as the *Jews* do, in
,, the common acceptation of the words, I bluſh to
,, own, that God ever gave fuch Laws; for mere
,, human conſtitutions, as thofe of the *Romans*, *Athe-*
,, *nians*, or *Lacedemonians*, will feem more reafonable
,, and proper; but if the Law of God is to be under-
,, ftood in the fenfe the Church teaches, then truly
,, it exceeds all human ordinances. ,,  For which
reafon he makes the allegorical way of interpreting
Scripture to be the key of knowledge; & following
the letter of the Law, the direct way to *Infidelity* &
vain Superftition. § *Literam fequentes in Infidelitatem,*
*& varias Superftitiones incurrunt.*  And he objects to
*Marcion* the *Heretick*, that he was againft the allegorical way of interpreting Scripture. ¶

B. Do

---

* *Stroma l.* 2. *e.* 19. *p.* 403. B, *l.* 6. *c.* 15. *p.* 678. *B.*
*Adv. Marc. l.* 2. *c.* 19.

† *Le Clerc*'s Life of *Clem. Alexan.* Eng. Tranſl. p. 54.
& Biblioth. Univer. To. 10. p. 236.

‡ *Homl.* 7. *in Levit. To.* 1. *fol.* 73. *C.*    § *Homil.* 26.
*in Mat. fol.* 50. *E.*    ¶ *Epiſt. ad. Rom. c.* 2. *fol.* 147. *G.*

*B.* Do not these Fathers suppose God either a weak Being, who could not frame as wise Laws as Men; or else an ill-natur'd Being, who, in order to puzzle Mankind, speaks in *riddles & mysteries?* What should we think of a *Lawyer,* who said, he shou'd be asham'd of the Laws of his own country, if taken in a literal sense; but that there was an allegorical sense which could one but hit, wou'd discover profound wisdom?

*A.* Thus the Fathers sufficiently acknowledg'd the sovereignty of Reason, in allegorising away matters of fact, that were in truth, uncapable of being allegoris'd; tho' that is but running into one unreasonable thing, to get rid of another: And how can we depend on any thing said in the Scripture, if we can't on its facts? One wou'd think nothing was a plainer fact, than that of *Lot's* lying with his two Daughters, yet St. *Irenæus* * allegorifes that away, and is so fond of allegorising, that for the sake of it, he contradicts the Scripture, & says, † ,, The Harlot *Raab* entertain'd *three* Spies; ,, and had he not made them three, he wou'd have been at a loss, how to say as he does, that *this Harlot hid in her House, Father, Son, & Holy Ghost.* ,, How can we be edily'd, says ,, *Origen,* ‡ in reading that so great a Patriarch as ,, *Abraham,* not only ly'd to King *Abimelech,* but also ,, betray'd to him the chastity of his Wife? What in- ,, structions can we reap from the Wife of so great ,, a Patriarch, if we think she was expos'd to be de- ,, bauch'd by her Husband's contrivance. Let the ,, *Jews* believe such things, & those with them, who ,, are greater friends to the letter than to the spirit.

He asserts, § ,, That there are even in the Gospel ,, things said, which, according to the letter, or taken ,, in their literal sense, are mere falsities, or lies; as

where

* *Lib.* 4. *c.* 51. *per totum.*
† *Lib.* 4 *c* 37. *p.* 336. *col.* 1. *l.* 36. *&c. Josh.* 2. 1.
‡ *Hom.* 6. *in Gen. to.* 1. *fol.* 12. H. 13. *A.*
§ *Hom.* 6. *in Isa. fol.* 106. D --

,, where our Saviour fays, *He that believeth in me,*
,, *the works that I do, ſhall he do alſe; & greater works*
,, *than theſe ſhall he do.* John xiv. 12. *&c.*,, which,
he ſhews, was not verify'd literally, but ſpiritually.
And,

,, \* T H A T it was want of knowledge in the Scrip-
,, tures, to think, that God ſpent ſix real days in the
,, work of the Creation.

H E deſires any one to ſhew, † ,, how the truth
,, of the Goſpels can be maintain'd, or their ſeeming
,, contrarieties clear'd by any other than the anago-
,, gical method; which he affirms neceſſary for that
,, purpoſe.

H E ſays, ‡ ,, The pair of *turtle-doves,* or two young
,, *pidgeons,* offer'd for Jeſus, were not ſuch as we ſee
,, with our carnal eyes; not *Birds,* ſuch as fly in the
,, air; but ſomething divine & auguſt, beyond human
,, contemplation, *&c.*

I F you deſire to be more plentifully furniſh'd with
Inſtances of the like nature with thoſe abovemention'd,
conſult the *Philocalia* of *Origen.* §

S T. *Auſtin,* a Man of the greateſt authority of all
the Fathers, ſays, ¶ ,, We muſt not take the ſtory
,, of *Jacob*'s cheating his Father, by perſonating his
,, Brother *Eſau,* literally, leſt the Scripture ſhould
,, ſeem to encourage *lying;* ,, and ſpeaking of Jeſus
curſing the *fig-tree,* ſays, ✠ *Hoc factum, niſi figuratum*
*ſtultum invenitur.* And he, with the reſt of the Fathers,\*
not only moſt unnaturally allegoriſes away the hiſtory
of the Fall, but even of the whole Creation; & *ſays,* †
,, The whole World was created in an inſtant; ,,
&

---

\* *Orig. contra Celſ l.* 6. *p.* 310, 311. *See Philocal.* 6. 1.
*p.* 12.         † *Tom.* 10. *in Joh. p.* 150. D, E.
‡ *Hom.* 14. *in Luc. p.* 101. B. 10. 3.         § *Cap.* 1. *p.* 12
*& ſeqq. Edit. Cantab.* 1658.         ¶ *Contra Mendacium.*
*c.* 10. *p.* 44, 45. 10. 4.         ✠ *Serm.* 74. *l.* 2. *de Gen.*
\* *Contra Maniche. c.* 17. *& d.*
† *Tom.* 3. *lib. impsrf. de Gen. ad Lit.* 6. 7. - *&c.*

& tho' there is not one word about Angels in the text, yet this angelical Doctor makes part of the six days labour relate to the Creation of Angels.

B. But how could he account for God's instituting the Sabbath, upon his resting from his six days labour, if all things were created in an instant?

A. How happy he was in allegorising, you may judge from his explaining that passage of *Genesis*, iii. 14. where the *Latin* Version which he follow'd, runs thus; * *Upon thy breast, & upon thy belly shall thou go, & dust shalt thou eat all the days of thy life.* By the *breast*, says he, is to be understood *pride*; by the *belly*, *the lusts of the flesh*; & by that which is added, *dust shalt thou eat*, is meant *curiosity*, which extends only to things temporal & earthly; & by *curiosity*, he means *Avarice* And,

St. *Ambrose* will not allow the *Rainbow* to be the *bow*, which God plac'd in the *clouds*; and saith, †
„ Far be it from us to call this *God*'s *bow*; for this *bow*,
„ which is call'd *iris*, is seen indeed, in the day, but
„ never appears in the night: „ For which weighty reason, he substitutes in its room, a strange, allegorical *bow*, out of his own imagination.

If the Fathers could allegorise away the most stubborn matters of fact, they could have no difficulty in allegorising away any other matter, where the words are capable of various senses. One would think, it was difficult to find out an allegorical meaning to this text, ‡ *O Daughter of* Babylon, *happy is he, who taketh, & dashes thy little ones against the stones*; yet nothing is too hard for *Origen*, who assures us, that the text intends, *The Man who dashes his vicious thoughts against the solid rock of reason.*

And indeed, the Fathers have so turnd, & twisted the Scripture, with a pious intention to make it speak
nothing

* *Lib. 2. de Gen. contra Manich. c.* 17, 18. *p.* 841. *B. To.* 1.
† *Lib. de Noe & Arca,* 27.
‡ *Origen contra Celsum, l.* 7. *p.* 347. -

nothing but what they thought agreeable to Reason, that they have render'd it like *Aristotle's Materia prima*; *nec quid, nec quale, nec quantum, nec aliquid eorum quibus ens det rminatur* : For by making the Scripture, in so many places, say one thing, & mean another, they have destroy'd its certainty; since as *Le Clerc* observes, * ,, If, according to this method, the sacred ,, Writers had said quite another thing than what ,, they said, or, if you will the quite contrary, yet ,, one might find as good sense in them; as those ,, that will try it will presently observe. -- There-,, fore the *Christians*, & the *Jews* wou'd have done ,, much better to keep close to the letter, than to use ,, so uncertain a method, to defend the holy Scrip-,, ture against the *Pagans*.

*B.* A L L the Fathers do not allegorise like *Origen*; *Justin Martyr*, for instance, asserts, that the threatning, that † *In the day thou eatest thereof thou shalt surely dye*, was literally fulfill'd, in that *Adam* did not live out a thousand years, which, with God, is but one day. But to go no further than the story of *Abraham's* prostituting his Wife; St. *Ambrose*, ‡ to justify *Abraham's* conduct, roundly asserts, adultery to be no crime before the giving of the Law by *Moses*. And St. *Austin* § makes adultery still lawful, if Husband & Wife consent. St. *Jerom*, indeed ¶ runs into the other extream, & approves the conduct of those, who kill'd themselves, to preserve their chastity. But the most eloquent St. *Chrysostom* ✠ enlarges very much in commendation of *Abraham* & *Sarah*, & says, ,, Tho' nothing ,, gives a Husband more uneasiness, than to imagine ,, his Wife has to do with another; yet this just Man ,, did what he cou'd, even to accomplish the act of adul-

---

* Life of *Clem. Alexand.* p. 54, 55. Engl. Transl. & Bibl. Univer. To. 10. p. 236. 237.   † *Dialo. cum Tryph. p. 89.*
‡ *Lib.* 1. *de Abr. Patriar. c* 4. See Daillé *de usu Patr.* p. 271, 272.   § *De civit. Dei, l.* 16. *c.* 25.
¶ *Com. on Jon. To.* 6. *p.* 150. D.   ✠ *Hom.* 32. *in Gen*

,, adultery. -- And adds, that *Sarah* too, (whom he
,, sets as a pattern for all marry'd Women) accepted
,, the proposal very couragiously; and then crys out,
,, Who can enough admire this readiness to obey her
,, Husband? Who can sufficiently celebrate the praises
,, of *Sarah*, who, after so long continence, & at her
,, great age, readily consented to this act of adultery,
,, and to let the *Barbarian* have the use of her body,
,, to save her Husband?

*A.* MIGHT not those Fathers as well· have allegoris'd, as talk'd thus absurdly? 'Tis chiefly owing·
to the *Papists* taking some words in a literal sense,
relating to the *eating the Flesh, & drinking the Blood of
the Son of Man*, that they come to be of a different
Religion from the *Protestants*; and tho' two parties
may agree, in taking the same words in an allegorical
sense, yet by allegorising them differently, they may
be of different Religions.  By allegorising some texts,
the *Jews* have made the *Messiah* a temporal Prince,
the *Christians* a spiritual one.  Mr. *Whiston* must think
there are no words so plain, but are capable of being
allegoris'd; since, he supposes the Catholick Church
has all along allegorised plain love-songs, between
*Solomon* & one of his Mistresses, into spiritual Hymns
between Christ & his Spouse, the Church.  And what
Dr. *South* must have thought of the *Revelations*, I leave
you to judge, when he does not scruple to call it †
*a mysterious, extraordinary Book; which, perhaps, the
more 'tis study'd, the less 'tis understood; as generally
finding a Man crack'd, or making him so.* And had not
the *Mahometan* Divines had the knack of allegorising
nonsence, fools, & frantick persons wou'd not have
been had in such honour and reverence among the
*Mussehmen*, ‡ *only because their Revelations & Enthusiasms transported them out of the ordinary temper of*
hu-

---

* *See Supplem. to his Essay, ab initio.*
† *South's* Serm. Vol. 2. pag. 467.
‡ *Ricaut's* pref. State of the *Ottom.* Emp. B. 2. c. 4.

*humanity.* Therefore, upon the whole, I muſt needs ſay, happy is the Man, who is ſo far, at leaſt, directed by the *Law of Reaſon,* and the *Religion of Nature,* as to ſuffer no myſteries, or unintelligible propoſitions, no allegories, no hyperboles, no metaphors, types, parables, or phraſes of an uncertain ſignification, to confound his underſtanding. And certainly, the common Parent of Mankind is too good & gracious, to put the happineſs of *all* his Children on any other doctrines, than ſuch as plainly ſhew themſelves to be the will of God, even to the ignorant and illiterate; if they have but courage & honeſty to make uſe of their Reaſon: Otherwiſe the Scripture wou'd not be plain in all neceſſary things, even to *babes & ſucklings.*

*B.* You ſuppoſe then, that the bulk of Mankind are taught by God himſelf, to know what Religion comes from him: even tho' they want letters, to make 'em capable of underſtanding thoſe external proofs, on which all traditional Religions do, & muſt depend.

## CHAP. XIII.

*The Bulk of Mankind, by their Reaſon, muſt be able to diſtinguiſh between Religion & Super-ſtition; otherwiſe they can never extricate them-ſelves from that Superſtition they chance to be educated in.*

*A.* RELIGION either does not concern the majority, as being incapable of forming a judgment about it, or it muſt carry ſuch internal marks of its truth, as men of mean capacity are able to diſcover; or elſe notwithſtanding the infinite variety of Religions, all who do not underſtand the original languages their traditional Religions are written in, which is all Mankind, a very few excepted, are alike

O                    bound

bound in all places to pin their Faith on their Priests, & believe in Men, who have an interest to deceive them, and who have seldom fail'd to do so, when occasion served.

Can People, if incapable by their Reason to distinguish truth from falsehood, have any thing more to plead for the truth of their Religion, than that they believe it to be the true Religion, because their Priests, who are hir'd to maintain it, tell them it was a long while ago reveal'd to certain Persons, who, as they, on their *Priestly* words, assure them, were too wise to be impos'd on themselves, & too honest to impose on others: And that no change cou'd have been made in their Religion in after-times; the care Men have of their own souls, as well as their natural affections for posterity, obliging them from generation to generation, to hand down their Religion just as they receiv'd it: And that it was morally impossible, innovations shou'd creep in, since it wou'd be the highest folly in any to attempt to introduce new doctrines, as a tradition receiv'd from their Ancestors, when all must know they had receiv'd no such tradition. As this is all, the bulk of Mankind, if they are not capable of judging from the Doctrines themselves of their truth, can say for their Religion, so they, in all places, make use of this argument, & with equal confidence aver, that, tho' all other traditionary Religions are full of gross falsehoods, & most absurd notions, which their Priests impudently impose on them as divine truths, yet our own Priests are such faithful representers of things, that one may as well question the truth of all History, as the truth of things believ'd on their authority. Priests of other Religions, we know, will lie for interest, & conscious that their traditional Religion will not bear examination, guard it with penal Laws; but we can never suspect, that our own Priests, tho' they take the same methods, act on the same motives.

THIS

THIS boasted argument, in which Men of all Religions so much triumph, if it proves any thing, wou'd prove there never was, nor cou'd be any false Religion, either in whole, or part; because Truth being before Falsehood, and Mens Ancestors having once possess'd it, no change cou'd afterward ever happen: Whereas, on the contrary, tho there have been at times great numbers of traditional Religions, yet as far as it appears, no one of them has long remain'd the same; at least, in such points as were merely founded on tradition.

I see no middle, but that we must either own, that there are such internal marks fix'd to every part of the true Religion, as will enable the bulk of Mankind to distinguish it from all false Religions; or else that all traditionary Religions are upon a level: Since those, who, in every country, are hir'd to maintain them, will not fail to assert, they have all external marks; such as *uninterrupted traditions, incontested miracles, confession of adversaries, number of proselites, agreement among themselves*, and all those other external arguments, that the *Papists* & *Mahometans* set so high a value on. In this case, what can the common people do, who understand not a word of the language, their Religion, & its external proofs are writ in, but be of the Religion in which they are educated; especially, if nothing is suffer'd to be publish'd, which may, in the least, tend to make them question its truth; and all other Religions are represented as full of the grossest absurdities.

HAD the People of *Rome*, in the primitive times of Christianity, been govern'd by external marks, none of them had quitted their old Religion, which had every external mark proper to recommend it; and under which they were so bless'd, as to become Masters of the best part of the known world. But,

BECAUSE this is a point, wherein the greatest part of Mankind are, at all times, nearly concern'd,

I

I shall beg leave to mention, tho' it be somewhat long, what Mr. *Lock* says on this head.

„ * H a v e the bulk of Mankind no other Guide,
„ but accident, & blind chance, to conduct them to
„ their happiness, or misery ? Are the current opinions,
„ & licensed Guides of every Country sufficient evi-
„ dence and security to every Man, to venture his
„ greatest concernments on ; nay, his everlasting hap-
„ piness, or misery ? Or, can those be the certain &
„ infallible oracles & standards of truth, which teach
„ one thing in *Christendom*, and another in *Turkey* ?
„ Or shall a poor Country - man be eternally happy,
„ for having the chance to be born in *Italy* ; or a
„ day-labourer be unavoidably lost, because he had
„ the ill luck to be born in *England* ? How ready
„ some Men may be to say some of these things,
„ I will not here examine ; but this I am sure, that
„ Men must allow one or other of these to be true ;
„ ( let them chuse which they please ) or else grant,
„ that G o d has furnished Men with faculties suffi-
„ cient to direct them in the way they shou'd take,
„ if they will but seriously employ them that way,
„ when their ordinary vocations allow them the lei-
„ sure. -- † There can't be a more dangerous thing
„ to rely on than the opinion of others, nor more
„ likely to mislead one ; since there is much more
„ falsehood & error among Men than truth & know-
„ ledge : And if the opinions & persuasions of others,
„ whom we know, & think well of, be a ground of
„ assent, Men have reason to be *Heathens* in *Japan* ,
„ *Mahometans* in *Turky*, *Papists* in *Spain* , *Protestants*
„ in *England*, and *Lutherans* in *Sueden*.

W a s there a set of Priests, on whose authority the common people were every where to depend for their religious sentiments, they must be known by some plain, external marks : To say the People must

follow

---

* *Of human Underst. l. 4. c. 19. Sect. 3. p. 399. Edit. 2.*
† *Ibid. l. 4. c. 15. Sect. 6. Edit. 2.*

follow thofe Priefts that are in the right, is to fuppofe
People muft judge what is right; and then judge
(if that concern'd them) whether any fet of Priefts
are in the right: and if Men can't believe, when they
fee no reafon for believing, what reafon can the bulk
of Mankind have to prefer one Religion before a
number of others, on the account of fuch things, as,
upon Prieftly authority, are believ'd to belong to
every one of them; fuch as *vifions, dreams, trances,
extacies, infpirations, conference with Spirits, traditionary
report about miracles, &c.*? And fhou'd the chance of
education throw Men into the *true* traditionary Religion, yet confidering its ftyle is not very exact, there
being generally more exprefs'd than is meant, & things
of the greateft confequence are often fo treated, as
that Men can't from thence perceive the nature and
extent of their duty; & even Precepts of the greateft
moment are fometimes fo far from being deliver'd
plainly & fimply, that they are exprefs'd after a general, undetermin'd, nay, hyperbolical manner; fo
that even in this cafe, there's a neceffity for the
common people to have recourfe to the Reafon of
things.

Are not the unlearned wholly unacquainted with
thofe *keys of folution* (as they are call'd) which the
learned have fuch frequent recourfe to; fuch as thofe
of a *tranfpofition of words,* or *claufes, errors of copies,
various readings, various meanings of the-fame word,
punctuation, taking away,* or *adding of the negative particle; allufion to cuftoms, confideration of the matter in
hand, exaggeration, interrogation, parenthefis, literal fenfe,
figurative fenfe; want of exactnefs in the facred Writers,
prudence in concealing fome things,* or *in complying with
fome opinions prevailing in their times; condefcention to*
Pagans or Jews; *ufing fuch ideas as prevail'd in fuch a
Religion, prejudication in the hearers, anfwers fuitable
to their needs, rather than to their queries, compendious
expreffions, phrafeology of that time, the author's nation,*

*or native country, parallel passages, precepts peculiar to
the Apostles, advices to perfection, censures against certain
Hereticks, the circumstances of the subject, the scope of
the author, what goes before, & what follows, the bar-
renness of the* Hebrew *tongue, and* consequently, *its
ambiguity, its particular idioms, the various senses of the
same verb in different conjugations, the want of certain
ways of expression us'd in other tongues, the sublime, &
metaphorical expressions most frequent in the oriental languages, the imitation of the* Hebrew *idiom in the* LXX
Version, *and in the original text of the New Testament
Greek of the Synagogue,* &c.

THE bulk of Mankind being incapable of *meta-
physical* speculations, and their underftandings giv'n
them to difcern thofe rules of action which God prefcribes them, he has, no doubt, adjufted one to the
other; and confequently, the fimplicity, the reafonablenefs, the conveniency & ufefulnefs of thefe Rules,
point them out to be the will of God, to Men in all
places, and conditions of life; but to carry things
further, can only ferve the defigns of ill Men, who
have taken an occafion from thence to abufe their
credulity to the vileft purpofes.

CAN, for inftance, the common people, who underftand not a word of the language, the *Jewifh* Books
are writ in, be better judges than the *Jews* themfelves of the meaning of their own Books; and of
their own Prophets fpeaking in their own language?
Or, are the common People capable of judging of
the innumerable difputes among *Chriftians*; if thofe
likewife depend, not on the Reafon of Things, but
on the critical underftanding of Books, written in
dead languages; nay, what do they know of the
diftinguifhing doctrines of their own Churches? They,
indeed, on all fides, know whom their leaders would
have them hate, but little, or nothing of thofe opinions which divide their leaders.

B,

*B.* Is there any Divine of note, who makes Revelation thus difficult to be underſtood by the ignorant, & unlearned?

*A.* I ſhall mention one, againſt whom you have no exception, who repreſents it thus obſcure, even to the learned. Is not Biſhop *Taylor* (highly eſteem'd for his devotional, as well as polemical works) a competent judge in this matter? And he (ſumming up, & that very briefly, what he had ſpent ſeveral chapters to prove at large) *ſays*, \* ,, Since there are ſo many ,, copies with infinite varieties of reading; ſince a ,, various interpunction, a parentheſis, a letter, an ,, accent may much alter the ſenſe; ſince ſome places ,, have divers literal ſenſes, many have ſpiritual, ,, myſtical and allegorical meanings; ſince there are ,, ſo many Tropes, Metonomies, Ironies, Hyperboles, ,, proprieties and improprieties of language, whoſe ,, underſtanding depends upon ſuch circumſtances, ,, that it is almoſt impoſſible to know the proper in- ,, terpretation; now that the knowledge of ſuch cir- ,, cumſtances, & particular ſtories is irrecoverably loſt: ,, † Since there are ſome myſteries, which, at the beſt ,, advantage of expreſſion are not eaſy to be appre- ,, hended, and whoſe explication, by reaſon of our ,, imperfections, muſt needs be dark, ſometimes un- ,, intelligible. And laſtly, ſince thoſe ordinary means ,, of expounding Scripture, as ſearching the originals, ,, conference of places, parity of reaſon, analogy of ,, faith, are all dubious, uncertain, & very fallible; ,, He that is the wiſeſt, & by conſequence, the like- ,, lieſt to expound trueſt, in all probability of reaſon, ,, will be very far from confidence, becauſe every ,, one of them, & many more, are like ſo many de- ,, grees of improbability & incertainty, all depreſſing ,, our certainty of finding out truth in ſuch myſteries, ,, & amidſt ſo many difficulties.

AND

---

\* *Polem. Works, pag.* 452. † *Ibid. pag.* 453.

And in another place, * ,, The obscurity of some ,, questions, the niceties of some articles, the intricacy ,, of some Revelations, the variety of human under- ,, standings, the windings of logick, the tricks of ad- ,, versaries, the subtilty of sophisters, the engagement ,, of educations, personal affections, the portentous ,, number of writers, the infinity of authorities, the ,, vastness of some arguments, consisting in an ennu- ,, meration of many particulars, the incertainty of ,, others, the several degrees of probability, the diffi- ,, culties of Scripture, the invalidity of probation, of ,, Tradition, the opposition of all exterior arguments ,, to one another, and their open contestation, the ,, publick violence done to Authors and Records, ,, the private arts and supplantings, the falsifyings, ,, the indefatigable industry of some Men to abuse all ,, understandings, and all persuasions into their own ,, opinions: These, & a thousand more, have made ,, it impossible for any Man in so great a variety of ,, matter, not to be deceiv'd. ,, And I might add in confirmation of the Bishop's sentiments, & demonstrate too, were it not endless to go through particulars, that there's scarce a text, except in things of their own nature evident, where Commentators do not differ. Whether there considerations alone, be not a sufficient reason for the unlearned to adhere to those plain, simple truths the Light of Nature dictates, I leave you to judge?

And do not other Divines, in effect, say the same, when they make Religion not to be implanted in human-nature, but an art so far above the capacity of common people, that it requires great learning and labour to be competently skill'd in it; and tell us, that they, who have spent their time in studying it, can't have too much honour, or too great rewards given them for deciding for the People, points of Re- ligion, as the common Law Judges do points of property;

* *Ibid. pag. 521.*

perty; & that People juftly incur the dreadful *Anathema* pronounc'd in Synods & Councils, againft thofe who refufe to fubmit to their decifions; and that 'tis the duty of the Magiftrate to fee their decrees put in execution.

A right in Priefts, whether in, or out of *Convocations*, to judge, & determine for the People, what they fhall believe & profefs, fuppofes it a duty in them fo to believe, & fo to profefs; and confequently, that the Religion of the *Laity* confifts in believing in their Priefts, and that whatever they decree, is to be the rule of their actions.

*B.* This is too fevere, they only claim a power of interpreting the Laws of Chrift, not of making new Laws themfelves.

*A.* There's only a verbal difference between a Lawmaker, and a fovereign Interpreter of Laws, to whofe interpretation all are oblig'd to fubmit; fo that ever fince the Council of -- People have been taught to renounce both Natural & Reveal'd Religion; and become Prieft-worfhippers, & to have a divine faith in their dictates, and indeed, fo they ought, if thefe Priefts had, as they claim, a judicial power to determine of Mens condition hereafter, and thereby make God a meer executioner of their Sentences, by which they bind, or loofe Mens fins to eternity.

As this notion carries with it the higheft blafphemy and idolatry, fo I think it is treated too gently by Mr. *Chillingworth*, in faying, * „ This prefumptuous „ impofing of the fenfes of Men upon the words of „ God, the fpecial fenfes of Men upon the general „ words of God, & laying them upon Mens Con- „ fciences together under the equal penalty of death „ & damnation, this vain conceit, that we can fpeak „ of the things of God better than the words of God, „ this deifying our own interpretations, & tyrannous

O 5            in-

* *Chillingworth*'s Relig. of Proteft. Part. I. c. 4. Sect. 16. p. 152. Edit. 5.

,, inforcing them upon others, this reftraining of the
,, word of God from that latitude & generality, and
,, the underftanding of Men from that liberty, wherein
,, Chrift & the Apoftles left them; is, & hath been
,, the only fountain of all the *Schifms* of the Church,
,, & that which makes them immortal; the common
,, incendiary of *Chriftendom*, and that which tears in
,, pieces, not the coat, but the bowels and members
,, of Chrift, *Ridente Turca, nec dolente Judeo.*

In fhort, True Religion can't but be plain, fimple, and natural, as defign'd for all Mankind, adapted to every capacity, & fuited to every condition and cir-cumftance of life; and if it be render'd otherwife, is it not owing to thofe, who have made it their bufinefs to puzzle Mankind, & render plain things obfcure; in order to get the confciences, & confequently, the properties of the People at their difpofal; and to be in a manner ador'd, notwithftanding the groffeft im-moralities, as the fole difpenfers of fuch things, as no ways relate to the good of the community; and to deftroy all that will not comply with their pernicious defigns, as enemies of God, and his holy Church? And,

Tho' the Clergy have taken all poffible methods for a blind fubmiffion, & a forc'd uniformity, yet they have not been able to hinder *Chriftians* from being endlefly divided, even in what they call *fundamentals*; and tho' no one Sect, as far as I can find, have ven-tur'd to give us a compleat fet of their *fundamentals*, yet all Sects unanimoufly own, that thofe things which are neceffary to the falvation of *Chriftians*, muft be fo plain. as that all *Chriftians*, even thofe of the meaneft capacities, may apprehend them. Would not one think, that a little honeft reflection fhou'd carry them further, and make them fee, that it is inconfiftent with the univerfal & unlimited goodnefs of the common Parent of Mankind, not to make that which is neceffary for the falvation of all Men, fo plain, as that all Men

may

may know it; tho' one wou'd be apt to think, that by the number & oddnefs of thofe things, which in moft Churches Divines have made neceffary to falvation, they were more zealous to damn others than to fave themfelves, or at leaft, that they thought there was no room in Heaven for any, but Men of their own narrow principles. But,

LET me ask thefe charitable Gentlemen, Whether the happinefs of others wou'd make *Chriftians* unhappy? Or, what prejudice it will be to them, to fuppofe *God is no Refpecter of Perfons*, but that all may come to him, who believe that *he will reward thofe* in all nations, and at all times, *who have diligently fought him?*

NATURAL Religion, which is of the greateft importance to Mankind, & is a perpetual ftanding Rule for Men of the meaneft, as well as higheft capacity, carries its own evidence with it, thofe internal, infeparable marks of truth: but can that be faid of any Religion, which depends on tradition? Does not that want foreign aid & affiftance? Ought we not to be certain, that the firft propagators of it cou'd not be impos'd on themfelves, or wou'd not impofe on others? Or in other words, were infallible, and impeccable? But fince numbers have taken their reveries for divine infpirations, ought we not to have certain marks to diftinguifh one from the other? Nor is this alone fufficient, for if evil Beings can imprefs notions in Mens minds as ftrongly as good Beings, and caufe miracles to be done in confirmation of them; is there any way to know, to which of the two notions thus imprefs'd are owing, but from their nature and tendency, or thofe internal marks of wifdom & goodnefs, by which they plainly fhew themfelves to be part of Natural Religion? If fo, can external proofs carry us further than the internal proofs do? But,

'TIS not enough to be certain, thefe Men were not impos'd on, we muft be as certain, they wou'd

on

on no occasion whatever impose on others, or in other words, were not Men of like passions & infirmities with other mortals. Does not the Scripture give very many instances of inspir'd persons as much govern'd by their passions, as uninspir'd? Was not *Abraham*, tho' a Prophet, & so dear to God, that he wou'd not destroy a neighbouring Town * without acquainting him with it, guilty of an incestuous marriage, his Wife being his Sister by the Father's side? † And did he not endeavour to betray her chastity to two Kings, ‡ in disowning her to be his Wife, by which conduct, he got from one of them, who § *entreated him well for her sake, Men & Maid-Servants, sheep, oxen, asses, & camels*; and from the other, ¶ *a thousand pieces of Silver*, besides, *Sheep, Oxen, Men & Women-Servants*? And immediately after ✳ *his Faith was counted to him for righteousness*, did he not doubt of God's promise, till God spoke to him *in a deep sleep?*

Was not *David*, tho' a Prophet, & a Man after God's own heart, guilty of many enormous crimes, from the time he design'd to have murder'd all the males in *Nabal*'s Family, * because he wou'd not pay contributions to him, & those Men, † who out of debt, discontent & distress join'd him? tho' *Nabal*, by so doing, might have incurr'd the fate of those Priests, from whom, *David*., by several falsehoods, got both *Shew-bread*, ‡ and *Goliath*'s Sword. What cou'd be more treacherous, than his invading people, that were at least, in peace, if not Allies of the King of *Gath*, § to whom he fled for safety; and having neither sav'd Man or Woman alive to bring tydings, told his generous Protector, he had been making an in-road into *Judea?*

I N

---

* *Gen.* 18. 17.  † 20. 12.  ‡ 12. 19.  20. 2.
§ - - 12. 16.  ¶ 20. 16.  ✳ 15. 6. 8. - 12. 13.
* 1 *Sam.* 25. 22.  † 22. 2.  ‡ 21. 6. 9.  § 27. 8-12.

In a word, (not to mention his treatment of *Uriah*, which no brave Man can think of without horror,) did he not leave the world in a very unforgiving temper, when the laſt thing he commanded his Son *Solomon* was, \* to put *Shimei* to death; tho' he had *ſworn before the Lord*, that he † *wou'd not put him to death*, & that *he ſhou'd not dye?*

S o l o m o n, tho inſpir'd with wiſdom from above, & had conferences with God himſelf, yet his paſſion for Women, made him guilty of groſs Idolatry. And not to multiply inſtances, we find one Man of God lying to another Man of God in the name of God, purely for the pleaſure of making him ‡ *eat bread, & drink water with him*. And if we go to the New Teſtament, 'tis plain, by what our Saviour ſays to thoſe, who § *had prophecy'd, & caſt out Devils, & done many wonderful works in his name, depart from me, ye that work iniquity*, that neither prophecies, nor miracles are abſolute ſecurities for Men to depend on. Nay, do we not find one of the Apoſtles, tho' he, with the reſt, had the power of doing Miracles, even to the ¶ *raiſing of the dead*, betraying his Maſter for the paltry ſum of thirty pieces of ſilver? And the other Apoſtles not only fled, & deſerted him, but the chief of them *forſwore him*, ✠ as often as he was ask'd about his being one of his followers; and he, as well as *Barnabas*, \* was afterwards guilty of a mean piece of diſſimulation. And *Paul* & *Barnabas* † had ſuch a *ſharp contention*, tho' about a very indifferent matter, as to cauſe a ſeparation: And even St. *Paul* ſays, ‡ *The good that I would, I do not; but the evil which I would not, that I do. -- But I ſee another law in my members, warring againſt the law of my mind, and bringing me into captivity to the law of ſin, which is in my members.* And a great deal more to the ſame purpoſe.                              Do

---

\* 1 *Kings* 2. 8, 9.    † 2 *Sam.* 19 23.    ‡ 1 *Kings* 13. 18.
§ *Mat.* 7. 22, 23.    ¶ 10. 8.    ✠ 26. 72.
\* *Gal.* 2. 13.    † *Acts* 15. 39.    ‡ *Rom.* 7. 19. 23.

Do not thefe inſtances, tho' many more might be added, plainly ſhew, that inſpir'd Perſons, whether Prophets or Apoſtles, are ſubject to the ſame paſſions, even to diſſembling & lying, as other Men? And that we ſin againſt that Reaſon, which was given us to diſtinguiſh between Good & Evil, Religion & Super-ſtition, if we do not by it examine all doctrines what-ſoever, and by whomſoever deliver'd? But ſuppoſing Prophets & Apoſtles impeccable as well as infallible; yet what certainty can people have, that thoſe things which were taught by them have been faithfully con-vey'd down for many generations together by Men, who were far from being infallible, or impeccable? So that here, certainly, they ought to make uſe of their Reaſon, in judging of all doctrines thus convey'd. Admitting Tradition has been a faithful conveyancer, yet how can the common People be certain the Scrip-ture has been truly tranſlated? But, granting even that; yet ſince moſt texts have vaſtly vary'd, & ſometimes contrary interpretations, & the literal ſenſe very often *kills*, how can they be confident they do not miſtake their meaning, except the Reaſon of Things makes it evident? But ſuppoſing no ſuch uncertainty in the meaning of texts, yet ſince the Scripture contains ſome Precepts, which are occaſional, obliging only certain perſons, upon certain occaſions, & in certain circumſtances, and others that are of an eternal obli-gation, & makes no diſtinction in delivering them; can Men, even the moſt learned, have any other way of knowing one from the other, but from the nature of the precepts; & that thoſe only are of an eternal obligation, which are founded on the eternal Reaſon of Things; & which wou'd eternally oblige, whether deliver'd in Scripture, or not? And,

Let me further add, that to make external Re-velation of any uſe, muſt we not, as I have already obſerv'd, be able to determine, whether God is oblig'd to act, as he declares in it he will do? And in order

to

to settle this important point, which Revelation itself can never do, must not our Reason tell us, that infinite Wisdom can have no Commands, but what are founded on the unalterable Reason of Things? And if God cou'd command at one time for commanding-sake in any one point, he might do so in all points, and times; and consequently, that an arbitrary will, which might change every moment, wou'd govern all things? And can they, who plead that their external Revelation is the unchangeable Will of God, any otherwise do it, but by having recourse to the nature of God, by which they can't but perceive, that the Will of God before, as well as since any external Revelation, must be as immutable as God himself, as being founded on the eternal Reason of Things? So that they who make the Will of God, whether reveal'd by himself, or by any Messenger, not to be unchangeably the same, destroy all possible proof, that any external Revelation cou'd be, or at least, continue to be the Will of God. Thus you see, that take what *hypothesis* you please, yet you can prove nothing to be his will, but what the nature of God, and the nature of things point out to all Men, who dare use their Reason, to be his Will, his immutable Will.

AMONG the numerous Answerers of the *Grounds and Reasons of the Christian Religion*, Mr. *Chandler* is deservedly reckon'd to stand in the foremost rank; and this judicious Divine says, * that „ Natural Reli-
„ gion is the only foundation, upon which Revela-
„ tion can be supported, and which must be under-
„ stood, before any Man is capable of judging either
„ of the nature or evidence of Christianity: And I am
„ persuaded, *says he*, that 'tis to the want of a due
„ knowledge of the first principles of all Religion,
„ those mistakes about the Christian are owing, that
                                                    have

* *Chandler's* Dedic. to Serm. preach'd in the *Old Jury*, pag. 3.

,, have obfcur'd the fimplicity of it, and prejudiced
,, many againft entertaining, and believing it. - -
,, If Natural Religion is not part of the Religion of
,, Chrift, 'tis fcarce worth while to enquire at all what
,, his Religion is. If it be, then the preaching Na-
,, tural Religion is preaching Chrift. - - * The Reli-
,, gion of Chrift muft be underftood, before it can,
,, or ought to be believ'd; and it muft be proved to
,, be a confiftent, & rational Religion, before they can
,, be under any obligation to receive it.

,, And, indeed, why fhou'd not every Man infift
,, upon thofe things? The only confequence that I
,, can imagine can flow from it is, not that the caufe
,, of Chriftianity will fuffer, which will ftand the teft
,, of the moft impartial inquiry, but that the rigid
,, directors of the faith and confciences of Men will
,, lofe their authority, and human fchemes & creeds,
,, that have been fet up in the room of Chriftianity,
,, will fall into the contempt they fo juftly deferve.

,, --'Tis my hearty prayer to *the Father of Lights*,
,, and *the God of Truth*, that all human authority in
,, matters of Faith, may come to a full end; and that
,, every one, who hath Reafon to direct him, & a
,, foul to fave, may be his own Judge in every thing
,, that concerns his eternal welfare, without any pre-
,, vailing regard to the dictates of fallible Men, or
,, fear of their peevifh, & impotent cenfures.,, And
in this prayer, I believe, every honeft Man will join.

The Reverend and judicious Mr. *Bullock*, in fum-
ming up what I have been endeavouring to prove at
large, fays, † ,, A Revelation coming from God, unlefs
,, it cou'd be known to be fuch, is in effect the fame,
,, as having none at all. - - Shall a Man, *fays he*,
,, embrace the firft Religion that offers itfelf to him,
,, & without feeking any further, ftick clofe to the
,, principles of his education? If this were fafe, then
,, all the contradictory notions that are in the world,
would

* *Ibid. pag.* 9, 10, 11.          † *Serm. pag.* 3, 4.

,, would be equally fafe & true; and there could be
,, no fuch thing as a falfe Religion, or the fpirit of
,, error any where: But this will not be admitted.
,, Is truth, then, confin'd to any certain country, or
,, to any particular fet of Men? No: But if it were,
,, ftill there would remain this difficulty, to be affur'd
,, to what country, or to what fort of Men it belong'd.
,, If this were all the rule we had to go by, every
,, Man (no doubt) would be partial to his own
,, country, & to thofe Men he is beft acquainted with.
,, And fo the principles of education muft prevail
,, every where, inftead of true Religion.

　　In anfwer to thefe, & fuch like objections, he fays,
,, * We are well affur'd, that God is the Author of
,, our beings, & all our faculties; and we cannot but
,, acknowledge, that our underftanding is the moft
,, excellent faculty he has given us: It is in that we
,, excel the beafts that perifh; & it was plainly given
,, us with this intent, that by a due ufe and applica-
,, tion thereof we might difcern truth from error;
,, that which is juft & fit to be done, or obferved by
,, us, from that which is not. -- Should we, there-
,, fore, admit any thing, as a Revelation coming
,, from him, which contradicts the evident dictates
,, of our Reafon, we facrifice one Revelation, that
,, which God gave us with our very beings, to make
,, way for another, which is inconfiftent with it. It
,, is in effect admitting, that the judgment of our own
,, minds is in no cafe to be depended upon; that the
,, faculties thereof, the very beft gift which God has
,, given us, are of no real ufe & fervice to us; no,
,, not even in difcerning which doctrines come from
,, God, and which do not: For, if I cannot depend
,, upon the plaineft dictates of Reafon, how can I be
,, affur'd, that any doctrine is a Revelation from God?
,, If I receive it without confulting my Reafon, then
,, for ought I know, it may be an impofture; and I

　　　　　　　　　　　　P　　　　　　　　　　am

* *Serm. pag* 18, 19

,, am every way as liable to embrace an error, as the
,, truth. But if I embrace it upon the tryal & con-
,, viction of my Reason, then 'tis plain, I admit the
,, principles of Reason are to be depended upon;
,, which if I do, I cannot consistently admit any thing
,, as true, which contradicts it.

To apply this Author's reasonings, God is frequently said *to swear*, nay, in both Old and New
Testament, * to *swear in wrath*. Now, if we are to
admit nothing that is repugnant to the natural notion
we have of God, ought we not to examine by our
Reason, whether God, who has no superior to invoke,
can swear at all, much less be in a passion, & swear
in wrath?

Again, If there are ever so many texts, which
seemingly confine salvation to a belief, to which the
greatest part of Mankind are utter strangers, or else
have not had sufficient reason to see they were oblig'd
to examine into it; or if they did, could not find out
its truth; must it not, by this Author's reasoning, be
my duty to consider, whether this is consistent with
the character we have from the Light of Nature, of
the impartial & universal goodness of God, to damn
Men for impossibilities? Or, whether one can be said
to be sent as a Saviour of Mankind, if he comes to
shut Heaven's gates against those, to whom before
they were open, provided they follow'd the dictates
of their Reason?

If, besides these, there are innumerable texts, which,
in the plainest manner words can express, impute human parts, human infirmities, and human passions,
even of the worst kind, to God, does not this suppose, that even all have a right to examine, & consequently, sufficient understanding to judge, when texts,
taken in their plain, obvious meaning, are, or are not
consistent with what the Light of Nature teaches them
of the character of the supreme Being? What Notions
must

* *Deut.* 1. 34. *Psalm* 95. 11. *Heb.* 3. 11.

muſt the Vulgar have of God, if the Light of Nature can't direct them right, when they find he is ſaid * to be *jealous & furious?* And God himſelf ſays, † *My fury ſhall come up in my face, for in my jealouſy, & in the fire of my wrath have I ſpoken*; with a number of other expreſſions of the like nature? Nay, does not the Scripture, if taken literally, ſuppoſe, that God does things of the greateſt moment in anger & fury? Was it not thus he gave his favourite People, ‡ *ſtatutes, which were not good, and judgments, by which they could not live?* And does not St. *Peter* (to mention no other Apoſtle) tho' a *Jew,* call the *Jewiſh* Law, given by God, § *a yoke, that neither we, nor our Fore-fathers could bear?* In what a number of places is God ſaid to do things *to try* people; & yet notwithſtanding this caution, how often is he ſaid *to repent?* Does he not even repent of the firſt action he did in relation to Man? ¶ *He repented that he made Man, & it grieved him at his heart.* Nay, does not the Scripture ſuppoſe he has ſo often repented, that he is ✠ *weary of re-penting?* What ſtrange notions muſt the bulk of Mankind cou'd not their Reaſon direct them right, have of the ſupreme Being, when he is ſaid * to have *reſted,* & to be *refreſhed*; & that † *Wine cheareth both God & Man?* And what is yet ſtranger, ſuch actions are attributed to him, as can only belong to the loweſt ranks of Creatures, ſuch as *hiſſing*; God being in three places ‡ in the Prophets ſaid *to hiſs*; and in one place *to hiſs for the Fly, that is in the uttermoſt part of the River of* Egypt, *& for the Bee, that is in the land of* Aſſyria?

B. DIVINES tell us, we muſt recede from the letter, when the nature of the thing requires it; that is, when it contains any notion, or fact, which our Reaſon tells us, is unworthy of God, as being in-

P 2　　　　　con-

* *Nah.* 1. 2.　† *Ezek.* 38. 18, 19.　‡ *Id.* 20. 21. 25.
§ *Acts* 15. 10.　¶ *Gen.* 6. 6.　✠ *Jer.* 15. 6.
* *Exod.* 31. 17.　† *Judges* 9. 13.
‡ *Iſa.* 5. 26. *Zach.* 10. 8. *Iſa.* 7. 18.

confiftent with his Wifdom, Goodnefs, Juftice Immutability, impartial and univerfal Benevolence, or any
other of his perfections; or any ways clafhes with
thofe duties, that Men as Men, or Creatures of the
fame Creator, owe their Fellow-Creatures.

*A.* I fhou'd think that Man was unreafonable, who
requir'd a greater fcope in reading any book, than
what thefe Divines allow him in reading the Scripture;
efpecially, confidering the frequent occafion he will
have to exercife his reafoning faculty, in allegorifing
away facts deliver'd after the plaineft manner: As for
inftance, If Reafon tells us, that God, the only true
God is *invifible*, we muft not interpret thofe numerous
texts literally, which fuppofe him to have been fo
often feen by mortal eyes: No, not even thofe which
reprefent him for many days together vifible on Mount
*Sinai*, where what was under his feet is mention'd;
and that the * *Nobles on whom God laid not his hand,
faw God, & did eat; & drink.* And Bifhop *Patrick* fays, ¶
,, That after they faw God, they were fo far from
,, receiving any harm, that they feafted with him
,, upon the relicks of the Peace-Offerings, with great
,, joy & gladnefs. ,,  And tho' 'tis faid, † *God fpake
to* Mofes *face to face*, as a Man does to his Friend,
yet for the fame reafon, that text muft not be interpreted literally.

*B.* THAT's certain, fince God, in the fame Chapter,
fays to *Mofes*, ‡ *Thou can'ft not fee my face, for there
fhall no Man fee me, & live.*

*A.* DOES not God immediately add, § *Behold there
is a place by me, & thou fhalt ftand upon a rock. And
it fhall come to pafs, while my glory paffeth by, that I
will put thee in a clift of the rock; and I will cover thee
with my hand, while I pafs by. And I will take away
mine hand, and thou fhalt fee my back-parts; but my
face fhall not be feen:* And fince Reafon tells us, God
has

* *Exod.* 24. 10, 11.    ¶ *Comment on the Place.*
† *Exod.* 33. 11.    ‡ *Ibid.* 33. 20.    § *Ib. ver.* 21, 22, 23.

has neither fore-parts, nor back-parts, muſt not the *rock*, the *cliſt of the rock*, & the *hand that cover'd* Moſes *in this cliſt*, and the *back-parts* ſeen upon taking away the hand, be underſtood by Men of the meaneſt capacity, in a ſpiritual ſenſe?

According to the acknowledg'd Maxims, you have laid down from Divines, we muſt not take literally the two conferences mention'd in the firſt & ſecond of *Job* between God and Satan; when *Satan, in very good company, with the Sons of God, preſented himſelf before the Lord*; who, when Satan wou'd not otherwiſe be ſatisfy'd of *Job's* integrity, permitted him to *ſlay* Job's *Children & Servants*, & reduce him to extremity to make the experiment. The ſame may be ſaid of the Lord's ſaying at another time to Satan, *ſtanding at the right hand of the Angel of the Lord, to reſiſt the High Prieſt* Joſhua, *ſtanding likewiſe before him,* \* *The Lord rebuke thee, O Satan :* And muſt we not think it as unworthy of God, to *talk to a Serpent* as to *Satan?* Or, how can we conceive a Serpent cou'd talk to *Eve,* & delude the Mother of Mankind, tho in the high ſtate of perfection; even tho' the Apoſtle ſays, † *The Serpent deceiv'd* Eve *by his ſubtilty*

Some are induced to imagine, that the Author of the Book of *Geneſis* thought, that words had ideas naturally fix'd to them, and not by conſent: Otherwiſe, ſay they, how can we account for his ſuppoſing, that God brought all animals before *Adam,* as ſoon as he was created, to give them names; & that ‡ *whatſoever* Adam *call'd every living creature, that was the name thereof*; and that the *Serpent* & *Eve,* almoſt as ſoon as created, entertain'd one another in the ſame language : And ſome think, that this Author did not know the reaſon of the neceſſary variety of language upon the increaſe of Mankind, by making God to come down to ſee *the City and Tower, whoſe*

P 3

---

\* *Zech.* 3. 1, 2.　　† 2 *Cor.* 11. 3.　　‡ *Gen.* 2. 10.

*top* was defign'd *to reach to Heaven*; and then.faying, *this they begin to do; and now nothing will be reftrain'd from them, which they have imagin'd to do. Go to, let us go down, and there confound their Language.* \*
And, perhaps, the not knowing the natural caufe of the *Rain-bow*, occafion'd that account we have in *Genefis* of its inftitution.

As to the ftory of an Angel of God's wreftling all night with *Jacob*, † and then *laming, & bleffing him, & changing his name*; „ Interpreters of note, whether „ *Jews* or *Chriftians* (as Mr. *Nye* obferves) ‡ under-„ ftood it done, not in fact, but in vifion only; „ tho' one would imagine the *Jews* thought it literally true, becaufe the text fays, § *They eat not of the finew,* that finew, *which fhrank, unto this very day.*

WHAT a number of ideas muft *Balaam*'s Afs have had, to be able to reafon with his Mafter, when he faw, & knew an Angel? And tho 'tis faid by *Peter*, ¶ that *the dumb Afs fpeaking with Man's voice, forbad the madnefs of the Prophet*; yet in the ftory itfelf, there does not appear any thing like madnefs: For that Prophet did nothing but what the Lord enjoin'd him; and declares, tho' *Balak wou'd give me his houfe full of filver & gold, I cannot go beyond the word of the Lord, my God.* And when he went with *Balaam*'s fecond meffengers, it was by the exprefs command of God; and yet the text fays, ✠ *God's anger was kindl'd becaufe he went:* And then follows the dialogue between the Afs and his Mafter.

How many commands did God give his Prophets, which if taken according the letter, feem unworthy of God, as making them act like mad-men, or idiots? As for inftance, the Prophet *Ifaiah* \* *walk'd for three years together naked for a Sign. Jeremiah* is commanded
*to*

---

\* *Gen.* 11. 4. 6, 7.    † *Ibid.* 32. 24, 25. 28, 29.
‡ *Nye* of Nat. & Rev. Relig. p. 203.    § *Gen.* 32. 32
¶ 2 *Pet.* 2. 16.    ✠ *Num.* 22. 22.    \* *Ifa.* 20. 3.

*to carry his girdle as for as* Euphrates, * *and there to bury it in the hole of a rock; and after many days he is sent to dig it up again.* So he is commanded † *to make bands & yokes, and put them about his neck, and send them to several Kings. Ezekiel* is commanded by the Lord *to draw* Jerusalem ‡ *on a tile, & lay siege to it, build a Fort against it, set a Camp against it, and set battering Rams against it round about.* Moreover, *to take an iron pan, and set it for a wall of iron between him & the City:* And immediately after he is commanded *to lye three hundred & ninety days on one side, & forty days on the other; & then to mix Man's dung with his bread.* And afterwards the Lord said, § *I have given thee cow's dung for Man's dung.* At another time he is commanded ¶ *to dig a hole through the wall of his house, & carry forth his goods in the twilight, & cover his face, as not to see the ground.* And as St. *John* was commanded ✠ *to eat a book,* so the Prophet was commanded *to eat a roll* *; and likewise *to clip his hair,* † and *to dispose of the clippings* after a very odd manner; and several other things as strange, too many here to mention. And the Prophet *Hosea,* ‡ who was likewise a Priest, was bid to take *a Wife of whoredoms;* (tho' that by *Moses's* § Law was forbid a *Priest,*) and *Children of Whoredoms;* and had three children by this Wife, to whom *the Lord himself gave names.*

No *Mathematician* cou'd give a more exact description of a city, than *John* does of ¶ *that great City, the holy* Jerusalem; which *from an high mountain he saw descending out of Heaven from God;* and he was so near it, as to describe the *Gates, Wall* and *Streets;* and to measure its length, breadth, & height *with a*

---

* *Jer.* 13. 4. 6.   † *Id.* 27. 2, 3.   ‡ *Ezek.* 4. 1, 2, 3, &c.
§ *Ezek.* 4. 12. 15.   ¶ *Id.* 12. 5, 6.   ✠ *Rev.* 10. 9.
* *Ezek.* 3. 1. 3.   † *Id.* 5. 1, 2, 3, 4.   ‡ *Hof.* 1. 2. &c.
§ *Lev.* 21. 14.   ¶ *Rev.* 21. 10. &c.

*reed.* And *Tertullian* assures us, * ,, that in his time, ,, there was seen for forty days together, a City ,, hanging in the air over *Judea.* ,, And yet Interpreters have since allegoris'd this great City into a meer Castle in the air. But,

To come to things of greater moment; did not the Scripture suppose Reason was able to teach Men of the meanest capacity, that God cou'd not be deceiv'd himself, or deceive us, the Prophet *Jeremiah* wou'd not have said, † *O Lord, thou hast deceiv'd me, and I was deceiv'd; thou art stronger than I, and hast prevailed.* -- ‡ *Wilt thou be altogether unto me as a Liar, and as waters that fail?* And in another Prophet the Lord says, § *The days are prolonged, and every vision fails.* And tho' the Lord adds, *There shall none of my words be prolonged any more, but the word which I have spoken shall be done;* yet he afterwards says, ¶ *If the Prophet be deceived when he hath spoken a thing, I, the Lord, have deceived that Prophet.* And if the Prophet is deceived, must not the people, who rely on that Prophet, be deceived? And does not the Prophet *Jeremiah* say, ✠ *Ah! Lord God, surely thou hast greatly deceived this people?* And to the same purpose the Prophet *Isaiah,* * *O Lord, thou hast made us to err.*

There are other texts which go further, and, if taken literally, represent God not only falsifying his word, but his Oaths. To mention two, the first relates to the Children of *Israel,* to whom the Lord said, † *Ye shall not come into the land concerning which I sware to make you dwell; & ye shall know my breach of promise.* The second is in *Psalm* 89. in the first part of which is largely set forth the promises of God to *David* by covenant & oath; and in the other part *David* complains of God's breach, both of his covenant, & his oath; and in summing up those breaches he

* *Contra Marcion. l. 3. c. 24.*   † *Jer. 20. 7.*   ‡ *Id. 15. 18.*
§ *Ezek. 12. 22. 28.*   ¶ *Id. 14. 9.*   ✠ *Jer. 4. 10.*
* *Isa. 63. 17.*   † *Num. 14. 30. 34.*

he fays , * *Thou haft made void the Covenant of thy Servant:* † *Lord, where are thy former loving kindneſſes which thou ſweareſt to* David *in thy truth?* And there are ſeveral facts mention'd in Scripture, which, if taken literally, look as tho' the Prophets either were deceiv'd themſelves, or were willing to deceive others. The Propheteſs *Hilda* aſſures good King *Joſiah* from the Lord, ‡ *that he ſhou'd be gather'd to his grave in peace;* and yet ſoon after he receiv'd a *mortal wound* §, of which he dy'd. The Prophet *Eliſha* ¶ ſends word to *Benhadad*, the King of *Syria*, who conſults him about his recovery, that he may, ( or rather ſhall, or will, for ſo it ought to be render'd,) certainly recover; yet he tells *Hazael*, who had a deſign on his Crown and life ( and who before had been anointed King of *Syria* by the Prophet *Elijah*, ✠ ) that *he ſhould ſurely die*. And this look'd the more ungrateful in the Prophet, becauſe he had receiv'd *forty Camel loads of the good thing of* Damaſcus , * to tell the King the truth. But I need not mention ſingle Prophets deceiving, or being deceiv'd , when the Scripture tells us of four hundred being deceiv'd at once , † to the deſtruction of a number of innocent perſons. *I ſaw,* ſays the Prophet *Micaiab,* ‡ *the Lord ſitting upon his throne, & all the Hoſt of Heaven ſtanding on his right hand, and on his left. And the Lord ſaid, who ſhall entice* Ahab King of Iſrael. *that he may go up, and fall at* Ramoth - gilead? *And one ſpake, ſaying after this manner, and another ſaying after that manner. Then there came out a Spirit, & ſtood before the Lord, & ſaid, I will entice him. And the Lord ſaid unto him, wherewith? And he ſaid I will go out, & be a lying Spirit in the mouth of all his Prophets. And the Lord ſaid, thou ſhalt entice him, & thou ſhalt alſo prevail. Go out, & do even ſo.*

P 5

As

* *Pſal* 89. 39. † *Ib. ver.* 49. ‡ 2 *Chron.* 34. 28. § *Ib.* 35. 23. ¶ 2 *Kings* 8. 7-10. ✠ 1 *Kings* 19. 15. *2 *Kings* 8. 8, 9. † 2 *Chron.* 18. 5. 22. ‡ *Ibid.* 18. 5. 18. 21, 22.

As to the new-Testament, I shall now only observe that tho' St. *Jude* \* quotes (besides the assumption of *Moses*) a Prophecy of *Enoch*, the seventh from *Adam*, and the Book containing this Prophecy was then in being, yet, becaufe there were things in it, which feem'd unworthy of God, & cou'd not be well allegoris'd, the authority of an infpir'd perfon quoting it as an infpir'd Book, cou'd not fupport its credit, but it fell into contempt, & was loft.

B. Tho' you allow Reafon to be the proper Judge in things of morality, as falling under its cognizance; yet as to Prophecies, you muft own, we are entirely to rely on authority.

A. I have hitherto faid nothing in relation to Prophecies, defigning to fpeak of them at another feafon; but fince you mention them, I muft, as to the Prophecies in the Old-Teftament, confefs my ignorance, that I do not underftand them; and Divines themfelves, as far as I can find, are infinitely divided about interpreting them: And as to thofe Prophecies, if they may be fo call'd, in the New Teftament, relating to the *fecond coming of Chrift*, and *the end of the World*, the beft Interpreters and Commentators own, the Apoftles themfelves were grofly miftaken; there fcarce being an Epiftle, but where they foretell that thofe times they wrote in, were *tempora noviffima*; & the then Age the laft Age, & thofe days the laft days; and that the *end of the World was nigh*, & *the coming of Chrift at hand*; as is plain, among other texts, from I *Cor.* 10. 11. *Rom.* 13. 11, 12. *Heb.* 9. 26. *Jam.* 5. 7, 8. I *Joh.* 2. 18. 2 *Pet.* 3. 12, 13. And they do not affert this as a meer matter of fpeculation, but build motives & arguments upon it, to excite people to the practice of piety, and all good works; as *Phil.* 4. 5. *Let your moderation be known to all Men, the Lord is at hand.* And to the fame purpofe are *Heb.* 10. 24, 25. I *Pet.* 4. 7, 8. I *Cor.* 7. 29. 2 *Pet.* 3. 11, 12.

And

\* *Jude* 9. 14.

And tho' they do not pretend to tell the very day &
hour, when these things must happen, yet they thought
it wou'd be during their time, & continually expected
it. *Timothy* \* is charged to *keep this Commandment --
till the appearing of the Lord.* So *Paul* says to the Co-
rinthians, † *as' oft as ye eat this bread, & drink this cup,
ye do shew the Lord's death till he comes.* And I think,
'tis plain, *Paul* himself expected to be alive at the
coming of the Lord, & that he had the word of God
for it. ‡ *For this we say unto you by the word of the
Lord, that we which are alive, & remain unto the coming
of the Lord, shall not prevent them which are asleep. --
The dead in Christ shall rise first. Then we which are
alive, & remain, shall be caught up together with them
in the clouds, to meet the Lord in the air; and so shall
we ever be with the Lord. Wherefore, comfort one another
with these words.* And there are other texts to the
same purpose, as 1 *Cor.* 15. 51, 52. 2 *Cor.* 5. 4.

B. D o e s not St. *Paul* § suppose, that before the
coming of Christ, *Antichrist must appear?*

*A.* T h a t does not in the least hinder, but he
might believe both wou'd happen in his time; *For,*
says he, ¶ *the Mystery of iniquity does already work.*
And St. *John* puts this matter out of dispute, in saying,
✠ *Little Children, it is the last time; and as ye have
heard that Antichrist shall come, even now are there many
Antichrists; whereby we know that it is the last time.*

B. D o e s not St. *Peter* say, \* *There shall come in
the last days, Scoffers -- saying where is the promise of
his coming?*

*A.* S a i n t *Peter* owns those to be the last days, &
the promise of his then coming he confirms, by saying,
† *God is not slack concerning his promise, the day of the
Lord will come as a Thief in the night: -- What manner
of*

---

\* 1 *Tim.* 6. 13, 14.        † 1 *Cor.* 11. 26.
‡ *Thes.* 4. 15, 16, 17, 18. See *Grotius* in loc.
§ 2 *Thes.* 2. 3.        ¶ *Ibid. ver.* 7.        ✠ 1 *John* 2. 18.
\* 2 *Pet.* 3. 3, 4.        † *ibid. ver.* 9, - 13.

*of perfons ought ye to be in all holy converfation and god-linefs, looking for, & hafting unto the coming of the day of God, wherein the Heavens being on fire fhall be diffolved, and the elements fhall melt with fervent heat: Neverthelefs we according to his promife, look for new Heavens, and a new Earth.*

*B.* DOES not St. Peter fay, * *Beloved be not ignorant of this one thing, that one day is with the Lord as a thoufand years, & a thoufand years as one day?*

*A.* THIS, as in the margin, feems to be quoted from *Pfalm* 90. 4. where 'tis faid, *A thoufand years in thy fight, are but as yefterday when it is paft* And furely St *Peter* cou'd not imagine, that God affected to fpeak unintelligibly, & by one day meant a thoufand years, and by a thoufand years one day; and refer to this place as a proof.

*B.* DIVINES are at a lofs how to account for the Apoftles fo frequently declaring, the *end of all things to be at hand, & Chrift to be then a coming;* when our Saviour fays, † *Of that day & hour knoweth no Man; no, not the Angels of Heaven, but my Father only.*

*A.* THOSE Divines wou'd not make thefe reflections, did they but confider what our Saviour declares to his Difciples, when they came to him privately, faying, ‡ *Tell us when thefe things fhall be, & what fhall be the fign of thy coming, and of the end of the world.* Does he not in anfwer to their queftion, tell them what thofe figns wou'd be? withal adding, § *So likewife ye, when ye fhall fee all thefe things, know that it is near, even at the doors. Verily, I fay unto you, This Generation fhall not pafs, till all thefe things be fulfill'd.* And to affure them of the truth of what he declares, *Heaven & Earth,* fays he, ¶ *fhall pafs away; but my words fhall not pafs away.* And his adding, ✠ *But of that day & hour knoweth no Man; no, not the Angels of Heaven, but my Father only,* was not
meant

* 2 *Pet.* 3. 8.    † *Mat.* 24. 36.    ‡ *Ib. ver.* 3.
§ *Ver.* 33, 34.    ¶ *Ver.* 34.    ✠ *Ver.* 36.

meant to contradict what he just before declar'd, that
* *this Generation shall not pass till these things be ful-*
*fill'd;* but to warn his Disciples not to be surpris'd as
the old World was, *when the Flood came, and swept
them all away; Watch therefore, for ye know not what
hour your Lord will come: But know this, that if the
good Man of the house had known in what watch the
Thief wou'd have come, he wou'd have watch'd.* - -
And the Apostles agreeable to this admonition of the
Lord, say, † *Yourselves know perfectly, that the day of
the Lord cometh as a Thief in the night.* And after the
resurrection our Saviour says to *Peter,* who asks him
concerning the beloved Disciple; ‡ *If I will, that he
tarry 'till I come, what is that to thee?* And the last
thing his Disciples ask'd him on his ascension, is, §
*Wilt thou at this time, restore again the Kingdom to Israel?*
And the answer he gave them is very consistent with
the Kingdom, even the temporal Kingdom of *Israel's*
being restor'd again during their lives. And by our
Saviour's saying, when the last supper was ended, ¶
*I will not drink henceforth of the fruit of the vine, until
that day I drink it new with you in my Father's Kingdom,*
they no doubt, believ'd this happy time was not far
off. But,

  I f most of the Apostles, upon what motives soever,
were mistaken in a matter of this consequence, how
can we be certain, that any one of them may not be
mistaken in any other matter? If they were not inspir'd in what they said in their writings concerning
the then coming of Christ, how cou'd they be inspir'd
in those arguments they build on a foundation far
from being so? And if they thought their times were
the last, no direction they gave, cou'd be intended to
reach further than their own times. And if *John* the
Evangelist, and *John* the Divine are the same person,
he must believe what is mention'd in the *Revelation,*
wou'd

---

* *Mat.* 24. 34.   † 1 *Thes.* 5. 2.   2 *Pet.* 3. 10.
† *John* 21. 22.   § *Act.* 1. 6.   ¶ *Mat.* 26. 29.

wou'd have happen'd within the compaſs of that Age in which he writ. But leaving theſe matters to another time, let us return to the conſideration of thoſe duties, which Reaſon ſhews us from the nature of God and Man, and the relation Men ſtand in to him, and one another.

As I have already ſhown you by a number of inſtances, where Divines themſelves own, that tho' the literal ſenſe of the Scripture be ever ſo plain, yet it muſt not ſtand in competition with what our Reaſon tells us of the nature & perfections of God; ſo I ſhall now ſhew you, the ſame in relation to thoſe duties Men owe to one another; and that if Men are not well grounded in the reaſon & nature of things, and from thence judge of their duty, in relation to one another; there are things either commanded, or approv'd of in the Scripture, which might be apt to lead Men aſtray. A Man, who looks no further than that, might think it no crime to cheat his elder Brother, impoſe on his aged Parent, and by a lie obtain his bleſſing: nay, hope that God wou'd confirm it, when he ſees how *Jacob* * obtain'd the greateſt bleſſing from God.

If Men flatter themſelves, that they are true *Iſraelites*, & thoſe of a different Religion, mere *Egyptians*; will they not be apt to imagine, when they ſee how the *Iſraelites* ſpoil'd the *Egyptians* by the command of God himſelf, who made them borrow what they were not to repay, that this might be a good precedent for them?

*B.* I muſt own, that a Command to † *lend, hoping for nothing again*, & a Command to *borrow, without returning* any thing *again*, ſeem to be very different Commands.

*A.* When Men find the Harlot *Rahab* celebrated, even in the *New Teſtament*, ‡ for lying to the Government,

* *Gen.* 27.  † *Luke* 6. 35. *Exod.* 3. 21, 22. - 22. 35, 36.
‡ *Heb.* 11. 31. *Jam.* 2. 25.

ment, and betraying her Country to its most cruel Enemies; are they not in danger, if they find their advantage in it, & 'tis for the service of those they judge to be true *Israelites*, to do the same? since 'tis not pretended the Harlot had any more a special command for so doing, than *Jael* had for an act of the highest treachery; for which, because it serv'd the interest of *Israel*, she is declar'd by the Prophetess *Deborah* to be *bless'd above Women*. *

W H A T Prince can ever want a pretence of going to War, & totally extirpating those he invades, when he sees, *Saul* † was commanded by God to destroy the *Amalekites*, *Men and Women*, *Infants & Sucklings*, *Ox & Sheep*, *Camel & Ass*, for an injury done ‡ four hundred years before? And how for sparing *Agag*, § (whom *Samuel* hew'd to pieces before the Lord;) and preserving some of the cattle for sacrifice, the Lord rejected him from being King; ¶ nay, order'd *Samuel*, least *Saul* shou'd suspect the design, to pretend a Sacrifice, when he sent him to anoint *David*?

W o u'd not people, if like the Children of *Israel*, they were destitute of an habitation, be apt to think what the *Israelites* did to the *Canaanites*, a good precedent; and that they might invade a neighbouring, idolatrous Nation, that never did them the least harm; and extirpate not only Men & Women, but even their innocent Infants, in order to get possession of their Country? And I question, whether the *Spaniards* wou'd have murder'd so many millions in the *Indies*, had they not thought they might have us'd them like *Canaanites*.

H o w many precedents, besides that of *Ehud*, ✠ (who, on a message from the Lord, stabb'd the King to whom his people sent him with a present) did the *Popish* Priests plead from the *Old Testament*, for the assassination of the two *Henries* of *France*? And had
the

* *Judg.* 5. 24.   † 1 *Sam.* 15. 2, 3.   ‡ *Exod.* 17. 8. &c.
§ 1 *Sam.* 15. 9. &c.   ¶ *Id.* 16. 2. &c.   ✠ *Jud.* 3. 15, 20, 21.

the *Gun-Powder-Plot* succeeded here, they wou'd, no doubt, have made use of the same plea to justify it.

Tho' the Lord bids the *Jews* to *pray for the peace of* Babylon, \* *whither he had caus'd them to be carry'd away captives*; & that *in the peace thereof they shou'd have peace*; yet is it not said in the *Psalms*, † O *Daughter of* Babylon, *happy shall he be, who taketh, and dasheth thy little ones against the stones*; and this for no other reason, but because *she desir'd of her Captives one of the songs of* Zion. ‡

THE holier Men in the *Old Testament* are represented, the more cruel they seem to be, as well as more addicted to cursing; How plentifully does *David* in the 109th *Psalm* bestow the bitterest curses on his Enemies? And how cruelly did he treat the *Ammonites*, when he took their Cities, § *cutting the people with saws, & with harrows of iron, & with axes?*

WHO is not surpris'd to find the holy Prophet *Elisha* cursing, *in the name of the Lord, little Children* for calling him *bald pate?* And what is still more surprising, ¶ *Two she Bears*, upon his cursing, *strait devour'd forty two little Children.*

AND he likewise entail'd the curse of leprosy on his Man *Gehazy, & his seed for ever*, ✠ for accepting, without his Master's knowledge, a small present from *Naaman*, the *Assyrian*; tho' the Prophet himself afterwards took \* *forty Camel loads of the good things of* Damascus, to tell their King the truth, in relation to his recovery; and yet deceiv'd him.

*Elijah's* causing *Fire to come down from Heaven*, to destroy two Captains with their Companies, for no other fault, but bluntly delivering a message from the King, & perhaps, in the very words they were commanded, was not so cruel, as his hindering it from † *raining upon the Earth for the space of three years and*

                                                            *six*

* *Jer.* 29. 7.    † *Psal.* 137. 8, 9.    ‡ *Ibid. ver.* 3.
§ 1 *Chr.* 20. 3.    ¶ 2 *Kings,* 2. 23, 24.    ✠ *Ib.* 5. 27.
* *Ibid.* 8, 9. *&c.*    † *Jam.* 5. 17.

*six months*; since a drought of that continuance, without dew or rain *, in such a barren country as *Judea*, must have, without miracles, destroy'd every thing; and yet St. *James* from hence takes occasion to recommend the efficacy of prayer. †

If God will not, in this life, miraculously alter the course of things, for the sake of the innocent, he, certainly, will not do it for the guilty; nor break in upon the ordinary methods & laws of his Providence, to punish one Man for the crime of another, the innocent for the guilty. If God cou'd act thus, it wou'd be no crime in Man to imitate him: nay, how cou'd we be sure, if God deals thus with his Creatures in this life, he will not act so in the life to come? since if the eternal Rules of Justice are once broke, how can we imagine any stop? And yet,

Are there not examples in Scripture, which, taken in their literal sense, seem to make God break in upon the common course of Nature, & the ordinary rules of his Providence, to punish Men for crimes they were not guilty of; as God's causing, in the latter end of *David*'s Reign, ‡ *a Famine for three years together*, for the crime of *Saul* and *his bloody House*, *in slaying the* Gibeonites: And that *God smote* Israel, *& destroy'd seventy thousand* of them for *David*'s fault, in causing *the innocent sheep*, as he justly calls them, *to be number'd*.

*B.* I believe there must be some mistake in this last story; for is it not fit for several important reasons, that Kings shou'd know the numbers of their People? Are they not the strength & riches of their Kingdom? And was not the People of *Israel*, by being frequently number'd, & sometimes by God's own appointment, a good precedent for *David*? But passing that by, how can we reconcile this story with itself? § In one place 'tis said, *God mov'd* David *to number* Israel; ¶

Q

in

in another *Satan provok'd* David. Did God confpire with Satan in this act, in order to deftroy a number of innocent perfons? But do thefe two places any more agree in the account *Joab* gives in of the number of the People? * nay, if in the beginning of *Saul's* Reign, the numbers were rightly calculated, 'tis morally impoffible, to fay nothing of the deftruction made by continual War, that either account fhou'd be true. Befides,

Can God change his mind, & that fuddenly too? Yet 'tis faid, *God fent an Angel to* Jerufalem *to deftroy it*; and as he was deftroying it, *the Lord beheld, and repented him of the evil.* And can any one think this to be a meer Peftilence, when a real Angel is faid to be miraculoufly fent to execute God's anger? † *And* David, *with the Elders of* Ifrael, *fell on their faces, & faw the Angel of the Lord ftand between the Earth and the Heavens, having a drawn fword in his hand, by the threfhing-floor of* Ornan, *the* Jebufite; & is there *commanded to build an Altar.*

*A.* What you fay may be true, fince there are feveral miftakes crept into the Old Teftament, where there's fcarce a chapter, which gives any hiftorical account of matters, but there are fome things in it, which cou'd not be there originally; ‡ and even in this Book of *Chronicles*, there are things mention'd, too late to be inferted by *Ezra*, or *Nehemiah*. And I might add, that the *Jewifh* Hiftory being for the moft part taken from larger accounts, 'tis no wonder its abftracts are not always very exact.

I cou'd give you many more inftances of this nature, but I am afraid fome will think thefe too many; tho' I have faid nothing, but what Archbifhop *Tillotfon* does in effect, in affirming, § ,, The difference be-
,, tween the Style of the Old and New Teftament is
so

* 1 *Sam.* 11. 8.　　† 1 *Chr.* 21. 15, 16. 18.
‡ See *Prideaux's* Connect. Part 1. B. 5. p. 343. & B. 8.
p. 574.　§ *Serm. Vol.* 2. *p.* 185.

,, so very remarkable, that one of the greatest Sects
,, in the primitive times did upon this very ground,
,, found their Heresy of *Two Gods:* The one evil,
,, fierce, and cruel, whom they call'd *The God of the*
,, *Old Testament* ; the other good, kind, & merciful,
,, whom they call'd *The God of the New Testament:*
,, So great a difference is there between the represen-
,, tations, which are made of God in the books of
,, the *Jewish* & *Christian* Religion, as to give, at least,
,, some colour, and pretence for an imagination of
,, two Gods.,, But,

I⊤ must be own'd, that the same spirit (I dare not
call it a spirit of cruelty) does not alike prevail
throughout the Old Testament; the nearer we come
to the times of the Gospel, the milder it appear'd;
for tho' God declares in the Decalogue, that he is a
*Jealous God, visiting the iniquity of the Parents upon
their Children, to the third and fourth generation*; and
accordingly *Achan*, * with all his Family, was destroy'd
for his single crime; yet the Lord afterwards says,
† *The Soul that sinneth, it shall dye; the Son shall not
bear the iniquity of the Father,* &c.

Oʋʀ Saviour, by saying, *He came not to destroy
Mens lives, but to save them*; condemns their taking
away the lives of any, except in defence of their own,
& of what is necessary for their support; and this he
declares, upon a most remarkable occasion : Some of
his Disciples, upon his not being receiv'd into a *Sa-
maritan* Village, ‡ *because his face was towards Jerusalem*, straight cry'd, *Wilt thou we command fire from
Heaven, and consume them,* as *Elias* did? § *He rebuk'd
them, and said, Ye know not what manner of spirit ye
are of; for the Son of Man is not come to destroy Mens
Lives, but to save them.* If any precedent might have
been pleaded from the Old Testament, it wou'd, no
doubt, have been that of *Elias*, the Fore-runner of

Q 2                                        our

* *Josh.* 7. 24.          † *Ezek.* 18. 20.
‡ *Luke* 9. 54.          § *Ibid. ver.* 55, 56.

our Saviour; who came from Heaven (to which he
went up by a Whirlwind in *a Chariot of fire*, with
*Horses of fire* \*) to meet our Saviour on a *high
mountain*. †

And if it be contrary to the spirit of the Gospel,
even to wish to imitate that great Prophet so favour'd
of God; the same will hold as strongly, in relation
to all the actions that are of a like nature of other
holy men, tho' quoted with approbation in the New
Testament; as *Moses* is for acting the part of a
Magistrate, ‡ when a private Man, in destroying his
fellow Subject. And if there's a contrast between the
spirit of the Old, & the spirit of the New Testament,
ought not we *Christians* to stick to the latter; & not
suppose the texts, which require doing good even to
the *Gentiles*, & dealing with them as ourselves expect
to be dealt with, to relate to *Christians* only before
they had power to act otherwise; & that after they
were to be govern'd by precedents from the Old
Testament?

*B*. Are there any so absurd, as to endeavour thus
to reconcile the Old & New Testament?

*A*. We find the Orthodox, as soon as they had a
Prince, who refus'd submission to their decisions in
the Council of *Nice*, in express terms own'd as much.

*Lucifer Calaritanus*, then a must orthodox Bishop,
in several discourses address'd to the Son of *Constantine*
the Great, does not scruple to tell the Emperor himself, that it was the duty of the Orthodox to kill him,
on the account of his *Arianism*; which he calls *Idolatry*:
And for this he quotes *Deut*. 13. 6. & 1 *Maccab*. 1. 43.
to ver. 29th of Chap. 2. and then insultingly says, §
„ If you had been in the hands of *Matthias*, or *Phineas*,
                                            they

---

\* 2 *Kings* 2. 11.    † *Mark* 9. 2. 4.    ‡ *Acts* 7. 24.

§ See *S. Johnson*'s Answer to *Hick*'s *Constant*, where
the Story is at large, p. 56. &c. & *Val*. p. 75, 76, 77.
taken out of *Biblioth. vet. Patr*. To. 4. Colen. pag.
164. &c.

„ they wou'd have kill'd you. You fay you fuffer
„ defpiteful ufage from us, contrary to the admoni-
„ tions of holy Scripture. -- If ever any one of the
„ worfhippers of God fpared Apoftates, let what you
„ fay of us be true. -- Pray fhew me but one of them,
„ that ever fpar'd the Adverfaries of his Religion: „
And the texts for obedience to Magiftrates from
*Titus* 3. 1. he evades, by faying, „ That the Apoftle
„ fpoke of thofe Princes & Magiftrates, who as yet
„ had not believed in the only Son of God; that they
„ by our humility, and meeknefs, & fuffering long
„ under adverfity, & all poffible obedience in things
„ fitting, might be won over to Chriftianity.

*Athanafius*, & the Confeffors that were with him
highly applauded *Lucifer*'s difcourfes, and fays, „ We
„ plainly fee the picture of an Apoftle, the boldnefs
„ of a Prophet, the magiftery of truth, the doctrine
„ of true Faith. -- You feem to be the true Temple
„ of our Saviour, who dwelling in you, fpeaks thefe
„ things by you. --

„ BELIEVE me, *Lucifer*, You alone did not fay
„ thefe things, but the Holy Ghoft with you; how
„ came you to remember Scripture at that rate?
„ how came you to underftand the fenfe & meaning
„ of it fo perfectly, if the Holy Ghoft had not affifted
„ you in it?

THEY, who defign a new Religion, in oppofition
to eftablifh'd ones, wou'd, no doubt, as thefe Fathers
fuppofe, begin with Precepts of the greateft humanity
& tendernefs, & doing the utmoft good to Mankind,
tho' of ever fo different perfuafions; but to think, as
thefe Fathers then did, (and the Orthodox, if we
judge from their actions, have ever fince thought)
that all the Precepts of the Gofpel of this nature were
defign'd only to draw *Jews* & *Gentiles* into the Church,
as Gallants gain their Miftreffes by obfequioufnefs, &
that after they were once in, the Church (as all Sects
and parties term themfelves) had a right to murder.

nos

not only private perfons, but even their Sovereigns, for not holding the orthodox Faith; and that this is the only way to reconcile the Old & New Teftament, is a notion highly injurious to the Chriftian Religion.

'Tis, no doubt, the intereft of wicked Priefts, to have God reprefented under oppofite characters; and to give in one Teftament Rules contrary to thofe in the other; that they, as it ferves their turn, may make ufe of either: But is it not aftonifhing for Saints and Confeffors upon the firft occafion, to renounce their former principles, and in defiance of their oaths of Allegiance, reprefent a Man *infpir'd by the Holy Ghoft,* & fay, that *Chrift fpoke in him,* when he declares it the duty of Chriftians to murder an heretical Emperor?

*B.* Those holy Fathers, I fuppofe, thought, they faw things of the greateft confequence, tho commanded in the Old, forbidden in the New Teftament; and that to make the Old & New Teftament to contradict each other in thefe things, was to deftroy the authority of both; and therefore concluded, this expedient was the only way to fupport both.

*A.* By reafoning thus, inftead of reconciling both, they deftroy'd both, & natural Religion too; in fuppofing Things are not good and evil in themfelves, but that all depends on the Will of an arbitrary Being, which might endlefly change. But,

If there's a Law of Nature, with the obferving of which God can't difpenfe either in himfelf, or in his Creatures; * & no Religion can be true, that in the minuteft circumftances is contrary to it's Righteoufnefs; and the Gofpel inculcates all fuch Precepts of Natural Religion, as require doing good to *Jew* and *Gentile,* even the fame we expect from them: and that we are indifpenfably bound to allow all others the fame right of judging for themfelves, as we claim for ourfelves;

* See *Prideaux's* Lett. to the *Deifts,* pag. 127. Edit. 7. 8vo.

felves; muft we not, if we will fupport the credit of the Old Teftament, fuppofe it to contain nothing inconfiftent with this natural right confirm'd by the Gofpel? If this be not fo, pray fhew me my miftake: but if it be juft reafoning, tel me how you can account for the conduct of the *Jews*, in invading, and that too without any Declaration of War, the *Canaanites*, a free and independant Nation, and againft whom they had not the leaft caufe of complaint, and on pretence of their being idolaters, deftroying not only the Men & Women, but Infants incapable of idolatry, or any other crime. This, you know, has given great advantage to the Enemies of our Religion, who reprefent the whole proceeding, as an unparallell'd piece of injuftice & cruelty, & therefore, I fhould be glad to know what our Divines, if they do not interpret this fact allegorically, or as only done in vifion, fay, to fhew tis not contrary to the Law of Nature, & thofe Precepts of the Gofpel which are founded on it.

*B.* I wonder you can be ignorant, with what eafe our Divines folve this feeming difficulty, by having recourfe to a pofitive Command for treating the *Canaanites* as they did.

*A.* Such a Command is pleaded in vain, except it can be fhewn, that the thing fuppos'd to be commanded, is not inconfiftent with the Law of Nature: which if God can difpenfe with in any one cafe, he may in all, nor cou'd his Wifdom then prefcribe any certain Rule of conduct, either for himfelf or his Creatures, but all wou'd depend on an uncertain, fluctuating, arbitrary Will.

*B.* May not a thing, which is unlawful for Men to do of themfelves, become lawful, by the Command of the fupreme Being?

*A.* Suppose any fhou'd now plead that they had a divine Commiffion to deftroy their next Neighbours, whom they judg'd to be Idolaters, Man, Woman &

Q 4

Child,

Child, in order to poſſeſs their country, wou'd not our Divines ſay, no Man cou'd be as certain he had any ſuch poſitive Command from God, as he was, that God had forbid it him by the Light of Nature? Nor cou'd miracles be a proof of any ſuch Commiſſion; ſince we can only know from the nature of the things themſelves, whether Miracles are done by a good, or evil Being; and we are to compare what we are told of God, with what we know of him; otherwiſe we believe in Men, & not in God. And if the Light of Nature, (the voice of God himſelf) teaches us, even to demonſtration, that God is infinitely wiſe and good, does it not likewiſe demonſtrate, that no Command, not ſtamp'd with theſe characters, can come from him, much leſs a Command inconſiſtent with all thoſe duties that Men as Men owe to one another?

B. MAY not God puniſh ſome wicked Nations with death, to fright others from committing the ſame crimes?

A. GOD has a thouſand ways of doing this, without commanding Men to do any thing, which, by the Law of Nature, he had forbid them; and if God deſign'd what he did to be a terror to others, wou'd he not act after ſuch a ſignal, & ſuper-natural manner, as all ſhou'd ſee it was his own doing; and the reaſon of his ſo doing: And in order to it, diſtinguiſh between the guilty, & the innocent?

IF God wou'd puniſh the *Canaanites*, for acting contrary to the Law of Nature, wou'd he, in order to do this, require the *Iſraelites* to act contrary to the ſame Law, in murdering Men, Women, & Children, that never did them the leaſt injury?

BESIDES, were not the *Jews*, conſidering their circumſtances upon their coming out of *Egypt*, the moſt improper People to convince the world, that they did not act out of a private intereſt, but purely to execute God's vengeance on an idolatrous Nation;

Wou'd

Wou'd God, in such a case, choose People as prone to Idolatry as the *Canaanites* themselves? Some question, whether, in this case, the plea of a divine Command, if taken literally, will not destroy all the internal proofs of the falsehood of any Religion; for can that, *say they*, which is consistent with the truth of any one true Religion, prove another Religion to be false? And do not all our Divines, when they are speaking against other Religions, maintain, that their commanding, or approving any thing contrary to the Law of Nature, is a demonstration of their falsehood? since it destroys all the internal proofs of the truth of any Religion, & confounds all the essential marks, by which we discern good from evil; and supposes God may command a Son to sacrifice his Father, or do any thing, tho' ever so repugnant to the Light of Nature.

*B.* These Men carry their reasoning too far; for has not Providence frequently made use of ill Men, not only to punish ill Men, but for other good purposes?

*A.* In the course of things it can't but happen, that some ill Men may be a scourge to others; yet that can't excuse them, if in so doing they act against the eternal Rules of Justice & Equity. Tho' a thing may be said to be done by the determinate Council of God, yet that will not justify, or excuse those that did it, if not consistent with the Law of Nature. St. *Peter*, speaking of the holy Child *Jesus*, says, * — *The People of Israel were gathered together, for to do whatsoever thy hand, & thy Counsel determined before to be done:* And yet were not they, & their Posterity punish'd for that fact, which God's hand & Counsel had determin'd shou'd be done? Besides,

If the *Israelites* had a divine Commission to extirpate the *Canaanites*, ought not the *Canaanites* to have known it, to prevent their resisting Men acting by a

Q 5                              divine

* *Acts* 4. 27, 28.

divine Commiſſion? Otherwiſe wou'd there not be two oppoſite rights at the ſame time; a right in the *Jews* by revelation, to take away the lives of the *Canaanites*, & a right in the *Canaanites* by the Law of Nature, to defend their lives?

*B.* WAS not the * *Sun's ſtanding ſtill for a whole day together*, at the command of *Joſhua*, that he might have light enough to deſtroy his Enemies, a ſufficient proof they ought to have offer'd up their throats?

*A.* THAT did not happen till they were defeated before *Gibeon*, and conſequently till then, it cou'd be no direction to them, and even after that, † *the Lord harden'd their hearts, that they ſhould come againſt* Iſrael *in battle*; and tho' 'tis ſaid, ‡ that *the living God is among you*, and that *he will not fail to drive out before you the* Canaanites, *&c.* yet *Iſrael* cou'd not drive them out of ſeveral places: And in one inſtance 'tis ſaid, § *The Lord was with* Judah, *& he drove out the inhabitants of the mountain, but could not drive out the inhabitants of the valley, becauſe they had chariots of iron.*

A Reverend Author, to ſolve the difficulties attending this matter, ſays, ¶ ,, The *Criticks* & *Rabbins*
,, take notice, that it is not ſaid by the Hiſtorian,
,, that *Joſhua* commanded the *Sun* & *Moon* to ſtand
,, ſtill; but he recites the words of a certain book
,, (ſuppoſed to be a *Poem*, written by one *Jaſher*)
,, in which the Poet, becauſe of the great and long
,, ſlaughter, that *Joſhua* made of the *Ammorites*, in-
,, troduces *Joſhua*, as requiring the *Sun* & *Moon* to
,, ſtand ſtill, while he, and his Army deſtroy'd the
,, Enemies of the Lord. Which, indeed, was an
,, elegant fiction, & very proper in a Poem that was
,, written on ſuch an occaſion.

AND

---

* *Joſh.* 10. 12, 13.     † *Ibid. cap.* 11. 20.
‡ *Ibid. cap.* 3. 10. - 16. 10. - 17. 12.     § *Judges* 1. 19.
¶ *Nye* of Nat. and Rev. Relig. pag. 102.

And now let me ask you, Whether the very endeavouring to reconcile this, or any other facts mention'd in the Old Testament, with the Light of Nature & the Evangelical Precepts, is not a plain confession what Men ought to think of them, if they cou'd not be reconcil'd; and that we are to use our Reason, in judging of the actions of the most celebrated persons of old? Else, to give no other instances, than the Transactions between *Judah* & *Tamar*, we might approve her stratagem, in getting to lye with her Father-in-law; for tho' before he knew himself to be the Man, he was resolv'd to burn her; yet after he cry'd, * *She has been more righteous than I:* And for this righteousness she was bless'd with twins, from whom the noble house of *Judah*, with all its Kings, & the *Messiah* himself, was descended.

I think, I cou'd not say less than I have, in vindication of the Precepts of the Gospel; by shewing that they were not design'd merely to draw People into the profession of the Christian Religion, and then to be laid aside, except where they serv'd the interest of the local orthodoxy; but that they are Rules in their own nature obligatory, which, from their internal excellency, always bound Mankind; & consequently, all Men, even those of the meanest abilities, must have been capable of knowing them, and out of danger, were it not their own fault, of being misled by any precedents whatever.

If what has been already said, may not be sufficient to shew, that it can't be imputed to want of Wisdom, or Goodness in God, or to any defect in Reason, which he has at all times given Mankind for the discovery of his Will, that the nature of Religion is so little understood, and so many things, which do not shew themselves to be the Will of God, are mix'd with it, let me ask you, whether God has a greater kindness for the brute, than the rational creation?

B.

* *Gen.* 38. 27.

*B.* THAT, certainly, muſt be a needleſs queſtion.

*A.* IF God, then, in the very frame & make of thoſe Animals we term irrational, has implanted the ſenſe of every thing neceſſary to anſwer the end of their creation, can we imagine, he has not as great a care of his Creatures endow'd with Reaſon, & made after his own image, and for ends infinitely more noble than the brute creation? When we ſee with what skill & contrivance, Birds, without being taught by any, but the God of Nature, build their neſts; and how artfully the Spiders frame their webs, the Bees their little cels, and the Beaſts avoid all noxious herbs: And not to multiply inſtances, how all Animals are endow'd with ſufficient ſagacity, for preſerving themſelves & ſpecies; muſt we not own, that what we call *Inſtinct*, is a certain & infallible Guide for inferior Animals? and can we doubt, whether Man, the Lord of the Creation, has not from his ſuperior Reaſon, ſufficient notices of whatever makes for his great ſt, his eternal happineſs?

IF we can't charge God with acting thus partially, muſt we not be oblig'd to own, that Reaſon is as certain a Guide for *rational* Creatures, as Inſtinct is for irrational? And conſequently, that thoſe Men are below Brutes, who, wanting Inſtinct, will not govern themſelves, nor ſuffer others to be govern'd by Reaſon? And

THO' they place the higheſt value on themſelves for being rational, & by virtue of it religious, yet are they ever contriving how to hinder the free exerciſe of Reaſon in religious matters; as if Reaſon & Religion were irreconcileable, and that the method God propoſes for the diſcovery of all other truth, was a moſt certain way to confound religious truth, and endleſly to multiply error. But,

THO' Divines in all Ages have, for the moſt part, ſhewn themſelves mortal enemies to the true exerciſe of Reaſon, yet now, God be thank'd, there are thoſe among them, who dare do it juſtice.           THAT

That eminent Divine, Mr. *S. Nye*, tho' writing in defence of Revelation , says, * ,, 'Tis obvious to ,, every one, that Natural Religion intimates to us, ,, & comprises *the whole* duty, that we owe to God ,, or Men: Whatever is to be believ'd, or done by us, ,, is declar'd & comprehended in Natural Religion; ,, God has instructed all Men every where, in the ,, whole of their duty, by a connate Light, even by ,, the talent of Reason common to all. And,

The judicious Mr. *Butler* says, † ,, That nothing ,, can be more evident, than that exclusive of Reve- ,, lation, Mankind can't be consider'd as a Creature ,, left by his Maker to act at random - - but from ,, his make, constitution, or nature, he is in the ,, strictest & proper sense a Law to himself. There ,, are as real, and the same kind of indications in ,, human-nature, that we were made for society, and ,, to do good to our fellow-creatures, as that we were ,, intended to take care of our life, health, & pri- ,, vate good.

*B.* If what you, and these reverend Authors say, be true, the Principles, on which all Religion is founded must be so obvious, that all Men, even of the meanest capacity, may from thence discern their duty both to God & Man.

*A.* You shall confess there are such Principles, by my asking you a question, or two: Is not the foundation of all Religion, the believing there's only one self-existent Being, to whom all others owe their being, & their continuance in being? And is it not as certain, as there is such a Being, that he did not create Mankind to supply any wants of his own; or give them rules for their conduct, but to oblige them to act for their common good? If then an action is for their good, is not that alone an infallible test of its being approv'd by God? And if it tends to their hurt,

is

* *Nye* of Nat. and Rev. Relig. p. 95.
† *Serm. preach. at the Rolls. p.* 47. & *p.* 50.

is not that as certain a mark of its being difapprov'd
by him? But if it tends to neither, does not that fufficiently fhow it to be neither approv'd, nor difapprov'd? Since it is as inconfiftent with the goodnefs
of God, to punifh Men for not doing an indifferent
thing, as it is with his wifdom, to reward them for
doing it.

*B.* T Ho' all rational Creatures, who, to their utmoft, imitate their great Creator and Benefactor, in
communicating happinefs to each other, do all that
God requires of them; yet 'tis on fuppofition, that
they do not judge wrong in relation to their common
good?

*A.* I F Men, according to the beft of their underftanding, act for their common good, they then govern
themfelves by the fame rule God governs them; their
will is the fame with his, & they concur in the fame
defign with him; and fhould they, in fome nice &
difficult cafes, miftake in applying the rule, yet in being
intirely govern'd by it, they have done all that God
requires; who, having made Men fallible, will not
impute to them want of infallibility: And the beft
way not to miftake, in applying this rule, is to confider duly all circumftances, & follow what upon the
whole feems beft. As this is the rule both of God &
Man, fo is it in common to the unlearned as well as
learned; for have not all alike faculties given them
by God, to diftinguifh between good & evil, right &
wrong, and to know, that, as they wou'd not fuffer
wrong themfelves, fo they ought not do wrong?

*B.* T H E common people may have fufficient abilities to know their duty to Man, but can they as well
know what they owe to God?

*A.* I N what point is it, that Men of the meaneft
abilities may not know their duty, whether it relates
to God, or Man? As to the firft, can't they tell what
fentiments infpire them with love and reverence for
the Deity? And need they much reflection to know,

that

that the more any sentiments do this, the more they ought to be cherish'd? And that every notion, which tends not to raise in them the highest conceptions of the divine Being, is derogatory to his perfection; and that the highest honour and worship they can render him, is solemnly to own him to be what he is? And that as they ought themselves to have the highest ideas of love & veneration for their Creator & Benefactor, so they should on all proper occasions endeavour to excite the same in others? And that as they cannot but see, it would be in them affronting God, to offer him a worship, which they believe he abhors, so they must think it the same in others?

As to their duty to one another, can't they perceive, that 'tis fit in the nature of things, & agreeable to the mind of their Creator, (who has endow'd them with Reason for this end) to introduce into his creation as much happiness as they can, by being ready to assist, and prevent one another in all good offices? And indeed, the reciprocal duties are so very evident, that even children are sensible of doing as they would be done unto; and the mind, with the same ease, sees the agreeableness or disagreeableness of moral & immoral actions, as the eye discovers agreeableness, or disagreeableness in outward objects. And,

The meaner people are, & the lower their station, the fewer are the things their duty consists in; & those so very plain, that they cannot well mistake, with relation either to God, or Man; were they not impos'd on by artful Men, who, in all ages and places, have mix'd with pure Religion, things tending, indeed, to their own honour, & their own good, but far from being consistent with the honour of God, & the good of Man; and then pretended they were necessary to influence the common people, who wou'd not be satisfy'd with plain, simple truths: And from this source have issu'd out most of those absurdities, which, to the scandal of human-nature, have over-run Mankind;

and

and which, for the most part, were too subtle, & me taphysical for the common people, if left to themselves, ever to have thought of; much less to have rais'd commotions about them : They, it must be own'd, peace and quiet being their interest, are naturally good Subjects & good Neighbours, and upon all accounts most useful members of the community; except when their Priests, on pretence of the good of the Church, work them up to tumults, mutiny, sedition, & rebellion; because their Governoyrs presume, without their leave, to give equal protection to all their Subjects, notwithstanding their different opinions. And if we consult Ecclesiastical History, we shall find the worst of Princes, have been most sure of their assistance, even in carrying on the vilest designs, provided the Church found their interest in so doing; and the best, of their opposition, when they design'd the interest of pure Religion, free from Priestcraft & Superstition. And the Laity, certainly, can't be too much on their guard, when they find extraordinary favours, (such as those in a former Reign,) are design'd for the Clergy.

I do not wholly confine this remark to the Priests of any one Religion, since by the influence they have on the multitude, they have at all times done sufficient mischiefs. Hence *Grotius* says, * ,, That, as ,, *Curtius* observ'd of old, the Multitude, ensnar'd by ,, Superstition, are more apt to be govern'd by their ,, Priests than Princes; and that the Kings and Em- ,, perors have learnt this at their cost, insomuch that ,, to produce examples of this kind, wou'd in a man- ,, ner, be transcribing the History of all Nations.

They, I think, wou'd do no small service to Mankind, who wou'd improve this hint of *Grotius*, and shew how the Priests in all Religions, and in all times, have impos'd on the credulity of the People;

nor

* *Grotius* de Imper. summ. Potest. circa sacra. c. 1. Sect. 13.

nor cou'd it but be very acceptable to a Clergy, who abhor all such vile methods.

*B.* You all along argue, that the Rule of action, in order to human happiness, being every where the same, as founded on the nature of God and Man, and the relation we stand in to him, & one another, true Religion, in all places & times, must ever be the same; eternal, universal, & unalterable; and such as every intelligent Creature, must have sufficient understanding to discover, & abilities to comply with; except we suppose a Being perfectly wise, & infinitely good, requires of his Creatures, things which he has not enabl'd them to know, or perform: And hence you conclude, that external Revelation can only be a republication of this unchangeable rule of life. But Divines, you are sensible, for the most part, are of a different sentiment  nay, highly complain of the imperfection & insufficiency of this Rule.

*A.* In order to shew the absurdity of such complaints, let me ask you, had Mankind, before any traditional Religion commenc'd, any Religion, or not?

*B.* It must be own'd, that they had a Religion, which, as coming from the Author of all perfection, must, as worthy of its divine original, be wholly perfect; nor cou'd there be a greater mark of its perfection, than that of its being universal, unchangeable, & indelibly implanted in human-natuie.

*A.* I will not ask you, whether any Religion, that wants those marks of perfection, can come from a Being of infinite perfection, but desire to know wherein the perfection of this universal, & unchangeable Religion consists?

*B.* It can't be deny'd, that the end for which God implanted this Religion in human-nature, was to make Men happy here as well as hereafter; (God's will in relation to Man & human happiness being equivalent terms) & therefore, he cou'd not, at any time, leave them destitute of the most proper means to answei this end.                 R                          *A.*

*A.* Does not the undeniable perfection of this universal Religion, sufficiently expose all your pretences to a new Religion, giv'n by God to any small part of Mankind in these last Ages?

*B.* We say, there was need of a new Religion, tho' the old was ever so perfect, because Men did not observe it.

*A.* If that was a reason for a new Religion, we might expect new Religions daily, \* ,, But, *as the* ,, *present Bishop of* Bangor *observes,* tho' the World was ,, the worse for abusing the Religion of Nature, and ,, might want to be reform'd by a divine Instructor, ,, yet the Religion of Nature was not the worse for ,, being abus'd, but still retain'd its first purity and ,, simplicity; ,, and consequently, its native efficacy to make us happy: But Men not paying a due regard to this most perfect Religion, but mixing with it human inventions, it might, then, be agreeable to the divine goodness, to send persons to recal them to a more strict observation of it ; which, had it been observ'd, must have destroy'd all contentions, but of outvying one another in all good offices, as the corrupting it has done the contrary.

Which *Hypothesis,* think you, is most for the honour of God, & the good of Man; (those certain tests by which we are to judge of the truth of all matters relating to Religion; ) that all God's Laws shou'd carry with them such evident marks of goodness and kindness for the whole race of Mankind, as that Men of the meanest capacities, even tho' they can't read in their own native language, may know their duty? Or that their Religion, & the proofs on which it depends, shou'd be originally writ in languages they understand not, which, by putting all traditional Religions on a level, obliges them in every Country,

to

---

\* *Sherlock's* Sermon for Propagating the Gospel in Foreign Parts. pag. 14.

to pin their faith on Men, who are but too apt to abuse the peoples credulity to their own profit?

*B.* There can be no doubt, but 'tis for the honour of God, & the good of Man, that all his Laws shou'd have such a signature impress'd on them, as may shew his infinite wisdom & goodness: but can you say, all his Laws bear this character?

*A.* Yes, if they are all of a piece: And since God had no other end in creating Mankind, but their good; or in giving them Laws, but as they conduce to that good, and has given, and requires 'em to use their understanding to distinguish between good and evil, Men, in doing all the good they can, whether they know any thing of the institutions, which prevail in this, or that Age or Country, or not, fully answer the end of their creation, & do in the best manner recommend themselves to the favour both of God & Man.

Without the common people are govern'd by those plain, obvious principles I contend for, they would always be in a state of uncertainty; since as Bishop *Taylor* justly observes, & all History confirms, „ * There's no Church that is in prosperity, but alters „ her Doctrine every Age, either by bringing in new „ Doctrines, or by contradicting her old, which shews „ they are not satisfy'd with themselves, nor with their „ own Confessions. „ † „ Let none of the Heathen, „ *says an antient Church-Historian*, deride us, because „ the latter Bishops depose the former, & always find „ out something which they add to the Faith.

*B.* Is there nothing in *Theology*, but what Divines have alter'd?

*A.* Mr. *Le Clerc* observes, that ‡ „ Theology is „ subject to revolutions as well as Empires: but tho' „ it has undergone considerable changes, yet the hu- „ mour of Divines is much the same.

R 2

What-

* *Dedication to Liberty of Prophesy.* pag. 32.
† *Evag. Eccles. Hist. l. 1. c. 11. p. 267. B.*
‡ *Life of Nazianzen* pag. 28. Eng. Transl.

WHATEVER noise *Ecclesiasticks* make about Creeds, or other fundamentals, there's very often something else at the bottom ; as whoever is conversant in Church History must know: However to give one instance,
,, * When the *Eastern* & *Western* Churches in the 9th
,, Century, fell into an humour of quarreling upon
,, the account of Jurisdiction, after some time of
,, anger, in which they seem'd to be searching for
,, matter to reproach one another with, they found
,, out this difference. The *Greeks* reproach'd the *La-*
,, *tins*, for adding to the Faith about the procession of
,, the Holy Ghost, & corrupting the ancient Symbol,
,, and that too contrary to the Decree of a General
,, Council. The *Latins* on the other hand, charg'd
,, them for detracting from the dignity of the *Son*.
,, And this became the chief point in controversy
,, between them.,, I can't but mention Bishop *Bur-*
*net*'s remark on this dispute, † ,, We of this Church,
*says he*, ,, tho' we abhor the cruelty of condemning
,, the *Eastern* Churches for such a difference, yet do
,, receive the Creed according to the usage of the
,, *Western* Churches.,, Which is in effect, receiving
that Creed, which damns the *Eastern* Churches.

AND it's plain from Church History, that *Creeds* were the spiritual arms, with which contending parties combated each other; and that those who were the majority invented such unscriptural terms, as they thought their adversaries wou'd most scruple, in order to the stripping them of their preferments; and it wou'd have been well if they had stuck there, & not made use of more cruel methods.

NONE, who consider how differently the circumstances of human affairs, which are continually changing, affect Men, but must see 'tis scarce possible, that the Doctrines which were originally taught, or the practice originally us'd in any institution, shou'd long continue the same; nothing being more easy

than

* *Expos. of* 39. *Art. p.* 70. *Art.* 5.     † *Ibid.*

than to vary the fignification of words. The infinite divifions which prevail'd, even in the primitive and apoftolical times, fufficiently prove this; without having recourfe to thofe alterations & additions, which the Clergy have fince been continually making in Chriftianity; efpecially in the *Greek* & *Latin* Churches. But we need go no further back than the *Reformation*; did not the whole body of the people, Laity as well as Clergy, in the compafs of twelve years, change their Religion three times? And it wou'd make no fmall book, to fhew how fince that time, our Clergy, tho' their *Calviniftical* Articles continue the fame, have vary'd, both as to *Doctrines* & *Difcipline*. What a quick change have we feen of thofe paffive principles, once the characteriftick of the Church? And if we judge by the prefent difputes now on foot, the Clergy are not like to be more fix'd for the future. But of all Clergy men, they, certainly, are not upon any account to be rely'd on, who, tho' by their whole conduct they fhew their great zeal for Perfecution, yet talk againft an implicit Faith, and recommend *Chriftianity* as *requiring no further favour, than a fair, and impartial inquiry into its grounds and doctrines.* This not only fhews their great hypocrify, but that they are more cruel than thofe, who exprefly forbid all examination; fince they firft tempt Men to examine, & then punifh them for fo doing, if they prefume to differ from their leaders; & thofe that forbid all examination can do no more. And herein they act the part of Satan, firft tempt people, & then punifh them for being tempted; fo that, ftrictly fpeaking, 'tis not always true, that Priefts of all Religions are the fame; fuch hypocritical, perfecuting Priefts are worfe than all others; who, while they charge the *Papift*, or *Mahometan*, with a confcioufnefs of his Religion's being a cheat, becaufe he will not permit it to be examin'd; not only practife the fame themfelves, but contend 'tis neceffary for the fupport of the true Religion:

How eafily the fenfe of words may be miftaken, the Apoftles themfelves are a fufficient inftance, for had they the fame ideas of the words which Jefus fpake, as Jefus himfelf had, 'tis impoffible that after three years converfe they fhou'd be ignorant of the end of his Miffion: And if his familiar Friends, who daily convers'd with him in the fame language, and had every minute an opportunity of being fatisfy'd of their doubts, cou'd yet fo grofly miftake; well may we at this diftance of time, if we are to be govern'd by words, & not by the unalterable Reafon of things: And how long was it, till they underftood the meaning of *Teach all Nations, Preach the Gofpel to every Crea-ture?* And St. *Peter* himfelf needed a Miracle to open his underftanding, to comprehend a moft evident truth.   * *Then* Peter *opened his Mouth, & faid, Of a Truth, I perceive that God is no Refpecter of Perfons: But in every Nation, he that feareth him, and worketh righteoufnefs, is accepted with him.* Till this happen'd, he, tho' fill'd with the Holy Ghoft, confin'd Salvation to the name of a perfon, *viz.* the Name of *Chrift,* † *There is none other Name under Heaven given amongft Men, whereby we muft be faved.*

Had there been but one language, and a Book writ in that language, in indelible characters, (fo that there cou'd be none of thofe thirty thoufand various readings, which are own'd to be crept into the New-Teftament) and all cou'd have accefs to it; yet even then, confidering how uncertain the meaning of words are, and the intereft of defigning Men, to put a wrong fenfe on them, it muft be morally im-poffible this Religion cou'd long continue the fame, And,

   ,, If, *as St.* Jerom *fays,* ‡ a falfe interpretation of ,, the Gofpel of Chrift, may make it become the ,, Gofpel of Men, nay, which is worfe, of Devils; ,, how can they, who, not underftanding the original, must

* *Acts* 10. 34, 35.   † *Id.* 4. 14.   ‡ *On Galat.* 1.

must trust to the interpretation of others, be certain; had they not a sufficient inward Light to direct them, what Doctrines are from God, what from Men, and what from Devils?

Is it not notorious, that Popish Priests, not to mention other persecuting Priests, have propagated such destructive notions, as if the Devil himself had been to contrive a Religion, he cou'd not have invented more pernicious?

WORDS are the arbitrary marks of Mens ideas, & the meaning of words, as well as the words themselves, are perpetually changing, & 'tis as impossible to fix one as the other. We see by the innumerable verbal disputes, which happen even among learned Men, how different their ideas are; and perhaps, there are not three persons, who, when they talk abstractedly, have precisely the same ideas, tho' they use the same words. No one can doubt of this, who considers how much the Divines of the same Church differ in explaining what they mean by *Divine Person, Essence, Trinity, Messiah, Incarnation, Hypostatical Union, Original Sin, Satisfaction, Justification, Predestination, Grace, Free-will,* & all other technical terms, if I may so call them. Bishop *Taylor* quotes *Osiander* for saying,

,, * There are twenty several opinions concerning
,, *Justification,* all drawn from the Scriptures by the
,, Men only of the *Augustine* Confession; & there are
,, sixteen several opinions concerning *Original Sin*;
,, & as many distinctions of the *Sacraments* as there
,, are Sects of Men that disagree about them.

THAT excellent Critick *Daillé* says, † ,, We have,
,, indeed, these words *Pope, Patriarch, Mass, Oblation,*
,, *Station, Procession, Mortal Sins, Penance, Confession,*
,, *Satisfaction, Merit, Indulgence,* as the Ancients had,
,, and make use of an infinite number of the like
,, terms; but understand them in a sense almost as

R 4 far

* *Polem. Disc. pag.* 452.
† *Daillé de Usu Patrum.* l. 1. c. 5. p. 149.

s, far different from theirs, as our Age is remov'd
s, from theirs.

To give one remarkable inſtance of this nature;
the primitive Fathers did not believe a Spirit to be
immaterial, but only a thinner ſort of body: And this
they did not only apply to the Souls of Men & Angels,
(who, they ſuppos'd, lay with Women, & got Children
in abundance;) but they 'thought that God himſelf
was corporeal. * *Melito*, who was believ'd to be a
Prophet, & flouriſh'd about 170, wrote a book about
the *imbodied God*. And *Tertullian* ſays, † *Quis negabit
Deum corpus eſſe, etſi Deus Spiritus eſt?* And again,
*Nihil incorporale niſi quod non eſt.* And St. *Hilary*, even
in the fourth Century affirms, ‡ *There's nothing but
what is corporeal.* And 'tis very probable, that from
ſome words of our Saviour, they thought that a *Spirit
was a thinner ſort of Body, that cou'd be ſeen, but not
felt.* And from St. *Paul*'s ſaying', § *In this dwelleth
the fulneſs of the Godhead bodily*, and talking in ſeveral
other places of *a ſpiritual body*, they concluded that
that was the ſame with *a bodily Spirit*; tho' our Divines now very well know how to diſtinguiſh between
*a bodily Spirit* & *a ſpiritual Body.*

In ſhort, there are ſcarce any words in any one
language, except of ſuch things as immediately ſtrike
the ſenſes, that are adequately anſwer'd in another,
ſo as exactly to comprehend the ſame ideas; and if
the ideas are only fewer, or more, what confuſion
may not that occaſion? How great, & frequent muſt
the miſtakes then be, in tranſlating the antiquated
languages of people, who liv'd at a vaſt diſtance of
time, as well as in countries far remote; & affected
hyperbolical, parabolical, myſtical, allegorical, & typical ways of expreſſing themſelves, as oppoſite to the
usage

* *Cotell. Not. ad Script. Apoſt. p. 429.*    † *Tertul. adver.
Prax. c. 7. De Carne Chriſti. c. 11. & adver. Hermo. c. 35.*
‡ See *Daillé* de Uſu Patrum. l. 2. c. 4. p. 269. & 268.
§ *Coloſ. 2. 9.*

ufage in other parts, as *Eaft* is to *Weft?* And not only this, but it will be likewife neceffary to have an accurate knowledge of their manners, cuftoms, traditions, philofophy, religious notions, fects, civil and ecclefiaftical polity; of all which the common people know as little, as they do of the original languages; and having very obfcure, & incompetent conceptions of the principal words, & phrafes us'd in the verfions, their Religion muft needs be a very odd jumble of confus'd & inconfiftent notions, were it to depend on words, & their precife meaning, & not on the things themfelves, and their relations, which are plain and obvious to common capacities; they wou'd be in a manner intirely govern'd by founds, fome of which, fuch, as they us'd to hear fpoken of with refpect, they wou'd highly reverence, while others, tho' of the fame fignification, they wou'd as much abhor, till cuftom had made them familiar. And,

WERE Men not to be govern'd by things, but words, the confequence now wou'd be much worfe than what happen'd on the confufion of languages at *Babel*; becaufe no written Religion, for want of an univerfal language, cou'd become univerfal, & people muft, without a competent skill in dead languages, be oblig'd to take their Religion on truft, from Men too, as fubject to be deceiv'd, as they are often ready to deceive: Nay, the univerfality of language, cou'd it have preferv'd Religion uncorrupt, wou'd have done fo in the *Antidiluvian* world, & before that confufion of language, which happen'd at *Babel*.

IF skill in languages cou'd make even the Learned certain, how comes it to pafs, that what goes for orthodox in one Age, fhall be heterodox in another? What is fundamental in one Church, be damnable error in another? Nay, muft not every one, if at all vers'd in Church-Hiftory, fay with Mr. *Chillingworth* ," * I fee plain, & with my own eyes, that there are

R 5                                                    Popes

* *Relig. of Proteftants. c. 6. Sect. 56. p. 290.*

„ Popes againſt Popes, Councils againſt Councils;
„ ſome Fathers againſt others, the ſame Fathers
„ againſt themſelves, a conſent of Fathers of one Age,
„ againſt a conſent of Fathers of another Age, the
„ Church of one Age, againſt the Church of another
„ Age?„ And do not the Clergy themſelves think
there's ſuch uncertainty in the Scripture-language,
even in things of the greateſt moment, when they
generally uſe unſcriptural terms to expreſs thoſe things?
And that they can't even here agree among themſelves, there needs no better proof than the diſputes
of our Divines about Fundamentals; tho' they are,
to prevent all controverſies of this nature, enacted,
guarded with penal Laws, & all the Clergy, at every
turn, oblig'd to ſubſcribe 'em in the ſame words.

I cou'd name two eminent Biſhops, who, if they
were to give a true account of their religious tenents,
'tis thought, wou'd appear to differ very widely, even
in what themſelves term Fundamentals. But are not
ſuch differences utterly unavoidable as long as Men
found their Religion on words and phraſes thus dubious, and not on the eternal Reaſon, & unalterable
Relations of Things, obvious to the meaneſt capacity?

Notwithstanding the wide difference there
is between all Chriſtian Sects, from the *Papiſt* down
to the *Quaker*, I can't help thinking, that an infinitely wiſe and good God has adapted the rules & evidences, of what he really requires from Mankind,
to their general capacity, and that the certainty of
every command, muſt be equal to the importance of
the duty. How can we ſuppoſe ſome of the moſt neceſſary duties of Religion, are only to be found in
voluminous books, which the greateſt part of mankind
have, perhaps, never heard of, & of thoſe that have,
not one in a thouſand underſtands a tittle of the languages they are writ in, or is capable of examining
into thoſe records, from which the authority of theſe
books are to de deriv'd?

Is

Is not that an admirable *Hypothesis*, which, tho' it suppofes God has endow'd Mankind with Reafon to enable them to diftinguifh between Religion & Super-ftition, yet admits that almoft all Mankind are in-capable of doing it, but muft alike, in all countries, depend on the authority of Men, hir'd to maintain the traditional Religion of the places where they live; who, perhaps, will tell them, that there was a time (happy thofe who liv'd in it) when Religion was fuited to the capacities of the vulgar; being preach'd by infpir'd Men in the languages they underftood, & miracles for their conviction wrought in their fight; but that now the fcene was entirely chang'd, they had no miracles, no infallible Men to have recourfe to, to fet them right; & that their Religion by diftance of time was not only become obfcure, but that the whole of it, & the proofs on which its validity de-pends, are writ in languages, of which the people underftand not a word; and that * ,, the evidence ,, arifing from particular types & prophecies, is now, ,, by length of time, & diftance of place, & change ,, of cuftoms, become obfcure & difficult to the ge-,, nerality of people, & cannot be thoroughly difcufs'd ,, without a great variety of knowledge concerning ,, the ancient *Jewifh* cuftoms, and the authority of ,, their writings, & the exact calculation of time,,, Which is in effect to fuppofe, that the Religion of the Vulgar muft confift, in taking the words of their Teachers, however divided among themfelves, for the word of God; and their Tranflations, for *Law* & *Gofpel*; and that believing in them, is having a di-vine Faith; tho' one would think, whatever depended on human Traditions, & Tranflations, cou'd be but a human Faith.

*B.* Tho' fomething of this nature is unavoidable, where Religion is writ in antiquated languages; yet in the main, are we not now more certain of the truth

* Bp. of *London's* Paft. Lett. pag. 20, 21.

truth of our traditional Religion, than thofe who liv'd in former Ages, we having the authority of every paft Age in confirmation of its truth?

*A.* Mr. *Lock*, fpeaking concerning *Affent* in mat-ters, wherein teftimony is made ufe of, *fays,* * ,, I think,
,, it may not be amifs to take notice of a Rule ob-
,, ferv'd in the Law of *England*, which is, that tho'
,, the attefted copy of a Record be good proof, yet
,, the copy of a copy never fo well attefted, and by
,, never fo credible witneffes, will not be admitted as
,, a proof in judicature. This is fo generally approv'd
,, as reafonable, and fuited to the wifdom & caution
,, to be ufed in our enquiry after material truths,
,, that I never yet heard of any one that blamed it.
,, This practice, if it be allowable in the decifions
,, of right and wrong, carries this obfervation along
,, with it, *viz.* That any teftimony, the further off
,, it is from the original truth, the lefs force & proof
,, it has. The being & exiftence of the thing itfelf,
,, is what I call the original truth. A credible Man
,, vouching his knowledge of it, is a good proof:
,, But if another, equally credible, do witnefs it from
,, his report, the teftimony is weaker; and a third
,, that attefts the hear-fay of an hear-fay, is yet lefs
,, confiderable. So that *in traditional truths, each re-*
,, *moves weakens the force of the proof.* And the more
,, hands the tradition has fucceffively paffed through,
,, the lefs ftrength & evidence does it receive from
,, them. ,, -- † ,, This is certain, that what in one
,, Age was affirmed upon flight grounds, can never
,, after come to be more valid in future Ages, by
,, being often repeated. ,, I hope you will pardon
me, if I prefume to think, that God, at all times, is
fo good & impartial, that his will, on which the happinefs of Mankind at all times depends, is at all times
equally knowable; & confequently, muft be founded
on

* *L. 4. c. 16. Sect. 10. pag. 382. al. pag. 562.*
† *Ibid. pag. 383. al. pag. 563. Sect. 11.*

on what is always alike difcernable, the Nature and Reafon of Things. Can a Religion, defign'd for every one, not be within the reach of every one? Or can that, which above all things it concerns A L L Men to know, not be knowable by A L L?

> - - - id, quod
> *Æque pauperibus prodeſt, locupletibus æque;*
> *Æque neglectum pueris ſenibusque nocebit.* *
> *Hoc opus, hoc ſtudium parvi properemus & ampli;*
> *Si patriæ volumus, ſi nobis vivere cari.* †

> \* Hor. l. 1. Ep. 1. 24.　　† Ib. Ep. 3. 28.

A n d certainly, nothing can be a greater libel on the true Religion, than to fuppofe it does not contain fuch internal marks, as will, even to the meaneft capacity, diftinguifh it from all falfe Religions; fo as that a Man, tho' unable to read in his Mother-tongue, may, without pinning his faith on any fett of Priefts, know what God requires of him.

I have faid nothing of the plainnefs, fimplicity, & even univerfality of Religion, but what is agreeable to the defcription, which St. *Paul*, from the Prophet *Jeremiah*, gives of the Gofpel difpenfation; the exprefs terms of which run thus, ‡ *I will put my Laws into their mind, & write them in their hearts; and I will be unto them a God, & they ſhall be to me a People :* § *And they ſhall not teach every Man his Neighbour, & every Man his Brother, ſaying, Know the Lord; for all ſhall know me, from the leaſt to the greateſt.* As thefe words are too plain to need a comment, fo I fhall defer drawing any confequences from them, till I have firft endeavour'd to free the Scripture from that obfcurity, in which artful Men have involv'd it. And,

I fhall, now, by way of recapitulation, mention what Mr. *Barbeyrac*, a Perfon of no fmall note in the learned world, fays concerning the *Practical Science*
of

‡ *Heb.* 8. 10, 11.　　§ *Jer.* 31. 33, 34.

*of Morality*; * ,, None can reasonably doubt, but that
,, every Man, who will be happy, must needs, in
,, order to make himself so, regulate his conduct after
,, some certain manner; and that God, as the Author
,, & Parent of all human race, does prescribe to all
,, Men without exception, the duties which tend to
,, procure them that happiness, which they so pas-
,, sionately seek after. Now, from hence it necessarily
,, follows, that the natural principles of this science
,, are such as may be easily discover'd; and such too,
,, as are proportionate to the capacities of all sorts of
,, persons: So that to be instructed in this science,
,, there will be no occasion to mount up to Heaven,
,, or to have from thence any extraordinary Revela-
,, tion for that purpose. -- It must be own'd, to the
,, eternal glory of the supreme Legislator of Mankind,
,, as well as to the utter confusion of themselves;
,, that none can complain without injustice, that God
,, has given him Laws, either impracticable, or in-
,, viron'd with such obscurity, as cannot be penetrated
,, by one who really has his duty at heart, notwith-
,, standing all his pains & application. This the wisest
,, Heathens have acknowledg'd; — (and) the *Stoicks*,
,, who made Morality their principal study, maintain'd,
,, that their Philosophy was not above the reach of
,, Women & Slaves; and that as the way to Virtue
,, lies open to all Men without distinction; so there
,, is no estate, or condition, with peculiar priviledges
,, exclusive of others, as to the faculty of knowing
,, the principles & rules, as well of those duties which
,, are common to all, as of those which belong to
,, each particular. - - † The idea of a Creator,
,, boundless in power, wisdom & goodness; and the
,, idea of ourselves, as intelligent reasonable, and so-

ciable

---

* Historical and Critical Account of the Science of Morality, in his prefatory Discourse to *Puffendorf*, of the *Law
of Nature* & *Nations*, Engl. Transl. Sect. 1. p. 1. col. 1, 2.
† *Sect*. 3. *pag*. 10. *col*. 2.

„ ciable Creatures: Thefe two ideas, I fay, if well
„ look'd into, and compar'd together in their whole
„ extent, will always furnifh us with fteady grounds
„ of duty, & fure rules of conduct; notwithftanding
„ it may fometimes fo fall out, that, for want of care
„ & attention, we may, in fome uncommon cafes,
„ not know how to apply them ; or cannot metho-
„ dically demonftrate the neceffary connexion of
„ fome remote confequences, with the firft principles
„ of Morality. -- * 'Tis certain, that the intire con-
„ formity of the Chriftian Morality, with the cleareft
„ dictates of right Reafon, is one of the moft con-
„ vincing proofs of the divinity of the Chriftian Re-
„ ligion; as has been acknowledg'd by all, who have
„ wrote with any folidity on that fubject. -- And if
„ we duly weigh, & confider it, we fhall find, that
„ this is the proof, which of all others is the moft
„ affecting; & the beft proportion'd to the common
„ capacities of the bulk of Mankind. - - [Who]
„ When they come at length to confider the Evan-
„ gelical Morality, & find it intirely conformable both
„ to their true interefts, and to all thofe Principles,
„ of which every Man has by nature the feeds in his
„ own heart, they cannot then help concluding, that
„ the Author of it muft neceffarily be that very Being,
„ who has giv'n life, & brought 'em into this world,
„ only to make 'em happy; provided they will not
„ be wanting to themfelves, but contribute on their
„ part, all that lies in their own power, towards the
„ attainment of their own felicity.
„ I might here commend to your perufal, what he,
„ in feveral fections, affirms of the „ extreme negli-
„ gence of the *publick Minifters of Religion*, in culti-
„ vating the fcience of Morality ; which, *as he fays*, †
„ being by them almoft banifh'd out of the world,
„ took fanctuary among the Laicks, or undignify'd
„ Men of Letters, who gave it a much better recep-
tion.

* *Sect.* 32. *p.* 87, 88. † *Sect.* 12. *p.* 36. *col.* 1, 2.

,, tion. -- * No fooner did that admirable Treatife
,, of *Grotius*, of *The Right of War & Peace*, appear in
,, the world, but the Ecclefiafticks, inftead of returning
,, thanks to the Author for it, every where declar'd
,, againft him; and his Book was not only put into
,, the expurgatory Index of the *Roman Catholick* In-
,, quifitors, but many, even *Proteftant* Divines, labour'd
,, to cry it down. And thus it far'd too with Mr. *Puf-*
,, *fendorff*'s Book of *The Law of Nature and Nations*;
,, the *Jefuits* at *Vienna* caus'd it to be prohibited;
,, and many *Proteftant* Divines, both of *Sueden* and
,, *Germany*, did their beft, to make this excellent
,, work fhare every where elfe the fame fate?

*B.* IF thefe great Men were thus dealt with, for
fetting the *Science of Morality* in its due light; can you,
who place Religion in the practice of Morality in
obedience to the Will of God, & fuppofe there can
be no other diftinction between Morality & Religion,
than that the former is acting according to the Reafon
of things confider'd in themfelves, the other, acting
according to the fame Reafon of things confider'd as
the Will of God? Can You, I fay, hope to efcape
being pelted by fome of the fame profeffion for fuch
a crime as this?

*A.* THAT, I muft own, wou'd be a favour I
neither hope, nor wifh for; fince I am fenfible, the
fhewing Religion to be no arbitrary Inftitution, but
founded on the Nature of things, and their Relations,
obvious to the capacity of all that dare ufe their Reafon, muft provoke all Ecclefiafticks of what denomination foever, who expect a blind fubmiffion from
the Laity: tho' was it not for the authority that the
High Church Clergy among the Reform'd lay claim
to, when from *Proteftant* principles they draw *Popifh*
conclufions, the pretences of the *Popifh* Priefts for the
neceffity of *an Infallible Guide*, wou'd appear ridiculous.

THE

* *Sect.* II. *pag.* 36. *col.* 2.

The substance of what the *Papists* say, is in short,
„ That if the Principles of *Protestants*, relating to
„ private judgment, are true, the bulk of Mankind
„ can't go beyond such plain rules of Religion as
„ carry their own evidence with them; since other-
„ wise they wou'd be oblig'd to admit things, about
„ which they are incapable of judging.

„ If, *say they*, the Religion of Peasants & Mecha-
„ nicks, Men & Maid-Servants, the ignorant & illi-
„ terate, must depend on books written in antiquated
„ languages, of which they understand not one word,
„ and are incapable of judging of the historical evi-
„ dences of remote facts, on which the authority of
„ those Books is founded, nor can know whether a
„ Religion thus founded, has been faithfully convey'd
„ down to them, must they not either be of that
„ traditional Religion, which obtains in the Country
„ where they live, (as none is without one) Or else
„ must there not be some persons appointed to judge
„ for them in matters of Religion, in whose deter-
„ mination they may safely acquiesce? If this be
„ *Popery*, there can be no mean between Popery &
„ Natural Religion.

„ If, in the earliest times, Christians were split
„ into many Sects, & each Sect had their particular
„ Scriptures; are the common Christians now (when
„ all the historical evidence is lost but of one side
„ only, and that too they understand not) competent
„ Judges in this matter? Or to condescend to par-
„ ticulars, are they capable of judging in the Con-
„ troversies between *Catholicks* & *Protestants*, about
„ the number of Canonical Books, Oral Tradition,
„ the Authority of the Church, the uninterrupted
„ Succession, & a thousand other things; especially
„ such as relate to Mysteries; about which they are
„ so far from being competent Judges, that they are
„ not capable of understanding even the terms, in
„ which the Learned choose to express themselves,

S                    when

„ when they endeavour to explain their inexplicable
„ Mysteries?

„ OUGHT not the illiterate, if they had a just
„ sense of their own ignorance, to have been frighted,
„ upon their pretended Reformation, at the very
„ thoughts of leaving a Church, to which their An-
„ cestors had been so long united; (and which most
„ of their Adversaries own'd to be a true Church,
„ and deriv'd their authority from her;) upon the
„ account of opinions, they were no more capable
„ of judging, than they were of judging, after they
„ had left the Church, to which of the numerous
„ Sects they shou'd join, themselves?

„ ALL *Protestant* Churches, have taken the same
„ methods to make people pay an absolute submission
„ to their decisions, as the Church of *Rome*, by ex-
„ communicating, & condemning, when they had
„ power, to perpetual imprisonment, or otherwise
„ punishing those who wou'd not renounce their
„ private opinions, when contrary to their decisions;
„ which is either condemning their own principles,
„ or their own practices so directly opposite to their
„ principles. But if this power of judging for the
„ People is, as the Protestant Clergy pretend, so ne-
„ cessary to preserve unity, that it must belong to
„ every particular, & *Protestant* Church, tho' founded
„ on the breach of Catholick unity, how came the
„ Church itself, before the pretended *Reformation*,
„ to want this power so necessary to preserve itself?

B. *Protestant* Divines, when press'd on this head,
usually distinguish between a just Authority, and an
absolute Authority.

A. CAN the Church of *Rome*, say its *Votaries*,
claim a greater authority, than the Church of *England*
does in her *Canons* of 1603; where she declares, *
„ All are *ipso facto* excommunicate, who shall affirm
„ she is not an orthodox & Apostolical Church; not

is

* *Can.* 3.

„ to be abſolv'd, but by the Archbiſhop, after having
„ publickly renounc'd this their impious error; and
„ after the ſame manner excommunicates.   * All,
„ who ſhall affirm the *Articles* of 1562, made to avoid
„ diverſity of opinions, *ulla ex parte ſuperſtitioſos aut*
„ *erroneos exiſtere;*  † All that ſpeak againſt her Rites
„ & Ceremonies, or condemn her Ordination, and
„ her Diſcipline ‡ (tho' ſhe herſelf complains of want
„ of godly Diſcipline) by *Biſhops*, *Deans*, *Arch-*
„ *deacons*, &c. All *Schiſmaticks*, & all Congregations
„ not eſtabliſh'd by Law, if they aſſume to themſelves
„ the name of a *true*, & *lawful Church :* „ Does not
this, ſay the *Papiſts*, ſhew, that tho' the principles of
the Church of *England* were *anti-popiſh*; yet that her
practices, her Laws Civil as well as Eccleſiaſtical,
before the *Revolution*, were popiſh; § ſince the Laws
againſt all *Separatiſts* then extended to the loſs, not
only of eſtate & liberty, but even of life itſelf?

Fʀᴏᴍ theſe, & ſuch like reaſons, the *Papiſts* conclude, that if the People are oblig'd to go a ſtep
beyond the plain & obvious rules of Natural Religion,
there is, in the judgment of all Churches whatever,
a neceſſity for them to have recourſe to others to
judge for them, unleſs there are to be as many Religions as Judges.

*B.* Hᴏᴡ did our Reformers anſwer theſe objections?

*A.* Tʜᴇʏ being chiefly concern'd for the Authority of the Scripture, & withal willing in their diſputes
with the *Papiſts* to ſupport private judgment, *ſaid*,
„ That the Scriptures themſelves, from their innate
„ evidence, & by the illumination of the ſame holy
„ Spirit which indited them, ſufficiently ſhew'd them-
„ ſelves to be the Will of God.

Tʜᴇ *Dutch* Confeſſion publiſh'd in 1566, in the
name of the *Belgian* Churches, after having recited a

S 2                              Ca-

* *Can.* 5.      † *Can.* 6. &c.      ‡ *Commination.*
§ See Mr. *Lock*'s 3d Letter for Toleration, c. 4. p. 226.

Catalogue of the Books of Scripture, *says*, * „ Thefe „ we receive as the only facred & canonical Books; „ not becaufe the Church receives them as fuch, „ but becaufe the holy Spirit witneffes to our con- „ fciences, that they proceed from God, and them- „ felves teftify their authority.

THE *Gallican* Churches, in their Confeffion, go fomewhat further, not only † „ declaring their faith „ in the Scriptures, to depend on the teftimony of „ the internal perfuafion of the Spirit, but that thereby „ they know the Canonical from the Ecclefiaftical, *i.e.* „ Apocryphal Books. And,

THE Affembly of Divines at *Weftminfter*, maintain'd, that ‡ „ Our full perfuafion and affurance of the in- „ fallible truth thereof, (the Scriptures) is from the „ inward work of the Holy Spirit, bearing witnefs „ by, & with the words in our hearts.

As to foreign Divines, I fhall only mention that great Reformer *Calvin*, who *says*, § „ All muft allow, „ that there are in the Scriptures manifeft evidences „ of God fpeaking in them. -- The Majefty of God „ in them will prefently appear to every impartial „ examiner, which will extort our affent: So that „ they act prepofteroufly, who endeavour by any ar- „ gument to beget a folid credit to the Scriptures. -- „ The Word will never meet with credit in Mens „ minds, till it be feal'd by the internal teftimony of „ the Spirit who wrote it.

OUR learned *Whittaker*, in his Controverfy about the Scripture againft *Bellarmine*, gives this account of the Doctrines of the Church; ¶ „ The Sum, *says he,* „ of our opinion is, that the Scriptures have all their „ authority & credit from themfelves; that they are „ to be acknowledg'd and receiv'd, not becaufe the
Church

---

* *Harm of Confef. p.* 12, 13.    † *Art. of Harm of Con-fef. pag.* 10.    ‡ *Chap.* 1. *Sect.* 5.
§ *Inftitut. Chrift. Relig. l.* 1. *c.* 7. *Sect.* 4, 5.
¶ *Controv. de Script. Quæft.* 3. *c.* 1. *p.* 286.

„ Church has appointed or commanded fo, but be-
„ caufe they came from God; but that they came
„ from God, cannot be certainly known by the
„ Church, but from the Holy Ghoft. And.

INDEED, our Church fuppofes no Man can be a good Chriftian, without being infpir'd; by faying, * *Works done before the Grace of Chrift, & the infpiration of his Spirit, are not pleafing to God: -- yea, -- we doubt not, but that they have the nature of fin.* And,

AS to the *Diffenters*, I fhall only quote Dr. *Owen*, a Man not long fince very eminent among them, who is as zealous in maintaining this opinion as any of the firft Reformers; his words are, † „ The Scrip-
„ tures of the Old & New Teftament do abundantly,
„ and uncontroulably manifeft themfelves to be the
„ Word of the living God; fo that merely on the
„ account of their own propofal to us, in the name
„ & Majefty of God as fuch, without tho contribu-
„ tion of help, or affiftance from Tradition, Church,
„ or any thing elfe without themfelves, we are oblig'd
„ upon the penalty of eternal damnation, to receive
„ them with that fubjection of foul, which is due to
„ the word of God. The Authority of God fhining
„ in them, they afford unto us all the divine evidence
„ of themfelves, which God is willing to grant us,
„ or can be granted to us, or is any way needful
„ for us. „ And left the *Quakers* fhould take it amifs, if while I quote other Sects, I fhou'd overlook them; *R. Barclay* fays, ‡ „ How neceffary 'tis to feek the
„ certainty of the Scripture from the Spirit, the in-
„ finite janglings, and endlefs contefts of thofe who
„ feek their authority elfewhere, do witnefs to the
„ truth thereof: „ And then proceeds to prove thofe infinite janglings, & endlefs contefts.

S 3

THE

---

* *Artic.* 13. † Dr. *Owen's* Dif. of the div. Orig. of the Script. c. 2. Sect. 5. & c. 4, 5.

‡ Prop. 3 pag. 70.

THE Reform'd wou'd have argu'd unanswerably, had they contented themselves with saying, that there are no Doctrines of a divine original contain'd in the Gospel dispensation, but what by their innate excellency are knowable to be such, as being *writ in our minds*, and *put into our hearts* by God himself; as is expresly declar'd by the Prophet *Jeremiah*, * & repeated and reafferted by the Apoftle, and by Chrift himself. But,

OUR Divines, it seems, at laft found out, that the Reformers, and their Succeffors, had embrac'd Chriftianity on fuch grounds, as they believ'd wou'd equally ferve any other Religion, where there was a ftrong perfuafion; and being zealous for certain things, which do not carry any internal marks of their truth, or in other words, of being *taught of God*, they fell into ftrange inconfiftencies; fometimes talking like *Hobbifts*, of the power of the Magiftrate; fometimes like *Papifts*, of the authority of the Church in religious matters; and fometimes maintaining both, and private judgment too, in the fame difcourfe, if not in the fame fection; which made their Adverfaries treat them as a pack of tricking, chicaning wretches, who had no regard to truth, or confiftency, or any thing but their private intereft.

THE opinion, now, which feems to be efpous'd by fome, who wou'd be thought the only true Churchmen, is, what the late learned Dr. *Rogers* maintains; who, tho' he agrees with the *Papifts*, that the People are incapable of judging for themfelves in moft points of Religion; yet, to do him juftice, he puts the Church of *Rome* but upon a level with all other Churches of what Religion foever, that chance to be uppermoft, for he lays it down as a Principle, † ,, That tho' no ,, Man ought upon any Authority to believe contra-,, dictions, or profefs an affent to evident falfehoods;

yet

---

* *Jer.* 31. 33.   *Hebr.* 10. 16.   *John* 6. 45.
† Pref. to Dr. *Roger's* 8 Serm. pag. 53, 54.

„ yet in queſtions, where he muſt in the event be
„ determin'd by ſome Authority or other, he may rea-
„ ſonably prefer the Authority appointed by publick
„ wiſdom, and may juſtly be requir'd ſo to do. --
„ * The bulk of Mankind are manifeſtly unable to
„ form a judgment either of the arguments by which
„ he (his Antagoniſt) endeavours to ſubvert our Re-
„ ligion, or eſtabliſh his own; whether they adhere
„ to us, or go to him, they muſt unavoidably rely
„ on his, or our Authority for the truth of the ſug-
„ geſtions on which their concluſion depends; & we
„ preſume our word will go as far as his.„   This is
aſſerting that people are oblig'd to take their Religion
on truſt, & then to change it as often as there's any
change in the State-Religion; or as often as they
change their reſidence; and in all theſe changes to be
govern'd by Men, who are hir'd, not to find out truth,
but to make that Religion, to which their Preferments
are annex'd, to paſs for true. And if People will not
be govern'd, the Legiſlature, or in the Doctor's phraſe,
*Publick Wiſdom may juſtly require them ſo to do.* Nor is
the matter mended, by excepting contradictions and
evident falſehoods, ſince here too, if private perſons
& Authority differ, publick Wiſdom will certainly be
on the ſide of the Authority it ſets up, & 'tis in ſuch
things that the publick Wiſdom in moſt Chriſtian
Countries has exerted itſelf with the utmoſt cruelty.
So that the whole queſtion between the *Papiſt* & the
Doctor (both ſides agreeing that Men can't believe
contradictions & evident falſehoods; and that there
are things, which the People are incapable of knowing,
or if known, can't judge whether they are true or not,)
is, on whom the People in theſe points muſt pin their
Faith? Whether there are certain ſtanding Judges appointed by Chriſt, who ſhall infallibly lead them into
the truth? Or whether in every Chriſtian Country,
the People are bound to be of the Religion of thoſe

S 4

fal-

fallible, not to fay, felf-interefted Guides, Publick Wifdom has authoris'd. Here it muft be confefs'd, the Doctor is againft the Pope of *Rome*, but 'tis to fet himfelf up in his ftead; & he accordingly maintains, that thofe who are committed to his care, are in things of which they can't judge, to follow his judgment; and fays, * ,, tho' he may miftake, & in confequence ,, of it miflead them, yet they will have this defence ,, before Chrift, that they have fought his Will in the ,, methods which he has directed, and, where they ,, wanted a Guide, preferr'd one appointed to that ,, office according to his Inftitution. ,, But why may not a Parifh-Prieft appointed by Publick Wifdom in *North-Britain, France,* or any other country, fay the fame to people incapable of judging in thefe points? Is not this fuppofing, that the Chriftian Religion in many points, is fo fram'd, that in every Parifh the People muft follow the Judgment of their Parifh-Prieft, becaufe they are to feek (and what more can be requir'd of them) Chrift's will in the manner the Parifh-Prieft tells them Chrift directs. And is not this *Popery*, even worfe than *Roman Popery*, as it is fetting up a *Pope* in every Parifh? And obliging the People as often as any of them change their Parifh, or he his Parifh, or his mind, to change their Religion too, in every thing that is not felf-evident, or a manifeft contradiction, in compliance with their prefent *Parifh-Pope?*

I can't but remark, how *good Wits*, tho' they liv'd in very diftant times, & feem of very different Religions, have luckily hit on the fame thought; I mean *Vergerius*, who, in *Luthers*'s days, was *Nuncio* to the Pope; and Dr. *Rogers*, late Chaplain to a *Proteftant* King, at the Head of the *Proteftant* Intereft. The former faid to *Luther*, † *If you wou'd have had any thing innovated in the Faith, in which you were bred up*

* *Vindic. of Civil Eftablifh. pag.* 205.
† Father *Paul's* Hift. of the Counc. of *Trent.* p. 75.

*up for* 35 *years, for your conscience and salvation sake, it was sufficient to have kept it to yourself.* The latter asserts, *, , That in the Christian Religion, the Apostle's , , Rule is, Haft thou Faith, have it to thyself?* And yet 'tis plain, the Apostle was persecuted by the *Rogerians* of those days, for not keeping his Faith to himself.

*E.* WHATEVER *Vergerius* might deserve from *Popish* Publick Wisdom, for misapplying this text, to put a stop to the Reformation; A *Protestant* Divine could deserve nothing but contempt from *Protestant* publick or private Wisdom, for so notoriously perverting its meaning, and openly bantering our first Reformers; and not only condemning them, for not keeping their Religion to themselves, but asserting, that all, † who (without a special commission) from the beginning of the world to this day, have ‡ , , labour'd by publick preaching, or writing, to with-, , draw Mens submission to the establish'd Religion, , , whether *Pagan*, *Mahometan*, or *Popish*, and gather , , Congregations in opposition to it, contrary to the , , command of the Magistrate; , , have been guilty of the damnable sin of disobedience & sedition. So that if *Popery* had been establish'd by Law in King *James's* Reign, all *Protestants* must have kept their Religion in their own breasts, since publickly professing a Religion can't but be unlawful, where there's no coming at it, but by unlawful means. The *Papists*, sure, need no other arguments, to shew the unlawfulness of the Reformation in most places, than what this Reverend Divine has furnish'd them with. And tho' he declares himself an enemy to all persecution, & owns, § , , that , , if there be no publick worship, there must be all , , the appearance that can be of absolute Irreligion; , , yet the chief design of his *Vindication of the Civil* , , *Establishment* is to prove, that all Magistrates, of

S 5       what

* *Pref. to his* 8 *Serm. pag.* 63.    † *Pag.* 158. ‡ *Pag.* 125.    § *Pag.* 29.

,, what Religion foever, have a right to oblige all,
,, but thofe of their own Communion, to keep their
,, Religion to themfelves. ,,   Which is declaring for
Perfecution as well as Irreligion ; fince all Men believe
'tis their duty publickly to worfhip God, tho' contrary
to all human commands; and he himfelf dares not
fay he would obey fuch commands.

AND his diftinction between Mens acting with, or
without a fpecial commiffion, is impertinent in relation to a Magiftrate, who owns no fuch commiffion;
& the whole is inconfiftent with that authority, which,
in another place , he gives to the Church or Clergy,
of prefcribing what Doctrines fhall be taught, & what
not. But if the Magiftrate, for the fake of the State,
can forbid the publick profeffion of all Religions but
one, why not that one ? fince I believe, there's fcarce
any inftance where the profeffion of but one has been
permitted , but that Religion foon degenerated into
Prieftcraft, to the entire deftruction of Mens civil liberties; and the Magiftrate , as well as his Subjects ,
has been forc'd to fubmit to the arbitrary , and vile
impofitions of his own Priefts.

IN fhort, this noble fcheme, if there's any confiftency in it, is, that in all matters of Religion, where
people are capable of judging, they muft not, if the
Magiftrate thinks not fit, openly profefs their Religion ;
and in all other things , which depend on Book-
learning , they are to be govern'd by their refpective
Parifh-Popes. And if fuch a fcheme as this, cou'd recommend the perfon that publifh'd it , to a much
larger Parifh-Popedom than he had before; 'tis high
time for the Laity to confider, whether all the blood
& treafure which have been fpent to keep out but one
Pope, has not been fpent in vain , if, inftead of that
one, we are now to have thoufands?

*A.* I do not find, that the Apoftles taught there was
any thing in Religion, of which People were incapable
of judging; for tho' Men cou'd not well be lower in
point

point of underſtanding, than thoſe to whom the Goſpel was firſt preach'd; yet even theſe are commanded to *judge for themſelves, to prove all things, to take heed to what they hear, to try the Spirits, to avoid falſe Prophets, Seducers, & blind Guides.* And if this was their duty in the Apoſtolick times, it was, certainly, ſo in all after-Ages; and if there are now any ſuch things, by what Authority ſoever introduc'd, as make the Apoſtolical Rule impracticable, I ſhall, with ſubmiſſion to Dr. *Rogers*, venture to affirm, they are no part of the Chriſtian Religion, & that thoſe who teach them are *falſe Prophets, Seducers, & Deceivers*, and as ſuch, are to be ſhunn'd by all Chriſtians.

Sᴛ. *Chryſoſtom* thinks Religion ſo very plain, that he ſays, * ,, Were it not for our ſloth, we had no ,, need of Teachers. ,, And we do not find that even the Fathers thought the People, as not being able to judge for themſelves, were to believe in their Pariſh-Prieſts. *Lactantius*, for inſtance, ſays, † ,, That in ,, thoſe things, eſpecially which concern our life ,, eternal, it becomes every Man to ſearch, & examine ,, the truth of them by his own ſenſe & judgment, ,, rather than to expoſe himſelf by a fooliſh credulity, ,, to the hazard of being ſeduc'd into other Mens errors. And St. *Baſil* tells us, ‡ ,, It is the duty of auditors ,, not to believe implicitly, but to examine the words ,, of thoſe that inſtruct them. ,, And all our Divines, I mean ſuch as are, what they pretend, *Proteſtants*, ſhew they have not ſo mean an opinion of the under-ſtanding of the People, by frequently exhorting them *to judge for themſelves*; & telling them, ,, They have ,, no reaſon to expect Heaven, if they will not be at ,, the pains of examining what wou'd bring them ,, thither, and that the luckineſs of the accident, ,, ſhou'd they ſtumble on truth, wou'd not atone for ,, the neglect of this grand duty.

A

* *Hom.* 3. *on* 2 *Theſ.* To. 4. *pag.* 234. Ed. Sav.
† *Inſt. l. 2. c.* 7.   ‡ *Baſil* Mor. Reg. 72. To. 2. p. 372.

A judicious Divine of our Church very juſtly obſerves * „ That they, who have a good cauſe, need
„ no diſingenious arts; they will not fright Men from
„ conſidering what their Adverſaries ſay, by denoun-
„ cing damnation againſt them; nor forbid them to
„ read their Books, but rather encourage them ſo to
„ do; that they may ſee the difference between
„ truth and falſehood, between Reaſon & Sophiſtry,
„ with their own eyes. -- And whenſoever Guides
„ of a party do otherwiſe, they give juſt cauſe to
„ thoſe who follow them to examine their Doctrines
„ ſo much the more carefully, by how much they
„ are unwilling to have them examin'd. 'Tis a bad
„ ſign, when Men are loth to have their opinions
„ ſeen in the day, but *love darkneſs rather than light.*

T H E fault of the People, even from the beginning,
has been, as the memorable Mr. *Hales* obſerves, that
„ † They, thro' ſloth and blind obedience, examin'd
„ not the things they were taught; but, like beaſts
„ of burden, patiently couch'd down, & indifferently
„ underwent whatever their Superiors laid upon them.

H A P P Y wou'd the Laity have been, if they had
giv'n no juſt occaſion for this infamous character:
tho' if they had follow'd the example of their Clergy
in this one thing, of being as true to their common
intereſt, as theſe have always been to the ſeparate intereſt of their own order, that alone wou'd have pre-
ſerv'd Religion in its native ſimplicity; as being a thing
wholly deſign'd for their general good; and then it
wou'd have been out of the power of the Prieſts to
corrupt it.

*B.* Is not this ſuppoſing, moſt, if not all, the corruptions of Religion, which have prevail'd in any
Church, are owing to their impoſitions, & the blind
deference of the Laity?

*A.*

* *Clagget*'s Perſuaſive to an ingenuous Tryal of Opinions in Relig. p. 25.   † *Tract of Schiſm.*

*A.* IF you think I fpeak this without juft grounds, examine into the prefent, & paft ftate of *Chriftendom* ; & fee whether all thofe grofs depravations, & perverfions of Religion, which have prevail'd in moft places, were not contriv'd to advance the feparate interefts of the Ecclefiafticks ; and Religion been corrupted, in an exact proportion to the number, riches, influence, & power of thefe Reverend Gentlemen? Now thefe corruptions being calculated for their intereft, cou'd a majority without a *miracle*, (as Bithop *Burnet* fays, * in relation to our *Reformation*) agree in correcting thofe abufes? And I may add, that in all Countries, where people have not had the liberty to judge for themfelves in religious matters, no other liberty has been preferv'd ; but Men have been flaves both in body & mind: Such power has the united force of Ecclefiafticks !

A Judicious Author fays, † „ It was not unreafonable „ in the beginning of the Reign of *Edward* VI. and „ Queen *Elizabeth*, to think the Lord and Commons „ better Judges of Religion than the Bithops & Con- „ vocation. The whole body can have no finifter „ intereft to blind them ; but the whole Clergy, „ which is but a part of the whole body, may; and „ therefore the whole body is to judge of this. The „ meaneft Man is as much interefted, and concern'd „ in the truth of Religion, as the greateft Prieft ; for „ tho' his knowledge thereof be not in all refpects „ equally eafy, yet in fome refpects it may be eafier. „ For want of learning does not fo much hinder the „ light of the layman, as wordly advantage & faction „ fometimes does the Prieft ; & the examples of thefe „ are infinite. Corruption in the Church before our „ Saviour, and in our Saviour's days, & ever fince, „ has oftner begun among the greateft Priefts, Rabbies, „ & Bithops, than among the meaneft Laity.

WHAT

* *Introduct. to his Expofit. of the Art. pag. 5.*
† *Of the true grounds of Eccl. Regimen, pag. 84.*

WHAT St. *Paul* says to the Christians of *Corinth*, in relation to false Apostles, has been verify'd in all Ages: * *Ye suffer Fools gladly, seeing ye yourselves are wise. -- Ye suffer if a Man bring you into bondage; if a Man devour you, if a Man take of you, if a Man exalt himself, if a Man smite you on the face.* And, indeed, the *Laicks* have so seldom thought of asserting their natural rights in religious matters, that they have generally sacrific'd to the malice of the Priests, all, who have endeavour'd to maintain these rights; & if the People threw off one set of Ecclesiastical Tyrants, 'twas only to be slaves to another; and were ever ready to join against any one, that endeavour'd to set them free from all Ecclesiastical Tyranny, under which the whole Christian World wou'd still have groan'd, had not so many accidents concurr'd at the *Reformation*.

WE pray against being *led into temptation*, but do we not lead the Clergy into almost irresistable temptation, to impose what they please on the People? What may not Men, who, in a manner, engross the teaching of the young, & instructing the old; (& have great powers, & vast revenues, & those too daily encreasing) bring about by their joint endeavours; and that much more easily, than when they had nothing to depend on but the alms of the people? What is it, that such a confederacy, so modell'd, may not effect, especially where they are caress'd by all parties, nay, even by that, which is by too many of them despis'd, & hated for their unpardonable crime of being against persecution? Are the Clergy less selfish, & designing, than they were in those times some call the *purest?* Or, are the Laity grown wiser, & by the experience of so many Ages, more upon their guard?

PEOPLE abroad were surpris'd to find a Nation, in former times so miserably oppress'd by the Ecclesiasticks, capable, even under a *Whigg* administration,

of

of repealing that Statute of *Mortmain*, which their Predecessors thought absolutely necessary to prevent an all-devouring Corporation from swallowing every thing; and at the same time to see the *First-Fruits* & *Tenths*, granted at the *Reformation* to the Crown, as a just acknowledgement of the Regal supremacy, to be given for ever to this insatiable Corporation; and at a time too, when their revenues were daily encreasing. These surprising favours made foreigners very inquisitive to know, how the conduct of the Clergy had merited more since the *Revolution*, than it did at the *Restoration*; or any other time since the *Reformation*? But begging pardon for this necessary digression, I shall now shew, from the confession of that great Divine & Philosopher, Dr. *H. More*, how little reason the Laity, tho' of the meanest capacity, have to depend upon the authority of Church-men: His words are,

,, * THERE's scarce any Church in *Christendom*
,, at this day, which does not obtrude not only plain
,, falsehoods, but such falsehoods as will appear, to any
,, free spirit, pure contradictions and impossibilities;
,, and that with the same gravity, authority, & im-
,, portunity, as they do the holy Oracles of God. ,,
If this be true, what a miserable condition must the People be in, if they are to depend on this *gravity, authority*, and *importunity* of their respective Priests; who, 'tis possible, may not believe the *Creeds* & *Articles* they subscribe, & yet be against making the least change, for fear of putting the People upon examining into other things, wherein the interest of the Clergy is more nearly concern'd; which may occasion them to assume to themselves the unpardonable crime of seeing with their own eyes, & judging with their own understandings. That *Convocation* † very well knew what they did, which in 1689 with so much indignation rejected those proposals, that some of our most eminent

nent

* *Mystery of Godliness, pag. 495.*
† See Dr. *Clarke's* Script. Doctrine, &c. p. 450.

nent Divines were by the Crown authoris'd to offer them, for making alterations in the *Liturgy*, particularly, in leaving the Clergy at liberty with relation to the *Athanasian* Creed.

In short, whoever in the least reflects, must needs see, that in most Churches, many of their fundamental articles are design'd to impose on the credulous Laity, and that the Priests themselves can't believe them. Can the Pope of *Rome* any more believe himself infallible, than the *Tartarian* Pope, or *Lama*, believes himself immortal? Or than *Protestant* Priests (whose Churches are founded on private judgment) can believe they have a right to make *Creeds* & *Articles* for the People? Can even the *Romish* Priests any more believe they can pardon sins, than the *Bonzees* believe the money they borrow in this world, shall be repaid to their Creditors in the next? Or can the *Popish* Priests, tho' they made the Laity for many Ages renounce their senses, have different ideas of the *Bread* & *Wine*, after they have mumbl'd over certain words, than they had before? Or can the *Lutheran* Priests believe they have the power of *Consubstantiation*? Or the *Calvinistical* Priests think, they can make the body and blood of Christ to be, not figuratively, or, not indeed, but *verily*, & *indeed, taken by the faithful*? Or can any of these Priests believe they give the Holy Ghost? Or that they have an *indelible character*? Or that there can be *Imperium in Imperio*? Or can the *Popish* Priests any more believe their *legendary Traditions*, than the *Pagan* Priests did their Oracles? Or some other Priests the doctrine of *passive-obedience*? Or the *Calvinistical* articles they so solemnly subscribe? Or that *awes* on one hand, & *bribes* on the other, is the way to promote the *Protestant* principle, of every Man's being oblig'd to judge for himself in all religious matters, without prejudice & partiality? Or an hundred other things, which, with this same *gravity*, *authority*, & *importunity*, they impose on the People?

If

IF Men, notwithstanding they pretend to be *inwardly mov'd by the Holy Ghost*, go into Orders, as they take to a trade, to make the best of its mysteries (and all trades have their mysteries;) and are bound for the sake of their maintenance, to maintain those doctrines which *maintain* them, and lest they shou'd not do so, are shackl'd with *subscriptions* upon *subscriptions*; can these Men, I say, under all the prejudices this world affords, be proper persons for the Laity to depend on in the choice of their Religion? Or, are they, who are not permitted to choose their own Religion, fit to choose a Religion for others? In this case, wou'd not *the blind lead the blind into the ditch of Popery*, &c.? And I think, I may venture to say, that Men may as safely trust the choice of their Religion to the chance of a dye, as to the chance of education; considering who, for so many Ages, have had the cooking up of Religion. And every one must see, that those things, which are brought into Religion, contrary to the end of it, as they are inconsistent with the interest of the People, so they savour more of art & learning, than to belong to simple Men, especially in those times they were introduc'd. And as *Adam* said to God, * *The Woman, whom thou gavest to be with me, she gave me of the tree, and I did eat*; so might the People say of their Priests, did they believe them *jure divino*; ,, The Priests thou gavest us, ,, deceiv'd us, & we have been deceiv'd.

*B.* THIS is too severe.

*A.* YOU know, that those few good Men among the Ecclesiasticks, have said as much of their own body, and therefore, I shall only mention what *Picus Mirandula* had the courage to say to *Leo* the Tenth, & the *Lateran* Council: He, after having complain'd, that all Orders of Men were debauch'd by the Clergy, says, † *Nec sane mirum, quando malum omne prodire de*

T *Templo*

* *Gen.* 3. 12.    † See *Fascic. Rerum. Expet. & fugiend.*
*to. I. pag.* 418, 419.

*Templo Johannes Chrysostomus censet; & Hieronimus scribit, se invenisse neminem qui seduxerit Populos, præterquam Sacerdotes.* Tho' 'twas not always they cou'd corrupt them, for the celebrated St. *Ambrose* says, * *Plerumque Clerus erravit, Sacerdotis nutavit sententia, Divites cum seculi istius terreno rege senserunt, Populus fidem propriam reservavit.*

THIS can be no reflection on the Ecclesiasticks among us, who abhor all these principles, by which their predecessors enslav'd Men both body and soul; & who maintain no opinions, however advantagious to the Order, that are against the publick good, and are so far from promoting persecution, that by their example as well as writings, they have highly contributed to that humanity, charity, and benevolence, which, to the great grief of others, is daily increasing among Men of the most different persuasions. Thus, where the Clergy are good, the People of course will be so; & therefore, such Clergymen (of which, perhaps, we now have more, than have ever been in the Church since *Constantine*'s time,) can't be too much esteem'd, for conquering the strong prejudice of education, & the stronger of interest. And they, certainly, ought to be as much valu'd by the Laity for so unusual a generosity, in defending the common rights of Mankind, as they are hated by their Brethren, for giving up those claims, by which they have at all times commanded the purses, as well as the consciences of the people; when too, they cou'd not but be sensible, what they were to expect from their restless enemies, whenever they shou'd be permitted to exert themselves.

AND here I can't omit saying, that, if he, who best defends the Church, best deserves to rule it, Justice has eminently appear'd in the promotion of that person, now happily presiding over it, who so early put a stop to the boasted Triumphs of the ablest adversary

our

* *Ambros.* Serm. 17. To. 4. pag. 725.

our Church ever had; & has since protected it against its worst, its domestick Enemies, treacherously under-mining the Constitution; who, as he treats all with that condescending goodness inseparable from true greatness, so he encourages Piety & Virtue, without distinction of parties; and tho' he has with equal pru-dence expos'd both *Popish* & *Protestant persecution*; * yet both the *Sorbonne* & *Geneva*, however differing in most other things, agree in owning so illustrious a merit. And I may challenge all Church - History to show three such Bishops, as to the honour of the *Re-volution*, have, since that blessed time, succeeded one another at *Lambeth*.

I must beg your patience for adding, on this in-exhaustable subject, one reason more, for Mens being govern'd by things, rather than words. It has been a general practice with the introducers of civil tyranny, tho' they chang'd the form of Government, to retain the old names; the better to hinder people from being sensible of the change: And may not this have happen'd in Church - matters? And may not Eccle-siastical tyranny be brought in, & supported by the same means? Has not this very term *Church*, had a different meaning put on it, from what it has in the original? And is not the *Greek* word sometimes trans-lated *Assembly*, sometimes *Church*; the better to con-found the *rights of the Church*, or *People*, as that word in Scripture always signifies? In one of our Articles, *the Church* is defin'd to be a *Congregation of the Faith-ful*, &c. yet is it not every where else taken for the *Clergy*? When 'tis said in the very next Article, ,, The Church has power to decree Rites and Cere-,, monies, and Authority in matters of Faith; ,, is it meant of the *Congregation of the Faithful*? And is it not a constant practice with some Men, to talk of the power & authority of the Church, when they only mean their own, in hopes to make that, which other-

T 2　　　　　　　　wise

* *Wake's* Serm. Vol. 3. pag. 4.

wife people might ftart at, go down under its facred name?

Are the People now taught to conceive the fame thing by the word *Bifhop*, as it means in the original, where *Bifhop* and *Presbyter* are fynonimous terms? Is it not to prevent their feeing it, that we tranflate the *Greek* word fometimes by *Overfeer*, fometimes by *Bifhop*? For the firft three, or four centuries, every Congregation had its own Bifhop, who was conftantly oblig'd to refide, & to officiate in the Parifh Church: And as among the *Jews*, the *Ruler of one Synagogue* had nothing to do in any other; fo among the primitive Chriftians (whofe difcipline was accommodated to that of the *Jews*,) it wou'd have been thought highly anti-chriftian, and invading the rights of his Brethren, for one Bifhop to have more than one *Altar*, or *Communion-table*. But things continually changing, a Parifh Bifhop, maintain'd by the Alms of his congregation, commenc'd a Bifhop, not only of many Parifhes, but of a whole Province; nay, of many Provinces, with the titles, pomp, & grandeur of Princes, and at laft, to an *Univerfal Bifhop*, *Pope*, or *Vice-God*.

The only Church that has now any pretence to primitive Epifcopacy, is that of *North Britain*; where fince the *Bleffed Revolution*, a parity of Parifh-Bifhops has been eftablifh'd. If you want fully to underftand the Conftitution of the primitive Church, in this, & all other points, you need only read the *Inquiry into the Conftitution, Difcipline, Unity, and Worfhip of the Primitive Church*, &c. written by the greateft Critick, Divine, & Lawyer of this, or, perhaps, any other Age.

What other reafon can be affign'd, why διακον⊙-, *Rom.* 16. 1. is not render'd *Deaconefs*, as well as elfewhere *Deacon*, but *Servant of the Church*; except it be to hinder the people from perceiving, that there was in the days of the Apoftles, an *Order of Women*, who had fomething more to do in the Church than to fweep it, and who, even at the Council of *Nice*
(Can.

(*Can.* 19.) are reckon'd among the Clergy? Did *Herefy*, or *Schifm*, (thofe religious *Scare-crows*, as the memorable Mr. *Hales* calls them; ) fignify any fuch thing in the days of the Apoftles, as afterwards, to the infinite prejudice of *Chriftendom*, they were made to mean? Why do we give the name of *Prieft* to the *Jewifh Sacrificer*, as well as to the *Chriftian Elder* (things fo widely different,) but to make People believe the latter have a *Divine Right* to every thing, which, under the *Theocracy*, belong'd to the former? And as in the New Teftament the *Preachers of the Gofpel* are never term'd Ἱερεῖς, or *Priefts*, fo *Scaliger* * remarks that the word fo apply'd, is not to be met with till after *Juftin*'s time.

Has the word *Clergy* the fame meaning now, as in the New Teftament, where 'tis taken in oppofition to thofe we now call fo? And did not Ecclefiaftical tyranny, & the ingroffing that name by the Minifters of the Church commence together?

Nor is it difficult to fee the reafon, why the word, βαπτίζω was not tranflated but naturaliz'd, fince the People would then have perceiv'd, that, not *fprinkling*, but *dipping*, or *immerfing*, was meant by it; but fhould any now (fo much cuftom has prevail'd) fay *John* the *Dipper*, inftead of *John* the *Baptift*, the People would think it profane.

If words have been thus artfully manag'd in relation to things, have not people much more reafon to fupect the fame management in relation to fpeculative points, where words allow a greater latitude? If *zeal* had had the fame meaning in after times, as in the Scripture, it had never occafion'd fo much mifchief. And what mifchief have not thofe two mifinterpreted words, *Zeal* & *Church*, by the artful management of defigning Men, occafion'd? Nay, Is not *Religion* made to fignify fomething very different from what it does in Scripture? How few, when they hear that word,

T 3                                        think

* *Scaligerana*, Ἱερεῖς.

think of the defcription given by St. *James*, * of *pure & undefil'd Religion*? What abfurdities have not people brought into Religion, by fixing a fenfe on the word *myftery* unknown to the Scripture? Nay, have not fome people, if the Univerfity of *Oxford* is a good Judge, advanc'd falfe, impious, & heretical doctrines concerning the Godhead, in declaring the † *three Perfons are three diftinct, infinite Minds or Spirits*; tho' now reviv'd by Dr. *W---d*, with the applaufe of thofe who before condemn'd it? And did not they, who efpous'd thofe doctrines, reprefent their adverfaries as abfurd *Sabellians*; in either making the three Perfons in the divine Being, to be analogous to three poftures in a human being; (for this was the utmoft Dr. *South's* Divinity could reach to) Or with Dr. *Wallis*, *three famewhats*, of which they themfelves had no idea? Good God! what pains Men take to deface the idea, which the Light of Nature as well as the Scripture gives of God; and which every one conceives, when he hears him mention'd on either a natural, political, or religious account.

I n fhort, was it not running too far from our prefent purpofe, it would not be very difficult to fhew, that there are very few terms in Scripture, which have things of moment depending on them, but what have loft their original meaning, to become orthodox.

I f they, who have the tranflating any old Book capable of vaftly different fenfes, make it fpeak what is moft for their intereft, muft not others be very good Men indeed, who will find fault with a tranflation in fuch points as make for their common advantage; or be at the pains in fuch cafe, to difcover any favourable additions, fubftractions or alterations that might have been made in the Scriptures, or other antient writings? efpecially if it be true what

Mr.

---

*. *Jam.* I. 27.    † *Oxford* Decree made by the Heads of Colleges and Halls in 1693.

Mr. *Whiston* complains of, * ,, That it is frequently ,, in the mouths of the Writers for the Church, that ,, some things are to be conceal'd for fear they gra- ,, tify *Atheists* & *Deists*, and *says*, Certainly, nothing ,, prejudices them more than such procedure & ex- ,, pressions, while they thereby perceive remains of ,, pious frauds every where, & suspect it has been so ,, from the beginning. They see they are not to be ,, let plainly into the truth of facts, but to be manag'd ,, with cunning & worldly prudence, for fear of being ,, disgusted at Christianity.

MUST not the People be at a loss, when they see how differently the texts in the most momentous parts are interpreted? Dr. *S. Clark* has reckon'd up more than 1250 texts relating to the doctrine of the *Trinity*; and how few of them are interpreted alike by the contending parties? 'Tis chiefly owing to these dif- ferent interpretations, that, where force has not inter- pos'd, it has from Age to Age been disputed, whether we have but one, or more than one object of supreme worship. A point, which, was Reason allow'd to be a competent Judge, would not meet with the least difficulty; & had we a Bible translated by *Unitarians*, many texts would be very differently translated, from what they are at present; & some left out as forg'd. When so judicious a Divine and Critick as the now Bishop of *A*— says, † ,, We should have more of the ,, true text by being less tenacious of the printed one; must not that give great uneasiness to those, who have nothing to trust to, but the printed text? And will this uneasiness be abated by his affirming, ,, that it ,, may with great truth be said of *Chillingworth*, ‡ ,, (the greatest Champion the *Protestant* cause ever had) ,, that he was abler at pulling down than building up; ,, towards which little can be expected from one,

T 4 who

* *Postscript to the Convoc. Proceedings, pag. 90.*
† *Clergyman's Thanks to Philol.*
‡ *Defen. of his Serm. against the Bp. of Bangor, p. 31.*

,, who is by his own arguments push'd so hard in
,, the defence he would make of *Protestantism*, that
,, he has nothing left, but to cry out, *The Bible*, I say,
,, *The Bible is the Religion of* Protestants.,, Nay, must
not that uneasiness be very much increas'd by Divines,
perpetually endeavouring to mend by their criticisms
several capital places in the sacred Writers; nay, who
pretend daily to make new & momentous discoveries?
How must their hearers be edify'd, when they tell
them 'tis *thus* or *thus*, in such an antient *Manuscript*,
*Father*, or *Assembly of Fathers*; or cry, *'tis render'd
more agreeable to the mind of the Holy Ghost* in the *Septuagint*, *Vulgar Latin*, *Syriack*, *Chaldaick*, *Ethiopick*,
*Coptick*, *Gothick*, or some other version.

I f no Court of Judicature, tho' in a thing of small
moment, will admit of a copy, tho' taken from the
original, without oath made by a disinterested person
of his having compar'd it (because the least mistake,
a various pointing, a parenthesis, a letter misplac'd
may alter the sense) how can we absolutely depend
in things of the greatest moment, on voluminous
writings, which have been so often transcrib'd by Men,
who never saw the original; (as none, even of the
most early Writers pretend they did;) And Men too,
who even in the earliest times,· if we may judge by
the number of forg'd passages, & even forg'd books,
would scruple at no pious frauds. And tho' there have
been innumerable copies of the New Testament lost,
which, no doubt, had their different Readings, yet as
it stands at present, we are told, there are no less
than 30000 various readings.

B, T h o' there are so many various readings, yet
does not that great *Critick*, Doctor *Bentley*, in his
Proposal for printing by subscription, a new edition
of the New Testament, assure the world, * ,, That out
,, of a labyrinth of 30000 various readings which
croud

* *Proposals for Printing by Subscription a new Edit.
of the New Testament.*

,, croud the pages of our prefent beft editions, all put
,, upon an equal credit to the offence of many good
,, perfons, that his *clue*, as he calls it, fo leads & ex-
,, tricates us, that there will be fcarce 200 out of fo
,, many thoufands, that can deferve the leaft confi-
,, deration.

*A.* HAS this Critick loft his *clue*, and fo forc'd to
drop the noble defign of afcertaining the Text of the
New Teftament, and *let the* 30000 *various Readings
remain on an equal foot to the offence of many good perfons?* who will now as much defpair of feeing it done,
as they do of Mr. *Whifton's* * reftoring the true text
of the Old Teftament; ,, which, *he fays*, has been
,, greatly corrupted both in the *Hebrew & Septuagint*
,, by the *Jews*, to make the reafonings of the Apoftles
,, from the Old Teftament inconclufive & ridiculous.

DR. *Bentley*, certainly, ought to go on with his
propofal; becaufe the world will hardly take the Doctor's word, that in a Book, where moft things are
own'd to be of the greateft moment, there fhould be
fo many various Readings of no moment; tho one,
or two, may be of that confequence, as to deftroy
the defign of the whole book. In a prefcription where
there are ever fo many wholefome drugs. yet if a
poifonous one happens to be mix'd, it may turn the
whole into rank poifon. If the Doctrine of the *Trinity*
is of the greateft moment, was not the Church highly
concern'd to prevent various readings in that important point, as well as fome forg'd texts?

HAD the Scripture been better guarded in many
other matters of confequence, there could not have
been fo many texts feemingly clafhing with one
another. That there are fuch, is deny'd by none:
Dr. *Scot* lays it down as certain, that † ,, That opinion
,, is falfe, or of little moment, that has but one, or
,, two texts to countenance it; & that very dubious,
T 5                    which

* *Whifton's* Effay pag 10.
† *Chrift. Life,* P. 2. *Vol.* I. *Ch.* 6. *p.* 384.

,, which has none but obscure texts to rely on; but
,, when there are more, & much plainer texts against
,, it than for it, it must be false.

A N D another judicious Divine says, that * ,, Our
,, Faith is not to be built on single texts, because they
,, may have been corrupted; tho' we have no ma-
,, nuscript to point out to us, that the other manuscripts
,, have been so corrupted in these passages. ,,  But,

I F we can't depend on single texts; & where there
are several, tne plainest are to carry it; the difficulty
will be to know which are the plainest ; since the
different Sects of Christians have ever pretended, that
the plainest texts are on their side, & wonder'd how
their Adversaries cou'd mistake their meaning.

T H E plain texts from St. *Austin*'s days, at least in
the *West*, were all in favour of *Predestination* ; & upon
those plain texts the Articles of our most excellent
Church, & all other *Protestant* Churches are founded.
It's true in Q. *Elizabeth*'s Reign, there were some
few among the inferior Clergy for *Free-will*; † but
then those *incorrigible Free-will* Men, as they were
call'd, were, by the direction of the Bishops, sent to
prison, there to live on hard labour, till they repented
of their errors: But since the Court in *Charles* I's Reign,
help'd to open the eyes of our Divines, they, no longer
blinded by their Articles clearly see, that all those plain
texts (and what a number are muster'd up on both
sides) are all for *Free-will*; against which, now, there
are none but are look'd on as *incorrigible*.

B. T H o' those Books, which contain the traditional Religions of other Nations, have, notwithstanding all the care taken to prevent it, been mix'd
with Fables & monstrous tales : yet we say, that the
Scripture, especially the New Testament, tho' there
are ever so many various readings, must needs be free
from all errors of consequence; because that being
                                                    design'd

defign'd by God for a plain, & unalterable Rule, for the actions of Mankind, cannot but be fo guarded by Providence, as to hinder any miftakes of moment.

*A.* YOUR reafoning, I grant, holds good in relation to the Law of Nature, which equally obliges, at all times & places, the whole Race of Mankind; but then that depends not on the knowledge of any language dead, or living; or on the skill, or honefty of Tranfcribers, or Tranflators; but on that, which as it as apparent to the whole World, fo it is not in the power of Mortals to alter; *viz.* the unchangeable Relation of Things, and the Duties refulting from thence.

„ * The Tranfcribers of books (as that learned & judicious Critick *Daillé* obferves) „ have been guilty „ of innumerable miftakes; & that St. *Jerom* † (the moft learned of the Fathers) complains, „ they wrote „ not what they found, but what they underftood; „ and he gives inftances of attempts made on the New Teftament by the Orthodox themfelves; particularly. St. *Epiphanius*, for faying, ‡ „ that in the true, and „ moft correct copies of St. *Luke*, it was writ, that *Jefus Chrift wept*; & that this paffage had been alledg'd by St. *Ireneus*, but that the *Catholicks* had blotted out the word, fearing that the *Hereticks* might abufe it. The fame St. *Jerom* fays, the laft twelve verfes in the laft Chapter of *Mark* were left out in moft *Greek* Bibles; § *Omnibus Græciæ Libris pene hoc capitulum non habentibus.* *Grotius* imputes this omiffion to the Tranfcribers: But *Maldonat* will not allow of *Grotius*'s reafon, becaufe he fays, *Luke* & *John* differ more with *Matthew* than *Mark* does. ¶ *Major enim inter illos & Matthæum, quam inter* Matthæum *& Marcum apparet repugnantia.*

*Hilary,*

* De ufu Patr. P. 1. l. 1. c. 3.   † Epift. 28. ad Lucum. p. 247.
‡ L. 1. c. 4.   § Epift. ad Hedib. Queft. 3. Grot. in loc.
¶ Maldonat. in loc.

*Hilary*, speaking of Chrift's bloody fweat, and the Angel fent to comfort him, fays, * *Nec fane ignorandum nobis eft, in Gracis & Latinis codicibus compluribus, de adveniente Angelo, vel de fudore fanguineo nihil fcriptum reperiri.* This St. *Jerom* † feems to confirm.

For my part, I think, that at leaft, till we are extricated by Dr. *Bentley's* clue, the beft way not to be miftaken, is to admit all for diviñe Scripture, that tends to the honour of God, and the good of Man; and nothing which does not. This clue, I think, will extricate the learned as well as unlearned out of many otherwife infuperable difficulties; and make the Laws of God, which way foever reveal'd, entirely to agree; & deftroy that abfurd notion of God's acting arbitrarily, and commanding for commanding-fake. And does not St. *Paul* ‡ fuppofe no Scripture to be divinely infpir'd, but *what is profitable for doctrine, for reproof, for correction, for inftruction in righteoufnefs?* And if this be the teft, ought we to admit any thing to be writ by infpiration, tho' it occurs ever fo often in Scripture, till we are certain it will bear this teft? And, indeed, was it otherwife, we fhou'd be in a fad condition, fince there's fcarce any opinion, tho' ever fo abfurd, or ridiculous, but has its vouchers, who quote texts on texts, for its fupport. Good Lord! what a load have the different parties laid on it, by their not obferving this Rule? But,

Cou'd we fuppofe any difference between *Natural* & *Traditional* Religion, to prefer the latter, wou'd be acting irrationally; as that Prophet did, who went contrary to what God had commanded § him by an immediate revelation, becaufe a known Prophet affur'd him, he had afterwards a different revelation for him. A crime fo heinous in the eyes of the Lord, that

* *Hilary l.* 10. *de Trin.*    † *Lib.* 2. *adver. Pelag.*
‡ 2 *Tim.* 3. 16. See *Grotius* in loc. and the 5 Letters about Infpiration. pag. 100. &c. Eng. Tanfl.
§ 1 *Kings* 13.

that he deftroy'd this Prophet after a moft fignal manner; tho' he had to plead for himfelf, that the Prophet, who fpoke to him in the name of the Lord, cou'd have no intereft in deceiving him; & that there was nothing in the command, but might as well come from the Lord, as what himfelf had receiv'd. And 'tis worth obferving, that the lying Prophet was fo far from being punifh'd, that the Lord continu'd to him the gift of Prophecy; nay, pronounc'd by his mouth the Doom of the Prophet, he fo *fatally deceiv'd*.

*B.* W H Y is this more worth obferving than the cafe of *Abimelech*, who, upon both *Abraham*'s & *Sarah*'s lying to him, took *Sarah*, as the Lord himielf owns, * *in the integrity of his heart*; & tho' he fent her back untouch'd, & gave confiderable prefents both to Wife and Husband, yet neither *he*, nor *his*, were to be pardon'd, till *Abraham* the offending perfon) being a Prophet, was to pray for him; † *fo* Abraham *pray'd unto God, & God heal'd* Abimelech, *and his Wife, and Maid-fervants; and they bare Children:* And yet this holy Prophet was foon after guilty of a very barbarous action, in fending out ‡ *Hagar, whom* Sarah *had giv'n him to Wife,* & *his Son* Ifhmael, *to perifh in the wildernefs*; for no other reafon, but becaufe *Sarah* had feen § *the Son of* Hagar *mocking*; and 'tis likely they had both perifh'd, had not *an Angel, calling out of Heaven,* directed ¶ *Hagar* to *a well of water*. And perhaps, the fame Angel, who, when fhe before fled from *Sarah*, who ✠ *had dealt hardly with her*, bid her * *return, and fubmit:* But in this laft domeftick quarrel, God himfelf miraculoufly interpofes, & fays, † *In all that* Sarah *hath faid unto thee, hearken unto her voice.* But begging pardon for this interruption, pray go on.

*A.* W E, certainly, ought to adhere ftrictly to the Light of Nature; if, (as a Learned & Reverend Critick

tick obferves) * ,, It muft be allow'd by the judicous
,, and impartial, that many corruptions are found in
,, our prefent copies of the holy Bible; and that we
,, have not now this bleffed book in that perfection
,, & integrity, that it was firft written. It is alter'd
,, in many places, & in fome of the greateft moment.
,, -- I cou'd prove, I think, by undeniable and un-
,, avoidable inftances, what Mr. *Gregory* of *Oxford*
,, fays in his Preface, to fome critical notes on the
,, Scripture, that he publifh'd. There's no Author
,, whatfoever fays this learned Critick, that has fuffer'd
,, fo much by the hand of time as the Bible has. ,,
If this, I fay, muft be allow'd, ought we not, in order
to prevent all miftakes, in the firft place to get clear
ideas of the moral character of the Divine Being;
and when by reafons much ftronger than any drawn
from human tradition, we have difcover'd this character, ought we not to compare what we are told
of him, by what we already know of him, and fo
judge of what Men teach us concerning God, by what
God himfelf teaches us; for *we are all taught of him*:
And then we fhall be as certain, as there is a God
perfectly wife, & infinitely good, that no doctrines
can come from him that have not thefe characters
ftamp'd on them. Thus were there more falfe readings
crept into the Scripture than thefe Divines fuppofe,
yet we might ftill know our duty; and be certain
that by doing our beft to promote our mutual happinefs, we anfwer the end of our creation; and that
if we deviate from this rule for the fake of what depends on human tradition, we quit certainty for that,
which is not pretended to amount to more than probability.

A N D it is no fmall incouragement for us to obferve
this rule, fince we find, that Men, if like Pedants,
or School-Mafters, they read books, not to examine
the force & cogency of the arguments they meet with,

but

* *Nye* of Nat. and Rev. Relig. pag. 198, 199.

but for the fake of words & phrafes, without confidering the nature, reafon, and tendency of things, underftand very little of things. Have not great numbers from Age to Age, tho' Men of good natural parts, had their underftandings confounded by thus unjudiciously employing them; & inftead of clearing doubts increas'd them, and fill'd the world with ufelefs criticifms, and trifling difputes? while they, who made words give place to things, & argu'd from the relation things bear to each other, have fhewn themfelves able *Cafuifts*, & inrich'd the World with moft ufeful difcourfes, for promoting the honour of God, and the good of Man. And, therefore we are often caution'd by the beft Authors, not to ftick too clofe to the letter in reading the Scripture; fince they fay the ftyle of Holy-writ is far from being exact; & that the laying too great ftrefs on words, has been the occafion of moft of the Difputes among Chriftians.

To fhew how little we are to depend on words and phrafes; they fay, a number of Texts might be produc'd to prove *Mofes* to be a God: ,, For he is ,, call'd * *God*, & *Lord*; and pray'd to, under that ,, appellation, *to forgive Sin* †; has attributed to him ,, the fame miraculous work of *bringing the Children* ,, *of* Ifrael *out of* Egypt, as is afcrib'd to God ‡; that ,, the Ifraelites did *believe in him*, as well as *in the* ,, *Lord* §, & were requir'd fo to do; that *he promis'd* ,, *Rain in due feafon to fuch as kept his commandments* ¶, ,, and to *Jofhua*, that *he wou'd be with him in carrying* ,, *the People into* Canaan ✠; altho' as a Man, he was ,, to die before; that he did *great works*; yea, *miracles* ,, *in the fight of the* Ifraelites, on purpofe *that they* ,, *might know that he was the Lord their God* *; that ,, *Aaron* is faid to be *his Prophet* †, which is proper

to

* *Exod.* 7. 1. *Id.* 4. 16.    † *Num.* 12. 11. *Exod.* 10. 16, 17.
‡ *Exod.* 32. 7.  *Id.* 33. 1.    § *Exod.* 14. *ult. Id.* 19. 9.
¶ *Deut.* 11. 13, 14, 15, &c.    ✠ *Id.* 31. 23.
* *Deut.* 29. 5, 6.    † *Exod.* 7. 1.

„ to the true God only ; & in fine, that the *Israelites*
„ were *baptiz'd unto,* or *into* Moses \*.

THESE Authors tells us, that in the *Ethicks* of
*Aristotle,* in the *Offices* of *Tully,* in the *Moral Treatises*
of *Grotius, Puffendorff,* &c. the nature & reason of our
duties, the connexion between them, & the dependance they have on one another are plainly seen,
but in the Scripture, things, *say they,* are not generally so treated, as that Men may precisely know the
nature, & extent of their duty. Are they not, *say they,*
for the most part, deliver'd in such a general, undetermin'd, nay, sometimes parabolical, and hyperbolical
manner, as did we not consult our Reason, & learn
our duty from thence, the letter might lead us wrong :
nay, the Apostle himself says, *the Letter killeth.*

*B.* I can't believe things of any moment are thus
represented, because, as God cou'd have no other end
in giving us a Revelation, than the rightly directing
our minds, so that end cou'd not have been answer'd,
except it was deliver'd in a way most plain, & easy
to be understood in all times & places; for if there
are propositions in Scripture, which naturally tend to
mislead us, or if the use of languages is perverted in
some instances, how can we certain, but it may be in
others ?

*A.* Is not the New Testament full of Parables, nay,
is it not said, † that *without a Parable Jesus spake not to
the multitude;* and for this remarkable reason, ‡ *That
seeing they might see, & not perceive, and hearing they
might hear, and not understand, lest at any time they
shou'd be converted, & their sins be forgiven them.* Is not
St. *John*'s Gospel, for the most part, writ after an
obscure, allegoricall manner, especially in relation to
the Person of Christ ? And do not Commentators own,
we labour under much the same difficulties in interpreting St. *Paul ?* The honourable Mr. *Boyle* says,
„ That

* I *Cor.* 10. I, 2.    † *Mat.* 13. 34.    ‡ *Mark* 4. 12.

,, * That fometimes in St. *Paul's* writings many paf-
,, fages are fo penn'd, as to contain a tacit kind of a
,, dialogue; and that unskilfully by Readers, & even
,, Interpreters, taken for an argument, which, indeed,
,, is an objection. It's faid it was the way of the *Eaft*,
,, to make ufe of dark, & involv'd fentences, figura-
,, tive & parabolical difcourfes, abrupt, and maim'd
,, ways of expreffing themfelves, with a neglect of
,, annexing tranfitions.

As for hyperbolical expreffions, it was cuftomary
among the *Eaftern* nations to exprefs themfelves after
a moft pompous, & high-ftrain'd manner. This way
of fpeaking was a main part of Learning, taught in
the Schools of the Prophets among the *Jews*; and
happy was he, who cou'd moft excel in this elevated,
romantick way; & both the Old & New Teftament
abound with expreffions of this nature. *Ifaiah*, in pro-
phecying the deftruction of *Babylon*, fays, † *The Stars
of Heaven fhall not give their light, the Sun fhall be
darkned.* -- ‡ *I will fhake the Heavens, & the Earth
fhall remove out of her place, in the wrath of the Lord
of Hofts, & in the day of his fierce anger.* And the deftruction of the City of *Jerufalem* in the New Teftament is defcrib'd after fuch a manner, as if Nature
was unhing'd, & the Univerfe diffolving.

Bp. *Fleetwood* on *Pfalm* 18. fays, § ,, That without
,, remembring *David's* hiftory, one wou'd imagine
,, Heaven & Earth were mov'd on his behalf; and
,, that the courfe of Nature had been overthrown,
,, & his life cover'd by continual miracles: ,, And he
,, there obferves, that the *Jewifh* expreffions, & the
,, expreffions of all people that dwelt *eaftward* are
,, full of pomp, & amplification of fancy & hyper-
,, bole. ,, And, I think, under this head we may
reckon thefe texts, that ¶ *All the Kings of the Earth*
V
*fought*

* *Boyle's* Stile of Script. p. 64. † *Ifa.* 13. 10. ‡ *Ib. ver.* 13.
§ Thankfgiv. Serm. *June* 7. 1716.
¶ 2 *Chron.* 9. 23.

*fought the prefence of* Solomon. That \* *If the things which Jefus did were written, the World itfelf could not contain the books.* And are not moft of the expreffions of St. *John* as figurative, as *Eating the Flefh, & drinking the Blood of the Son of Man?* And what monftrous practices did thofe words, taken literally, produce, even in the primitive times; & what fenfles difputes fince? And,

Must we not put under this head a number of other texts, † *Whatfoever you fhall ask in my name, that will I do.* ‡ *If two of you fhall agree on Earth, touching any thing they fhall ask, it fhall be done for them of my Father, which is in Heaven.* § *If you have Faith as a grain of muftard feed. you fhall remove mountains, & nothing fhall be impoffible to you.* ¶ *And you may fay to this* Sycamine *tree, Be thou plucked up by the roots, & be thou planted in ths Sea, & it fhall obey you.* ✠ *Whatfoever thou fhalt bind on Earth, fhall be bound in Heaven.* \* *He that is fpiritual, judgeth all things,* (which the *Papifts* fay is the *Pope*) *yet he himfelf is judg'd of no Man.* † *Things prefent, & things to come, all are yours.* ‡ St. *John's little Children* are faid to *have an unction, & to know all things.* And what more cou'd be faid of the *Anointed*, or Chrift himfelf? Men are bid to be § *partakers of the divine nature;* and to be as ¶ *perfect as their heavenly Father is perfect.* What bleffings are not Chriftians promis'd, even in this life? Is it not faid, ✠ *Chrift has made us Kings & Priefts unto God; -- \* & we fhall reign on the Earth?* And are not the † *Meek to inherit the Earth? And, is not* ‡ *every one that hath forfaken houfes, or Brethren, or Sifters, or Father, or Mother, or Wife, or Children, or Lands, for my name fake, to receive an hundred fold, & to inherit everlafting life?* What one is fent to declare

---

\* *John* 21. 25.  † *Id.* 14. 13.  ‡ *Mat.* 18. 19.  § *Id.* 17. 20.
¶ *Luke* 17. 6.  ✠ *Mat.* 16. 12.  \* *Cor.* 2. 12.  † *Ib.* 3. 22.
‡ 1 *John* 2. 20.  § 2 *Pet.* 1. 4.  ¶ *Mat.* 5. 48.
✠ *Rev.* 1. 6.  \* *Ib.* 5. 10.  † *Mat.* 5. 5.  ‡ *Ib.* 19. 29.

clare is to be done, that he is said to do: So *Jeremiah* is said to be * *set over the Nations, & over the Kingdoms, to root out, pull down, & destroy.* What is design'd to be done, shall be said to be actually done: As † *the Lamb slain from the Foundation of the World.* ‡ *Before* Abraham *was I was*; or as we (to make it more mysterious) render it, *I am:* § Nay, a Creature not born long before, is said to be *the First born of every Creature.* Advice is call'd Submission, Subjection, & Obedience; ¶ *Ye younger submit yourselves to the elder; yea, be subject to one another.* ✠ *Obey them that have the rule over you; and submit yourselves.* Persuasion is call'd compulsion, as * *Compel them to come in.* And what rooting work have not the *Papists* made from this text; † *Every plant my heavenly Father hath not planted shall be rooted up;* and such other misapply'd places? Is not God's *permitting evil,* call'd *doing it?* ‡ *Shall there be evil in a City, & the Lord has not done it?* Nay, is not the Lord said to § *have created evil?* And to *have harden'd Mens hearts*; and then *to punish them* for their being harden'd? And *to tempt Men?* Are we not to pray against God's *leading us into temptation?* Nay, is not God, if the words are to be taken literally, represented as an arbitrary Being, ¶ *hating Children not yet born, neither having done any good, or evil?* ✠ *Jacob have I loved, but* Esau *have I hated.* -- * *Therefore hath he mercy on whom he will have mercy, & whom he will he hardeneth.* † *Hath not the Potter power over his clay?* --

A R E not things in Scripture absolutely condem'd, which are only so conditionally: As the *Jewish* Rites & Sacrifices are, in the Old Testament, represented as ‡ *an iniquity, & an abomination to the Lord.* Things

V 2          com-

* *Jer.* 1. 10.   † *Rev.* 13. 8.   ‡ *John* 8. 58.   § *Col.* 1. 15.
¶ 1 *Pet.* 5. 5.   ✠ *Heb.* 13. 17.   * *Luke* 14. 23.
† *Mat.* 15. 13.   ‡ *Amos* 3. 6.   § *Isaiah* 45. 7.
¶ *Rom.* 9. 11.   ✠ *Ib. ver.* 13.   * *Ib. ver.* 18.   † *Ver.* 21.
‡ *Isaiah* 1. 13.

commanded are positively said not to be commanded;
* *As I spake not to your Fathers, nor commanded them
in that day I brought them out of the Land of* Egypt,
*concerning Burnt - offerings & Sacrifices.* What can be
more figurative than Jesus's saying, † *If any Man come
to me, & hate not his Father, & Mother, & Wife, and
Children, & Brethren, & Sisters; yea, and his own life
also, he can't be my Disciple.* Things spoken in an unlimited, are to be taken in a restrained sense : ‡ *Swear
not at all.* § *Children & Servants, obey your Parents
& Masters in all things.* ¶ *The love of money, is the root
of all evil.* ✠ *Whatsoever the Pharisees bid you do,
that do, & observe.* * *Rejoice evermore. Pray without
ceasing. Prove all things.* And sometimes a short duration is express'd by the words *for ever*; or *for everlasting*; or for the *end of the World* : So *Jonah*, after
he came out of the Fish's Belly, says, † *The Earth
with her bars was about me for ever*, & an hundred
other such texts: So that whether any *duration* is to
be *everlasting*, (in the sense we that take that word)
can't be known from the words of Scripture; but it
must be judg'd of from the nature of the things that
are said thus to endure.  But,

WHAT can be more surprising, than Christ's declaring in most express terms, he came to do that,
which we must suppose he came to hinder : *Think not,*
(says he) ‡ *I am come to send Peace, I come not to
send Peace, but a Sword. For I am come to set a Man
at variance with his Father*, &c. And, § *Suppose ye,
I am come to give peace on Earth, I tell you nay; but
rather division.* And again, ¶ *I am come to send fire
on Earth, and what will I, if it be already kindled?*
And has not that fire burnt outragiously ever since,
being blown up by those, whose business it was to
have extinguish'd it? And have they not so acted as
if

* *Jer.* 7. 22.  † *Luke* 14. 26.  ‡ *Mat.* 5. 34.  § *Eph.* 6. 1. 5.
¶ 1 *Tim.* 6. 10.  ✠ *Mat.* 23. 3.  * *Thes.* 5. 16, 17. 21.
† *Jonah* 2. 6.  ‡ *Mat.* 10. 34.  § *Luke* 12. 51.  ¶ *Ib. Ver.* 49.

if this was a prophetick saying, they were at all times bound to see fulfill'd, tho' to the destruction of all moral duties whatever?

Another difficulty in understanding both the Old and New Testament, is, that most things, tho' owing to second causes, are referr'd immediately to God. In the New Testament, *Pilate* is said * to *have his power from above*, even while he was condemning Jesus. And † *there is no power but of God, the Powers that be, are ordain'd of God:* ‡ *Take heed, therefore, unto yourselves, & to all the Flock, over the which the Holy Ghost had made you Overseers.* Nay, every good motion is imputed to the Spirit, whether with, or without understanding. § *I will pray with the Spirit, & with the Understanding also: I will sing with the Spirit, and with the Understanding also.* Or, if a Man talk'd in an unknown tongue, & cou'd not interpret what he said; or any of the congregation understood him; yet it was *Prophesying*, & the *gift of the Spirit*. And St. *Paul* calls a Heathen Poet a Prophet. And is not *Spirit*, nay, the *Spirit of God*, ¶ taken, at least, in twenty different senses in the Scripture?

In short, *the words of Scripture*, on which things of the greatest consequence depend, *are*, as is shewn by a learned Author, ✠ *sometimes taken, not only in a different, but contrary sense.* However, to give one instance, *Nature* in *Rom.* 2. 14. & *Nature* in *Eph.* 2. 3. if rightly translated, are taken in opposite senses, and that word in 1 *Cor.* 11. 14. is taken in a sense different from both.

How can we know from Scripture, what things are owing immediately to God, or to second causes; since every thing that was thought to be good, not only the powers & faculties of Mens minds, but voluntary actions themselves, are immediately ascrib'd to

* *John* 19. 11. † *Rom.* 13. 1. ‡ *Acts* 20. 28. § 1 *Cor.* 14. 15.
¶ *See* Tractat. Theol. Polit. pag. 14, &c.
✠ *Stapleton* of Controv. l. 4. c. 10.

to God  For inſtance, *Bezaleel* is ſaid to be * *fill'd with the Spirit of God in wiſdom, & underſtanding*, be-caufe he cou'd *deviſe cunning works of gold, & ſilver*, &c. And the Prophet *Iſaiah*, after he had defcrib'd the whole art of plowing & fowing, ſays of the plowman, † *His God does inſtruct him to diſcretion, & teach him.* -- And ſpeaking of the art of threſhing, he ſays, ‡ *This alſo comes from the Lord of Hoſts, which is wonderful in counfel, & excellent in working.* Can the Clergy have a better pretence to a *Jure-divino-ſhip*, than the Plow-man and Threſher? Where is it faid of them, that *their God inſtructs them to diſcretion, & teaches them?* Or, that *their art comes from the Lord of Hoſts, which is wonderful in counfel, & excellent in working?*

As fome things are immediately referr'd to God, fo others are as immediately referr'd to Satan; § nay, the fame action is imputed both to God and Satan. Thefe few, among numberlefs inſtances, I mention, to ſhew, that the Scripture ſuppoſes, that from our Reaſon we have ſuch infallible teſts, to judge what is the Will of God, that we are fafe from being miſled by any expreſſions of this nature.

*B.* Surely, the moral Precepts deliver'd by our Saviour, are not expreſs'd thus obſcurely.

*A.* These, no doubt, are the plaineſt, yet even thefe, generally ſpeaking, are not to be taken in their obvious & literal meaning: As for inſtance, ¶ *Lend, hoping for nothing again.* ✠ *He that takes away thy coat, let him have thy cloak alſo.* * *Of him, who takes thy goods, ask them not again.* And ſhou'd we not, without having recourfe to the Reaſon of things, be apt to think, that the Poor, as fuch, were the only favourites of Heaven: † *Bleſſed be ye poor, for 'yours is the Kingdom of God. Bleſſed are ye that hunger, for yo ſhall be filled.* And ſhou'd we not likewife be apt to ima-

*. *Exod.* 31. 3, 4.    † *Iſaiah* 28. 26.    ‡ *Ibid. ver.* 29.
§ 2 *Sam.* 24. 1 *Chron.* 21.    ¶ *Luke* 6. 35.
✠ *Mat.* 5. 40.    * *Luke* 6. 30.    † *Ib.* 6. 20, 21.

Imagine, that the Gospel was an enemy to the Rich as such; & consequently, to all those methods which make a Nation rich: As, * *Woe unto you rich, for you have receiv'd your consolation.* † *It is easier for a Camel to pass through the eye of a needle, than for a rich Man to enter into the Kingdom of God.* And that no Man might be rich, it was a general precept, ‡ *Sell what ye have, & give alms:* Nay, the *Woman that cast into the treasury her two mites* is commended, because she cast in § *all she had, even all her living.* And to shew that none were exempt from this precept, Jesus says to the Man, who ¶ *had observ'd all the precepts from his youth, One thing thou lackest, sell whatsoever thou hast, & give to the Poor.* This precept is impracticable in a Christian State, because there cou'd be no buyers where all were to be sellers; & so is a community of goods, tho' in use among the *Essenes,* & the Christians at first.

T I s certain, that such passages, as ✠ *Blessed are they that mourn;* * *Blessed are ye that weep;* † *Woe unto you that laugh now, ye shall mourn, & weep.* And other texts about ‡ *self-denial, and taking up the cross,* and *Take no thought for your life, what ye shall eat, or what ye shall drink.* § *Take no thought for the morrow,* ¶ *Consider the ravens, for they neither sow, nor reap.* — ✠ *Consider the lillies, how they grow, they toil not, they spin not, and yet, I say,* Solomon, *is all his glory, was not array'd like one of these.* 'Tis certain, I say, that such like texts have, by being interpreted literally, run Men into monstrous absurdities?

F R O M this text, * *Resist not evil, but whoever shall smite thee on thy right cheek, turn to him the other also,* and some others of the like nature, not only the pri-

mitive

---

mitive Fathers, but a confiderable Sect, even how among the *Proteſtants*, think all felf-defenſe unlawful.

FROM theſe ſayings of our Saviour, * *There are ſome Eunuchs, which were ſo born from their Mothers womb, and there are ſome Eunuchs, which were made Eunuchs of Men, & there be Eunuchs, which have made themſelves Eunuchs for the Kingdom of Heaven's-ſake*; the primitive Fathers, who thought they ought not to put a different meaning on the word *Eunuch* in the latter end of the verſe, from what it had twice before, believ'd it a piece of heroick virtue for Men to caſtrate themſelves: And tho' by the *Roman* Law no one cou'd be caſtrated without leave of the Preſident, as *Juſtin* obſerves; † yet he commends a Youth, who perform'd this operation on himſelf without it. And you know, that the Biſhop of *Alexandria* highly approv'd this action in *Origen*, as an inſtance of heroick virtue, tho' afterwards, when he became his capital Enemy, he as much condemn'd it. Do not theſe things ſufficiently ſhew, that we muſt not deviate one tittle from what our Reaſon dictates in any of theſe important points. Nay, even the Precept of ‡ *forgiving injuries, not only ſeven, but ſeventy times ſeven*, except interpreted conſiſtently with what the light of Nature dictates to be our duty, in preſerving our reputation, liberty, & property, & in doing all we can in our ſeveral ſtations, to hinder all injury & injuſtice from others, as well as ourſelves, wou'd be a Doctrine attended with fatal conſequences So that the expediency, or even lawfulneſs of forgiving injuries, depends on ſuch circumſtances as human diſcretion is to judge of.

As I am a member of the Common-wealth I can't be a Judge in my own cauſe, and tho' I may legally proſecute a Man who has injur'd me, yet if the injury be but ſlight, & by my over-looking it, he may become my Friend, common prudence will oblige me me to forgive him : But, if he, taking advantage of my good nature, injures me the more, & more frequently, becaufe he may do it with impunity; the Precept of *forgiving*, tho' it forbids me to punifh for punifhment-fake, does no more in this cafe bar me of a legal remedy, than it does Nations of refenting national injuries : And all good Governments oblige people, for the fake of the common good, to profecute thofe who have injur'd them by robbing, ftealing, or any other ways cheating, or defrauding them. So that 'tis the Reafon of things, which, in all circumftances, muft determine us how to act; & confequently, when this Precept is truly ftated, there is nothing new in it: But if it be not truly ftated, it is fuch a new doctrine, as may be attended with fatal confequences.

*Celfus*, fays, * that ,, the Doctrine of *forgiving in-* ,, *juries*, was not peculiar to the Chriftians, tho' they ,, taught it after a groffer manner.,, And *Confucius* thus expreffes this doctrine, † ,, Acknowledge thy ,, benefits by the return of benefits; but never revenge ,, injuries.

*B. Confucius*, tho' he forbids the revenging injuries, yet he did not carry things to that ftate of perfection, as to teach the *loving our Enemies*; but on the contrary maintains, ‡ ,, We may have an averfion for ,, an Enemy without defiring revenge, the motions ,, of Nature are not always criminal; § & 'tis only ,, the good Man, who can love, & hate with reafon.

*A.* ARE not the paffions of love & hatred given us by God, to be exercis'd on proper objects ? Actions, abftractedly confider'd, are not the objects of love and hate, but perfons for the fake of their actions; and are not the actions of fome Men too deteftable to create in us any fentiments, but of averfion; fo as to oblige us to bring them to condign punifhment ?

V 5                    Nay,

* *Origen contra Celfum. l. 7. p. 373.*
† *Max.* 23. in the tranflated Morals of *Confucius.*
‡ *Max.* 63.        § *Max.* 15.

Nay, muſt we not learn to hate ourſelves, before we can learn to love thoſe that hate us?

IF we ought not, nay cannot love the Devil, becauſe our Enemy, how can we love thoſe Devils incarnate, thoſe Enemies of God & Men, who hate, & perſecute Men for ſhewing their love to God, in following the dictates of Conſcience? If love carries with it complaiſance, eſteem, & friendſhip, & theſe are due to all Men, what diſtinction can we then make between the beſt, & worſt of Men? Tho' God, it's true, makes the *Sun to ſhine*, and the *rain to fall on the evil, & the good*; and, indeed, how cou'd it be otherwiſe in the preſent ſtate of things? yet, certainly, he does not love evil Men, tho' he bears with them for a time.

I am ſo far from thinking the Maxims of *Confucius*, and Jeſus Chriſt to differ; that I think the plain and ſimple Maxims of the former, will help to illuſtrate the more obſcure ones of the latter, accommodated to the then way of ſpeaking. Our Saviour's ſaying, * *Ye have heard that it hath been ſaid, Thou ſhalt love thy Neighbour, & hate thine Enemy*; Divines have, in vain, puzzl'd themſelves to find out that text in the Old Law; for cou'd they find it as they do other texts, that our Saviour in the ſame chapter, by this way of ſpeaking, refers to, it wou'd only ſhew, that the Divine precepts were not conſiſtent with one another. Indeed, St. *Paul* ſays, † *If thy Enemy hunger, feed him, if he thirſt, give him drink, for in ſo doing thou ſhalt heap coals of fire on his head:* ‡ But treating him thus, can't ſure be an argument of love; ſince 'tis in order to have divine vengeance fall on his head.

*B.* COMMENTATORS agree, that theſe Precepts of our Saviour are not to be taken in the plain, obvious, & grammatical meaning of the words, but are to be ſo explain'd, limited, and reſtrain'd, as beſt ſerve to promote human happineſs. *A.*

* *Mat.* 5. 43.  † *Rom.* 12. 20.
‡ *Pſalm* 18. 8. 13. 120. 4. 140. 10,

*A.* Suppose thofe Precepts are capable of being thus paraphras'd, yet how do we know this was the defign of the Preacher? The *Effenes* (a Sect our Saviour never found fault with) had, as is plain from *Philo* & *Jofephus*, rules much the fame, which they interpreted according to the plain & literal meaning, and the Chriftians, as I fhall fhew hereafter, for fome Centuries, underftood moft of thefe Precepts after the fame manner, believing that the nature of moral rules requir'd they fhould be thus interpreted, efpecially fuch as are defign'd to govern the actions of the moft ignorant and illiterate, and taught too by a perfon, whofe infinite knowledge muft enable him fo to exprefs himfelf, as that his words fhould not be liable to the leaft mifconftruction.

*B* However, Chriftians at firft depending on the grammatical, & obvious meaning of the words, might miftake, yet Reafon taught them afterwards how they were to be interpreted.

*A.* Reafon, then, muft be our Guide, and we muft know our duty from the Light of Nature, antecedently to thofe Precepts, otherwife we cou'd never know it was our duty to put fuch fenfes on words, as they otherwife feem not to bear. Befides,

Should not Rules concerning Morality, be fuited to Mens particular circumftances, plainly defcribing that conduct which they require? Is not this the defign of the Municipal Laws in every Country? What Benefit cou'd Subjects have from Laws written in fuch a loofe, general, and undetermin'd manner; as *Lend, hoping for nothing again*, *If any Man will fue thee at Law, & take away thy coat, let him have thy cloak alfo: Of him who takes away thy goods, ask them not again*; or thofe other texts, which feem to condemn the Rich as fuch, & require, not the fetting the poor at work, but the *felling all, & giving to the Poor*, or thofe other Precepts, which feem to forbid *felf-defence*, or require us to *take no thought for our life*,

or

or for *the morrow?* And that too by arguments drawn from *Lillies, neither toiling, nor spinning?* The same may be said of all general, & undetermin'd Rules in the New Testament, tho' more plainly deliver'd: As for instance, tho' 'tis said, * *Servants, obey your Masters in all things;* & † *please them well in all things;* yet is the measure of obedience due from Servants to Masters any otherwise to be learnt, than from the agreement of the parties, or the custom of the Country? 'Tis said, *We are to render to* Cæsar, *the things that are* Cæsar's; but must we not learn from the Laws in every Nation, who is *Cæsar?* And what is his due? Otherwise we shou'd act like those wicked Priests, who, not long since, from general words of *obedience,* wou'd have destroy'd our happy Constitution, and treacherously invested the Prince with an absolute power. We are to *render all Men their dues;* but what those dues are, we are to learn *from* the Reason of things, & the Laws of the Country.

I N a word, 'tis the tendency of actions, which makes them either good or bad; they that tend to promote human happiness are always good, & those that have a contrary tendency are always bad. And 'tis the circumstances Men are under, by which we are to judge of the tendency of actions. As for instance, the killing a Man, consider'd without its circumstances, is an action, neithe. good or bad; but by the Magistrate, when the publick good requires it, or by a private Man, when necessary for self-defence, is an Action always good: But done when the publick good does not require it, when there is no such danger, & with malice prepense, 'tis always evil. Taking up arms against a person entrusted with the protection of the Common-Wealth, can't be determin d to be good, or bad, without considering circumstances; if he has not abus'd his trust, it will be Rebellion, the highest of crimes, but if he has betray'd that trust, & oppress'd the

* *Col.* 3. 22.   † *Titus* 2. 9.

the Community, then a juft and neceffary defence. Injoying a Woman, or lufting after her, can't be faid, without confidering the circumftances, to be either good, or evil; that warm defire, which is implanted in human-nature, can't be criminal, when perfu'd after fuch a manner, as tends moft to promote the happinefs of the parties, & to propagate & preferve the fpecies. What we call *Inceft*, is now for many good reafons not to be allow'd of, yet it was a duty in the Children of *Adam* & *Eve*: And if the neareft of kin were now thrown on a defert Ifland, I fee no reafon, but that they might act as the firft-born pair did.

Tho' there were ever fo many texts in the New as well as Old Teftament againft ufury, & thofe too back'd by the unanimous authority of all the Fathers, yet the forbidding it, efpecially in trading Nations, wou'd now be immoral, fince without it induftry wou'd in a great meafure be difcourag'd, arts unimprov'd, and trade & commerce, confifting chiefly in credit, deftroy'd: Befides, what reafon can be affign'd, why a Man fhou'd any more lend his money, than lett his lands for nothing. And even that common rule of doing as we would be done unto, fuppofes an action fit to be done, or at leaft, without any ill tendency. Nay, to go a little further, was not the Command of *abftaining from blood*, given after the Deluge to the then whole race of Mankind, & often repeated in the Law? And in the New Teftament, is not this fame Precept enjoin'd the *Gentile* Converts, by the unanimous Decree of the Apoftles, & by the Holy Ghoft too, as neceffary; nay, equally fo with the abftaining from fornication; and thought by all Chriftians, for many Ages, to be of perpetual obligation? yet who is now fo ridiculous, as out of Religion to abftain from black-puddings? Who now, to give another inftance, thinks it a duty to wafh his neighbour's feet; tho' a thing, not only commanded by a dying Saviour, after the moft folemn manner,

&

& under no leſs penalty than *having no part in him*;
but enforc'd, & inculcated by his own example. Our
Saviour commands Men· \* *not to ſwear at all*; and
St. *James* impreſſes the ſame precepts, by ſaying, †
*Above all things, ſwear not*; and by the manner of its
being introduc'd by our Saviour, it ſeems chiefly to
relate to oaths taken on ſolemn occaſions ; ‡ *It is
ſaid of old, thou ſhalt not forſwear thyſelf, but ſhall perform unto the Lord thine oaths: But I ſay unto you,
ſwear not at all.* — And yet, who now, beſides *Quakers*,
refuſe to ſwear at all? By theſe, you ſee, tho' ſeveral
other inſtances might be produc'd, how Chriſtians have,
in the main, taken the tendency of actions to be the
rule, to judge of their lawfulneſs or unlawfulneſs,
goodneſs or badneſs: And in thoſe few things Superſtition has made them judge otherwiſe, has it not always been to their Prejudice?

*B.* Is there no exception to this Rule? Muſt not
Men, at all times, make their words & thoughts agree;
and never ſpeak, but juſt as they think?

*A.* THE Rule I have laid down holds even here;
for tho' ſpeech was given Men to communicate their
thoughts, and 'tis generally for their common good,
that Men ſhou'd ſpeak as they think; yet this common
good preſcribes certain reſtrictions. Deceiving an
Enemy in a juſt War, either by words or actions, if
it tends to bring about the end of War, Peace, is certainly a duty: And the ſame reaſon obliges people not
to keep thoſe promiſes, tho' ſworn to, which they
have been forc'd to make to Robbers and Thieves:
And ſome go ſo far, as to think, that thoſe who wou'd
force others to declare their opinions to their own
prejudice, in ſuch matters where the Government has
no concern, have no more right to truth than Robbers,
& other publick Enemies.

FRIENDSHIP will ſometimes oblige Men to deceive people, when it manifeſtly tends to their good,

&

* *Mat.* 5. 34. † *James* 5. 12. ‡ *Mat.* 5. 33, 34.

& none are prejudic'd by it; and all practife it with relation to Children, fick people, & Men in paffion. Muft he not be an ill Man, indeed, who would not fave an innocent perfon, by telling his purfuer a falfehood? This is a duty he owes to both, the perfuer & perfu'd. And if Men, (as none fcruple it) may bid their Servants fay, *They are not at home*; & do feveral other things of this nature, why may they not, when filence will be interpreted to their prejudice, deceive impertinent people, in fuch matters where they have no concern? Thus, you fee, there are certain exceptions to this Rule, which, as well as the Rule itfelf, are built on the good of Mankind; and yet thefe exceptions will by no means juftify mental refervations, or equivocations.

The Children of *Ifrael*, in the time of the *Judges*, were certainly none of the beft *Cafuifts*; who, when in a quarrel, (the oddeft that ever was) having \* *fworn before the Lord at* Mifpath, *not to give any of their Daughters to Wife to* Benjamin; *and*, in purfuance of this quarrel, *deftroy'd them with their Wives & Children*, except 600, who efcap'd by *flying to a cave*; and then reflecting that a whole Tribe would be loft, if they did not give them Wives; and their oaths, accompany'd with a curfe, violated, if they did; found out thefe two expedients: The Men of *Jabefh Gilead*, not concerning themfelves in this quarrel, † *nor coming to the general Affembly, they deftroy'd with their Wives & Children, except* 400 *Virgins*; ‡ *whom they gave for Wives to* thefe Benjamites; but thefe not being a fufficient number, they advis'd, nay, § *commanded them, to feize on fome of their Daughters as they were dancing*, & to *carry them off*: Thus thefe merciful, & religious People preferv'd their Oaths, and their Brother *Benjamin*.

B.

\* *Judges* 21. 1.    † *Ibid. ver.* 8.
‡ *Ibid. ver.* 12.    § *Ibid. ver.* 20, 21.

*B.* The *Hebrew* Midwives, no doubt, acted according to your Rule in deceiving *Pharoah*, by not destroying the *Hebrew* male-children; because they said, * *They feared God, & God dealt well with them, & made them houses;* but there's another precedent in the same history, which seems very surprising: The Lord, tho' he told *Moses*, † and the Elders of *Israel*, his real design of *bringing his People out of* Egypt *into the Land* of the *Canaanites*, ‡ yet bids them say to the King of *Egypt*, § *Let us go three days journey into the Wilderness, that we may sacrifice to the Lord our God; left he fall upon us with Pestilence, or with the Sword:* ¶ *We can't sacrifice in the Land, for we shall sacrifice the abomination of the* Egyptians; ✠ *Our Cattle must go with us, for thereof we must serve the Lord.* And at last, when *Pharoah*, whose heart God had frequently harden'd, comply'd with their request, he bids them go * *serve the Lord, as ye have said;* and upon this occasion, they borrow'd of the *Egyptians*, as the Lord order'd them, † *Jewels of Gold & Silver, & raiment,* even to the *spoiling of them*; and when *Pharaoh* (who all along seem'd jealous of their design, & bids them ‡ *not go far away*) found that this solemn Sacrifice was a meer pretence, & that they really fled with all they had borrow'd of his people, he persu'd the fugitives, the consequence was, that the *Egyptians,* instead of obtaining restitution, were miraculously destroy'd, & *Pharaoh* lost his life as well as his Subjects, & those who had dealt thus treacherously with them, were as miraculously preserv'd.

*A.* As to this point, I can only advise you to consult our learned Commentators, who will satisfy you in this matter, as well as why the § *Terror of the Lord* hinder'd justice to be done upon the two Sons of *Jacob*, for the vilest piece of cruelty and treachery, they

---

* *Exod.* 1. 17. 20, 21.   † *Ibid.* 3. 8.   ‡ *Ib. ver.* 18.
§ *Exod.* 5. 3.   ¶ *Ib:* 8. 26.   ✠ *Ib.* 10. 26.   * *Ib.* 12. 31
† *Exod.* 12. 35, 36.   ‡ *Ib.* 8. 28.   § *Gen.* 35. 5.

they committed on the *Shechemites*. But not to meddle with things foreign to our purpose,

I will venture to say, that this Rule of acting according as the circumstances we are under, point out to us, to be for the general good, is a Rule without exception; whereas all other general Rules are of little use, when apply'd to particular cases; because of the many exceptions to them, founded on other Rules, equally general: And further, that this universal, & unexceptionable Rule is highly necessary, in explaining all the Precepts of our Saviour; especially those relating to *loving of Enemies*, & *forgiving Injuries*. And the rather, because

THE Ecclesiasticks, tho' they cry up the Precepts of Mens *loving their* own *Enemies*, yet they effectually evade this, and all other moral Precepts, by telling them 'tis their duty to *hate God's Enemies*; (and those to be sure, are God's Enemies, who refuse blindly to submit to their dictates, especially in matters relating to their power and profit:) And have also found out many ways of making the Precept of forgiving injuries useless, more particularly by telling Men, that 'tis for the correction of manners, for the good of their own, as well as their neighbours souls, that the *Spiritual Courts* are erected, where People, for such hasty & angry words, as no action (there being no real damage) will lye for at *Common Law*, are to be censur'd: And thus numbers of ordinary people are, on this pretence, to the great benefit of those Courts, frequently undone; and spiteful persons gratify their malice, without any satisfaction, but that of ruining their Neighbours, & very often themselves.

I might shew you, in support of my never-failing Rule of judging of actions by their tendency, that we are carefully to distinguish between the actions of Jesus himself; since in some (these being no otherwise to be accounted for) he, as Divines themselves own, acted by virtue of his prophetical office; these,

X  con-

confequently, can be no precedent for us; but of this hereafter.

B. You have already, I muft own, taken a great deal of pains, to fhew, that God, in creating Mankind, had no other defign than their happinefs, and that all the Rules he gave them (it being repugnant to his nature to have any arbitrary commands) cou'd have no other tendency; and that by making them moral Agents, he made them capable of knowing wherein their happinefs confifts, or in other words, of difco-vering whatever the relations they ftand in to God, and their fellow - creatures make fit to be obferv'd. And from thence you conclude, Mens happinefs, at one time as well as another, confifting in the fame things, that the Gofpel (which can make no altera-tion in the relations Men ftand in to God, and one another, or the duties that flow from thence,) cou'd only be a Republication, or Reftoration of that Reli-gion, which is founded on the eternal Reafon of things: which, you fuppofe, is what we are ftill go-vern'd by; fince we are oblig'd to recede from the *Letter*, tho' the words are ever fo plain, if that recedes from the Reafon of things, as all own the *Letter* does, in innumerable places relating to God himfelf; by imputing human parts, human infirmities, & human paffions, even of the worft kind, to him; & making thofe the caufe of many of his actions: And that as in the Old Teftament there are feveral things, either commanded, or approv'd, which wou'd be criminal in us to obferve, becaufe we can't reconcile our doing them with the Reafon of things, fo in the New Tefta-ment, its Precepts are for the moft part deliver'd either fo hyperbolically, that they wou'd lead Men aftray, were they govern'd by the ufual meaning of words; or elfe exprefs'd in fo loofe, general, & un-determin'd a manner, that Men are as much left to be govern'd by the Reafon of things, as if there were no fuch Precepts: And the Scripture not diftinguifhing

be-

between thofe Precepts which are occafional, & thofe which are not, we have no way to diftinguifh them, but from the Nature of things; which will point out to us thofe Rules, which eternally oblige, whether deliver'd in Scripture, or not. Thefe fentiments you fo ftrongly inforce, that I fhou'd find it difficult not to yield, had I not fo able a Combatant as Dr. *S. Clark*, for my Second; who, in his excellent *Difcourfe of the unalterable obligation of Natural Religion, & the truth, and Certainty of the Chriftian Revelation*, not only fhews, that they are diftinct Religions, but the infinite advantage the latter has above the former: And tho' this good, as well as great Man is dead, whereby the Church has fuftain'd an irreparable lofs, yet he will for ever live in this immortal Work.

# C H A P.  XIV.

*Dr.* C L A R K'*s Difcourfe of* The unchangeable Obligation of Natural Religion, and the Truth, & Certainty of the Chriftian Revelation, *confider'd; and from thence is shewn, how inconfiftent foever with the defign of that Difcourfe, that nothing can be a part of Religion, but what is founded on the Nature, and Reafon of Things.*

*A.* I Own, the Dr. got immortal honour by that Difcourfe; how 'tis admir'd, the feventh Edition fhews: And we may well imagine, an Author, who ufually exhaufts the fubject he writes on, has here omitted nothing that makes for his purpofe. And, therefore, fince 'tis your pleafure, I will fully confider this Difcourfe, & begin with the Character he gives of the *Law of Nature* ; and fee whether he does not re-

prefent

present it so absolutely perfect, as to take in every thing that God requires of Mankind: And then examine what he says in behalf of Revelation, in contradistinction to the Religion of Nature.

The Dr. not only maintains, that * ,, the Law ,, of Nature is eternal, universal, and absolutely un- ,, changeable; ,, but has two Sections to prove, ,, † that the *Will of God* always determines itself to act ,, according to the eternal *Reason of Things*, ‡ & that ,, all *rational Creatures* are oblig'd to govern them- ,, selves in all their actions by the same eternal *Rule* ,, of Reason; ,, which supposes, that all rational Creatures are not only capable of knowing this eternal Rule of Reason, but likewise of knowing there can be no other Rule, for the actions both of God & Man. In his previous Discourse of the *Being of a God*, he affirms, that § ,, They, who are not govern'd by this ,, Law, are for setting up their own unreasonable self- ,, will, in opposition to the Nature, and Reason of ,, things. — acting contrary to their own Reason & ,, knowledge, attempting to destroy that order, by ,, which the Universe subsists; and by consequence, ,, offering the highest affront imaginable to the Crea- ,, tor of all things, who himself governs all his actions ,, by these Rules, & cannot but require the same of ,, all his reasonable Creatures. ,, And in this Discourse he says, ¶ ,, The All-powerful Creator, & Governour ,, of the Universe, who has the absolute, & uncon- ,, troulable dominion of all things in his own hands, ,, and is accountable to none for what he does, yet ,, thinks it no diminution of his power, to make this ,, *Reason of things* the unalterable Rule, & Law of all ,, his own actions in the government of the world, ,, and does nothing by mere will and arbitrariness. ,, And indeed, if God does nothing by mere will and arbitrariness, tis impossible there can be any other Rule
but

* *Edit.* 4. *pag.* 82.    † *Pag.* 47.    ‡ *Pag.* 48.
§ *Pag.* 131.    ¶ *Pag.* 49.

but the Reason of things. And accordingly he says, „ * The eternal & unchangeable Nature, & Reason „ of the Things themselves are the Law of God, „ not only to his Creatures, but also to himself, as „ being the Rule of his own actions in the govern- „ ment of the world. „ † „ And, as a learned Prelate „ of our own has excellently shewn, not barely his „ infinite Power, but the Rules of this eternal Law, „ are the true foundation, and the measure of his „ dominion over his Creatures. Now, for the same „ reason, that *God*, who hath no *Superior* to determine „ him, yet constantly directs all his own actions by „ the eternal Rule of Justice and Goodness; 'tis evi- „ dent all *intelligent Creatures* in their several spheres „ and proportions, *ought* to obey the same Rule ac- „ cording to the Law of their nature. „ Which is supposing it wou'd be Tyranny in God to have any arbitrary Commands, or give Man any other Rules, but the Rules of this eternal Law, the *true foundation*, & *measure of his dominion over his Creatures*. And again, „ ‡ God, who is infinitely self-sufficient to his own „ happiness, cou'd have no motive to create things „ at all, but only that he might communicate to them „ his goodness & happiness. „ If so, they, who do all the good they can to themselves, & Fellow-crea- tures, answer the end of their creation. § „ And, „ *he says*, that in matters of natural Reason & Mo- „ rality, that which is holy & good is not therefore „ holy & good, because it is commanded to be done, „ but it is therefore commanded by God, because it „ is holy & good:„ Which supposes that all God's Commands, if they are all holy and good (between which, I think, the distinction is only verbal,) are founded on the Nature, and Reason of things. And accordingly he says, ¶ „ that God has made (his in- „ telligent Creatures) so far like himself, as to endue

X 3 them

* *Pag.* 113.    † *Pag.* 87, 88.    ‡ *Pag.* 121.
§ *Pag.* 86, 87.    ¶ *Pag.* 48.

,, them with thofe excellent faculties of Reafon and
,, Will, whereby they are enabl'd to diftinguifh Good
,, from Evil, & to choofe the one, & refufe the other.
Which fuppofes thofe are the only things which God
commands, or forbids, otherwife thefe excellent faculties wou'd only enable them to know but part of
the Will of God, tho' God can will nothing but what
is for their good, that being the fole end of his
creating them.

AND he fuppofes, that ,, this Law of Nature is
,, not founded in the pofitive Will of God, but arifes
,, from the different relations & refpects which things
,, have to one another, which makes fome things fit,
,, and others unfit to be done.,, And fays, that *
,, the Law of Nature has its *full* obligatory power,
,, antecedent to all confiderations of any particular
,, *private*, & *perfonal reward* or *punifhment*, annex'd
,, either by natural confequence, or by pofitive ap-
,, pointment, to the obfervance, or neglect of it.
,, This alfo is very evident: Becaufe if Good & Evil,
,, Right & Wrong, fitnefs & unfitnefs of being prac-
,, tifed, be (as has been fhown) originally, eternally,
,, and neceffarily, in the nature of the things them-
,, felves; 'tis plain, that the view of *particular rewards*
,, or *punifhments*, which is only an after-confideration,
,, & does not at all alter the nature of things, cannot
,, be the original caufe of the obligation of the Law,
,, but is only an additional weight to enforce the
,, practice of what Men were before oblig'd to by
,, right Reafon.,, And to prove this he fays, that
,, † the judgment & confcience of a Man's own mind,
,, concerning the reafonablenefs, & fitnefs of the thing,
,, that his actions fhould be conformed to fuch, or
,, fuch a Rule, or Law, is the trueft, or formalleft
,, *obligation*, even more properly, & ftrictly fo, than
,, any opinion whatfoever of the authority of the
,, giver of a Law, or any regard he may have to its
fanc-

* *Pag.* 89. † *Pag.* 53.

„ sanctions by rewards & punishments. For whoever
„ acts contrary to this sense, & conscience of his own
„ mind, is necessarily self-condemned; & the greatest,
„ & strongest of all obligations is that, which a Man
„ cannot break through without condemning him-
„ self. „ And,

He likewise affirms, that * „ these eternal moral
„ obligations, as they are really in perpetual force,
„ merely from their own nature, and the abstract
„ Reason of things; so also they are moreover the
„ express & unalterable Will, and Command of God
„ to his Creatures, which he cannot but expect should,
„ in obedience to his supreme Authority, as well as
„ in compliance with the natural Reason of things,
„ be regularly, & constantly observ'd thro' the whole
„ Creation., Which not only supposes, that the
Reason of things, & the divine Commands are inseparable; but that 'tis the reason, or the fitness of the
thing, that makes it a divine Law; and consequently,
that they who never heard of any external Revelation,
yet if they know from the nature of things what's fit
for them to do, they know all that God will, or can
require of them; since his Commands are to be mea-
sur'd by the antecedent fitness of Things; & Things
can only be said to be fit, or unfit, as they are for
or against the common good. And if the Creator will
do every thing, the relation he stands in to his Creatures makes it fit for him to do; and expects nothing
from them, but what the relation they stand in to
him, and one another, makes likewise fit for them to
do, how can they be ignorant of their duty? Especially, if, as the Dr. demonstrates, † „ All the same
„ reasons & arguments, which discover to Men the
„ natural fitnesses, or unfitnesses of things, and the
„ necessary perfections, or attributes of God, prove
„ equally at the same time, that that, which is truly

X 4 the

,, the Law of Nature, or the Reason of things, is in
,, like manner the Will of God.,,  And,

He juſtly obſerves, that tho' * ,, This method of
,, deducing the Will of God from his Attributes, is
,, of all others the beſt and cleareſt, the certaineſt &
,, moſt univerſal, that the Light of Nature affords,
,, yet there are other collateral conſiderations, which
,, prove, & confirm the ſame.,,  And that

,, † The ſame may be prov'd from the tendency,
,, & practice of Morality, to the good and happineſs
,, of the whole World:,, Which, indeed, wou'd be
no proof, were any thing commanded that had no
ſuch tendency; for ſuch things, according to the penalties they were to be enforc'd by, wou'd be more,
or leſs to the hurt of Mankind.

To ſhew the natural connexion there is between
all the parts of Religion, he ſays, ‡ ,, Who believes
,, the Being, and natural Attributes of God, muſt of
,, neceſſity confeſs his moral Attributes alſo.  Next,
,, he who owns, and has juſt notions of the moral
,, Attributes of God, cannot avoid acknowledging the
,, obligations of Morality, & Natural Religion. In like
,, manner, he who owns the obligations of Morality
,, and Natural Religion, muſt needs to ſupport thoſe
,, obligations, and make them effectual in practice,
,, believe *a future ſtate of rewards and puniſhments.*
And he affirms, that § ,, the certainty of a future
,, ſtate of rewards & puniſhments, is in general de-
,, ducible, even demonſtrably, by a chain of clear,
,, & undeniable reaſoning;,, nay, he ſays, ¶ ,, 'tis a
,, propoſition in a manner ſelf-evident.,, And ſpeaking
of ſome arguments he had before mention'd, he ſays,
,, ✠ theſe are very good, and ſtrong arguments for
,, the great probability of a future ſtate; but that
,, drawn from the conſideration of the moral Attributes

* *Pag.* 119.    † *Pag.* 121.    ‡ *Pag.* 34.
§ *Pag.* 8.    ¶ *Pag.* 125.    ✠ *Pag.* 154.

,, butes of God, feems to amount even to a Demon-
,, ftration : Nay, to a compleat Demonftration. *

IN fhort, the Dr's *Hypothefis* is, That upon God's
framing Mankind after the manner he has done,
there are certain things refulting from thence, which
naturally, & neceffarily conduce to their good or hurt;
and that the way to know the Will of God, is to
know what thofe things are, in order to do the one,
and to avoid the other. For which reafon God gave
Mankind underftanding, which (without blafpheming
the infinite Wifdom and Goodnefs of God) muft be
allow'd to be fufficient to anfwer the end for which
it was given. And that a Being, infinitely wife & good,
as well as wholly difinterefted, can require nothing of
Men, but what they, for the fake of their own intereft, tho' there were no pofitive divine Commands,
were oblig'd to do; and confequently, that whoever
acts for his own good, in fubferviency to that of the
Publick, anfwers the end of his creation. As this
fcheme of things, to do the Doctor juftice, gives us
the higheft idea of the goodnefs, wifdom, & perfection of the divine Being; fo to compleat his moral
character, the Dr. reprefents the Laws of God, by
which Mankind are to govern all their actions, as moft
plain & obvious, & even imprefs'd on human nature.
And therefore fays,

,, † THAT all rational Creatures are oblig'd to govern
,, themfelves, in all their actions, by the eternal Rea-
,, fon of things, is evident from the fenfe, all, even
,, wicked Men, ‡ unavoidably have of their being
,, under fuch an obligation; § & from the judgment
,, of Mens Confciences on their own actions. ,,
And that ¶ ,, the moft profligate of all Mankind,
,, however induftrioufly they endeavour to conceal,
,, & deny their felf-condemnation, yet cannot avoid
,, making a difcovery of it fometimes when they are

X 5                    not

* *Pag.* 140, 141.      † *Pag.* 48.
‡ *Contents pag.* 52.   § *Ib. pag.* 54.   ¶ *Pag.* 57.

,, not aware of it.,,　And that every Man, * ,, by
,, the reason of his mind, cannot but be compell'd to
,, own, & acknowledge, that there is really such an
,, obligation indispensably incumbent upon him. ,,
And † ,, They who *do* evil, yet *see*, & *approve* what
,, is good, and condemn in *others* what they blindly
,, allow in *themselves*; nay, very frequently condemn
,, even themselves also, not without great disorder,
,, & uneasiness of mind in those very things wherein
,, they allow themselves.,,　And herein, give me leave
to say, consists the excellency of the Law of Nature,
that tho' a Man is so brutish as not to observe it himself, yet he wou'd have all others religiously observe it;
and no Rule can be calculated for the general good,
but what is so fram'd; and if Men wou'd make this a
test of the Will of God, how happy wou'd they be?

　T H E Dr. more fully to prove his point, says, That
,, ‡ the mind of Man naturally, & necessarily assents
,, to the eternal Law of Righteousness, may still bet-
,, ter, and more clearly, & more universally appear,
,, from the judgment that Men pass on each *others*
,, actions, than what we can discern concerning their
,, consciousness of their own.,,　And there he shews,
That § ,, the unprejudic'd Mind of Man as naturally
,, disapproves injustice in morall matters, as in na-
,, tural things it cannot but dissent from falsehood,
,, or dislike incongruities.,,　And again,

　,, ¶ T H E case is truly thus, that the eternal dif-
,, ferences of Good & Evil, the unalterable Rule of
,, Right & Equity, do necessarily, & unavoidably de-
,, termine the judgment, and force the assent of all
,, that use any consideration, is undeniably manifest
,, from the universal experience of Mankind. ✠ For
,, no Man *willingly*, and *deliberately* transgresses this
,, Rule in any *great*, & *considerable* instance, but he
,, acts contrary to the Judgment, & Reason of his own
mind,

*Pag.* 53.　†*Pag.* 60.　‡*Pag.* 58.
§*Pag.* 61.　¶*Pag.* 54.　✠*Pag.* 55.

,, mind, & secretly reproaches himself for so doing:
,, And no Man observes, & obeys it steadily, espe-
,, cially in cases of *difficulty* and *temptation*, when it
,, interferes with any present interest, pleasure, or paf-
,, fion; but his own mind commends, and applauds
,, him for his resolution, in executing what his Con-
,, science cou'd not forbear giving his affent to, as
,, just, & right. And this is what St. *Paul* means,
,, when he says, (*Rom.* 2. 14, 15.) that *When the* Gen-
,, tiles, *which have not the Law, do by Nature the things*
,, *contained in the Law.*,, And in another place he
fays, * ,, No Man does good, brave, and generous
,, actions, but the Reason of his own Mind applauds
,, him for his so doing; and no Man, at any time,
,, does things base, vile, dishonourable, and wicked;
,, but at the same time he condemns himself.,, And
he says, that † ,, the eternal Rule of Right ought as
,, indispensably to govern Mens actions, as it cannot
,, but necessarily determine their assent.

O n e wou'd be apt to think, that the Dr. believ'd
that Man without reflection, cou'd not but know the
Law of Nature, & be in love with it; since he says,
,, ‡ That in reading Histories of far & distant Coun-
,, tries, where 'tis manifest we can have no concern
,, for the event of things, nor prejudices concerning
,, the characters of persons; who is there that does
,, not praise, & admire, nay, highly esteem, and in
,, his imagination love, as it were, the equity, truth,
,, justice, & fidelity of some persons; and with the
,, greatest indignation & hatred, detest the barbarity,
,, & injustice of others? Nay, further, when the pre-
,, judices of corrupt minds lye all on the side of in-
,, justice, as when we have obtain'd some very great
,, profit, or advantage, thro' another Man's treachery,
,, or breach of faith; yet who is there, that upon that
,, very occasion, does not (even to a proverb) dislike
,, the *Person,* & the *Action,* how much soever he may
,, rejoice at the event. **These**

THESE reasons shew the infinite goodness of God, by not only thus deeply impressing that Law on human nature, by which God expects all Men shou'd govern all their actions; but in making the very observing this Law, to carry with it, distinct from the good it produces, the highest satisfaction, & rational enjoyment; and the contrary, that sorrow, remorse, & self-condemnation, which are the unavoidable consequence of acting against it: And of this the Philosophers of old, and I believe, all since, who do not adulterate Religion with things that are not moral (and consequently, carry no satisfaction with them) must be sensible. But as it wou'd be endless, to mention all the Dr. says of the irresistable evidence, as well as the absolute perfection of the eternal, & immutable Law of Nature, I shall recite but one passage more, which he supports by the Authority of Bishop *Cumberland*. ,, This, *says he*, * is that Law of Nature,
,, to which the Reason of all Men, every where, as
,, naturally, & necessarily assents, as all Animals con-
,, spire in the pulse, and motion of their heart & ar-
,, teries; or as all Men agree in their judgment con-
,, cerning the whiteness of snow, or the brightness of
,, the Sun.

B. THIS, indeed, is so full & home, that no ancient, or modern Deist cou'd have said more in praise of the unlimited Wisdom, and universal Goodness of God; than in supposing the common Parent of Mankind, has given all his Children, even those of the lowest capacities, and at all times, sufficient means, of discovering whatever makes for their present, and future happiness; and that no Man can plead ignorance of a Law as evident as that the Sun is bright, or snow white; and as inseparable from rational nature, as the pulse of the heart and arteries are from animal nature.

4.

* Pag. 83.

*A.* If this be talking like a Deift, all who write on this fubject talk thus; fince they all maintain, that „ there muft be a Law of eternal rectitude flowing „ from the Nature of things, otherwife there could „ be no actions good, or lovely in themfelves : no „ real diftinction between Virtue & Vice; Good or „ Evil; and that God can't difpenfe with his Crea- „ tures, or with himfelf, for not obferving it; other- „ wife an arbitrary will, which might change every „ moment, would govern every thing; „ and that „ this Law of eternal rectitude is implanted in Man „ at his very creation; & that no Man can act con- „ trary to it, but does violence to himfelf, and fins „ againft his very make, & conftitution. „ And can it be otherwife, when the only innate Principle in Man is the defire of his own happinefs; and the Goodnefs of God requires no more than a right cul- tivating of this Principle; in preferring a general, or publick, to a particular, or private good: And where there are two Evils, and both can't be avoided, to choofe the lefs *fub ratione boni.*

THE latter part of the Dr's Difcourfe is chiefly le- vell'd againft thofe he calls the *True Deifts,* and that you may know what fort of Men they are he com- bats, he gives you their Creed.

„ THESE Deifts, *fays he,* * did they believe what „ they pretend, have juft, and right notions of God, „ and of all the divine Attributes in every refpect, „ who declare they believe there is one eternal, in- „ finite, intelligent, all powerful, and wife Being; „ the Creator, Preferver, & Governor of all things; „ *That* this fupreme Caufe is a Being of infinite Ju- „ ftice, Goodnefs and Truth, and all other moral as „ well as natural perfections; *That* he made the World „ for the manifeftation of his Power and Wifdom, „ and to communicate his Goodnefs & Happinefs to „ his Creatures; *That* he preferves it by his continual all-

* *Pag.* 27.

„ all-wise Providence, & governs it according to the
„ eternal Rules of infinite Justice, Equity, Goodness,
„ Mercy & Truth; *That* all created, rational Beings,
„ depending continually upon him, are bound to
„ adore, worship, & obey him; To praise him for
„ all things they enjoy, & to pray to him for every
„ thing they want; *That* they are all obliged to pro-
„ mote in their proportion, and according to the
„ extent of their several powers & abilities, the gene-
„ ral Good and welfare of those parts of the World
„ wherein they are plac'd: In like manner, as the
„ divine Goodness is continually promoting the uni-
„ versal benefit of the Whole; *That* Men, in parti-
„ cular, are every where oblig'd to make it their
„ business, by an universal benevolence to promote
„ the happiness of all others: *That* in order to this,
„ every Man is bound always to behave himself so
„ towards others, as in reason he would desire they
„ should in the like circumstances deal with him;
„ Wherefore, he is oblig'd to obey, and submit to
„ his Superiors in all just, and right things, for the
„ preservation of society, and the peace & benefit of
„ the Publick; To be just & honest, equitable and
„ sincere in all his dealings with his equals, for the
„ keeping inviolable the everlasting Rule of Righ-
„ teousness, and maintaining an universal trust and
„ confidence, friendship and affection amongst Men;
„ and towards his inferiors to be gentle and kind,
„ easy, and affable, charitable and willing to assist as
„ many as stand in need of his help, for the preser-
„ vation of universal love and benevolence amongst
„ Mankind, & in imitation of the Goodness of God,
„ who preserves, and does good to all his Creatures,
„ which depend entirely upon him for their very
„ Being, and all that they enjoy. *That* in respect of
„ himself, every Man is bound to preserve, as much
„ as in him lies, his own Being, and the right use
„ of all his faculties, so long as it shall please God,
who

„ who appointed him his ſtation in this world, to
„ continue him therein : *That* therefore, he is bound
„ to have an exact government of his paſſions, and
„ careſully to abſtain from all debaucheries & abuſes
„ of himſelf, which tend either to the deſtruction of
„ his own Being, or to the diſorders of his faculties,
„ and diſabling him from performing his duty, or
„ hurrying him into the practice of unreaſonable, &
„ unjuſt things. Laſtly, *That* according as Men regard,
„ or neglect theſe obligations, ſo they are propor-
„ tionably acceptable, or diſpleaſing unto God ; who
„ being ſupreme Governor of the World, cannot but
„ teſtify his favour, or diſpleaſure, at ſome time,
„ or other ; and conſequently, ſince this is not done
„ in the preſent ſtate, therefore there muſt be a fu-
„ ture ſtate of rewards and puniſhments in a life to
„ come.

The Deiſts, no doubt, will own, that the Dr. has
done them juſtice ; ſince all their Principles, as he repreſents them, have a direct tendency to make them
good Men ; and contain nothing to divert them from
intirely attending to all the duties of Morality, in
which the whole of their Religion conſiſts ; & which
leaves them no room for thoſe endleſs quarrels and
fatal diviſions, which zeal for other things, has occaſion'd among their fellow-creatures ; and whom they
pity upon the account of that inſupportable bondage,
which ſuperſtition has, in moſt places, laid them under.
And muſt not a Religion, which the Dr. has prov'd
to be demonſtrably founded on the eternal Reaſon of
things, have a more powerful influence on rational
Beings, than if it was laid on any other bottom.
How can a Religion, which, as the Dr. deſcribes it,
carries in all its parts, ſuch evident marks of Wiſdom
and Goodneſs, fail to make Men in love with their
duty ; when they muſt plainly ſee, that, and their intereſt to be inſeparable ? If Princes requir'd no more
of their Subjects, & private Men of their Neighbours,

than to be govern'd by these Principles, how happy wou'd the World be, thus govern'd?

I do not perceive the Dr. himself finds any defect in their Principles; but only objects to their manner of taking them as they are discoverable by the Light of Nature, and the Reason of Things. *

*B.* Is not that a very just objection?

*A.* No t from one who supposes, that ,, the eternal ,, Reason of Things ought to be the Rule by which ,, all Men should govern all their actions; ,, & who, among other things of the like nature, affirms, that ,, † the original Obligation of all is the eternal Reason ,, of Things; That Reason, which God himself, who ,, has no Superior to direct him, or to whose hap- ,, piness nothing can be added, or any thing diminish'd ,, from it, yet constantly obliges himself to govern ,, the World by: And the more excellent, & perfect ,, his Creatures are, the more chearfully, & steddily ,, are their wills determin'd by this *supreme obligation,* ,, in conformity to the nature, and in imitation of ,, the most perfect Will of God.

*B.* W h y do you think this favours *Deism?*

*A.* B e c a u s e, if the eternal Reason of things is the *supreme Obligation,* must not that, if there's any difference between it and external Revelation, take place? And must not that Rule, which can annul any other, be not only the supreme, but the sole Rule; for as far as Men take any other Rule, so far they lose of their perfection, by ceasing to be govern'd by this Rule, in conformity to the nature, and in imita-tion of the perfect Will of God. And if this most perfect Will of God is to be thus known, can things that have another original; and are of a later date, be any part of the most perfect Will of God? Or, can the eternal Reason of Things extend to things that do not belong to Reason; or, as Divines love to speak, are above Reason? Or, can the Dr. suppose, there's

* *Pag.* 29.    † *Pag.* 54.

there's any other Rule, than the Nature, or Reason of Things, when he makes no medium between Mens being govern'd by it, and by their own unreasonable will? *

In short, 'tis the view with which an action is done, that makes it moral: He, who pays his debts out of a principle of honesty, does a moral action; while he, who does the same for fear of the Law, can't be said to act morally: And can he, who does a thing to avoid being punish'd, or in hopes of being rewarded hereafter (& for the same reason is ready to do the contrary) merit, at least, equally with him, who is in love with his duty, and is govern'd, not by servile motives, but by the original obligation of the moral fitness of things, in conformity to the nature, and in imitation of the perfect will of God? This the Dr. will not deny to be true Deism; and that they who do not act thus, deserve not the title of *True Deists.*

The Doctor, after he has himself, giv'n us a consistent scheme of *Deism*, says, † „ There is *now* no „ such thing, as a consistent scheme of *Deism:* That „ which alone was *once* such -- ceases *now* to be so, „ after the appearance of Revelation.„ If Christianity, as well as *Deism*, consists in being govern'd by the original obligation of the moral fitness of things, in conformity to the nature, and in imitation of the perfect will of God, then they both must be the same: but if Christianity consists in being govern'd by any other Rule, or requires any other things, has not the Dr. himself giv'n the advantage to *Deism?*

These *true Christian Deists,* as, I think, the Dr. ought to call them, say, that tho' the Dr's Discourse is chiefly levell'd against them, yet he can't differ with them, without differing from himself; & con-

Y                                    demning

---

demning in one part of his elaborate Treatise, what he has approv'd in the other. For,

IF Christianity has not, *say they*, destroy'd Mens moral agency, or forbid them to act as moral Agents, they must now, as well as formerly, judge of the Will of God, by that Reason given them by an all-gracious God, to distinguish between Good & Evil; the only things to which the Precepts of a Being, who, as the Dr. owns, is incapable of acting arbitrarily, can extend: And these *Deists* agree with the Dr. in his two first propositions, upon which, the whole of his reasoning is built: * ,, That from the eternal, & necessary dif-
,, ferences of things, there naturally arise certain
,, moral obligations, which are of themselves in-
,, cumbent on all rational Creatures, antecedent to all
,, positive institution, & to all expectation of reward
,, and punishment. ,, And,

,, THAT the same eternal moral obligations, which
,, arise necessarily from the natural differences of
,, things, are moreover the express Will & Command
,, of God to all rational Creatures: ,, And accordingly they judge of the positive Will of God, from those eternal moral obligations, which arise necessarily from the natural differences of things; which being incumbent on all rational Creatures, antecedent to all positive institution, can't but be so knowable by them: & having, agreeable to the Dr's direction, thus chosen their Religion, *they say*, 'Tis impossible for them (since there can't be two originals of the same thing) to choose that Religion from external Revelation, which they have already chosen from internal Revelation; and if external Revelation can't alter the nature of things, & make that to be fit, which is in itself unfit, and that to be necessary which is in itself unnecessary, it can only be a transcript of the Religion of Nature, and so every thing it says, is to be judg'd of by the Reason, and Nature of things:

other-

* *See the Contents of the Dr's Book.*

otherwife, fay they, we might be oblig'd to admit things, which, for ought we know, are as neceffarily falfe, as God is true; fince * ,, all Doctrines incon-
,, fiftent with Morality, are, *as the Dr. juftly obferves,*
,, as certainly, & neceffarily falfe, as God is true.

Besides, if thefe moral Obligations, which of themfelves are incumbent on all rational Creatures, & which likewife fhew themfelves from their internal excellency, to be the will of God, are as evident, as the Sun is bright; how can Men, fay thefe *Deifts*, believe on leffer evidence, what they know before to be certain on the greateft; in this cafe, muft not Faith be fwallow'd up by Knowledge, & Probability by Demonftration?

These *Deifts* intirely agree with the Dr, when he afferts, that † ,, Some Doctrines are in their own
,, nature *neceffarily, & demonftrably* true, fuch as are
,, all thofe which concern the obligation of plain
,, *moral Precepts*; and thefe neither need, nor can
,, receive any ftronger proof from miracles, than what
,, they have already (tho' not, perhaps, fo clearly
,, indeed to all capacities) from the evidence of
,, right Reafon. Other Doctrines are in their own
,, nature *neceffarily falfe, & impoffible to be true*; fuch
,, as are all *abfurdities & contradictions*, & all Doctrines
,, that tend to promote vice; and thefe can never
,, receive any degree of proof from all the miracles
,, in the world.,, But as to what the Dr. adds, ‡
,, That other Doctrines are in their own nature *in-*
,, *different*, or *poffible*, or, perhaps, *probable* to be true,
,, and thofe cou'd not have been known to be pofi-
,, tively true, but by the evidence of miracles, which
,, prove them to be certain.,, Here thefe *Deifts* beg leave to differ with him, as to any doctrines, in their own nature indifferent, being the Will of God; for that wou'd be to fuppofe, what the Dr. has prov'd to be impoffible, that God acts arbitrarily, & out of meer wilfulnefs. And here they wou'd ask him,

Y 2 fince,

fince, as he owns, * ,, Evil Spirits can do Miracles,
,, † and the nature of the doctrine to be prov'd to be
,, divine, muft be taken into confideration; how Miracles can prove a doctrine, relating to indifferent
things, to be from God? Or, how there can be any
fuch doctrines in the Chriftian Religion, if what he
fays be true; ‡ ,, That every one of the Doctrines it
,, teaches, as matter of truth, has a natural tendency,
,, & a direct powerful influence to reform Mens lives,
,, and correct their manners. This, *adds he*, is the
,, great end, & ultimate defign of all true Religion:
,, And 'tis a great and fatal miftake to think that any
,, Doctrine, or any belief whatever, can be any other-
,, wife of any benefit to Men, than as it is fitted to
,, promote this main end.

Tʜɪꜱ fuppofes Men, by their Reafon, are not only
able to know, that it is repugnant to the nature of
God, to require any thing of them, except it has a
natural tendency, and a direct powerful influence to
reform their lives, or correct their manners, but likewife to difcern what Doctrines have this tendency;
and that, if, upon examination, they find every Doctrine contain'd in Scripture has this tendency, they
may, then, fafely pronounce them all to be divine.
This previous examination, therefore, is highly neceffary to prevent what he juftly calls a *fatal miftake*.

Tʜᴇ difference between thofe, who wou'd engrofs
the Name of Chriftians to themfelves, & thefe *Chriftian Deifts*, as I may juftly call them, is, that the
former dare not examine into the truth of Scripture
Doctrines, left they fhou'd feem to queftion the veracity of the Scriptures; whereas the latter, who believe
not the Doctrines, becaufe contain'd in Scripture,
but the Scripture, on account of the Doctrines, are
under no fuch apprehenfion: For having critically
examin'd thofe Doctrines by that Reafon, which God
has giv'n them to diftinguifh Religion from Superftition,

---

* *Pag.* 306.     † *Pag.* 312.     ‡ *Pag.* 184.

tion, they are sure not to run into any errors of moment; notwithstanding the confess'd obscurity of the Scriptures, and those many mistakes that have crept into the Text, whether by accident, or design.

The Dr. says, * „ The moral part of our Saviour's „ Doctrine wou'd have appear'd infallibly true, whether „ he had ever work'd miracles, or no. The rest of „ his Doctrines was what evidently tended to pro- „ mote the honour of God, & the practice of righ- „ teousness amongst Men. Therefore that part also of „ his Doctrine was possible, and very probable to be „ true; but yet it could not from thence be known „ to be certainly true; nor ought to have been re- „ ceiv'd as a Revelation from God, unless it had been „ prov'd by undeniable miracles.

Here the *Deists* can, by no means, come into the Dr's distinction between the moral part of our Saviour's Doctrine, & that part which evidently tends to promote the Honour of God, and the practice of Righteousness; it being manifestly a distinction without any difference: And if the whole of Religion consists in the Honour of God, and the Good of Man, which he is far from denying; nothing can more effectually strike at the certainty of all Religion, than the supposing, that Mankind cou'd not be certain, that whatever evidently tended to promote the honour of God, & the practice of righteousness, was the Will of God, 'till they were convinc'd of it by undeniable Miracles.

'Tis possible, *say they,* a Man may doubt, whether there is a God; but none sure, who believe one, can doubt, but that 'tis demonstrably fit, just, & reasonable for Men, to do every thing, that evidently tends to promote the honour of God, & the practice of righteousness. And, „ if the mind of Man, *as the Dr. says,* † „ can't avoid giving its assent to the eter- „ nal Law of Righteousness; „ can the mind of Man avoid

* *Pag.* 314.        † *Pag.* 63.

avoid affenting to the practice of Righteousnefs as his indifpenfable duty? But if it be but probable, that whatever evidently tends to promote the honour of God, and the practice of righteousnefs, is from God; it can't be more than probable, that miracles done in their behalf are from God. Does not the Dr. here deftroy the certainty of thefe Doctrines, which he had before demonftrated, & this too only to prove their probability?

THESE *Chriftian Deifts* own the Dr. is in the right, for contending, that the neceffary relation that is between things, makes fome actions moral, & others immoral; but then they wou'd ask, Whether there be any other way to diftinguifh them, but from their nature & tendency? for they can't but conclude, that thofe which evidently tend to promote the honour of God, & the practice of righteoufnefs, are plain moral Duties, and perpetually oblige.   And,

,, IF no Miracles, *as the Dr. owns*, * can prove ,, a Doctrine that's vicious in its tendency & confe- ,, quences, to be from God;,, muft not, *fay they*, that. Doctrine, which has the contrary tendency and confequences, be from God, tho' ever fo many mi- racles are done in oppofition to it? And,

THEY likewife *fay*. As evidently as God is not only a good & perfect, but alfo the only perfect Being, fo evident is it, that every Doctrine, that carries any degree, much more the higheft degree of goodnefs and perfection in it, has the character of Divinity imprefs'd on it; & therefore, can't agree with the Dr. ,, † That neither can any degree of goodnefs, and ,, excellency in the Doctrine itfelf, make it certain, ,, but only highly probable to come from God.

IF no Miracles can prove any indifferent thing to be the Will of God, and all that evidently tends to promote the honour of God, and the practice of righteoufnefs, are plain, moral Duties, as the Dr. con- tends,

* *Pag.* 315.      † *Pag.* 221.

tends, and all such Duties neither need, nor can receive any stronger proof from Miracles, than what they have already from the evidence of right Reason, how can Miracles, *say these Deists*, have any other use, than to make Men consider the nature, & tendency of a Doctrine, and judge from thence whether it be from God? But,

ALLOWING the Dr. what *Hypothesis* he pleases, in relation to Miracles, yet if the Doctrines themselves, from their internal excellency, do not give us a certain proof of the Will of God, no traditional Miracles can do it, because one probability added to another will not amount to certainty.

*B.* I thought the Dr. had built his arguments in favour of Revelation, upon the obscurity of the Law of Nature, & wou'd not have declar'd, that * „ the „ Reason of all Men, every where, as naturally, and „ necessarily assents to it, as all Animals conspire in „ the pulse, and motion of their heart and arteries, „ or as all Men agree in their judgment concerning „ the whiteness of snow, or the brightness of the Sun.

*A.* HAVE patience, and you shall see, that *Snow is no longer white*, or *the Sun bright*; and in order to it I'll shew you, that the Dr's new scheme consists in supposing, that tho' † „ in the original uncorrupted „ state of human-Nature, right Reason may justly be „ suppofed to have been a sufficient guide, and a „ principle powerful enough to have preferv'd Men „ in the constant practice of their duty, yet upon „ the Fall, Mankind were in a very bad state, as „ wanting greater help, and assistance, than the Light „ of Nature could afford them. ‡ And *that* there „ was plainly wanting some extraordinary, & super- „ natural assistance, that was above the reach of bare „ Reason and Philosophy to procure. § There was „ plainly wanting a divine Revelation to recover „ Mankind out of their universally degenerate state,

Y 4                                           into

* *Pag.* 83.   † *Pag.* 196.   ‡ *Pag.* 197.   § *Ibid.*

,, into a ſtate ſuitable to the original dignity of their.
,, Nature. ,,    And again, * ,, There was plainly
,, wanting a divine Revelation, to recover Mankind
,, out of their univerſal corruption and degeneracy.,,
*And in the Margin,* ,, A divine Revelation abſolutely
,, neceſſary for the recovery of Mankind:,, But if a
divine Revelation was abſolutely neceſſary to this end,
Men were under an abſolute impoſſibility of recovering without it.

Tʜɪs is ſuppoſing, God had left all Mankind for
4000 years together, & even the greateſt part to this
day, deſtitute of ſufficient means to do their duty,
and to preſerve themſelves from ſinking into a corrupted & degenerate ſtate ; and that it was impoſſible
for them when thus ſunk, to recover themſelves; and
yet that God (their duty being the ſame after, as before the Fall,) expected impoſſibilities from them ;
*viz.* either to preſerve themſelves from thus falling;
or if fallen, to recover themſelves. But if they had
not power to do this, and it was not their fault, that
they at firſt were in , and after remain'd in what he
calls a ſtate of univerſal degeneracy and corruption ,
this muſt then be the ſtate God deſign'd they ſhou'd
be in ; and it wou'd ſeem not only to be in vain, but
a crime in them , to endeavour to change that ſtate ,
in which, God, of his infinite Wiſdom & Goodneſs,
thought fit to place them.   But,

Iғ Men alike, at all times, owe their exiſtence to
God, they at all times muſt be created in a ſtate of
innocence, capable of knowing, and doing all God
requires of them ; and we muſt conclude from the
Wiſdom & Goodneſs of God, that he will at no time
command any thing, not fit for him to command,
or for Man to do : and therefore, cou'd we ſuppoſe
ſome things commanded by external Revelation,
which were not commanded by the Light of Nature,
we muſt conclude, that 'till then it was not fit for
God

God to command them, or for Man uncommanded to do them.

The Dr. to shew the fault was not in Mankind, but in the Guide God gave them, says, * ,, The Light ,, of Nature, and right Reason, was altogether in- ,, sufficient to restore true Piety;,, and as tho' this was not enough, he adds, ,, that the Light of Nature ,, no where appear'd;,, which Sentences seem in- consistent, since the first supposes a Light, tho' in- sufficient, appearing to Mens minds, but the Dr. does not seem to know whether they had no light at all, or † ,, a Light, which, *he says*, has undeniable de- ,, fects in it.

*B.* May not the Law of Nature be very clear, tho' the Light of Nature may be so very dim, as to have undeniable defects?

*A.* Can the Law of Nature be clear, & the Light of Nature dim, when the Law of Nature is nothing, but what the Light of Nature, or Reason dictates? Or, as Dr. *Scot* expresses it, ‡ ,, Right Reason pro- ,, nouncing such actions good, and such evil, is the ,, Law of Nature, and those eternal reasons, upon ,, which it so pronounces them, are the Creed of ,, Nature, both which together make *Natural Reli-* ,, *gion.*

The Dr. to persue this point, & to shew that the fault was not in the Creatures, but the Creator; says, that § ,, Even those few extraordinary Men of the ,, Philosophers, who did sincerely endeavour to re- ,, form Mankind, were themselves intirely ignorant ,, of some Doctrines, absolutely necessary for bringing ,, about this great end of the reformation, & recovery ,, of Mankind; Their whole attempt to discover ,, the truth of things, and to instruct others therein, ,, was like wandring in the wide sea, without knowing

Y 5

whither

,, whither to go, or which way to take, or having
,, any guide to conduct them?

And that you might be sure, that the fault was in
the eternal, universal, & unchangeable Law of Nature;
he calls those Philosophers, who thus wander'd in the
wide sea, * ,, wise, brave, & good Men, who made
,, it their business to study, & practise the duties of
,, Natural Religion themselves, & to teach, & exhort
,, others to do the like;,, nay, one wou'd imagine
he thought them, notwithstanding their unavoidable
ignorance, inspir'd; since he says, † ,, There never
,, was a great Man, but who was inspir'd; *Nemo un-
quam magnus Vir sine divino afflatu fuit:* And for this
he quotes the authority of *Cicero*, who, if the Dr's
reasoning is just, was certainly inspir'd.

The Dr's Scheme outdoes that of the most rigid
*Predestinarians*, for that at all times saves the Elect:
But here are no Elect, but all, for many ages, are in-
extricably involv'd in a most deprav'd, corrupted, and
impious state.

The Dr. justly says, ‡ ,, Let none on pretence
,, of maintaining Natural Religion, revile, and blas-
,, pheme the Christian, lest they be found liars unto
,, God:,, And for the same reason, may not I say,
let none blaspheme Natural Religion? Tho, if Natural
& Reveal'd Religion can differ, it must be a greater
crime to revile a Religion, that is eternal, universal,
and unchangeable, than a Religion that is not so.
And,

Tho I pay a due deference to the Dr's deep penetration in matters of Religion, I dare not say,
there's the least difference between the *Law of Nature*,
& *the Gospel*; for that wou'd suppose some defect in
one of them, & reflect on the Author of both; who,
certainly, was equally good, and equally wise,
when he gave the one, as when he gave the other
(if

* *Pag.* 167.    † *Pag.* 197.    ‡ *Pag.* 241.

(if it may be call'd another) Law. * Nor dare I be so rash, as to charge the Light of Nature with *undeniable defects*, as the Dr. presumes to do; since, if that Light was sufficient to answer the end design'd by God, which was to be a competent guide to Men, in relation to their present, and future happiness, there cou'd be no deficiency: If not, then there must have been an undeniable default in the giver of it, in appointing means not sufficient to answer their design'd ends; tho' both means and ends were intirely in his power. Nor dare I say, „There are several „ necessary truths, not possible to be discover'd with „ any certainty by the Light of Nature; „ because God's means of information will, & must always bear an exact proportion to the necessity of our knowing what we are oblig'd to know, especially touching the *Nature*, and *Attributes of God*, which, he supposes, „ † were very difficult for the wisest Men to find out, „ & more difficult for them to explain. „ But here I must do the Dr. that justice, as to observe, that he, in another place, is so far from finding any such defect in this Light, even with relation to the nature & attributes of God, that he says, ‡ „ All the heathen „ World had certain means of knowing God, for „ § *That which may be known of God*, was *manifest* „ enough unto Men in all Ages. „ And if no Age can know more of God, than *that which* may *be known*, & if that which *may* be known of him was manifest enough in all Ages, what advantage can one Age in this grand point have above another? And, therefore, I must conclude,

I t can't be imputed to any defect in the Light of Nature, that the Pagan World ran into Idolatry, but to their being intirely govern'd by Priests, who pretended communication with their Gods, and to have thence their Revelations, which they impos'd on the credulous as divine Oracles: Whereas the business of the

* *Pag.* 214. † *Pag.* 178. ‡ *Pag.* 161. § *Pag.* 160.

the Chriſtian diſpenſation was to deſtroy all thoſe traditional Revelations, & reſtore, free from all Idolatry, the true primitive, and natural Religion, implanted in Mankind from the Creation.

THE Dr. however, ſeems afraid, leſt he had allow'd too much to the Light of Nature, in relation to the diſcovery of our duty both to God & Man, and not left room for Revelation to make any addition; he therefore, ſuppoſes, * ,, there are ſome Duties, which ,, Nature hints at only in general: ,, But, if we can't, without highly reflecting on the Wiſdom & Goodneſs of God, ſuppoſe, that he has not, at all times, giv'n the whole rational Creation a plain Rule for their conduct, in relation to thoſe Duties they owe to God, themſelves, and one another, muſt we not ſuppoſe Reaſon, and Religion (that *Rule* of all other *Rules*) inſeparable, ſo that no rational Creature can be ignorant of it, who attends to the dictates of his own mind, I mean, as far as 'tis neceſſary for him to know it. An ignorant Peaſant may know what is ſufficient for him, without knowing as much as the learned Rector of St. *James's.*

THO' the Dr. ſays, ,, the knowledge of the Law ,, of Nature is in fact, by no means, univerſal; ,, yet he aſſerts, that † ,, Man is plainly in his *own* na- ,, ture *an accountable Creature*; ,, which ſuppoſes that the Light of Nature plainly, and undeniably teaches him that Law, for breach of which he is naturally accountable: And did not the Dr. believe this Law to be univerſal, he cou'd not infer a future Judgment from the conſcience *all* Men have of their actions, or the judgment they paſs on them in their own minds; whereby ‡ ,, *They that have not any Law,* ,, *are a Law unto themſelves; their Conſciences bearing* ,, *witneſs, and their thoughts accuſing, or excuſing one* ,, *another;* ,, Which is ſuppoſing but one Law, whether that Law be written on paper, or in Mens hearts

* *Pag.* 239.   † *Pag.* 152.   ‡ *Ibid.*

hearts only; and that all Men, by the judgment they pass on their own actions, are conscious of this Law. And,

The Apostle *Paul*, tho quoted by the Dr, is so far from favouring his *Hypothesis* of any invincible ignorance, even in the wisest, & best of the Philosophers, that he, by saying, * *The Gentiles that have not the Law, do by Nature the things contained in the Law*, makes the Law of Nature and Grace to be the same: And supposes the reason why they were to be punish'd, was their sinning against Light and knowledge: † *That which may be known of God was manifest in them, & when they knew God, they glorify'd him not as God:* And they were likewise guilty of abominable corruptions, not ignorantly, but ‡ *knowing the Judgment of God, that they who do such things are worthy of death.* Had the Dr. but consider'd this self-evident Proposition, that *There can be no Transgression where there is no Law*; and that an unknown Law is the same as no Law, and consequently, that all Mankind, at all times, must be capable of knowing all (whether more, or less,) that God requires: It wou'd have prevented his endeavouring to prove, that, 'till the Gospel dispensation, Mankind were intirely, and unavoidably ignorant of their duty in several important points, and thus charging the Light of Nature with undeniable defects.

I think it no compliment to external Revelation, tho' the Dr. design'd it as the highest, to say, it prevail'd, when the Light of Nature was, as he supposes, in a manner extinct; since then an irrational Religion might as easily obtain, as a rational one.

The Dr, to prove that Revelation has supply'd the insufficiency, and undeniable defects of the Light of Nature, refers us to *Phil.* 4. 8. which he introduces after this pompous manner; § ,, Let any Man of an honest,

* *Rom.* 2. 14. † *Rom.* 1. 19. 21. ‡ *Ib. ver.* 32.
§ *Pag.* 229.

,, honeſt, and ſincere mind conſider, whether that
,, practical Doctrine, has not, even *in itſelf*, the greateſt
,, marks of a divine original, wherein * *Whatſoever*
,, *things are* true, *whatſoever things are* honeſt, *what-*
,, *ſoever things are* juſt, *whatſoever things are* pure,
,, *whatſoever things are* lovely, *whatſoever things are*
,, *of* good report, *if there be any* Virtue, *if there be*
,, *any thing* praiſe-worthy; all theſe, and theſe only,
,, are the things that are earneſtly recommended to
,, Mens practice.

I wou'd ask the Dr. how he can know what theſe
things are, which are thus alone earneſtly recommended
to Mens practice; or, why they have, in themſelves,
the greateſt marks of a divine original, but from the
Light of Nature? Nay, how can the Dr. know,
there are defects in the Light of Nature, but from
that Light itſelf? which ſuppoſes this Light is all we
have to truſt to; and conſequently, all the Dr. has
been doing, on pretence of promoting the honour of
Revelation, is introducing univerſal Scepticiſm: And
I am concern'd, and griev'd, to ſee a Man, who had
ſo great a ſhare of the Light of Nature, imploy it
to expoſe that Light, of which before he had giv'n
the higheſt commendation; and which can have no
other effect, than to weaken even his own Demonſtration, drawn from that Light, for the Being of a
God.

I ſhall mention but one text more, which had not
the Dr. thought it highly to his purpoſe, for ſhewing
the inſufficiency of the Light of Nature, he wou'd
not have uſher'd it in after this moſt ſolemn manner:
,, † When men have put themſelves into this temper
,, and frame of mind, let them try if they can any
,, longer reject the evidence of the Goſpel: ‡ *If any*
,, *Man will do his will, he ſhall know of the Doctrine,*
,, *whether it be of God.*

Is

---

* *Phil.* 4. 8.    † *Pag.* 341.    ‡ *John* 7. 17.

I s it not ſtrange, to ſee ſo judicious a Divine write after ſuch a manner, as if he thought the beſt way to ſupport the dignity of Revelation, was to derogate from the immutable, & eternal Law of Nature? and while he is depreſſing it, extol Revelation for thoſe very things it borrows from that Law? in which tho' he aſſerts there are undeniable defects, yet he owns, that God governs all his own actions by it, & expects that all Men ſhou'd ſo govern theirs. But,

I find the Dr's own Brother, the Dean of *Sarum*, is intirely of my mind, as to thoſe two texts the Dr. quotes; *viz. Rom.* 2. 14. & *Phil.* 4. 8. As to the firſt, *viz. Rom.* 2. 14. he ſays, * „ The Apoſtle ſuppoſes, „ that the moral Law is founded in the Nature and „ Reaſon of Things; that every Man is endu'd with „ ſuch powers and faculties of mind, as render him „ capable of ſeeing, and taking notice of this Law; „ and alſo with ſuch a ſenſe and judgment of the „ reaſonableneſs, & fitneſs of conforming his actions „ to it, that he cannot but in his own mind acquit „ himſelf when he does ſo, & condemn himſelf when „ he does otherwiſe. „ And as to the ſecond, *viz. Phil.* 4. 8. where the ſame Apoſtle recommends the practice of Vertue, upon the fore-mention'd principles of comelineſs & reputation: „ Theſe principles, *ſays he*, „ if duly attended to, were ſufficient to inſtruct Men „ in the whole of their duty towards themſelves, and „ towards each other: And they wou'd alſo have „ taught them their duty towards God, their Creator „ and Governor, if they had diligently perſu'd them: „ For according as the Apoſtle expreſſes it, *Rom.* 1. 20. „ *The inviſible things of God from the creation of the* „ *world, are clearly ſeen, being underſtood by the things* „ *that are made, even his eternal power & Godhead.* -- „ The ſame fitneſs & decency that appears in Mens „ regular behaviour towards each other, appears alſo
in

---

* *Enq. into the Cauſe & Origin of Moral Evil. p.* 154, 155, 156, 157.

„ in their behaviour towards God: And this, like-
„ wife, is founded in the Nature & Reason of Things;
„ and is what the circumstances and condition they
„ are in do absolutely require. Thus we see wherein
„ Moral Virtue, or Good consists, & what the obli-
„ gation to it is from its own native beauty and ex-
„ cellency.

B. IF God, as the Dr. asserts, does abhor all arbitrary Commands, and Natural Religion comprehends
every thing that is not arbitrary; and withal, is so
deeply impress'd on Mens minds, that they can't violate its precepts without self-condemnation; I can't
apprehend how these Philosophers, who made it their
business to study, & practise Natural Religion, cou'd be
intirely ignorant of any Doctrines absolutely necessary
for the Reformation of Mankind: Nay, that „ their
„ whole attempt to discover the truth of things,
„ was like wandring in the wide sea, without any
„ guide; and therefore, I shou'd be glad to know,
„ what are these absolutely necessary Doctrines, they
„ were thus intirely ignorant of.

A. „ These Philosophers, the Dr. says, * had no
„ knowledge of the whole scheme, order, and state
„ of things.„ This, I think, may be allow'd; since
I believe there's none at present, who have, or pretend to have so extensive a knowledge. „ But they
„ had no knowledge of the method of God's go-
„ verning the World.„  Then they must be blind,
if living in the World, they did not see how the things
of this World were govern'd by Providence. „ Then
„ they did not know the ground & circumstances of
„ Mens present corrupt condition.„  If so, they did
not understand human-nature, and how prejudices &
passions work on Mankind.  „ They did not know,
says he, „ the manner of the divine interposition ne-
„ cessary for their recovery, and the glorious end, to
„ which God intended finally to conduct them.„

It

It muſt be own'd, they were not in the leaſt acquainted with the Dr's glorious ſcheme, of all Mankind's being for four thouſand years together, & the greateſt part too, at preſent, by the very frame of their conſtitution, and the condition of their being, plac'd by God in a moſt deprav'd, degenerate ſtate; without poſſibility of recovering from it. ,, But they had, it ſeems, ,, no knowledge of God's deſign in creating Mankind. Sure, the Dr. had forgot what he quotes from *Cicero* to this purpoſe; * ,, *Ad tuendos conſervandosque homi-* ,, *nes hominem natum eſſe. Homines hominum cauſa* ,, *ſunt generati, ut ipſi inter ſe alii aliis prodeſſe poſſint.* ,, *Hominem, natura obedientem, homini nocere non poſſe.* And does not the Dr. maintain the ſame thing, in ſaying, that † ,, God cou'd have no motive to create ,, things at firſt, but only that he might communicate ,, to them his goodneſs & happineſs.

,, These Philoſophers, *he ſays,* ‡ were ignorant ,, of the original dignity of human-nature.,, And becauſe he frequently inſiſts on it, I ſhall further conſider this matter; and will confeſs, 'tis probable, they thought that human-nature, Men having at all times the ſame common faculties, was always the ſame. Had they known the ſacred ſtory of *Adam* and *Eve,* that wou'd have confirm'd them in their ſentiments. The moſt they cou'd perceive by it wou'd be, that the firſt pair came into the world in every ſenſe naked, deſtitute of all that knowledge, experience gave their poſterity; and therefore, God, the better to ſupport them in this ſtate of univerſal ignorance, planted a Garden for them, that they might live on the fruit of it. How weak was their Reaſon, how ſtrong their appetites! when they cou'd not abſtain (the ſole command giv'n them) from the Fruit of but one Tree; in a garden too, where muſt needs be an infinite variety, & the choiceſt Fruit!

7.      These

* *Pag.* 75. † *Pag.* 121. ‡ *Pag.* 171

THESE Philosophers might have been at a loss, to conceive, how *Eve* cou'd entertain a conference with a Serpent (incapable of human voice) even before consent had giv'n any meaning to sounds. And they wou'd be apt to ask, Why, (tho' custom hath made it shameful to go without cloaths in those places where cloaths are worn) the first Pair shou'd nevertheless, tho' they knew not what cloaths were, be asham'd to be seen uncloath'd by one another, & by God himself? So that, when * *They heard the voice of God walking in the Garden, in the cool of the evening,* (a strange representation these Philosophers wou'd think of God!) *they hid themselves from his presence:* Nay, *God* himself ( their *Fig-leave Aprons,* which *they,* having, it seems, all things necessary for sewing, *sew'd together,* not being sufficient to hide their shame) *made them coats of* the *skins* of the Beasts, newly created in pairs. And they wou'd, likewise, desire to be inform'd, how *Eve,* before her eyes were open'd, *saw that the Tree was good for food;* & that *it was pleasant to the eyes, & a Tree to be desir'd to make one wise.* †

UPON the whole, I grant, that these Philosophers wou'd be so far from finding out this original dignity in the first Pair, that they wou'd be apt to think, by the Serpent's so easily imposing on her, that the original serpentine nature, was too subtil for the original human-nature; & that there being nothing done by any Serpent since the fall, which cou'd occasion the Precept of Mens being bid to be as *wise as Serpents,* it must allude to this transaction between the Woman & the Serpent; tho' they cou'd never come into the belief of the *Ophitæ* ‡ (with whom the *Marcionites* may be join'd) who thought, that *Wisdom* herself was the Serpent, which they preferr'd to Christ, as teaching them to know Good & Evil; and designing for them Immortality and Deity; and foretelling that *Adam,* tho'

* *Gen.* 3. 8.       † *Id.* 3. 6.
‡ *Iren. l.* 1. *c.* 34. *Tertull. Præscript. c.* 47.

tho' threaten'd with certain *Death on the day he eat the forbidden Fruit*, *ſhou'd not* then *dye*; who accordingly liv'd after that ſentence about 900 years : And that *Moſes's* erecting the brazen, healing Serpent, was in honour of this Serpent, who deſign'd ſo much good to Mankind.

*B.* THESE Philoſophers wou'd be groſly miſtaken, did they believe this done by a Serpent : We ſay, it was the Devil, in the ſhape of a Serpent, that tempted them.

*A.* THESE Philoſophers, indeed, wou'd ſee, that the Chriſtians are now aſham'd of the literal interpretation of this ſtory ; tho' St. *Paul* was of another mind, who expreſly ſays, *The Serpent deceiv'd* Eve *thro' ſubtilty.* And they, perhaps, wou'd ask, Whether it was the Devil, who is ſaid to be *more ſubtil than any Beaſt of the field;* ſince it was this ſubtil Beaſt that ſaid to the Woman, * *Ye ſhall not ſurely die.* And it was upon the Woman's ſaying, *The Serpent beguiled me, and I did eat,* that the Lord ſaid to the Serpent, † *Becauſe thou haſt done this, thou art curſed above all the Cattle, and above every Beaſt of the field: ‡ Upon thy belly thou ſhalt go, & duſt thou ſhalt eat all the days of thy life.* Does this character agree to an immaterial, immortal Being ? Did he all the days of his life go upon his belly, & eat duſt ? Does not God, continuing his diſcourſe to the Serpent, ſay, *I will put enmity between thee, and the Woman; between thy ſeed, & her ſeed; it ſhall bruiſe thy head, and thou ſhalt bruiſe his heel?* And is not this the conſequence of Serpents going on their belly ? Do they not frequently bite Men by the heel; eſpecially in hot countries, where Serpents are numerous, & Mens heels bare ? Why ſhall *thy ſeed,* not ſignify *thy ſeed,* but the ſeed of a Being not mention'd in all this ſtory ; & who has no ſeed, but metaphorical ſeed; which, ſince the Woman's ſeed is taken literally, wou'd be immediately changing

Z 2                                    the

* *Gen* 3. 4, 5.    † *Ib. ver.* 13.    ‡ *Ib. ver.* 14.

the meaning of the word *feed?* Does this text afford the leaft argument, to imagine God did not as much fpeak to the Serpent, as to *Adam* & *Eve?* If a book is to be interpreted thus, efpecially in relation to hi- ftorical facts; how can we, thefe Philofophers wou'd fay, be fure of its meaning in any one place? Befides, wou'd they not ask, Why the whole race of Serpents fhou'd be curs'd for the crime of a fallen Angel?

*B.* They might as well ask, Why all other Animals fhou'd bring forth in pain, for the fault of *Eve?* For had Nature form'd all Females at firft, as they have been ever fince *Eve* eat the forbidden Fruit, none of them, except by Miracles, cou'd be deliver'd without pain; no more than Serpents, had they at firft, been form'd as at prefent, creep otherwife than they do.

*A.* THOSE Philofophers, perhaps, wou'd not think the matter a jot mended, by fubftituting (did the ftory afford room for it) a Devil, inftead of a Serpent; fince they cou'd not fee, how an infinitely good God cou'd permit a moft malicious cunning Spirit to work on the weaknefs of a Woman, juft plac'd in a new World; without interpofing in this unequal conflict, or giving notice of any fuch wicked Spirit; Angels, neither good, nor bad, being mention'd in the Hi- ftory of the Creation. And yet that after the fact was commited, God fhou'd thus revenge it on all their innocent pofterity for ever, by *curfing the ground,* &c.

WHAT wou'd feem to them moft unaccountable is, That God fhou'd continue to fuffer this fubtil, & malignant Spirit, endow'd with an univerfal know- ledge of what is paft, & a deep penetration into fu- turity, to range about deceiving, and circumventing Mankind; who, having a capacity vaftly fuperior to them, is continually fowing the feeds of mifchief, & fcattering the poifon of univerfal difcord, making ufe of thofe very Men as his inftruments, whofe profefs'd bufinefs it is, to promote univerfal concord.

THE

The poor *Indians*, you know, when our Missionaries give such an account of the Devil, say, „ Is not „ your God a good God, & loves Mankind? Why „ does he then permit this Devil to be continually doing „ them such infinite hurt? Why is he not put under „ confinement, if not depriv'd of a being, of which he „ has made himself unworthy? With us one, who „ does not hinder a mischief, when it is in his power, „ is thought not much better than he who does it.

But to return to the Dr, where is the difference in relation to the goodness of God, & the happiness of Mankind, between God's creating them in a state, as he calls it, of universal degeneracy & corruption: or causing them by the folly of *Adam*, which infinite Wisdom cou'd not but foresee, to fall unavoidably into this bad state? What dignity, what perfection cou'd *Adam*'s nature have, that the nature of his Posterity has not? Are they not as much fram'd after the image of their Maker? Are not their souls as much immediately from God as *Adam*'s? And are not their Bodies exactly made after the same manner? Were not all other Animals at first created by God as well as Men? Had these any dignity, or perfection in their animal-nature, which the same creatures since have not? Besides, is not this suppos'd high state of perfection in *Adam*, giving the lye to the History? since this very perfect Man, notwithstanding all the original dignity of his nature, had no better excuse for his yielding to the first temptation, than that * *the Woman, whom thou gavest to be with me, gave me of the tree, & I did eat.* How can we suppose his understanding was in the least impair'd by this crime, since God himself says (tho' to whom it does not appear) † *Behold the Man is become like one of us, to know good and evil*; and to prevent his being so, both for immortality as well as knowledge, ‡ *God placed Cherubims with a flaming sword, which turned every way to keep the way of the*

Z 3

trees

* *Gen.* 3. 12.     † *Ib. ver.* 22.     ‡ *Ib. ver.* 24.

*Tree of life.* Wou'd it not be very ſtrange, that his Poſterity (while his underſtanding receiv'd no hurt,) ſhou'd ſuffer ſo greatly in theirs, as the Dr. wou'd have it thought? Indeed, St. *Auſtin* * ſuppoſes, that *Adam* before the Fall cou'd have erected his *membrum genitale ad voluntatis nutum*; and that motions of the fleſh were perfectly ſubordinate to his will, like his fingers. But this notion not being orthodox at preſent, & the loſs of this faculty no ways inferring the loſs of underſtanding, I may venture to ſay, that the Dr's deſcription of human-nature in all, but one pair, (and that too, perhaps, but for a day,) is a Libel on the dignity of human-nature, and an high reflection on the Wiſdom & goodneſs of its Author; in placing them, without any fault of theirs, in an unavoidable ſtate of degeneracy & corruption for 1000 years together, & continuing the greateſt part ſtill in the ſame ſtate.

But let us ſee, whether the Dr. has better ſucceſs with his other arguments, by which he endeavours to curtail the univerſal goodneſs of God; and, therefore, I ſhall take notice of two other things, which he inſiſts on, to ſhew the groſs, & unavoidable ignorance of the Philoſophers, in the moſt momentous points of Religion: The firſt is, That, † ,, which ,, of all things the beſt, & wiſeſt of the Philoſophers ,, were entirely, & unavoidably ignorant of, and yet ,, was of the greateſt importance for ſinful Men to ,, know; viz. *The Method, by which ſuch as have erred* ,, *from the right way, and have offended God, may yet* ,, *reſtore themſelves to his favour.* ,, And here he con-cludes, ‡ ,, That there ariſes from Nature no ſuffi-,, cient comfort to ſinners, but an anxious, & endleſs ,, ſolicitude, about the means of appeaſing the Deity.

To anſwer the Dr, I need only quote what another able Divine, writing on the ſame ſubject of Natural,

&

* *De Civit. Dei, l.* 14. *c.* 23, 24,
† *Pag.* 182. ‡ *Pag.* 183,

& Reveal'd Religion, says, * „ I affirm, it is an Ar-
„ ticle of Natural Religion, that forgiveneſs does
„ certainly follow repentance. If God be a merciful,
„ & benign Being, he will accept the payment we
„ are able to make; and not infiſt on impoſſible de-
„ mands, with his frail, bankrupt creatures. No ge-
„ nerous Man, but will forgive his Enemy, much
„ more his Child; if he diſapproves the wrong he
„ has done, is really griev'd for it, is deſirous to make
„ amends, even by ſuffering for the honour of the
„ perſon injur'd. How much more ſhall God forgive
„ all perſons thus diſpos'd, & reform'd; ſince there's
„ no generoſity in Man, but what is, with his nature,
„ infus'd into him by God.

„ Not only Mercy, but Wiſdom will effectually
„ diſpoſe God to forgive the penitent, becauſe the
„ Creature reform'd by penitence is ſuch as it ought
„ to be, & ſuch as God willeth it; which being ſo,
„ it can be no wiſdom in God to afflict it unneceſſa-
„ rily. 'Tis not juſtice, but rage, to puniſh where the
„ perſon is already mended. When we argue thus,
„ from any of the known and certain attributes of
„ God, we are as ſure of the concluſion, as if the
„ thing was to be diſcern'd by ſenſe; ſince no ſenſible
„ thing is more certain, than the attributes of God.

Mr. Lock has the ſame ſentimens, & ſays, † „ God
„ had, by the Light of Reaſon, reveal'd to all Man-
„ kind, who wou'd make uſe of that Light, that he
„ was good, & merciful. The ſame ſpark of the di-
„ vine nature, & knowledge in Man, which making
„ him a Man, ſhewed him the Law he was under
„ as a Man, ſhewed him alſo the way of atoning the
„ merciful, kind, compaſſionate Author, and Father
„ of him, & his being, when he had tranſgreſſed that
„ Law. He that made uſe of this candle of the Lord,
„ ſo far as to find what was his duty, cou'd not miſs

Z 4                              to

* *Nye* of Nat. and Rev. Relig. p. 85, 86.
† *Reaſonab. of Chriſtianity*, &c. p. 255, 256.

,, to find alſo the way to reconciliation & forgiveneſs,
when he had fail'd of his Duty. --

,, ,, The Law is the eternal, immutable ſtandard of
,, Right : And a part of that Law is, that a Man
,, wou'd forgive, not only his Children, but his Ene-
,, mies; upon their repentance, asking pardon and
,, amendment. And therefore, he cou'd not doubt,
,, that the Author of this Law, & God of patience
,, & conſolation, who is rich in mercy, wou'd for-
,, give his frail offſpring; if they acknowledg'd their
,, faults, diſapproved the iniquity of their tranſgreſ-
,, ſions, begg'd his pardon, & reſolved in earneſt for
,, the future, to conform their actions to this Rule,
,, which they own'd to be juſt & right. This way
,, of reconciliation, this hope of atonement, the Light
,, of Nature revealed to them.

Had the Dr. only ſaid, that we can't know from
the Light of Nature, that *There's more joy in Heaven
over one Sinner that repents, than over ninety nine juſt
perſons, who need no repentance*; that, if ſtrictly taken,
might, perhaps, be better diſputed; but nothing, ſure,
can be more ſhocking, than to ſuppoſe the unchangeable God, *whoſe nature, and property is ever to forgive*, was not, at all times, equally willing to pardon
repenting Sinners; and equally willing they ſhou'd
have the ſatisfaction of knowing it.

If *God's Ways are equal*, & he has, at one time as
well as another, the ſame goodneſs for the Sons of
Men, in relation to their eternal happineſs; how can
we ſuppoſe he left all Mankind, for ſo many ages,
& the greateſt part, even at preſent, in a moſt miſerable ſtate of doubt, & uncertainty, about the pardon
of ſin; & conſequently, about the poſſibility of any
Man's being ſav'd? If this notion, that even the beſt,
& wiſeſt of Mankind, were, not only abſolutely, but
moſt abſolutely ignorant of that, which of all things,
it was of the greateſt importance for Mankind to
know, be not inconſiſtent with the divine goodneſs,
I am at a loſs to know what is ſo.      If

IF the defign of God, in communicating any thing of himfelf to Men, was their happinefs; wou'd not that defign have oblig'd him, who, at all times, alike defires their happinefs, to have, at all times, alike communicated it to them? If God always acts for the good of his Creatures, what reafon can be affign'd, why he fhou'd not, from the beginning, have difcover'd fuch things, as make for their good; but defer the doing it till the time of *Tiberius*? fince the fooner this was done, the greater wou'd his goodnefs appear to be: Nay, is it confiftent with infinite benevolence, to hide that for many ages, which, he knew, was as ufeful at firft to prevent, as afterwards it cou'd be, to put a ftop to any thing he diflik'd.

AND, indeed, unlefs we deny that God, at all times, intended Mankind that happinefs, their nature is capable of, we muft allow, that, at all times, he has giv'n them the means of obtaining it, by the rules he has prefcrib'd them for their conduct; & confequently, thefe Rules muft have been difcoverable at all times. For, if God acts upon rational motives, muft not the fame motives, which oblig'd him to difcover any thing that's for the good of Mankind, have oblig'd him to difcover every thing that is fo; and that too, after the fame plain manner: And not do this, as it were, grudgingly, little by little; here a bit, & there a bit; and that to one favourite Nation only, under the vail of types, allegories, *&c.* and at laft, tho' he difcover'd fome things more plainly, yet it was but to a fmall part of Mankind, the bulk of them to this day remaining in deplorable ignorance.

B. ANOTHER Argument the Dr. brings for the undeniable defect of the Light of Nature is, that tho' it is *evident* from this Light, that *God ought to be worfhipp'd*; yet * ,, *the manner*, in which he might ,, be *acceptably worfhipp'd*, the wifeft, and beft of the ,, Philofopheres *were intirely, and unavoidably ignorant of.*

* *Pag.* 178.

Z 5

*A.* WHO can forbear pitying thefe unhappy Philofophers, indifpenfably oblig'd to worfhip God acceptably; & yet, hard fate! unavoidably ignorant how to perform this acceptable worfhip? But,

IF God cou'd not will to be worfhipp'd, without willing fome way or other, of being worfhipp'd; and if he left it to the Light of Nature to difcover how he wou'd be worfhipp'd, cou'd that be for any other reafon, but becaufe it was acceptable to him, to be worfhipp'd as that Light directed? Is it not a contradiction, to fuppofe God wou'd be acceptably worfhipp'd, & yet let Men, even the beft, be intirely & unavoidably ignorant, how to worfhip him acceptably? Does not the Light of Nature tell us, that God is a Being of infinite wifdom & goodnefs; and that all his natural faculties are directed by thefe two attributes, to ferve the purpofes of benevolence? how then can we be ignorant, what worfhip, what fervice, we are to render him? Can we doubt, if we endeavour to have the fame frame of mind, & govern our actions by the fame Law of benevolence, whether we fhall obtain his favour? fince *to imitate him, is to pay him the higheft adoration; and to keep his commandments fhews the higheft veneration.* 'Tis for fuch reafons as thefe, that Dr. *Scot* intirely differs from this learned Author, and fays, * ,, If we truly underftand what ,, God is, we can't but apprehend what worfhip is ,, fuitable to him, from the eternal congruity & pro- ,, portion that there is between things & things, as ,, obvious to the mind, as founds & colours are to ,, the ears & eyes.

*B.* DR. *Clark* owns, that † ,, Obedience to the ,, obligations of Nature, & imitation of the moral at- ,, tributes of God, the wifeft Philofophers eafily knew, ,, was, undoubtedly, the *moft acceptable* fervice to God; & what he infifts upon as neceffary, is only fome external adoration. *A.*

* *Chrift. Life. P. 2. Vol. I. Ch. 6. p. 323.*
† *Pag. 178, 179.*

*A.* But since external adoration can't be perform'd, but by external signs, these must be different in different places; because what are marks of respect in one Country, are marks of disrespect in another, or, at least, look ridiculous.

*B.* The reason that the Dr. gives, why the wisest Men were intirely, & unavoidably ignorant, how God wou'd be acceptably worship'd with external adoration, is, because * *they fell lamentably into the practice of the most foolish Idolatry.*

*A.* Never any before, call'd the worshipping of Idols, the worshipping of the true God, tho' unacceptably. But however, since you lay such stress on this discourse, I shall consider what the Dr. says, to prove his paradox.

„ *Plato*, says he, † after having deliver'd almost di-
„ vine truths, concerning the nature, & attributes of
„ the supreme God, weakly advises Men to worship
„ likewise inferior Gods; nor dar'd to condemn the
„ worshipping even of Statues. -- ‡ And so he spoil'd
„ the best Philosophy in the world, by adding Ido-
„ latry to that worship, which he had wisely, & bravely
„ before prov'd to be due to the Creator of all things.
But cou'd he be intirely, & unavoidably ignorant of, what he had bravely & wisely prov'd?

„ *Socrates*, he says, § superstitiously offer'd a Cock
„ to *Esculapius*, unless it was done in mockery to him,
„ looking on death to be his greatest deliverance: „
But since he doubted what *Socrates* intended, why does he instance in him, as one intirely, and unavoidably ignorant, how God was to be acceptably worshipp'd?

„ *Cicero*, he says, ¶ allow'd Men to continue the
„ Idolatry of their Ancestors, advis'd them to con-
„ form themselves to the superstitious Religion of
„ their Country. -- In which he fondly contradicts
„ himself, by inexcusably complying with the prac-
„ tices of those Men, whom, in many of his writings,
he

* *Pag.* 179. † *Ibid.* ‡ *Pag.* 181. § *Pag.* 179. ¶ *Pag.* 180.

,, he largely, & excellently proves to be extremely ,, foolish, upon the account of those very practices. ,, But does this prove any unavoidable ignorance in *Cicero*, in relation to the worship of the true God? But only that he, as a Philosopher, not only knew, but spoke the truth; tho, as a Priest, he thought fit to dissemble. Perhaps, he suppos'd it not prudent, without some such softning expressions, so plainly to attack the reigning Superstition. But,

SINCE the reasoning of the ancient Philosophers fully shew'd their sense, these reflections might have been spar'd; were it but for the sake of some modern Philosophers, whose philosophical Faith is as little reconcileable with the *Creeds* & *Litanies*, they, as Priests, solemnly repeat, and the *Articles* they as solemnly subscribe, as any thing *Cicero*, the Priest, cou'd say in opposition to *Cicero*, the Philosopher; who describes our moral obligations after so beautiful a manner, and by such plain, and irresistable arguments, shews the necessary connexion between Virtue & Happiness, Vice & Misery, as can't but make us highly delighted with the one, and create in us a just aversion to the other.

THE Dr. had here a fair opportunity, of shewing the absurdity of arguing from what even the best of Men say, when 'tis not safe to talk otherwise. This had been more agreeable to his candor, than taking an handle from hence to expose the Light, & Law of Nature, as well as those great Men (to whom we are infinitely oblig'd, for writing under these disadvantages so freely as they have done) especially *Cicero*, from whom the Fathers have borrow'd their best arguments against Paganism. *Arnobius* says, * that if his Works had been read, as they ought, by the Heathens, there had been no need of Christian Writers. And in answer to those *Gentiles*, who seeing the use the Christians made of them, were for solliciting the

Senate

* *Arnob.* contra *Gent.* l. 3. p. 120.

Senate to burn, or otherwise suppress them: He says, *That were, not to defend the Gods, but to fear the testimony of Truth.* Which Pagan method has not only been us'd often since, by all who fear'd the testimony of truth, to the loss of an immense treasure of learning; but they have improv'd it too, and been for burning of Men, as well as Books; and thereby introduc'd a Superstition more abominable than Paganism. And give me leave to add, that

In Old *Rome*, as long as there was civil liberty, there was an intire liberty of conscience; & even the Priests of the National Church, provided they comply'd with its ceremonies, had no speculative *Creeds*, or *Articles*, to subscribe, but were intirely free to maintain what opinions they pleas'd. Of this, *Cicero* is a remarkable instance; who, in his Book *de Divinatione*, exposes the superstition of his own Countrymen, & ridicules those miracles, with which the Annals of the Church-Priests were fill'd: And he, tho' a Priest himself, every where treats his Brethren with great freedom; and in his address to them, speaking of an ambitious, intreaguing Priest, who wou'd hide his malice under the cover of Religion, (for some such there have been in all Religions,) says, * ,, If *Publius* ,, *Claudius* is to defend his pestilent, & deadly Ministry ,, by the sacred name of divine Religion, when 'tis ,, impossible for him to do it by human equity, 'tis ,, high time to look for other ceremonies, other Ministers of the immortal Gods, & other Interpreters ,, of Religion.,,   But to return,

The Dr. having thus expos'd the Light of Nature, and as he thinks, shewn its undeniable defects in the persons of these Philosophers; demands what grounds our modern Deists have to imagine, that if they themselves had liv'd without the Light of the Gospel, they shou'd have been wiser than *Plato*, *Socrates*, and *Cicero*. But sure no great wisdom is requir'd to know the

* *Orat. pro Domo sua ad Pontifices.* c. I.

the Law of Nature, was it but half as plain, as the Dr. from Bishop *Cumberland*, has represented it; and which no well-meaning *Gentile*, who *did by nature the things contain'd in the Law*, cou'd be ignorant of. And,

I am surpris'd to find the Dr. arguing as if that Law, „ * which is a most perfect Rule to the most perfect „ Being, is not perfect enough for his imperfect „ Creatures; „ tho' their whole perfection consists in imitating him, & governing their actions by the same Rule: A Rule, which, it can't be deny'd, had Mankind govern'd their actions by it, wou'd have render'd them as perfect as their nature was capable of. I shou'd be glad to know, why this Rule has lost its virtue, & will not now render Men as acceptable to God as ever. But cou'd we suppose a God of infinite perfection, might ordain an imperfect, or insufficient Rule, for the actions of his Creatures; or, which comes to the same, afford them no other Light for the discovery of it, but what had such undeniable defects, as made them incapable of knowing their duty; nor was sufficient to hinder them from falling into, and continuing from Age to Age, in a deplorable state of corruption; I wou'd ask, whether God did this knowingly, or ignorantly, not foreseeing the consequences? To suppose the first, is to make God act out of spite, & hatred to his Creatures, in bringing them into being, and making that being a Curse to them: Or if the last, why were not these defects supply'd as soon as discover'd? Or, were they not discover'd by infinite Wisdom till these latter times; & then reveal'd only to a small number, tho' all Mankind had equal need of them? And then too, so imperfectly, that Men have ever since been in continual quarrels, about the meaning of most of those things, which are suppos'd to have been added, to supply the defects of the Law of Nature?

WHAT

* *Pag.* 50.

What human Legiſlator, if he found a defect in his Laws, & thought it for the good of his Subjects to add new Laws, wou'd not promulgate them to all his People? Or, what Parent wou'd act after ſo partial a manner, as the Dr, in a ſelf-confounding ſcheme, ſuppoſes the common Parent of Mankind has done? And not let all his Children know as ſoon as poſſible, what was for their common good? eſpecially, if they were in ſuch a forlorn, & miſerable condition, as he repreſents all Mankind to have been in, almoſt as ſoon as created.

The Dr. very rightly obſerves, that * „ Even „ among Men, there's no earthly Father, but, in thoſe „ things he eſteems his own excellencies, deſires, & „ expects to be imitated by his Children ; how much „ more, ſays he, is it neceſſary, that God, who is in- „ finitely far from being ſubject to paſſions, and va- „ riableneſs, as frail Men are, and has an infinitely „ tenderer, & heartier concern for the happineſs of „ his Creatures, than mortal Men can have for the „ welfare of their Poſterity, muſt deſire to be imi- „ tated by his Creatures in thoſe perfections, which „ are the foundation of his own unchangeable hap- „ pineſs. „  How far this invariableneſs in God, and his great love for his Creatures, is conſiſtent with that ſcheme of things, which the Dr. has hitherto advanc'd, has, I think, been made appear. We will now examine what he adds, to ſhew that God has an infinitely more tender, and hearty concern for the happineſs of his Creatures, than mortal Men can have for the welfare of their Poſterity : What he ſays, is, that † „ both the „ neceſſities of Men, & their natural notions of God „ gave them reaſonable ground to expect, and hope „ for a divine Revelation, to recover Mankind out „ of their univerſally degenerate eſtate, into one ſui- „ table to the original excellence of their nature.

And

And that * „ it was agreeable to the dictates of Na-
„ ture, & right Reason, to hope for such a divine
„ Revelation; † That it is agreeable to the natural
„ hopes & expectations of Men, that is, of right Reason
„ duly improv'd, to suppose God making some par-
„ ticular Revelation of his Will to Mankind. — —
„ And that this was most suitable to the divine attri-
„ butes; „ yet notwithstanding these, and a great
many other fine sayings to the same purpose, he denies
that God was oblig'd to make such a Revelation:
But, with submission, what other reason have we
to say, God is oblig'd to do any one thing whatever,
but that 'tis agreeable to the natural notions we have
of his wisdom & goodness, & to the dictates of Nature & Reason, for him so to do; and if the necessities of Mankind have always been as great, and the
goodness of God always the same, wou'd not these
oblige him to have prescrib'd an immediate remedy to
the disease; & not to have deferr'd it for four thousand
years together, & then apply'd it but to a few, tho'
all had equal need of it? And a need occasion'd
( as the Dr. supposes ) by God himself, in not affording
them any other light, but what was insufficient to
answer the end for which it was giv'n.

*B.* THE Dr. supposes, that this Revelation was not
the effect of God's *Justice*; ‡ for then it must needs
have been giv'n in all Ages, and to all Nations;
*but of mercy, & condescending goodness.*

*A.* CAN a Being be denominated merciful, & good,
who is so only to a few; but cruel, & unmerciful to
the rest? And certainly, all the arguments the Dr. can
urge from the necessities of Mankind, & the abundant
Goodness of God, will equally prove, that this Revelation, did it teach a new Religion, shou'd be universal, as that it shou'd be at all. But,

IF Revelation was absolutely necessary to recover
Mankind, out of their universally degenerate, & corrupted

* *Contents. pag.* 201. † *Pag.* 214. ‡ *Pag.* 215.

rupted ſtate, & replace them in a ſtate ſuitable to the original dignity, and excellency of their nature; and more effectually to do this, there was inſtituted an Order of Men, who were to be, as the Dr. calls them, * *the Inſtruments of conveying extraordinary aſſiſtances for this purpoſe*; muſt not Revelation have had its intended effect; and made Chriſtians, eſpecially where theſe Inſtruments of conveying extraordinary aſſiſtances are in great numbers, and in great authority, much more perfect, & excellent, than Men cou'd poſſibility be, when under times of unavoidable corruption? And yet

The Dr. having taken a large paſſage from *Cicero*, where the Orator very rhetorically deſcribes the great corruptions of his time, & aſſigns the cauſes thereof, makes this remark, † „ *That a livelier deſcription of the* „ *preſent corrupt ſtate of human-nature is not eaſily to* „ *be met with*; „ which, I think, is ſufficiently owning, that human nature at preſent is far from being exalted to ſo high a ſtate of perfection, or in the leaſt mended. And tho' the Dr. frequently quotes *Cicero* for the ſupport of his opinion, yet *Cicero* is far from ſuppoſing any ſuch defect in Nature: For a proof of which, I need only mention theſe two ſhort paſſages. „ ‡ 'Tis „ impoſſible to err, as long as we follow the guidance „ of Nature. -- § There's no Man, who following „ the conduct of Nature, but may arrive at perfection. And the Dr. himſelf quotes a paſſage from him, to ſhew that Nature has not been wanting to declare her mind; ⁋ *Multis ſignis natura declarat quid velit.* And it might be as eaſily ſhewn, he as much miſtakes the meaning of thoſe other Philoſophers he quotes. And indeed, how cou'd any Men, except they had a very abſurd *Hypotheſis* to ſerve, aſſert, that any thing cou'd be Mens duty, they were unavoidably ignorant of? Yet,

A a                          The

THE Dr, to prove this invincible ignorance in the *Gentile* World, has frequent recourfe to the authority of *Lactantius*, a primitive Father, without fhewing that he had a greater regard for truth than other Fathers: And I am afraid the Dr. himfelf feems here not much to regard it, in maiming a fentence of *Lactantius*; * *Maximum itaque argumentum eft, philofophiam neque ad fapientiam tendere, neque ipfam effe fapientiam; quod myfterium ejus, barba tantum celebratur, & pallio.* Whereas the whole Sentence runs thus, † *Non eft ergo fapientia, fi ab hominum cœtu abhorret; quoniam, fi fapientia homini data eft, fine ullo difcrimine omnibus data eft; ut nemo fit prorfus, qui eam capere non poffit. At illi* [ *Philofophi* ] *virtutem humano generi datam fic amplexantur, ut foli omnium publico bonò frui velle videantur; tam invidi, quam fi velint deligare oculos, aut effodere cæteris, ne folem videant. - - Quod fi natura hominis fapientiæ capax eft, oportuit opifices, & rufticos & mulieres, & omnes denique qui humanam formam gerunt, doceri ut fapiant; populumque ex omni lingua, & conditione, & fexu, & ætate conflari.* Then follows what the Dr. quoted.

THIS had been a full anfwer to all the Dr. had taken from him, if not to all the Dr. has faid on this head, & it plainly fhews, this Father here thought, that Wifdom, as it was defign'd for all, was within the reach of all; & that which the loweft of Mankind cou'd not attain, was neither Wifdom, nor Virtue; and that thofe Philofophers, who wou'd confine this univerfal light to themfelves, were as envious, as if they wou'd exclude others from the light of the Sun. And that this alone was a fufficient proof, that their Philofophy confifted only in the beard, & the cloak.

THIS Father afferts nothing here, but what the wifeft of Men had long before own'd, in faying, that ‡ *Wifdom is eafily feen of them that love her, and found*

*of*

* *Pag.* 189. † *Lactant. Inft. Divin. l. 3. c. 25. N. 2-6. Edit. Cellar.* ‡ *Wifd. of Solomon* 6. 12. & 16.

*of such as seek her. — She goes about seeking such as are worthy of her, shews herself favourable to them in the ways, and meeteth them in every thought.* And,

WHAT impartial Man, who has compar'd the former, & present condition of Mankind, can think the World much mended since the times of *Tiberius?* or tho' ever so well vers'd in Church-History, can, from the conduct of Christians, find, that they are arriv'd to any higher state of perfection, than the rest of Mankind; who are suppos'd to continue in their degeneracy, & corruption? What was the opinion of a late eminent Philosopher, as well as Divine, is plain, by his saying, * *Si resurgerent Philosophi & Gentilium sapientes, & perlustrato orbe à nobis quærerent, quid profuerit humano generi religio Christiana, quoad mores & vitæ probitatem? quoad pacem & bonum publicum? nos utique appellatis Barbaros per opprobrium: sed nobis Barbaris quid præstatis vos Christiani?*

Monsieur *Leibnitz*, a great Statesman as well as Philosopher, in comparing the Christians at present, with the Infidels of *China*, does not scruple to give the preference to the latter, in relation to all *moral Virtues;* — and after having said of them, † *Dici enim non potest, quam pulchre omnia ad tranquillitatem publicam, ordinemque hominum inter se, ut quam minimum sibi ipsi incommodent, supra aliarum gentium leges apud Sinenses sint ordinata.* He adds, *Certe talis nostrarum rerum mihi videtur esse conditio, gliscentibus in immensum corruptelis, ut propemodum necessarium videatur missionarios Sinensium ad nos mitti, qui Theologia naturalis usum praxinque nos doceant, quemadmodum nos illis mittimus qui Theologiam eos doceant revelatam.* And the learned *Huetius* tells us, that ‡ ,, There's such a constant agreement between the *Chinese* themselves, ,, & their neighbours, as they seem to be all but one ,, Family. ,, And,

A a 2　　　　　　　Na-

* *Burnet de Fide & Offic. Christianorum. p. 98.*
† *Prefatio ad novissima Sinica.* ‡ *Alnetan quæst. l. 3. p. 419.*

*Navarette*, a *Chinese* Missionary, agrees with *Leibnitz*, & says, that * ,, It is God's special Providence, that ,, the *Chineses* did not know what is done in *Chri-* ,, *stendom*; for if they did, there wou'd be never a ,, Man among them, but wou'd spit in our faces. ,, And he adds, with respect to the manners of those *European* Christians, who come into the *East Indies*, & of the Converts made by the *Missionaries*; ,, That ,, there are few converted in those parts, where they ,, converse with the *Europeans*; and when it happens ,, that any are converted, they prove so bad, it were ,, better they had never been baptiz'd. And I am afraid, 'tis much the same in relation to the *West Indies*. And,

Bishop *Kidder* says of Christians in general, ,, That were a wise Man to choose his Religion by ,, the lives of those who profess it, perhaps, Christia- ,, nity wou'd be the last Religion he wou'd choose. ,, And who, that has been abroad, and compar'd the Lives of Believers & Unbelievers, does not say the same things?

And Dr. *Clark* himself, in the Discourse we are now considering, has sufficiently prov'd, that Man is naturally a social Creature, full of benevolence, pity, & tenderness; and he says, that † ,, Reason, which ,, is the proper nature of Man, can never lead Men ,, to any thing else than universal love, & benevolence; *and that* ,, wars, hatred, & violence can never arise, ,, but from extreme corruptions. ,, Tho' there's no part of Natural Religion, but highly tends to improve this social, and benign temper; yet alas! we find, that what, in most places, passes for the Christian Religion, if not the chiefest part of it, has transform'd this social, & benign Creature into one fierce, & cruel; and made him act with such rage & fury against those, who never did, or design'd him the least injury, as cou'd not have enter'd into the hearts of Men to conceive,

* *Navarrette*'s Acco. of *China*, in *Churchill*'s Collection of Voyag. V. 1. l. 2. c. 13. † *Pag.* 107.

ceive, even tho' they were in the Dr's unavoidable
state of degeneracy & corruption.

IF People are once persuaded, that what their Priests
call *Schism, Heresy, Infidelity*, &c. tho' held with the
utmost sincerity, are damnable Sins, it wants not much
skill to persuade them to hate those mortally, whom
God, they are already persuaded, will hate to all eternity; and that, as they regard the preservation of the
Orthodox Faith, & the saving their own Souls, & the
Souls of all that are dear to them, they ought to take
the most effectual methods to root out all such damnable opinions. 'Tis upon this common principle,
that the *Inquisition* is establish'd; and the *Papists*, to do
them justice, act up to it; tho' perhaps, even among
them, there are some Lay-men, where Nature is too
hard for Principles.

IF once pernicious opinions are believ'd to be contain'd in any Revelation, they will have the same effect, as if really there. Has not the belief of the iu-
dicial power of the Clergy, as to the next world,
and their independent power in this world, done the
same mischief, as if they had really been contain'd in
Scripture? And if they, who maintain these, & other
as vile maxims, have got possession of Mens Minds,
by ingrossing (not to mention other arts) the teaching
the young, as well as instructing the old; what less
than a new Revelation can expose their expositions,
or explain away their explanations of the present Revelation, which have prov'd more fatal to the happiness of Mankind, than all the superstitions of the *Pagan*
World. Had the *Bees* speech & reason, wou'd they,
think you, from age to age, have continu'd to give
the best part of their honey to such haranguing Drones,
who for the most part, employ'd their talents, to set
not only Hive against Hive, but the *Bees* of the same
Hive against one another, for such things as had no
other tendency, than to make the idle Drones lord it
over the industrious Bees? But not to deviate,

We

We have no great reason to hope, it will ever be so well with Mankind, but that there will always be too much room for such arguments, as the Dr. urges from the corruptions of Mankind, for new Revelations. Have not Impostors always made use of this plea? Was it not on the carnality of the primitive Orthodox Christians, that the spiritual *Montanus* founded his new Gospel; which divided the Christian World for no small time, & made the celebrated *Tertullian* say; * That ,, the Law & Prophets were to be look'd on as ,, the Infancy, & the Gospel, as it were, the Youth, ,, but that there was no compleat perfection to be ,, found, but in the instruction of the Holy Ghost, ,, who spoke by *Montanus*.

AND it was the ill lives of the Professors of Christianity, as 'tis own'd by Christian as well as Arabick Writers, which prepar'd the way for that success which *Mahomet* met with, whose Religion, as it gain'd in a short time, more Proselites than any other, so it is still gaining ground: For which Father *Maracci*, who has so well translated, and makes such just reflections on the *Alchoran*, gives this odd reason: † *Habet nimirum hæc Superstitio* ( Mahumedana ) *quicquid plausibile, ac probabile in Christiana Religione reperitur, & quæ Natura legi ac lumini consentanea videntur. Mysteria illa Fidei nostræ, quæ primo aspectu, incredibilia, & impossibilia apparent; & præcipue, quæ nimis ardua humanæ natura censentur, penitus excludit. Hinc moderni Idolorum Cultores, facilius ac promptius* Saracenicam, *quam* Evangelicam *Legem amplectuntur.* But,

THE Dr. is so far from solving the difficulties attending this scheme, that he quits it, and artfully introduces a new scene: and tho' he had before laid it down as a most evident truth, that God does nothing by meer will & arbitrariness, yet this NEW Hypothesis is wholly built on it, in supposing, that in these latter times,

---

* See *Reeve's* Prelim. Disc. to *Tertul.* Apologet. p. 149.
‡ *Marrac. Pref. ad Prodrom. p.* 4.

times, God intended to give some Men, without regard to their merits, an higher degree of happiness than he did the rest; and to shew how consistent this is with Reason, he says, * ,, As God was not oblig'd ,, to make all his Creatures equal, or to make Men ,, Angels, or to endow all Men with the same capa- ,, cities & faculties, so he was not bound to make ,, all Men capable of the *same degree*, or the *same kind* ,, of happiness; or to afford all Men the very same ,, *means* & *opportunities* of obtaining it.

*B.* But how comes this to be shifting the scene, & introducing a new Hypothesis?

*A.* Because his former supposes Men living & dying in a deprav'd, corrupted, degenerate, & impious state, incapable of reformation; whereas in this all Men are allow'd to have, in general, the means of attaining to a certain degree of happiness hereafter; whilst Christians alone have in particular the means & opportunites of gaining this higher degree, & kind of happiness.

Tho' infinite variety of Creatures, & consequently inequality, is necessary to shew the great extent of the divine goodness, which plainly appears from the beautiful, and well form'd System of the World, & the due subordination of things, all contriv'd for the happiness of the whole; yet sure, it does not from thence follow, that God will not either here, or hereafter, bestow on the rational Creation, all the happiness their nature is capable of, since that was the end why God gave it them.

Can God, who equally beholds all the Dwellers on Earth, free from partiality and prejudice, make some People his favourites, without any consideration of their merits, and merely because they believe certain opinions taught in that Country where they happen to be born; while others, far the greater number, shall, from Age to Age, want this favour, not upon

Aa 4                                          the

the account of their demerits, but becaufe deftin'd to live in places, where God, who always acts from motives of infinite Wifdom & Goodnefs, thought it beft to conceal from them all fuch opinions. What can more reprefent God as an arbitrary, and partial Being, than thus to fuppofe, that he vouchfafes not to afford, the greateft part of Mankind, the happinefs, of which himfelf had made them capable?

MUST not every one perceive, that this narrow notion is inconfiftent with the character of a Being of unlimited benevolence? Is not infinite Goodnefs always the fame? How then can it, in thefe laft days, make fuch inequality among Men? Is not this fuppofing inconftancy in the divine conduct? Is not this notion repugnant to the natural idea we have of the divine Goodnefs? As likewife to thofe exprefs texts of Scripture, which declare *God is no refpecter of Perfons*; that *Every one, of what Nation foever, fhall be rewarded according to his works?* And that *Men are accepted according to what they have, & not according to what they have not?*

IF God, as the Dr. contends, will judge Men as they are accountable, that is, as they are rational, muft not the judgment of the moft righteous Judge, hold an exact proportion to the ufe they have made of their Reafon? And if Mens ftate in this life be a ftate of probation, and for that caufe they are made moral Agents, capable of knowing good from evil, & confequently, of doing every thing that's fit to be done, muft they not be dealt with hereafter, according to the ufe they have made of their moral agency?

HOW can Men be fure, if God acts thus partially, that this partiality may not even now be in favour of other countries, than thofe they live in, & of other notions, which not flowing from the Nature & Reafon of Things, we may be wholly unacquainted with? If Men may lofe any part of God's favour for impoffibilities, or not obferving fuch Rules as he never

gave

gave them, where shall we stop? Cou'd I think God so partial & prejudic'd, as most Sects, for their own sakes, represent him, how cou'd I admire, love, and adore him, as I ought? Nav, how can any, who have such unworthy notions of God, be certain, God's prejudice and partiality will be in their favour? If you admit any one imperfection in God, how can you be sure of his veracity immutability, or any other perfection whatever?

Tho' Dr. *Clark* contends for what terminates in this gross partiality, as if the whole of Christianity was founded on it; yet some of our Divines, of the first rank too, are of a different opinion; from two of which, I'll give you the following quotations.

,, God's Goodness & Mercy (*says* Mr. Wharton) *
,, were, from all Ages, equal & uniform, his Justice
,, always impartial and universal, in excluding none
,, from his favour, but for reasons common to them
,, with all Mankind. — The universality, & impar-
,, tiality of the divine Justice & Favour, is founded
,, on the excellency of the divine Nature; which can't
,, be suppos'd to want that, which above all is ne-
,, cessary for the government of the World, impartial
,, Justice in the dispensing of rewards & punishments.
,, — All Men were equally created by God, and if
,, we respect that alone, all have an equal title to his
,, favour. — Otherwise we cou'd not but conceive
,, injustice in God; nor were it possible to reconcile
,, such a partiality with his infinite excellency. The
,, reason why *God is no respecter of persons*, is said to be,
,, because *There is no iniquity with the Lord.* † All
,, reasonable preference of one Person to another,
,, must be founded on some just cause; otherwise it
,, wou'd be trifling, & fond, nay, even unjust, and
,, foolish. — Far be it from us, to imagine any such
,, imperfections in God, in him there is no variableness,

Aa 5 or

* *Wharton's* Vol. of Serm. pag. 305. &c.
† 2 *Chron.* 23. 49.

,, or shadow of change. -- He ever proceeds upon
,, fixed, and immoveable principles, which equally
,, serve for all actions & causes. -- God has fix'd
,, most impartial Laws of government, which uni-
,, versally affect all the members of Mankind. -- It is
,, so pleasing a delusion, to fancy themselves dear to
,, God in an extraordinary manner, & for unaccoun-
,, table reasons, that 'tis no wonder many have been
,, tempted to entertain such a charming error. - -
,, This seduc'd the *Jews*. -- This prejudice has cor-
,, rupted great numbers of Christians. -- Is God the
,, God of the *Jews* & *Christians* only? Is he not the
,, God of the *Gentiles* also? Are not his Attributes
,, always unalterable, & the influence of these equally
,, deriv'd down to all his Creatures?

THAT celebrated Preacher, Dr. *Ibbott*, affirms,
that * ,, 'Tis not our being of any Nation, or any Sect,
,, members of any particular Church, or Society,
,, that will intitle us to God's favour; but our working
,, the work of God, living up to that light & know-
,, ledge which he has afforded us; and being most
,, punctual, & exact in the discharge of those moral
,, duties, which all Mankind, who have any true
,, notions of God and Religion, have ever thought
,, themselves oblig'd to. ,, -- *Again*, † Wherever Men
,, fear God, and love one another, they will be ac-
,, cepted without any regard to their country, or na-
,, tion; their tribe, or family; for this is what God
,, would bring all People to, *from the rising of the Sun*
,, *unto the going down thereof*. This is that inward
,, temper of mind, & that outward practice of life,
,, which he requires, & which, wherever he meets it,
,, will find acceptance with him.

THE contrary is a notion, which lays a foundation
for everlasting persecutions: for if Men flatter themselves, that they, upon the account of their particular
systems, are the Favourites of Heaven, & that others
shall

* *Serm. Vol.* I. *pag.* 207.    † *Pag.* 211.

shall want, even to eternity, many degrees of their happiness; will not that oblige them, as they love their Children, Families, Friends, Neighbours, & Relations, to use any means, come into any persecuting measures, to prevent such opinions from spreading, as they imagine, wou'd deprive them of that degree of happiness, which otherwise they might ever enjoy? And is it not chiefly owing to this absurdity, that even the most moderate of the different Sects, are far from treating one another with that benevolence, which the common ties of humanity require.

DID Men believe, that all who were equally sincere, were equally acceptable to God, there cou'd be no pretence for the least partiality, much less for persecution, either positive, or negative. Nor cou'd any Man love another the less, for the widest difference in opinions. And then of course, Mens indignation wou'd be wholly bent against immorality, discoverable by the Light of Nature, which, now alas! is but too often protected by zeal for mere speculations.

THIS principle, and this alone, wou'd cause universal love, & benevolence, among the whole Race of Mankind; and did it prevail, must soon produce a new, & glorious face of things; or, in the Scripture phrase, *a new Heaven, & a new Earth*: & wou'd free Men from that miserable perplexity, in which the fear of mistaking in speculative matters involves them.

WHAT assurance, upon any other ground, can even the generality of Christians have, that they do not err most dangerously; when they consider what divisions there have been, from the beginning, among Christians about such points? And that the Guides of their own Churches, even the most able, tho' they agree in saying, *Their Fundamentals are plain*, have not always the same set of *Fundamentals*, & when they have, widely differ in explaining them: Can they, I say, who consider this, be certain, that it is not the fear of loss of preferment, or some other political reasons, that keep up any sort
of

of verbal agreement among them, even in things
own'd to be of the highest consequence; and which,
as such, are plac'd in their *Creeds & Articles?* Consider
with yourself, what comfort, what satisfaction, it must
give a Man, especially, on his death-bed, to be certain, he is not accountable for any errors in opinion,
if he has, according as his circumstances permited, done
his best to discover the Will of God.

D r. *Prideaux* says, * ,, The main arguments *Ma-*
,, *homet* made use of, to delude Men into the impo-
,, sture, were his promises, & his threats, being those
,, which easily work on the affections of the Vulgar.
If the bulk of Mankind are so easily deluded by threats
and promises, when join'd to opinions as absurd as
those of *Mahomet*, can there be any other way to
avoid their being deluded in proportion to the greatness
of those promises & threats, but by annexing them,
not to any set of opinions, but to sincerity & insin-
cerity? For here, the only effect they can have, is to
make Men judge without prejudice, & partiality.

T h e present Bishop of *Sarum* says, † ,, God is just,
,, equal, and good; and as sure as he is, so he can't
,, put the salvation and happiness of any Man, upon
,, what he has not put it in the power of any Man
,, on Earth to be intirely satisfy'd of. ,, And much less
*say I*, can a just, equal, & good Cod put the salvation,
or any part of the happiness of the greatest part of
Mankind, upon that, of which, instead of being intirely satisfy'd, they are intirely ignorant. Is it possible,
a mistaken Christian can have a title to God's favour,
& a Man of another Religion not have the same title,
when that sincerity, on which the title depends, is
common to them both? ‡ ,, If the favour of God,
*as the Bishop says*, ,, follows sincerity, as such; & equally
,, follows every degree of sincerity; ,, must not Men
of all Religions whatever, if equally sincere, have the
same

* Life of *Mahomet*. pag. 25. Edit. 7. 8vo.
‡ *Preserv. pag.* 78.        ‡ *Ibid. pag.* 91.

same title to be equally favour'd by God? Who is the only infallible Judge of their sincerity, in the use of those talents, whether great, or small, he has endow'd them with.

Mr. *Chillingworth* was so far from thinking involuntary errors crimes, that he thought it criminal to ask pardon for them; and says, * ,, That wou'd be to ,, impute to God the strange Tyranny of requiring ,, bricks, were he has giv'n no straw; of expecting ,, to gather, where he has not strow'd; to reap, where ,, he sow'd not; of being offended with us for not ,, doing, what he knew we cou'd not do.,, And,

The *Romanists* themselves, tho' they own the common People can have but an imperfect knowledge, of what their infallible Church requires; yet say, that ,, a disposition to receive, & an endeavour to under- ,, stand what it teaches, is sufficient.,, And shall not the *Protestants* allow as much to such a disposition, in relation to the will of God, as the *Papists* do, to the will of Man? But since there are some, to whom these notions about sincerity, will appear shocking; for their sakes, I will quote a Divine, whom they have in a manner idoliz'd: I mean the famous Mr. *Lesley*, who says, † ,, *In the beginning God created Man, & left him* ,, *in the hands of his own Counsel.* (*Ecclef.* 15. 14.) ,, He set life & Death, Blessing & Cursing for him to ,, choose; and God will bless, or curse him, according ,, to what he has set before him; whether by Revela- ,, tion, or his own natural reason only: And who is ,, Judge of this but God, who always knows the sin- ,, cerity of any Man's intentions, & what endeavours ,, he has us'd towards the right informing his Judgment?

In a word, this is so evident a truth, that there are none, but who, with the Bishop of *London*, say, ‡ ,, Christianity requires no further favour, than a fair ,, & impartial inquiry into the grounds, & doctrines of

* *Answer to the Pref. of Charity maintain'd. S.* 16.
† *Lesley* of private judgm. p. 221. ‡ *Past. Leter. p.* 54.

,, of it; ,, even while they are defigning the further favours of *Fines, Pillories,* & *imprifonment,* &c. But to return to the Dr.

I wou'd be glad to know, whether the greater degree of happinefs, from which Dr. *Clark* wou'd exclude the reft of Mankind, belongs to all thofe innumerable Sects, that go under the name of Chriftians; or to one Sect, by virtue of its peculiar fundamentals; or elfe to all Chriftians, who, tho' ever fo much miftaken, fincerely endeavour to find out the Will of God? If the Dr. fays the latter, he can't think this favour depends on any fet of notions, but on fincerity, & confequently, muft equally belong to all that are equally fincere. But allowing that Chriftians are to be rewarded above others, equally fincere, yet if they are likewife fubject to be punifh'd above others for their miftakes, even about fuch abftrufe notions, as divide the moft eminent Men of the fame moft eminent Church, fuch as Dr. *Waterland,* & Dr. *Clark;* nay, Dr. *Clark,* in fome editions of his Book, & himfelf in other editions; where then, is the great advantage of the Dr's *Hypothefis?* But,

I F Chriftians are to be punifh'd hereafter, for not obferving fuch things, as the happinefs of Mankind in general does not depend on, God, certainly, is far from being partial in their favour; if not, where is the difference?

*B.* B u t does not the Dr. raife an argument, from Mens different capacities and abilities in this life, for their having different degrees of happinefs hereafter?

*A.* T h o' Men here have different capacities, yet if that depends on bodily organs, all Souls may in Heaven have equal capacities. But even this fuppofition will not ferve his purpofe, except the wifeft of the Philofophers had not abilities equal to the meaneft Chriftian; and fo (allowing a proportion between happinefs & abilities) were naturally incapable of the fame degree, or kind of happinefs. But,

T H E

The Dr. himself seems conscious of the weakness, even of this new *Hypothesis*; since he, after he had us'd it, to get rid of a troublesome objection, straight quits it in saying, * ,, That as no Man ever deny'd, ,, but that the benefit of Christ's death extended back- ,, ward, to those who liv'd before his appearance in ,, the world, so no one can prove, but the same bene- ,, fit may extend itself forward to those, who never ,, heard of his appearance, tho' they liv'd after it. ,, If both these, tho' knowing nothing of Christ, or his death, reap the benefit of his death; what more can the most perfect Believer expect? So that even on this supposition, the Dr. must have own'd, that all Men, living up to that light God has giv'n them, are upon a level in relation to their future happiness.

And indeed, if Sinners, since the coming of Christ are not to be sav'd without repentance & amendment, & Sinners, at all times, were to be sav'd on these terms, or else cou'd not be sav'd at all; must not repentance & amendment, which suppose a knowledge of what was to be repented of, & amended, put all Mankind, at all times, upon a level, with relation to their future happiness? Can any thing be more evident, than that, if doing evil is the only foundation of God's displea- sure, ceasing to do evil, & doing the contrary, must take away that displeasure. As long as Men continue in their sins, they must continue the proper objects of God's resentment; but when they, forsaking their sins, act a part suitable to their rational nature, they of course become the proper objects of his approbation. And this, sure, can't be deny'd, except you suppose, Christ, who *came not to call the righteous, but sinners to repentance*, propos'd some other way of reconciling them to God, than by persuading them to *bring forth fruits meet for repentance*; or, in other words, by obli- ging them to live up to the eternal, & universal Law of Righteousness.

Tho'

* *Pag* 270.

THO the Dr. says no more than our Articles affirm, *viz.* that * „the oblation of Chrift once made, „ is that perfect redemption, propitiation, and fatis-„ faction for the fins of the whole World, both ori-„ ginal, & actual; ,, yet I wifh the Dr. had been more explicit, & told us, what benefit thofe who never heard of Chrift's appearance, cou'd gain by his death.

*B.* THE Dr. fays, † that „ Chrift dy'd, to fhew God's „ irreconcileable hatred to fin, and to vindicate the „ honour of his Laws.

*A.* THESE reafons, fure, cou'd never influence thofe, who never heard of Chrift; or, if they had, perhaps, wou'd have been fo perverfe, as not to imagine, that pardoning the guilty, & punifhing the innocent, cou'd either fhew irreconcileable enmity to guilt, or love for innocence; and perhaps, govern'd by prejudices, might think very odly of a King, who, tho' he freely pardon'd his repenting Rebels, yet fhou'd caufe his moft loyal, & only Son to be put to death, to fhew his hatred to rebellion, and to vindicate the honour of thofe Laws, which forbid putting an innocent Perfon to death; or any Perfon to be any way inftrumental to his own death, much more to facrifice himfelf. Cou'd thefe Philofophers, who did not imagine any virtue in facrificing of beafts, ‡ to wafh away the fins of Men, eafily conceive, a human facrifice, which they believ'd human-nature abhorr'd, to be an expiation for fins? Or, that fins freely pardon'd, cou'd want any expiation? Or, that all was mere mercy, and pure forgivenefs, after a full equivalent paid, and adequate fatisfaction giv'n?

*B.* THIS, indeed, feems to me as great a miftery, as that the fame God fhou'd receive fatisfaction from, and give fatisfaction to the fame God; and that the fame God, who thus receives, and gives fatisfaction, fhou'd neither give, or receive any fatisfaction; fince the Holy Ghoft, the fame God with God the Father,

&

* *Article* 31.  † *Pag.* 259, 260.  ‡ *Pag.* 206. 287.

& God the Son, neither gives, or receives any satisfaction.

*A.* THO' I have omitted several things, which
well deserve to be criticis'd; yet, I think, I have said
enough to shew the inconsistency of the Dr's scheme;
and the weakness of all those arguments, by which he
attempts to destroy the all-sufficiency, absolute perfection, plainness, & perspicuity of the Law of Nature,
which he had before so fully demonstrated. Who
cou'd expect, after we had been told, that as God governs all his own actions by the eternal Rule of Reason,
so all his rational Creatures are oblig'd to govern themselves in all theirs, by the same eternal Rule: A Rule
too, own'd to be so plain, that the *Reason of all Men
every where naturally, & necessarily assents to it :* Who,
I say, after these, & a number of other such expressions,
cou'd imagine, that all this shou'd be unsaid, and the
utmost art employ'd, to shew the imperfection, insufficiency, obscurity, & uncertainty of the Light of
Nature; and that by reason of its many defects, all
Mankind, from age to age, were in an unavoidable
state of corruption? And that, even those few Men,
who made it their business to study Natural Religion,
were intirely ignorant of some doctrines, absolutely
necessary for the reformation of Mankind? Nay, that
they were (here the Dr, perhaps, describes his own
conduct;) ,, like Men wandring in the wide sea,
,, without knowing whither to go, or which way to
,, take, or having any Guide to conduct them? ,,
And, in support of his *Hypothesis,* make no scruple to
represent God, not alike good at all times & places;
& to have acted for many ages with so little foresight,
as to give Mankind no other light for their conduct,
than such, as disabl'd them from answering that end,
for which it was giv'n: And afterward, with so little
goodness, as when he saw this defect, still to continue
the greatest part of Mankind in that dismal state of
darkness, in which all before were involv'd? And them,

after

after he had made the moft of this ftrange *Hypothefis,* to quit it for the fake of another, no lefs ftrange? And, tho' he had declar'd, that *God does nothing in the government of the World, out of mere will & arbitrarinefs*; yet to fuppofe, that God acts thus with his rational Creatures; and without regard to merit, arbitrarily defigns Chriftians a greater degree of happinefs than others? And at laft quit too, even this *Hypothefis,* by fuppofing all Men, tho' they never heard of Chrift's death, to be upon a level, in relation to any benefits receiv'd from it? And, I may add,

WHEN Men confider, how often this Difcourfe has been reprinted, & review'd, by a Man, own'd to be as great a Mafter of Reafon, as ever appear'd in print, & withal, both a fubtil *Mataphyfician,* and excellent *Mathematician*; an acute *Philofopher*, as well as a deep *Divine*; one, who never fails to exhauft the fubject he handles: when Men, I fay, confider all this, will they not be apt to cry? *Si pergama dextra,* &c. *

B. I muft own, you have produc'd feveral weighty Arguments , many of them new, at leaft to me; to prove that Religion was, & always muft be invariably the fame. But fince you go out of the common road, & the path you take, is fcarce at all trodden , you muft expect, it will be faid of you, as of fome modern Writers, that you are better at pulling down , than building up.

*A.* WHEN any notion, in defence of which people have little to fay, is attack'd, they ufually cry , *Why will you pull down , except you build up?* When in reality, error muft be remov'd, in order to make way for truth: You muft pull down one, before you can build up the other. But here, I hope, there's no room for that objection ; becaufe, as nothing but rubbifh is remov'd, nothing but what is either inconfiftent with, or, at leaft, takes off from, the full exercife of piety, & virtue; fo every thing is advanc'd, which tends to
pro-

* *Virgil. Æn.* 2. 291.

promote the honour of God, & the happiness of human societies. And, I may add, that as in attacking the superstition of any one party, all the rest wou'd think me in the right; so here all parties, without coming into the *Hypotheses* of their adversaries, may, by equally receding from those arbitrary things they have brought into Religion, come to an happy agreement.

For my part, I think, there's none who wish well to Mankind, but must likewise wish this *hypothesis* to be true: & can there be a greater proof of its truth, than that it is, in all its parts, so exactly calculated for the good of Mankind, that either to add to, or take from it, will be to their manifest prejudice. And,

If, as Bishop *Chandler* remarks, * ,, They are de-,, ceivers, & true enemies to Mankind, who do not ,, teach a Religion most worthy of God, most friendly ,, to society, most helpful to government, and most ,, beneficial to every individual; ,, what need we run to his *Jewish Rabbies*, or any other *Rabbies*, to discover this true Religion? If 'tis by this test, that our Reason must judge of the truth of all Religion, are not they the best Friends to Mankind, who teach such a Religion, without the least mixture of those arbitrary things, that have caus'd such fatal contentions among Christians? And which, at the best, *serve only to divert them from attending to a Religion most worthy of God, most friendly to society, most helpful to government, and most beneficial to every individual*; and withal, is a Religion, as I hope, is here fully prov'd, founded upon such demonstrable principles, as are obvious to the meanest capacity, and most effectually prevents the growth, both of Scepticism & Enthusiasm.

I intirely agree with this Right Reverend Father, that ,, Christianity in itself, stripp'd of the additions ,, that policy, mistake, & the circumstances of time, ,, have made to it, is a most holy Religion; ,, but I

may

* *Introduct. to Def. of Christ. pag. 2,*

may add, that by reason of these additions, it is become, in most places, a most unholy Religion. And can we hope to get rid of these additions, but by bringing them to the Bishop's own test? I might here ask him, Who are they, that have brought in, & still defend these additions to Christianity; which, as all fair & candid Writers own, have giv'n great advantages to its Adversaries?

What good Christian is not ready to join with the excellent Dr. *Sykes*, in wishing, * ,, That Christians ,, wou'd not vend under the name of Evangelical ,, Truths, the absurd, and contradictory schemes of ,, ignorant, or wicked Men? That they wou'd part ,, with the load of rubbish, which makes thinking ,, Men sink under the weight, & gives too great a ,, handle to Infidelity? † The hands of Friends to ,, Christianity, *says he*, have been much embarrass'd, ,, thro' fear of speaking against local truths; and its ,, Adversaries have so successfully attack'd those ,, weaknesses, that Christianity itself has been deem'd ,, indefensible; when, in reality, the follies of Christians alone have been so. ,,   If this be true, have I not shewn some resolution, in daring to attack the darling weaknesses, and follies of false Christians; in proving that true Christianity is so far from being indefensible, that it carries its own evidences with it; or in other words, all its Doctrines plainly speak themselves to be the will of an infinitely wise, & good God; as being *most friendly to society, most helpful to government, & most beneficial to every individual*; or, in one word, free from all Priest-craft.

B. There's one objection which will always stick; you will be represented as an affecter of novelty; & that 'tis pride & vain-glory, which makes you go out of the common road.

*A.*

*A.* Th A - is a reflection all muſt expect, who endeavour to reform any prevailing abuſes. They little underſtand human-nature, who do not ſee, that novelty, in this caſe, can only ſerve to make a Man deſpis'd by the Majority, for his ignorance, in not being able to diſcover that truth, which they, at firſt ſight, clearly perceive; as well as hated by them, for propagating falſe Doctrine, & inhumanly treated for it, if it claſhes (& where does not Reformation claſh) with the intereſt of a certain ſet of Men, who have two thirds of Mankind, *viz.* the *bigots* and *immoral*, intirely at their devotion. But,

I am ſo far from being a *Novelist*, that all, except where they diſagree with themſelves, muſt agree with me. Are not all of my ſentiments, who own, that their Revelation contains all things worthy of having God for its Author? For that ſuppoſes, that Reaſon, antecedently to Revelation, can tell them what is, or is not worthy of having God for its Author. And do not all recede from Revelation, or, which is the ſame, recede from the plain, obvious, grammatical conſtruction of its words, whenever that, in the leaſt point, recedes from the Religion of Nature & Reaſon? Which being, *as Dr.* Prideaux *owns*, wrote in the hearts of every one of us from the creation; is * ,, the touch-,, ſtone of all Religion; & that, if the Goſpel varies ,, from it in any particular, or in the minuteſt cir-,, cumſtance is contrary to its Righteouſneſs, that is ,, ſtrong enough to deſtroy the whole cauſe, & make ,, all things elſe that can be ſaid for its ſupport, totally ,, ineffectual. ,, Which ſuppoſes, we can't judge of the truth of any Revelation, till we apply to it the touchſtone of all Religion, & ſee whether it agrees with that in all particulars. And do not all, without regard to the plain meaning of the words, in interpreting the precepts of the Goſpel (which are, for the moſt part, deliver'd in general, undetermin'd, & very

* *See pag.* 51, 52. *where the paſſages are as large.*

often, hyperbolical terms) fo explain, limit, & reftrain thefe Precepts, as to make them agreeable to the touch-ftone of all Religion, the Nature, & Reafon of Things, for fear, that otherwife they might depreciate morality? And in this cafe, they, as 'tis allow'd, are the beft Interpreters, who moft recede from the *killing Letter*. And is not this, in effect, faying with the prefent Bifhop of *Bangor*, * ,, That the Gofpel is a Republication of ,, the Law of Nature; & its Precepts declarative of ,, that original Religion, which is as old as the Creation. And, ,, 'Tis as reafonable to fuppofe, that three angles ,, of a triangle fhould be equal to two right ones in ,, one age, and unequal in another, as to fuppofe, ,, that the duties of Religion fhould differ in one age, ,, from what they were in another, the habitudes, ,, and relations from which they flow continuing al- ,, ways the fame.

The principles I maintain are fo evident, that they who are introducing things in oppofition to them, yet muft own their force. Dare any fay, that God is an arbitrary Being, and his Laws not founded on the eternal Reafon of Things: even while they are con-tending for his acting arbitrarily, and giving us fuch Laws as are founded on mere will & pleafure? Will any maintain, that our reafoning faculties were not giv'n us, to diftinguifh between good & evil, Reli-gion and Superftition? Or that they will not anfwer the end for which they were giv'n?

Will any affirm, that the nature of God is not eternally the fame? Or that the nature of Man is chang'd? Or that the relations God & Man ftand in to one another, are not always the fame; nay, even while they are making alterations in thefe relations, by fuppofing new Laws, & new Duties?

If all own, that God, at no time, cou'd have any motive to give Laws to Mankind, but for their good; & that he is, at all times, equally good, &, at all times,

acts

* *See the Quotation at large, pag.* 69. *&c.*

acts upon the same motives, must they not own with me, except they are inconsistent with themselves, that his Laws, at all times, must be the same? And that the good of Mankind is the test, the *criterion*, or the internal evidence, by which we are to judge of all his Laws? But,

IF, after all, I am still criminal, it must be in not owning, that God created the greatest part of Mankind to be damn'd; or, which is the same, made such things necessary to their salvation, as they were incapable of knowing? And in my asserting, that * *God is a Rewarder of those, who diligently seek him*, tho' they do not seek him under the direction of this, or that set of Men, who, provided they can make themselves necessary *here*, care not who they damn *hereafter*. And thus,

IN believing with St. *Peter*, † that *God is no Respecter of Persons, but in every Nation he that feareth him and worketh righteousness, is accepted with him*. And with St. *Paul*, ‡ that *the* Gentiles *do by Nature the things contained in the Law*; And that § *God will render to every Man* (whether Believer, or Unbeliever) *according to his deeds*; And that ¶ *the Grace of God, which bringeth salvation, --- teaching us, --- we should live soberly, righteously, & godly in this present World* ( which takes in the whole of our duty ) *has appear'd to all Men*, and at all times. And

IN believing with our Saviour, that ✠ *the Whole need not a Physician*, and that * *the Doctrine he taught* shews itself to be *the Will of God*, and that he *did not speak of himself*, and in believing the description, that God himself gives of the New Covenant, † *I will put my Laws into their minds, & write them in their hearts: -- ‡ They shall not teach every Man his Neighbour. -- They shall all know me from the least to the greatest*.

B b 4                    IN

In a word, All are forc'd to own these sentiments I contend for, except the *Anthropomorphites*; they, indeed, said, that *Fallible Reason must give place to infallible Revelation*; or in Dr. *Waterland*'s words, *
,, That to advance Natural Light, that is, *Pagan*
,, darkness, in opposition to Scripture evidence, is
,, setting up human Conjectures above divine Truths: And that, since the Scripture so frequently imputes human parts, and passions to God, we ought not to doubt of it; only because we can't reconcile it with that Philosophy, which the bulk of Mankind, for whom the Scripture was chiefly wrote, are intirely ignorant of.

In our next Conference (it being high time to put an end to this) I shall shew you, that all Mankind, *Jews, Gentiles, Mahometans,* &c. agree, in owning the sufficiency of the Law of Nature, to make Men acceptable to God; and that the Primitive Christians believ'd, there was an exact agreement between *Natural & Reveal'd Religion*, and that the excellency of the latter, did consist in being a Republication of the former.

For the present, take these few authorities: ,, If, says the renowned *Origen*, † ,, we admit the judgment
,, of God to be just, we must acknowledge, that there
,, can be no ground for the punishment of Sinners,
,, unless the common conceptions of all Men, are suf-
,, ficient to give them a sound understanding in the
,, duties of Morality. And, therefore, it is not to be
,, thought strange, that those things which God has
,, taught us by the Prophets, & by our Saviour, were
,, implanted by him in the minds of all Men; that so
,, every Man, having had the intention, & meaning
,, of the Law written in his own heart, shou'd be left
,, without excuse before the Divine Tribunal. And,

Lac-

* Remarks on Dr. *Clark*'s Exposit. of the Ch. Catechism. p. 66.  † *Origen contra Celsum. l. 1. p. 6.*

*Lactantius*, the most eloquent of the Fathers, seems ravish'd with the description *Cicero* gives of the Law of Nature; and therefore, chooses to express his own sense of it, in the words of that Philosopher. ,, The ,, Law of God, *says he*, * is necessary to be observ'd, ,, that will lead us into the way of happiness, that ,, holy & heavenly Law, I mean, which *Marcus Tullius* ,, has, as it were, divinely describ'd in his third Book ,, *de Republica*; and whose words, I will, therefore, ,, subjoin. Right Reason is a Law of Truth, consonant ,, to Nature, implanted in all Men, uniform & eternal. ,, -- This Law neither needs to be propos'd, nor can ,, it ever be, either in whole or part, repeal'd, neither ,, Senate, nor People, can discharge us from the obli-,, gation of it, we need not look abroad for an ex-,, positor, to make us understand it: It is not one Law ,, at *Rome*, another at *Athens*; one at this time, another ,, hereafter; but one, and the same immutable Law ,, continues, & extends itself to all times & nations; ,, and one God is the common Lord, & Governor of ,, all things. He it is, that has fram'd, propounded, ,, & establish'd this Law; & whosoever obeys not him, ,, abandons even himself, renounces his own nature, ,, & in so doing, suffers actually in himself the greatest ,, punishment, tho' he escape all things else which ,, are deem'd so.

St. *Austin* says, † ,, The reason why God has given ,, us a written Law, is not because his Law was not ,, already written in our hearts, but because Men let-,, ting out their appetites after things abroad, became ,, strangers to themselves; & therefore, we have been ,, summon'd, and call'd upon by him, who is every ,, where present, to return into ourselves: For what ,, is that the outward written Law calls for, unto ,, those who have forsaken the Law written in their ,, hearts; but ‡ *Return, O ye Transgressors, to your ,, own Hearts?*

I shall,

---

* *L. 6. c. 8.*   † *In Psal 57.*   ‡ *Isaiah 46. 8.*

I shall, likewise, shew you, that the Law of Liberty, that * *perfect Law of Liberty*, which we are oblig'd to maintain in all our words & actions, as † *the Law we are to be judg'd by*, does not consist in a freedom from things of a moral nature, for that wou'd be perfect Slavery; but from all those things as are not of such a nature: And that 'tis evident from the reasoning, which runs thro' all the Epistles, that the placing Religion in any indifferent things, is inconsistent with the nature of Christianity; 'tis introducing *Judaism*, or what (as Christians have found to their cost) is still more prejudicial.

And therefore, instead of transcribing the best part of the Epistles, I shall only mention a text, or two: The Apostle of the *Gentiles* not only says, ‡ *Stand fast in the Liberty, wherewith Christ hath made you free*; but declares, *Wherever the Spirit of the Lord is, there is Liberty*; and consequently, that they who impose any indifferent things, as part of Religion, sin against our Christian Liberty, & act by another Spirit than that of the Lord. And I am afraid, that in this, as well as in many other cases, the Spirit of the Lord, & the Spirit of the Church, in most places, have been very opposite. And lest we shou'd mistake in this important point, the Apostle likewise tells us, not only in what things the Kingdom of God does, but in what things it does not consist. § *The Kingdom of God is not meat & drink, but righteousness, peace, & joy in the Holy Ghost; for he that in these things serveth Christ, is acceptable to God, & approv'd of Man: Let us, therefore, follow after the things which make for peace, & things wherewith we may edify one another.* If these are the only things, by which we can serve Christ, and which will make us acceptable to God, & approv'd of Men, can such things, as have no tendency to promote righteousness, peace, & joy in the Holy Ghost, make us serviceable to Christ, or acceptable either to God, or Man?

THESE

* *James* 1. 25.   † *Ibid.* 2. 21.   ‡ *I Cor.* 16. 13.
§ *Rom.* 14. 17. 18. 10.

THESE words of the Apostle, tho' they need no paraphrase, yet I shall mention what *Calvin* says on this place, *Nam fieri non potest, ubi quispiam Deo acceptus est ac hominibus probatus, quin perfecte in ipso vigeat ac floreat regnum Dei. Qui tranquilla placidaque conscientia per justitiam servit Christo, tam hominibus quam Deo se approbat. Ubi ergo est justitia, & pax, & gaudium spirituale, illic regnum Dei suis omnibus numeris est absolutum.* And with him *Bucer, Musculus,* & others of our first Reformers, agree. And if the Kingdom of God, which has these things, is absolutely perfect, *omnibus suis numeris absolutum*, it can only be the Kingdom of Satan, which requires things of a different nature. And if 'tis in these things only we can serve Christ, others can't be introduc'd, but for the service of Antichrist.

HOWEVER, I shall, at present, content myself with saying, There are but two ways for any thing to oblige, either from the Reason of the thing, or else from a positive Command. Now, if there are no such things, as are commanded to be observ'd at all times, & by all People; & no Commands can oblige those, to whom they were not giv'n; we have no way left, to know what things oblige perpetually, but from their nature; which will sufficiently distinguish them from those, which (in so miscellanious a Book as the Bible, taking in such a vast period of time) might be given upon certain occasions, & particular reasons; in which we are no other ways concern'd, than like them, to act according as the circumstances we are in require. Without this, Christians wou'd have no certain Rule, to know what Precepts oblige perpetually; all being alike commanded in Scripture, without making any difference; no precepts being said to bind all Mankind, or to bind any for ever, except those relating to the *Jewish* oeconomy; which, in an hundred places, we are told, are to last for ever.

To

To comprise the matter in few words, what I have been endeavouring to prove, is,

*First*, THAT there are things, which, by their internal excellency, shew themselves to be the Will of an infinitely wise, and good God.

*Secondly*, THERE are things, which have no worth in themselves; yet because those that have, can't many times be perform'd without them, these are to be consider'd as means to an end; & being of a mutable nature, are left to human discretion, to be vary'd as best suits those ends, for whose sake alone they are instituted.

*Thirdly*, THAT there are some things so indifferent, as not to be consider'd either as means, or ends; & to place any part of Religion in the observance of these, is highly superstitious. And I may venture to say, He that carries these distinctions in his mind, will have a truer notion of Religion, than if he had read all the *Schoolmen*, *Fathers*, and *Councils*.

*B.* I own, 'tis time to give you some respite, & to thank you for a favour, which can't be too much acknowledg'd; in thus freely communicating your thoughts on this important subject; and doing it after such a manner, as cannot, were this Conference to be publish'd, offend persons, tho' of the greatest gravity, who have the interest of truth at heart.

*A.* BEFORE we part, I must remind you of the occasion of this Conference; for tho' you plainly saw, that God never intended Mankind shou'd be without Religion; or cou'd ordain an imperfect Religion; and therefore, did not see how to avoid concluding, there must have been, from the beginning, a Religion most perfect, which Mankind, at all times, were capable of knowing: yet you were at a loss, how to make out Christianity to be this perfect, this original Religion. How far I have gone in removing this difficulty, you best know: All I can say, is, I am willing, whenever you please, to resume the conference; & begging leave to repeat what I mention'd at first, am ready to give up my *Hypothesis*, if you can name one attended with fewer difficulties; and likewise, to assure you, that if I have advanc'd any notion, which does not naturally, and necessarily shew itself to be the will of God, by tending to promote his honour, & the Good of Men, I here intirely renounce it : And by not persisting to defend Error, give this uncommon mark of an ingenuous disposition, *Errare possum*, *Hæreticus esse nolo*.

## FINIS.

Made in the USA